Eric Christianson is Lecturer in Biblical Studies, Department of Theology and Religious Studies, University College Chester.

JOURNAL FOR THE STUDY OF THE OLD TESTAMENT
SUPPLEMENT SERIES
280

Sheffield Academic Press

A Time to Tell

Narrative Strategies in Ecclesiastes

Eric S. Christianson

Journal for the Study of the Old Testament
Supplement Series 280

In loving memory of my mother, Penny
(1943–1990)

Sweet is the light,
and it is good for the eyes to see the sun…
Remove vexation from your heart
and take away pain from your body,
for youth and the prime of life are fleeting.

Ecclesiastes 11.7, 10

Copyright © 1998 Sheffield Academic Press

Published by Sheffield Academic Press Ltd
Mansion House
19 Kingfield Road
Sheffield S11 9AS
England

Printed on acid-free paper in Great Britain
by Bookcraft Ltd
Midsomer Norton, Bath

British Library Cataloguing in Publication Data

A catalogue record for this book is available
from the British Library

ISBN 1-85075-982-0

CONTENTS

Preface   9
Acknowledgments   13
Abbreviations   15

Introduction
READING ECCLESIASTES AS NARRATIVE   19
  1. The Narrative Assumption   20
  2. Events and a Proleptic Plot Afoot   24
  3. Qoheleth's Autobiographical Adhesion   33
  4. Motif   42
  5. The Structure of Narrative Discourse   45

Part I
THE FRAME NARRATOR'S STRATEGY

Chapter 1
PUTTING THE FRAME IN PLACE   52
  1. The Frame Proper   52
  2. Frame Narratives   56
  3. The Production of Narrative Levels   69
  4. Narrative Level as a Cause of Amnesia   70

Chapter 2
THE OUTER BORDERS: I   73
  1. The Superscription (1.1)   73
  2. Plot and Desire (1.1-2)   77

Excursus
הבל AND QOHELETH'S NARRATED LIFE   79
  1. הבל outside Ecclesiastes   79
  2. הבל in Ecclesiastes   81
  3. הבל and הכל   88

Chapter 3
THE INNER BORDERS   92
  1. הבל הבלים in the Frame (1.2; 12.8)   92
  2. A Momentary Intrusion (7.27)   93

Chapter 4
THE OUTER BORDERS: II   96
  1. The Inclusio (12.8)   98
  2. The Final Portrait (12.9-10)   99
  3. Admonitions to a Preferred Epistemology (12.11-12) 105
  4. The Final Word (12.13-14)   114

Chapter 5
FRAMING THE FRAMER: FINAL REFLECTIONS ON *THIS* FRAME   118

Part II
THE NARRATIVE STRATEGY OF QOHELETH

Chapter 6
THE SOLOMONIC GUISE   128
  1. Scope and Strategy   128
  2. The Guise, the Canon and the Rabbis   148
  3. The Guise and Pseudonymity   154
  4. The Implied Author and/as Qoheleth/Solomon   159
  5. Solomonic Readings and Readers   165

Chapter 7
QOHELETH AND THE SELF   173
  1. Self-Presence?   174
  2. The Deconstructed Subject   179
  3. The Biblical Self   182
  4. Qoheleth on *the* Self and *his* Self   193
  5. Accounting for the Self   211

Chapter 8
QOHELETH'S QUEST   216
  1. Success, Failure and Many Questions   217
  2. 'And Move with the Moving Ships':
     Qoheleth's Physical Language   221
  3. Qoheleth's Search and the Actantial Model   227

  4. Gustave Flaubert's *Bouvard et Pécuchet*: A Comparison   235
  5. Redemption and Remembrance   242

Conclusion   255

Postscript
QOHELETH AND THE EXISTENTIAL LEGACY OF THE HOLOCAUST   259
  1. Existentialist Themes: Material for a Response   260
  2. The Existential Drama Made Real   262
  3. The Disillusioned Rationalist and the Holocaust   266
  4. Survival and Memory   272
  5. Conclusion   273

Bibliography   275
Index of References   286
Index of Authors   296

The conversation usually goes something like this (we join the dinner conversation partway through):

'So, you're finishing your book for publication?'

'Yep.'

'And what's the topic?'

'Uh, well, it has to do with reading the book of Ecclesiastes as a story.'

'Really. But isn't it just a gloomy bunch of badly arranged proverbs from a rather maladjusted scribe?'

Reaching for my wine, I take a moment to calm myself. 'My approach is based on a hunch, really, that what lends the book its cohesion is the main character who narrates his story in the first person and attempts to redeem the anguish of his youth through that retelling. So I establish that there are elements of narrativity (like autobiography, plot, motif and so forth) and then discuss the issues those raise. It's called, "A Time to Tell: Narrative Strategies in Ecclesiastes"' (this I utter with the kind of smile that suggests I think myself just a bit clever).

'Hmmm. Fascinating. So, how long have you and your wife lived in the UK?'

'Actually, my wife's British...'

To be fair, not a few people have shown what I have understood to be *genuine* interest in the programme of this book. But the initial idea takes most people by surprise. Although when I began I was fairly much alone in my overall assumptions about Qoheleth (with the exception of Michael Fox and perhaps Oswald Loretz), thankfully the situation has changed. Tremper Longman III had up to that point only given brief notice of a similar view but has recently developed his narrative approach more fully in his commentary in the NICOT series. (I note here that future scholars of Qoheleth are distinctly more advantaged than I due to the recent deluge of Qoheleth studies: they have access to the 1997 CBL proceedings, *Qohelet in the Context of Wisdom*, Long-man's provoking commentary and C.-L. Seow's encyclopaedic commentary, all of which I have only recently acquired and therefore only consulted at points I have deemed critical to my argument.) More specifically, Naoto Kamano has identified elements of narrative prolepsis similar to elements that I had identified independently (see p. 31 n. 50). Gary Salyer has carried out a full-blown literary-critical study of Qoheleth's discourse, focusing intently on reader-oriented questions, entitled, 'Vain Rhetoric: Implied Author/Narrator/Narratee/Implied Reader Relationships in Ecclesiastes' Use of First-Person Discourse' (PhD dissertation; University of California at Berkeley, 1997). Salyer's work is impressive, thorough and worthy of considerable attention. However, Salyer and I did not become aware of each other's work until July 1998, by which time the final manuscript of this book was already at press. I have made reference to Salyer's exceptionally relevant work where time and space have provided. Well, if only *they* had been at those dinner parties ...

Now a few more specific words are in order about my approach.

In the history of biblical scholarship Qoheleth's inconsistencies and strange sayings have long been hung on the lines of academic and popular works of all sorts for the world to see. Indeed, it is a rare thing to read an introduction to a work on Ecclesiastes that does not begin by airing them out again, and to state that the book is 'perplexing', 'enigmatic' and so forth is bordering on an insult to the reader's general knowledge. This work, however, does not rest on the fact that Ecclesiastes presents problems to readers. Rather, it is an experiment in what happens when a text is investigated with confidence in its narrative quality. Such an approach need not be contrived.

Many have allowed that Ecclesiastes has 'narrative elements', 'narrativity', 'narrative threads', autobiographical qualities and so forth (see the Introduction, sec. 1, for examples). However, few if any regard such elements to be suggestive of the book's overall quality. While the various wisdom themes and narrative elements vie for the reader's commitment, the latter are rarely allowed predominance. The even occasional reference to such notions as an overbearing 'persona' in Ecclesiastes, or the fact that most people consistently refer to 'Qoheleth' when referring to the speaker of Ecclesiastes (why do we not refer to 'Solomon' when referring to the speaker of Proverbs—even

Proverbs 1–9—when the set-up is basically the same?), suggests that an investigation of that persona is overdue. My programmatic question, then, could be phrased as follows: What happens when *narrative* elements are viewed as constitutive of the whole, as opposed to, say, the structure of wisdom sayings or the relationship between themes of wisdom/folly and birth/death, or indeed to any elements commonly found in a collection of wise sayings?

I have pre-empted a related though different question: How can a general narrative-critical approach to a text that is not commonly regarded as a narrative be justified? Hence the purpose of the Introduction is to establish the veracity of the statement, 'Ecclesiastes can be studied with confidence as a narrative text for the purpose of analysis.' That statement has arisen from a reading conjecture: that Ecclesiastes relates the *story* of Qoheleth (an assumption I have, again, found present, to varying degrees, in numerous readings of Ecclesiastes). To flesh out that conjecture I investigate four features of Ecclesiastes. Two are common to all narrative texts—the presence both of events and of plot—and two serve as indicators of a narrative quality but are not limited to narrative texts—first-person narration and motif.

Part I ('The Frame Narrator's Strategy', Chapters 1–5) isolates the frame narrator (in 1.1-2; 7.27; 12.8-14) as a character in his own right. More specifically this section explores the ways in which a structure is provided that both limits and opens up possibilities for readers. The frame narrator is in a paradoxical position in that he validates Qoheleth's radicalism by appearing to find his words worth relating. Even words of praise are offered. But from the summary of the epilogue, I argue at length, it is clear that the frame narrator did not agree with Qoheleth's approach to wisdom, God and tradition, bound as they were to his wholly different epistemology. Finally, the strategy of framing occurs on many levels, and one of its consequences is the bringing into question of the reader's relation to the framed material, as well as the relation of the framer to the one framed. The interpretive possibilities arising from the tension in these narratorial relationships are explored in detail.

Part II ('The Narrative Strategy of Qoheleth', Chapters 6–8) explores the telling of Qoheleth's narrative, the words of the disillusioned rationalist and storyteller. Here is addressed the fact that in reading Ecclesiastes an interaction seemingly takes place, one in which the reader feels the concern of identity and the formation of Qoheleth's character. In the guise of Solomon that concern is ironic (almost satirical) and somewhat playful. In the establishment of his self as perhaps the central concern of his narrative, Qoheleth shows that although he passionately observes the world's transience and absurdity he desires (in an ironic mode?) that his image would be fixed and remembered. After exploring such elements of self-expression, the linguistic characteristics and ideological categories of Qoheleth's quest are surveyed. Included in this investigation are the element of physicality in Qoheleth's language as well as the identification of the actors in the quest, the Subject, Object and Power (Sender) in particular. The final outcome of the quest is a redemption of Qoheleth's youth and folly in which Qoheleth implicitly invites readers to take part.

The Postscript explores thematic parallels between Qoheleth's narrative and the reflections and memories of Holocaust survivors. The three themes touched on find expression in the post-World War II existentialist literature that sought to respond to the incomprehensibility of the Holocaust: the role of extreme circumstances, (confrontation with) absurdity and (particularly in relation to the existential legacy of the Holocaust) the individual struggle with or against death and fate. Indeed, many of the themes covered in this book as a whole come together in the Postscript, most important of which is the autobiographical quality of Qoheleth's words, which, in part, makes the comparison possible.

ACKNOWLEDGMENTS

> Authors who always refer to their works as 'my book, my commentary, my history', sound like solid citizens with their own property who are always talking about 'my house'. They would be better to say: 'our book, our commentary, our history', seeing that there is usually more of other people's property in it than their own.
>
> *Blaise Pascal, Sayings* 1

Pascal's truism extends to the sometimes less obvious influence of friends and mentors through the years. It is therefore with appropriate gratitude that I begin by thanking Professor Sean McEvenue, a valued friend whose encouragement to me as an undergraduate at Concordia University in Montréal, to read the Bible critically and yet with *jouissance*, has had a lasting impression on me. Of equal influence was Professor Paul Garnet, whose passion for research and linguistic subtlety was always an impetus for my own work. His friendship and encouragement are deeply valued.

This book began life as a PhD thesis in 1991 at the University of Sheffield. I am grateful to my PhD supervisor, Philip Davies, who throughout the duration of my study was not only generous in his time and comments but helped me constantly to see the forest for the trees of my work. And thanks must go to my friend and colleague John Jarick, with whom I have enjoyed many a mini Qoheleth-seminar, and whose comments from a reading of the final draft of the thesis proved invaluable. Thanks also to Professor Leon Stein of Roosevelt University, Chicago, who offered a valuable critique of the Postscript. Bill Brown, Michael Fox, Jim Kanaris, my examiners—Cheryl Exum and the late Norman Whybray (whose presence and work in the biblical guild will be sorely missed)—all have at one stage or another provided valuable feedback on this work. In this last year colleagues in the Theology and Religious Studies department at University College Chester have provided me with ample support and encouragement. A different but no less valuable contribution was made by the staff at Sheffield Academic Press. In particular I would like to thank Chris Allen, Jean Allen, Steve

Barganski, Jeremy Boucher, Rebecca Cullen—and a special word of thanks to Vicky Acklam, who has seen the project through with efficiency and good humour.

For God's provision and evident grace in these last seven years of study I am grateful. Much of that provision comes through the love of family. And so this book is dedicated to my mother, Penny Christianson, who I know would have loved to have debated the finer points of Qoheleth's thought. I thank her here for the love of life, literature and critical thinking that she imparted to me. And thank you to my father and *belle-mère*, Dennis and Rose Christianson, who year after year have sent their encouragement and support over the miles. Thanks are also due to my grandmother, Lucille Beer, without whose support my final year of postgraduate study would have proven infeasible. Finally, thank you to my wife, Sonya Christianson, who has carefully read the majority of this book and offered her insightful comments (and rightly insisted on the deletion of not a few commas). Even more impressively, she has had no choice but to live with the Preacher at every waking moment and yet she has listened to my incessant monologues and still has not had me committed to a Home for Beleaguered Qoheleth Readers. By gracing me with her friendship, laughter and love she has imparted joy to my few days under the sun.

ABBREVIATIONS

AB	Anchor Bible
AEL	M. Lichtheim (ed.), *Ancient Egyptian Literature* (3 vols.; Berkeley: University of California Press, 1973)
ANET	James B. Pritchard (ed.), *Ancient Near Eastern Texts Relating to the Old Testament* (Princeton, NJ: Princeton University Press)
ASTI	*Annual of the Swedish Theological Institute*
AUSS	*Andrews University Seminary Studies*
AUUSSU	Acta Universitatis Upsaliensis. Studia Semitica Upsaliensia
BDB	Francis Brown, S.R. Driver and Charles A. Briggs, *A Hebrew and English Lexicon of the Old Testament* (Oxford: Clarendon Press, 1907)
BETL	Bibliotheca ephemeridum theologicarum lovaniensium
BibInt	*Biblical Interpretation: A Journal of Contemporary Approaches*
BKAT	Biblischer Kommentar: Altes Testament
BLS	Bible and Literature Series
BR	*Bible Review*
BT	*The Bible Translator*
BTB	*Biblical Theology Bulletin*
BTF	*Bangalore Theological Forum*
BZAW	Beihefte zur *ZAW*
CBQ	*Catholic Biblical Quarterly*
CL	*College Literature*
CRBS	*Currents in Research: Biblical Studies*
CritInq	*Critical Inquiry*
CTR	*Criswell Theological Review*
DCH	D.J.A. Clines (ed.), *The Dictionary of Classical Hebrew* (4 vols.; Sheffield: Sheffield Academic Press, 1993–98)
Enc	*Encounter* (Indianapolis)
EvQ	*Evangelical Quarterly*
EvT	*Evangelische Theologie*
Exp	*Expositor* (London)
ExpTim	*Expository Times*
FCB	The Feminist Companion to the Bible
GCT	Gender, Culture, Theory

GR	*The Germanic Review*
HAR	*Hebrew Annual Review*
HeyJ	*Heythrop Journal*
HS	*Hebrew Studies*
HUCA	*Hebrew Union College Annual*
HudR	*Hudson Review*
ICC	International Critical Commentary
ISBL	Indiana Studies in Biblical Literature
ITC	International Theological Commentary
Int	*Interpretation*
JAAR	*Journal of the American Academy of Religion*
JAdC	*Journal of Advanced Composition*
JBL	*Journal of Biblical Literature*
JBR	*Journal of Bible and Religion*
JPsT	*Journal of Psychology and Theology*
JQR	*Jewish Quarterly Review*
JR	*Journal of Religion*
JSOT	*Journal for the Study of the Old Testament*
JSOTSup	*Journal for the Study of the Old Testament*, Supplement Series
JTS	*Journal of Theological Studies*
KJV	King James Version
LAE	W.K. Simpson (ed.), *The Literature of Ancient Egypt* (London: Yale University Press, 1973)
MLN	*Modern Language Notes*
NCB	New Century Bible
NEB	New English Bible
NICOT	New International Commentary on the Old Testament
NIV	New International Version
OLA	Orientalia Lovaniensia Analecta (Uppsala)
OTL	Old Testament Library
OTWSA	Die Ou Testamentiese Werkgemeenskap in Suid Afrika
PRS	*Perspectives in Religious Studies*
PrtRev	*Partisan Review*
PTMS	Pittsburgh Theological Monograph Series
RL	*Religion in Life*
RSV	Revised Standard Version
SBL	Society of Biblical Literature
SBLSCS	SBL Septuagint and Cognate Studies
SBTh	*Studia Biblica et Theologica*
SCT	Studies in Continental Thought
SJT	*Scottish Journal of Theology*
TBS	The Biblical Seminar
TBT	*The Bible Today*

TDOT	G.J. Botterweck and H. Ringgren (eds.), *Theological Dictionary of the Old Testament*
TLB	The Living Bible
TOTC	Tyndale Old Testament Commentaries
TrinJ	*Trinity Journal*
TZ	*Theologische Zeitschrift*
VT	*Vetus Testamentum*
VTSup	*Vetus Testamentum*, Supplements
WBC	Word Biblical Commentary
WUNT	Wissenschaftliche Untersuchungen zum Neuen Testament
ZAW	*Zeitschrift für die alttestamentliche Wissenschaft*
ZDMG	*Zeitschrift der deutschen morgenländischen Gesellschaft*

Introduction

READING ECCLESIASTES AS NARRATIVE

I readily agree with the assertion of Mieke Bal that no narrative theory is capable of describing 'all the aspects of a narrative text',[1] and that it is therefore justifiable to approach any text that has narrative aspects (or 'narrativity') with the tools that narrative criticism offers. My purpose here, however, is to go further than such an approach might allow. Rather, I will investigate the possibility that Ecclesiastes meets certain narratological criteria that would commend it as a narrative text for the purpose of analysis, and not merely as a text with elements of narrativity.[2]

Central to my approach is the concept of 'strategy', one I consider more useful than the more common approach of structure. (Many have attempted to delineate the book's structure in order to discipline or rationalize its overt contradictions.[3]) By strategy I mean simply a

---

1. *Narratology: Introduction to the Theory of Narrative* (trans. C. von Boheemen; Toronto: University of Toronto Press, 1985), p. 9.

2. This will be pursued in the same spirit in which Bal herself goes on to delimit her definition of what constitutes a narrative (or what she would call a *fabula*), presumably so that she is able to make similarly decisive judgments about texts (*Narratology*, pp. 11-47).

3. One of the most influential structural studies is A.G. Wright's 'The Riddle of the Sphinx: The Structure of the Book of Qoheleth', *CBQ* 30 (1968), pp. 313-34 (supplemented by two later articles: 'The Riddle of the Sphinx Revisited: Numerical Patterns in the Book of Qoheleth', *CBQ* 42 [1980], pp. 38-51; 'Additional Numerical Patterns in Qohelet', *CBQ* 45 [1983], pp. 32-43). His work, although not widely accepted, is regarded as truly structuralist in approach, as evidenced by its presence in bibliographies representative of structuralist approaches to the Bible; for example, Robert Polzin, *Biblical Structuralism* (Philadelphia: Fortress Press, 1977); R. Barthes *et al.*, *Structural Analysis and Biblical Exegesis* (trans. A.M. Johnson, Jr; PTMS, 3; Pittsburgh: Pickwick Press, 1974 [1971]). For summaries of attempts to discern a structure in Ecclesiastes, see Wright, 'The Riddle of the Sphinx: The Structure of the Book of Qoheleth', pp. 314-20; M.V. Fox, *Qohelet*

scheme for achieving some purpose, an artful means to some end. *Narrative* strategy is the function a narrator intends to fulfil by the use of a narrative device, technique or overall design. More specifically, states Wolfgang Iser, it is the 'panoply of narrative techniques available' to the author, the ultimate function of which is 'to *defamiliarize* the reader' with topics and language that are old while familiarizing the reader with what is new and particular to *this* story.[4] I include under the rubric 'narrative strategy' elements such as first-person narration, framing and characterization. Sometimes my investigation is particularly structural, sometimes not. For example, while it is clear that the frame narrative suggests a structural strategy, the same cannot necessarily be said of first-person narration (or more precisely, the construct of self with which Qoheleth narrates). The concept of strategy therefore has the advantage of including structural considerations as well as those that are not evidently so.

To begin the discussion, then, it will prove helpful to survey a number of readers who have identified at least some elements of narrativity in Qoheleth's words.

1. *The Narrative Assumption*

> Qohelet constantly interposes his consciousness between the reality observed and the reader. It seems important to him that the reader not only know what the truth is, but also be aware that he, Qohelet, saw this, felt this, realized this. He is reflexively observing the psychological process of discovery as well as reporting the discoveries themselves.
>
> Michael Fox[5]

> [Qoheleth] is 'disillusioned' only in the sense that he has realized that an illusion is a self-constructed prison. He is not a weary pessimist tired of life: he is a vigorous realist determined to smash his way through every locked door of repression in his mind.
>
> Northrop Frye[6]

and his Contradictions (JSOTSup, 71; Sheffield: Almond Press, 1989), pp. 19-28; J. Crenshaw, 'Qoheleth in Current Research', *HAR* 7 (1983), pp. 41-56 (48-56); S. Breton, 'Qoheleth Studies', *BTB* 3 (1973), pp. 22-50 (38-40).

4. W. Iser, 'Narrative Strategies as a Means of Communication', in M.J. Valdés and O.J. Miller (eds.), *Interpretation of Narrative* (Toronto: University of Toronto Press, 1978), pp. 100-17 (101-102).

5. *Qohelet*, p. 93.

6. *The Great Code: The Bible and Literature* (Toronto: Academic Press Canada, 1982), p. 123.

[Qoheleth's] own personal experiences seem to supply the key to his outlook...He is a free-lance humanist...There may have been many a melancholy streak in his nature that disposed him to look at the shadier sides of life. He is the original 'gloomy dean'. He had hung his harp on the weeping willows and it moaned in the breeze.

John Paterson[7]

Qoheleth is an 'intellectual' in a sense otherwise unknown to the Old Testament. In his remorseless determination to probe the nature of things he belongs to a new world of thought, though...his sense of God's transcendence ('God is in heaven, and you upon the earth', 5.2) is a Jewish inheritance which distinguishes him quite radically from the secular philosopher.

R.N. Whybray[8]

I wish...that I could have spoken with Qohelet face to face, seen his emotion as he told his story, noted the tone of his voice, where he smiled or was tearful, whether he was hesitating or agitated, silent or effusive, have him repeat his tale, and note the variations, what he added and what he suppressed, what were his conflicts and his dreams especially...

Frank Zimmermann[9]

Each of the above statements presents a unique characterization of Qoheleth. To Fox he is a seeker of truth eager to communicate his experiences. To Frye he is a realist embarked on a critique of the way of wisdom. To Paterson he is a journal-keeping humanist. To Whybray he is a distinctly Jewish philosopher. To Zimmermann he is a melancholy storyteller. To each of them Qoheleth is a character who (according to Ecclesiastes) interacted with the world and left it with his consequent thoughts and judgments. In each instance the tendency is to assume the presence of a cohesive narrative character at the heart of Ecclesiastes.

So why is Qoheleth, to many readers, seen clearly as a character who interacted with the world? Is it because Ecclesiastes is a narrative?; that is, because it is 'the representation of real or fictive events or situations in a time sequence'[10] that tells the story of Qoheleth? Of course,

7. 'The Intimate Journal of an Old-Time Humanist', *RL* 19.2 (1950), pp. 245-54 (245, 250-51).

8. *Ecclesiastes* (NCB; Grand Rapids: Eerdmans, 1989), p. 7.

9. *The Inner World of Qohelet* (New York: Ktav, 1973), p. ix.

10. G. Prince, *Narratology: The Form and Functioning of Narrative* (Berlin: Mouton, 1982), p. 1. This definition is distinct from two other uses of the word: (1) the *subject* of the narrative discourse; i.e. the actual events themselves (akin to what I call 'story' below); (2) the event of narrating itself (see also G. Genette,

quotations about Qoheleth as a character are not in themselves evidence that Ecclesiastes is a narrative. Perhaps Ecclesiastes is only a group of *meshalim* collected and placed in a relatively random order by a redactor(s), all loosely structured by a frame narrator/epilogist/editor.[11] But if the above quotations show anything it is the justification of the question, Why has Ecclesiastes been understood to be otherwise?[12] While the narrative *assumption* is often made, relatively little effort has been taken to legitimate it. A brief survey will help to show what I mean.

Leland Ryken affirms that Ecclesiastes reads 'much like a story', citing some of Qoheleth's narrative style as evidence.[13] Less committedly, J.G. Williams admits that there is in Ecclesiastes the use of a kind of narrativity that is merely common (and necessary) to the poetics of all wisdom literature.[14] Also, there has been some significant study of the first-person form of Qoheleth's words which assumes a cohesive narrative element at work.[15] While not specifically narrative in

Narrative Discourse [trans. J. Lewin; Oxford: Basil Blackwell, 1980 (1972)], pp. 25-27). After consideration of a number of definitions of narrative I settled on Prince's as representative; that is, most definitions suggest that events in the relation of time are fundamental to a narrative. What *qualifies* such an entity (i.e. narration, plot etc.) will be explored further below.

11. Take, for example, John Barton's statement: '[Ecclesiastes is sapiential wisdom with a frame narrative], not a narrative overweighted with sapiential advice' (*Reading the Old Testament* [London: SCM Press, 1984], p. 132). For a convenient summary of redactional hypotheses that imply a similar sentiment, see Crenshaw, 'Qoheleth in Current Research', pp. 45-46.

12. My introductory quotes are profuse to make a point. The point is that such writing about Qoheleth is common. Similar statements about the narrative quality of Ecclesiastes can be found in many academic works, and one may take those I have here supplied to be representative.

13. 'Ecclesiastes', in *idem*, *Words of Delight: A Literary Introduction to the Bible* (Grand Rapids: Baker Book House, 1987), pp. 319-28 (321).

14. 'Proverbs and Ecclesiastes', in R. Alter and F. Kermode (eds.), *The Literary Guide to the Bible* (London: Collins, 1987), pp. 263-82 (273-75, 277).

15. E.g. O. Loretz, 'Zur Darbietungsform der "Ich-Erzählung" im Buche Qohelet', *CBQ* 25 (1963), pp. 46-59; George Castellino, 'Qoheleth and his Wisdom', *CBQ* 30 (1968), pp. 15-28; P. Höffken, 'Das EGO des Weisen', *TZ* 41 (1985), pp. 121-34; Bo Isaksson, *Studies in the Language of Qoheleth* (AUUSSU, 10; Uppsala: Almqvist & Wiksell, 1987), Chapter 2; C.-L. Seow, 'Qohelet's Autobiography', in A.B. Beck *et al.* (eds.), *Fortunate the Eyes that See: Essays in Honor of David Noel Freedman in Celebration of his Seventieth Birthday* (Grand Rapids: Eerdmans, 1995), pp. 275-87. These works focus mainly on the section known as the royal fiction (1.12-2.26; though for Seow, 1.12–2.11). Isaksson, however, does

approach, many studies have reviewed literary aspects of Qoheleth. For example, Edwin Good's 'The Unfilled Sea: Style and Meaning in Ecclesiastes 1.2-11', sets much emphasis on Qoheleth's sophisticated uses of common narrative devices.[16] Also, there is Frank Zimmermann's widely neglected psychoanalytic study. In order to carry out his study he must (and does) presume that the whole book is autobiographical, 'a complete representation of Qohelet himself'.[17] Harold Fisch has offered an insightful study suggesting sophistication in Qoheleth's use of irony. In doing so he relies heavily on the notion of an autobiographical coherence in Qoheleth's narrative.[18] Gary Salyer suggests that Qoheleth's discourse, while not a narrative, displays narrative qualities in that it gives 'the reader a narrative encounter with the weakness of staid traditionalism, empiricism and personal insight'.[19] Finally, Michael Fox's article, 'Frame-narrative and Composition in the Book of Qohelet',[20] explores 'the literary characteristics of *Qohelet* as narrative'.[21]

Such a brief survey shows that there are some, such as Ryken, who refer vaguely to Ecclesiastes as a story (although usually by implication), and some, such as Zimmermann, who make a real

go beyond this section to recognize an 'autobiographical thread', and, like myself (see sec. 3, below), Tremper Longman III has recognized that the whole work should be properly regarded as autobiographical (see *The Book of Ecclesiastes* [NICOT; Grand Rapids: Eerdmans, 1998], pp. 15-20). I have reviewed Longman's work in *HS* 40 (1999), forthcoming.

16. In J.G. Gammie *et al.* (eds.), *Israelite Wisdom: Theological and Literary Essays in Honor of Samuel Terrien* (Missoula, MT: Scholars Press, 1978), pp. 59-73. See also, P. Viviano, 'The Book of Ecclesiastes: A Literary Approach', *TBT* 22 (1984), pp. 79-84; and M. Payne, 'The Voices of Ecclesiastes', *CL* 15 (1988), pp. 262-68.

17. *Inner World*, p. xiii; also, cf. pp. ix-xiv.

18. H. Fisch, 'Qohelet: A Hebrew Ironist', in *idem, Poetry with a Purpose: Biblical Poetics and Interpretation* (ISBL; Indianapolis: Indiana University Press, 1988), pp. 158-78, esp. pp. 158-59.

19. 'Vain Rhetoric', p. 276 (cf. pp. 140-41).

20. *HUCA* 48 (1977), pp. 83-106. The article is reprinted in a shortened form with no modification as regards the narrative approach in *Qohelet*, pp. 311-21. His work has been helpful in laying some foundation for my own and I shall draw upon it accordingly.

21. 'Frame-narrative', p. 83. More recently, Longman has come close to such an overarching approach in his commentary, *The Book of Ecclesiastes*, identifying the whole as a 'framed wisdom autobiography' (p. 17).

assumption about Ecclesiastes' narrative quality. It is an assumption that has not been thought possible in work on Proverbs and yet has had not a few advocates in work on Job. However, few if any have examined that narrative quality critically in Ecclesiastes, or attempted to demonstrate it with any degree of conclusiveness with the aid of narrative criticism.

2. *Events and a Proleptic Plot Afoot*

The past is a foreign country: they do things differently there.
L.P. Hartley[22]

The story of any narrative can be 'transformed' into any medium: comic book, pantomime, film and so forth. For example, the story of Jesus (consisting of selected events, settings etc. from the Gospels) has been transformed into several types (stained glass, film, theatre etc.) of narrative discourse, each showing that story can be transferred from discourse to discourse. Similarly, the text of Ecclesiastes (its narrative discourse) is the tangible expression of its story.[23] That Ecclesiastes has been rendered as music,[24] poem,[25] slide show,[26] series of woodcuts[27]

22. *The Go-Between* (Harmondsworth: Penguin Books, 1958), p. 7.

23. Narratives are structures (discourses) 'independent of any medium', having 'wholeness, transformation, and self-regulation' (S. Chatman, *Story and Discourse: Narrative Structure in Fiction and Film* [London: Cornell University Press, 1978], pp. 20-21). This implicitly strict division between content and form has been criticized. For example, Wayne Booth argues that it is not legitimate to see events as simply 'clothed' in the form of narrative discourses. For this does not give justice to the real author who is far more complex in using his or her privilege to 'telescope' certain events while 'expanding' others, and is hence more in control of the shape of events as manifested in their narrative discourse (1983 Afterword to *The Rhetoric of Fiction* [Harmondsworth: Penguin Books, 2nd edn, 1983], pp. 437-38). In other words, there is no such thing as 'pure' transformation of content to form. Obviously, this is not the place to enter such a basic and hence large debate. Suffice to say that while I agree with Booth that there is no such thing as 'pure' transformation, the operative distinction (as long as we are aware of its limits) in Chatman (and others) is useful. Shlomith Rimmon-Kenan (*Narrative Fiction: Contemporary Poetics* [London: Methuen, 1983], pp. 6-8) concludes similarly.

24. For example, the classic 1960s rock song, *Turn, Turn, Turn!* (music written and words adapted by Pete Seeger; performed by The Byrds). Although I recall reading about a classical music suite based on Ecclesiastes, unfortunately I have been unable to locate the reference.

25. For example, *Ecclesiastes: Rendered into English Verse by F. Crawford*

and sketches[28] points at least to its transferability. Although not all forms demonstrate a narrative quality, the central events of the text to which I will be making reference are often evident.

Events, in any given text, are the most important distinctive quality that earns the title 'narrative', for events are the fabric of which stories are made. An 'event' is most simply described as 'something that happens'. Events entail a change from one state of affairs to another. This takes place in most verbal statements. Borrowing Seymour Chatman's term, such verbal phrases are 'process statements'.[29] While a process statement is an event, by itself it is not necessarily a narrative event. If verbal action were the only criterion the definition would be far too loose to be of value.

Events (actions) are only meaningful in relation to at least one other event in the relation of time. Narrative events are thus 'made' before the reader. This shows that the event in question has *functionality*. My own use of the word takes on board two of Mieke Bal's criteria for narrative events: *change* and *choice*.[30] The two concepts are closely

Burkitt (London: Macmillan, 1936). The first 'verse' reads, 'Bubble of bubbles! All things are a Bubble! What is the use of all Man's toil and trouble?' (p. 9).

26. For example, R. Short's photo-essay of Ecclesiastes, *A Time to Be Born—A Time to Die* (New York: Harper & Row, 1973).

27. For example, Stefan Martin's series of wood engravings, in J. Blumenthal (designer), *Ecclesiastes, or The Preacher* (New York: Spiral Press, 1965). There is an example on p. 76.

28. As can be seen from any number of attempts to augment Ecclesiastes with sketches demonstrating its narrativity. For example, see the illustrations of Emlen Etting, in *Koheleth: The Book of Ecclesiastes* (New York: New Directions, 1940).

29. So Chatman, *Story and Discourse*, pp. 32-33. Rimmon-Kenan challenges Chatman's distinction, wanting to include 'stasis' statements (statements that only describe the state of things and are therefore not events; e.g. 'Bob is hungry') in the definition of an event. She argues that 'an account of an event may be broken down into an infinite number of intermediary states... [for example,] "He was rich, then he was poor"', and that this implies a process of change, meeting Chatman's criterion (*Narrative Fiction*, p. 15). There are some stasis statements (as her example) that imply change and can therefore be considered process statements.

30. So Bal, *Narratology*, pp. 13-16. I have chosen not to use Bal's criterion of *confrontation* (pp. 16-18). This criterion demands that every event have a subject, predication and (direct) object. The subject and (direct) object must be 'confronted by each other' (p. 16). Furthermore, both the subject and (direct) object must be agents of action. This means that Bal can say that 'Liz writes a letter' meets such a criterion (p. 17). For it can be implied that a letter represents a person and that therefore two agents of action confront each other in the narrative. But in my view

related. An event must be functional in (produce *change* in or have an effect upon) the larger sequence of events that I have called a narrative. This can only be accomplished through the *choice*(s) made by characters in the narrative. Narrative events can have different types of functionality according to their context. Again, to borrow from Chatman, there are two types of such functional events: kernels and satellites. A *kernel* is an event that initializes narrative motion.[31] Kernels create the possibility for a change of story-line. That they do assumes their functionality to other events. If kernels are not in relation to another event in time, by which they can raise a question or further the plot, they are logically expendable. If they are logically expendable they have only an 'immediate functionality'. Such events are *satellites*; that is, one or more events that are directly related to the kernel but do not themselves further the story-line. The satellite is 'always logically expendable'.[32]

Does Ecclesiastes have functional narrative events? First it must be established whether the text in question narrates an event; that is, whether it meets the basic criterion of verbal action, change. Every time Qoheleth makes his opinion known, or relates what he has done in order to come to a certain conclusion, there is a *process* of change at hand. The first explicit appearance of this is in 1.12-13a:[33] 'I am Qoheleth.[34] I was king over Israel in Jerusalem. I set my heart to investigate and to search out by wisdom all that is done under the heavens.' The subject, Qoheleth, describes himself in a stasis statement: 'I was

this is included in the criterion of functionality. The letter can only be significant if the agent it represents is of any consequence in the larger structure of events. At any rate, functionality can only occur if at least two agents of action (not necessarily human) are involved.

31. *Story and Discourse*, pp. 53-56. Kernels '[advance] the plot by raising and satisfying questions... [and are] nodes or hinges in the structure, branching points which force a movement into one of two (or more) possible paths' (p. 53).

32. *Story and Discourse*, p. 54.

33. While I consider 1.1-2 to be an implicit event (see Chapter 2.2), I have chosen to discuss 1.12-13a for the sake of clarity, as it is the first explicit narrative event.

34. 'I am Qoheleth' (as opposed to the usual, 'I, Qoheleth...') seems the best translation of אני קהלת. This is the first self-introduction of the book and would hence deserve the slight pause this translation offers (so also, Fox—for the same reason, but also on the grounds that it resembles 'the opening of various royal inscriptions'; *Qohelet*, p. 174). Cf. Joseph's dramatic self-introduction, אני יוסף (Gen. 45.3; cf. also, 2 Sam. 19.23, of a king).

king'.[35] During the time of his reign to which the statement refers, Qoheleth gave his heart (לב) to investigate and to seek out (תור, 'spying out' or 'evaluating'; see Num. 13.32; 14.34 [of land]) an object; namely, 'all that is done under the heavens'. I will not investigate here the real Object of Qoheleth's quest (for this, see Chapter 8.3). What matters for now is the criterion of change. Qoheleth's state of knowledge at this narrative level is given a quality of self-determination, of the inevitability of change.

Second, functionality must be established in order to show how this event is meaningful in the larger structure of events. This event finds an immediate functional counterpart at 1.14: 'I observed all the deeds that have been done under the sun, and behold, everything is absurd[36] and a pursuit of wind.' The narrator, Qoheleth (unchanged from 1.3), has temporally linked two narrative events. Ecclesiastes 1.12-13a and the event of 1.14 are separate, and yet the former begs the conclusion: the event of finding what is searched for.[37] A story-line, however small, has been created and the criterion of functionality met. But does Qoheleth's seeking at 1.12-13a function as a kernel event? Qoheleth announces his intention to inform himself about what we must assume he did not know. His quest was 'successful' (he observed successfully all that is done under the sun) and his findings could have been expressed in a variety of ways: as moral treatise, as 'the bare facts', even as 'evil' report. At Num. 13.32 we are told that the report of the spies was evil (or 'cunning', דבה), which implies that a good report was possible. Qoheleth's seeking, like the spies' report, forces the logic of the story (eventually) to take a particular direction. His seeking creates numerous possibilities in the direction of the sequence of events and is hence a kernel event.[38] By claiming that he set his heart to discover things by

35. Or 'I have been king'. See C.-L. Seow, *Ecclesiastes: A New Translation with Introduction and Commentary* (AB, 18C; New York: Doubleday, 1997), p. 119, for the discussion. Both translations are stasis statements.

36. On translating הבל as 'absurd', see the Excursus.

37. To understand this as conclusive, כל־המעשים שנעשׂו תחת השמשׁ at 1.14a and כל־אשׁר נעשׂה תחת השמים at 1.13b are understood to refer to the same realm of experience. 'Under the heavens' and 'under the sun' are interchangeable throughout Ecclesiastes (see 2.3, 11; 3.1; cf. 5.2 [cf. n. 43, below]). Hence, the conclusion (והנה...) of Qoheleth's investigation is summized in the object of his 'I saw' at 1.14: [that which is] 'absurd and a pursuit of wind'.

38. One could perhaps add Chatman's recent measure that true narrative events are not simply subservient to Argument or Description. In other words, events at

wisdom, Qoheleth limited the scope of his quest while at the same time
opened wide the possibilities for story-direction and for the imagination
of the sequential reader (i.e. the reader who reads this text for the first
time, attentively, from beginning to end).

Obviously, events can have more than one functional counterpart.
There are several in 1.12-13a that the sequential reader discovers as the
narrative line unfolds. Indeed, every subsequent observation is
'covered' by the event of investigating 'all that is done under the heavens'.[39] While it could be argued that such a functional poetic is necessary to the opening verses of any book of wisdom literature, this would
depend on the strategy at hand. The prologue to Proverbs (1.1-3 in particular), for example, states the purpose of the entire 'book':

> The proverbs of Solomon, son of David, king of Israel.
> To know wisdom and instruction,
>   and to understand the sayings of insight.
> To acquire instruction in wise dealing,
>   righteousness, justice, and integrity.

By this the reader realizes that the purpose is primarily a didactic one.[40]
Content is given precedence over story, and the functional poetic of

the surface level often simply serve a point or moral (such as events we might find
in a fable), or are present only to establish some character trait pertinent to the plot
('No narrative event is cited by the verb "added" in "To good looks she added a
brisk intelligence... "'). Events are made meaningful only if they disclose new
questions and propel the story forward (see S. Chatman, *Coming to Terms: The
Rhetoric of Narrative in Fiction and Film* [Ithaca, NY: Cornell University Press,
1990], pp. 6-21 [18]). In this respect, Qoheleth's discourse is a narrative in that his
declaration to seek understanding is not subservient to a simple moral (quite the
opposite: Qoheleth's story raises more questions than it answers), nor is it the servant of description in that its function is not simply to establish what kind of sage
he is/was (for that sort of information we would look to the frame narrator). Rather
its function is to involve us in his quest and to invite us to reflect on its outcome, on
the myriad possibilities that such a quest enables.

39. For example, after the highly observational ch. 2, cf. 3.10, 16-22; 4.1, 4, 7;
passim.

40. That the infinitive constructs here may be taken to be purpose clauses (e.g.
לדעת = '*in order* to learn', so the sense of RSV and other translations) is evidenced
by the fact that there is no other referent for the infinitives except the opening
phrase, 'The proverbs of Solomon', without which the infinitives 'to know' etc.,
would stand rather meaninglessly on their own. Thus each of these verbs and their
nouns should be seen as qualifying the purpose of the משלים. The infinitives that
qualify the meaning of Eccl. 1.13, however, have an altogether different function.

events is neither present nor necessary.[41]

Other functional events in Ecclesiastes may here be indexed. Both the location of the event and the location of one event to which it is functional are shown. The selection of one event from each chapter shows that functional events are a *feature* of the book as a whole.[42]

Figure 1. *Narrative Events in Ecclesiastes*

Place	Description	E	I
1.2	Speech-act of Qoheleth (FC = 1.12; cf. 1.16; *passim*)		X
2.1	Test of שׂמחה (FC = 2.2-10; cf. 3.22; 5.18[43])	X	
3.16	Observation of משׁפט (FC = 1.13; 3.17; cf. 5.8)	X	
4.1-2	Observation of עשׁק (FC = 1.13; 4.3-4; cf. 5.8; 8.9)	X	
5.1	Shift to present;[44] admonition (FC = 12.9; cf. 8.2-4)		X
6.3-6	Didactic pericope[45] (FC = 6.1; cf. 4.13-16)	X	

41. This is not to say that there are not events in the book of Proverbs. Events are present as early as 1.7, 8 and following, but these are not functional to the whole.

42. E = explicit; I = implicit. Here is a plain example that demonstrates the distinction: E = 'Someone reported Qoheleth's words.' I = 'The words of Qoheleth.' The latter is an implicit form of the former explicit event. This can also be thought of in terms of the classic distinction between telling (E) and showing (I). Wayne Booth argues persuasively that showing is, in fact, a form of telling (*Rhetoric of Fiction*, Chapter 1, esp. pp. 18-20, 25-27). FC = functional counterpart. It is worth noting here that there is some non-narrative material in Ecclesiastes, particularly the two blocks of wisdom sayings in 7.1-14, 19-22 and 10.1-4, 8-20. Even these passages, however, are set firmly in a narrative context (see below, sec. 5).

43. In referring to ch. 5 I use the English versification which is one verse ahead of the MT.

44. The shift in narration at 5.1 (and the examples of 7.13-14; 11.9) constitutes a narrative event in that the shift occurs not only at the external structural level (of discourse) but at the narrative diegetic level (of story) as well. That is, that Qoheleth speaks suddenly to a character in the text not mentioned before (i.e. an implied reader) can be seen as an event of narration. It is because the reader can, in a sense, visualize Qoheleth changing his narrative stance that this meets the criterion of change (further on this reader-oriented event, see Salyer, 'Vain Rhetoric', p. 172). The functionality criterion is met in the link of 5.1 ('Guard your step whenever you go to the house of God... ') to 12.9b ('He [Qoheleth] continually taught the people knowledge... '). From 12.9 the didactic aspect of 5.1 and other addressee passages can be made sense of in a narrative context—that is, in the context of what Qoheleth *did*; his story.

45. A didactic pericope such as this (and the examples of 4.13-16; 9.13-15) is a virtual mini-story within itself (pericope). This particular pericope has its own

7.13-14	Shift to present; admonition (FC = 12.9; cf. 7.10)		X
8.16	Test of חכמה (FC = 1.13 [reiteration]; 8.17; cf. 7.23)	X	
9.13-15	Didactic pericope (FC = 9.16; cf. 4.13-16)	X	
10.5-7	Observation of רעה (FC = 1.13; cf. 5.13; 6.1; *passim*)	X	
11.9	Salient shift to present (FC = 12.9; cf. 9.7-10)		X
12.8	Conclusion/summary (FC = 1.3, 13; *passim*; cf. 1.2)	X	

Undoubtedly functional events are the most important feature of narratives. These separate the classified ads from the *roman*, the academic essay from the quest epic and the collection of sayings from the autobiography. When functionality is present in a text, the whole work necessarily exudes another feature: plot. The element of plot (which is not possible without functional events) is essential to any narrative. As Chatman puts it, 'A narrative without a plot is a logical impossibility...[The issue is not so much that a given work has] no plot, but rather that the plot is not an intricate puzzle, that its events are "of no great importance"...'[46] What, then, is the 'great importance' of events in Ecclesiastes? Is there something, for example, that instigates a readerly desire for resolution, or expansion of some generating thrust or idea?

Events constitute plot when they are arranged in an ordered time sequence of some kind. The arrangement of events is what gives a plot its particular type of suspense or narrative desire—its shape. Plot is also the product of tension *between* events (partly the result of the quality of their respective time relationships), and in Ecclesiastes that tension is expressed through anachrony; that is, *prolepsis*. Gérard Genette says of prolepses that 'Repeating prolepses...scarcely appear except as brief allusions: they refer in advance to an event that will be told in full in its place'.[47] Take, for example, the reflections of Scout, the primary narrator in Harper Lee's *To Kill a Mockingbird*:

> When he was nearly thirteen, my brother Jem got his arm badly broken
> at the elbow. When it healed, and Jem's fears of never being able to play
> football were assuaged, he was seldom self-conscious about his

characters (the man of 6.3a-b, 4, and the stillborn [הנפל; cf. Job 3.16] of 6.3c, 5)

and events functional to one another (the living [6.3a], dying [6.3b] and consequential experience [6.4] of the man and the 'experience' [6.3c, 5] of the stillborn).

46. *Story and Discourse*, pp. 47-48.
47. *Narrative Discourse*, p. 73.

injury... *When enough years had gone by* to enable us to look back on them, we sometimes discussed the events leading to his accident.[48]

Here the reader is clued into future events (looking back, discussing) not yet narrated but that have already had their effect on the narrator. Such prolepsis provides self-perpetuating questions for the plot.[49] The implication of Qoheleth's age at the moment of his narration forms a similar proleptic element in Ecclesiastes.[50] That is, by stating his observations at the outset in a past aspect, the reader is aware that it is 'old man Qoheleth' who is reflecting on his youth, the younger persona of the experiencing Qoheleth.[51] By placing his statements in the preterite Qoheleth places himself in a future stance, and places the reader both in the narrative telling *now* and in the time of his narrated world. Whenever the preterite is used the reader could easily prefix the sentence

48. *To Kill a Mockingbird* (Harmondsworth: Penguin Books, 1964 [1960]), p. 9 (italics mine).

49. Compare an example from the Prologue of Sirach: 'my grandfather Jeshua, *after devoting himself for a long time to the reading of the Law*... was led to write on his own account something in the line of instruction and wisdom... You are therefore invited to read it through... ' (*The Apocrypha* [trans. E. Goodspeed; Chicago: University of Chicago Press, 1938], p. 223). Although the Translator (the narrator here) is recalling a past event (*ana*lepsis), he is doing so from a perspective later than the production of the book itself, thereby perpetuating the question of the value of the words that follow.

50. It is worth noting here that N. Kamano has, independently of myself, recognized a proleptic aspect to some of Qoheleth's *hebbel* judgments (2.11b and 2.17b in particular) in which he 'presents a conclusion of his argument to his audience in the middle of the discourse without providing sufficient reasons for such a conclusion' ('Character and Cosmology: Rhetoric of Ecclesiastes 1,3–3,9', in A. Schoors [ed.], *Qohelet in the Context of Wisdom* [BETL, 136; Leuven: Leuven University Press, 1998], pp. 419-24 [421]).

51. The aspect of old age is discerned in 1.1-2 and 1.12 ('I was king'; the description of Qoheleth as Solomon [see Chapter 6] may imply the perspective of old age; cf. 1 Kgs 3.14; 11.4). Also, the test of toil in ch. 2 implies a significant amount of time to have elapsed in order for Qoheleth to have become great and surpass all who came before him (2.9; cf. 1.16). Passages such as 7.15; 8.16 and 9.1-3 also assume a wealth of experience at Qoheleth's disposal. This perspective is, of course, enforced by the extensive use of the preterite, which always keeps Qoheleth's narrative stance in a reflective mode (see Chapter 7.4). Finally, Qoheleth's injunction to remember one's creator in the days of youth 'before the years draw nigh when you will say, "I have no delight in them"' (12.1; cf. 9.7-10; 11.9-10), assumes (or even requires) from its narrator a life of deeply felt experience.

with, 'When I was younger...' The narrative stance, then, is one that perpetuates a readerly desire to 'fill-in'. In other words, such kernel events anticipate (prolepsis) a story to be unfolded in its fullness. A character has begun to act, to take shape in the reader's mind, and its actions demand consequences and resolution. (That Qoheleth does in fact relate a narrative resolution [see Chapter 8.5] brings this story element into sharp relief.)

In Figure 1 I suggested that 1.13 was the functional counterpart of each of the listed observational events (3.16; 4.1-2; 10.5-7). Each observation (of which there are many) has a necessary referent in 1.13. This connection, of course, transpires in reading. It is the interaction (in the mind of the reader) between the notion of quest (instigated at 1.13 and augmented by a host of cognate verses) and each of the *subsequent* observations that creates the sense of mystery and enquiry to which the quotes at the beginning of the previous section bear witness. Indeed, it is unlikely that those quotes could have emerged from anything other than the sense of mystery that this character-oriented plot creates. It is in and through this connection and interaction that the plot 'unfurls before us as a precipitation of shape and meaning'.[52]

There is another type of prolepsis in Ecclesiastes that engenders a fictitious effect. Upon reading Qoheleth's opening lamentation—indeed, denouncement—'Everything is absurd!' (1.2), it is easily surmised that Qoheleth himself is 'informed'. Already, he has lived and he has judged. From this juncture one may envisage an aged Qoheleth in hospital pining for youthful days, his body ravaged by time. Or would he be held captive in a prison for the unorthodox? Or perhaps one 'sees' in Qoheleth one of the 'Old Boys' in his club, smoking a cigar, content that he has 'been there', 'done that' and has nothing left to prove? The reader, envisaging Qoheleth in any such beginning feels assured of the final setting, and the natural inclination is to fill-in what is not known—what Qoheleth does not reveal. How did Qoheleth arrive at this sorrowful state of affairs? The twist comes when the reader later discovers (at 12.8) that Qoheleth's opening remarks (stated through the mouth of the frame narrator *before* Qoheleth begins to demonstrate them) are indeed his final and ultimate conclusions, thus underscoring that plot aspect. What the reader learns in the ensuing narrative (as one learns of Jem's circumstance from Scout's ensuing narrative in *To Kill a*

52. Peter Brooks, *Reading for the Plot: Design and Intention in Narrative* (Oxford: Clarendon Press, 1984), p. 35.

Mockingbird) is *how* Qoheleth arrived at that state of apparent cynicism.

All kinds of questions emerge from the nexus of the mystery of Qoheleth. Is there any completeness in his character? Are we led to believe (by his ominous conclusions) that all that is important has been disclosed? Is there anything left to say beyond the decree, 'Everything is absurd'? Is the quest of this enigmatic character ever over for the reader? Or is the reader left with his or her questions, burning with the unflexing observations that Qoheleth has related? To return to Chatman's criterion, this is the 'great importance' of events in Ecclesiastes. It is what Peter Brooks describes as 'the principle of interconnectedness and intention which we cannot do without in moving through the discreet elements—incidents, episodes, actions—of a narrative'.[53] So it is that the proleptic aspect propels the story ahead to a known, tragic conclusion. It will be seen as this study continues that the concern of plot permeates most of the narrative questions under discussion.

3. Qoheleth's Autobiographical Adhesion

> The first personal pronoun *I* is unduly prominent in this book: [Qoheleth] suffers from 'I trouble', and this ego seems to have few friends.
>
> John Paterson[54]

> ... autobiography may only be the acceptable face of megalomania.
>
> John Sturrock[55]

Qoheleth's narration in Ecclesiastes is fused together by an iterative first-person narrator. Its presence is so strongly embedded that it led E.H. Plumptre in 1880 to go as far as to read historical (as opposed to fictional) events into nearly every sentential statement of Qoheleth:

> Not without reason did the wiser thinkers of the school of Hillel... in spite of seeming contradictions, and Epicurean or heretical tendencies, recognize that in this record of the struggle, the fall, the recovery of a child of Israel, a child of God, there was the narrative of a Divine education told with a genius and power in which they were well content... to acknowledge a Divine inspiration.[56]

53. *Reading for the Plot*, p. 5.
54. 'Intimate Journal', p. 251.
55. *The Language of Autobiography: Studies in the First Person Singular* (Cambridge: Cambridge University Press, 1993), p. 13.
56. E.H. Plumptre, 'The Author of Ecclesiastes', *Exp* 2 (1880), pp. 401-30 (429-30).

So Plumptre read into the 'I' a historical figure. Whatever historicity
the reader may or may not assume, one comes from Qoheleth's narrative with an impression (one that some have thought overbearing) of
individuality.[57]

It should be clarified that by 'first person' I am referring to a distinction of narrative posture and not of grammar alone. The 'I' may be used
in something other than a first-person narrative. Take Gérard Genette's
example: 'when Virgil writes "I sing of arms and the man..." or [...]
when Crusoe writes "I was born in the year 1632, in the city of
York..." The term "first-person narrative" refers, quite obviously, only
to the second of these situations.'[58] The term also refers to the situation
in Ecclesiastes. Harold Fisch makes such a case by comparing the often
more impersonal 'I' of the Psalter: 'The "I" is there the function of a
relationship in which the reader can share; it is not the sign of an
autonomous ego. By contrast, Ecclesiastes gives us a radically individualized statement.'[59] This is an important distinction that Qoheleth
enjoys: his use of the 'I' is uniquely narrative-bound.

There is perhaps no other book in the Hebrew Bible that has such
relentless individualism and it is likely such a quality that has inspired
such titles of articles and books as 'Old Man Koheleth',[60] 'The Intimate
Journal of an Old-Time Humanist' (Paterson, 1950) or *The Inner World
of Qohelet* (Zimmermann, 1973). As Martin Hengel comments,

> one can...speak of a marked '*individuality*' of authorship. It is an indi-
> viduality which emerges with him for the first time among the wisdom
> teachers of the Old Testament, and later also appears in a kindred form
> in Jesus Sirach and is typical for the time of Hellenism.[61]

57. On the question of the relative importance of whether Qoheleth's narrative
reflects actual historical events, see below, Chapters 6.4, 7.1 and 7.4. Suffice it to
say that I agree with Salyer's distinction of Qoheleth's *fictional* autobiographical
form ('Vain Rhetoric', pp. 204-16).

58. *Narrative Discourse*, p. 244; see also, Bal, *Narratology*, pp. 121-26.
Although Genette goes on to discard the usage of 'first person', I will use it in the
traditional sense, to distinguish narrative posture and to maintain clarity.

59. 'Qohelet: A Hebrew Ironist', p. 158.

60. Elizabeth Stone, 'Old Man Koheleth', *JBR* 10 (1942), pp. 98-102.

61. M. Hengel, 'Koheleth and the Beginning of the Crisis in Jewish Religion',
in *idem*, *Judaism and Hellenism* (trans. J. Bowden; 2 vols.; London: SCM Press,
rev. edn, 1974 [1973]), I, pp. 115-30 (116-17) (italics Hengel's). Hengel argues that
the 'style' of Qoheleth's individuality can be traced mainly to Hellenistic sources,
placing Qoheleth's locale of writing firmly in a Hellenistic culture. It is obviously

Other wisdom-oriented books of the Hebrew Bible rarely employ this intimate narrative device.[62] This is not to say that Qoheleth's style is without precedent. First-person narratives abound in ANE literature, as well as in some Greek philosophical discourses.[63] Qoheleth's style on the whole, however, is more individualized than that of other ancient first-person narratives.[64] Indeed, the relentless individualism of his

precarious, however, to argue for any literary-historical relationship of dependence of one upon another, whether with Hellenic, Judaic or other ANE texts.

62. For example, Proverbs seems to strike up this personal narrative posture only twice: 7.6-27 where the story of a senseless youth is told and 24.30-34 where the narrator offers an aetiology for the saying, 'A little sleep, a little slumber… ' But cf. also, Prov. 4.1-3, the Dame Wisdom speeches (1.22-33; 8.4-36) and the dialogue of 'the man' (נאם) to Ithiel and Ucal (30.1-9).

63. This is widely noted. For example, Seow, in the most far-reaching comparative study yet on the form of Qoheleth's discourse in 1.12–2.11, suggests that Qoheleth's form is most like West Semitic and Akkadian first-person royal inscriptions ('Qohelet's Autobiography', esp. pp. 279-84). Longman relates his own work on Akkadian autobiography (*Fictional Akkadian Autobiography* [Winona Lake, IN: Eisenbrauns, 1991]) to the form of Ecclesiastes (*idem*, pp. 120-23; and *The Book of Ecclesiastes*, esp. pp. 17-20). L. Ryken also compares Qoheleth's narration to fictional Akkadian autobiography (in particular the Cuthaean Legend; 'Ecclesiastes', in L. Ryken and T. Longman III [eds.], *A Complete Literary Guide to the Bible* [Grand Rapids: Zondervan, 1993], pp. 268-80 [273-74]). Although Egyptian texts are not particularly relevant to the autobiographical form (note Seow's comments, 'Qohelet's Autobiography', p. 276), many of the texts are set in narrative frames with narratorial situations quite simalar to that of Qoheleth's (frame narrator speaking to son etc.), a feature I will compare in depth at Chapter 1.2.

64. For example, in *The Instruction for King Merikare* (*ANET*, pp. 414-18), although the second person of address implies first-person narration, the primary narrator, King Merikare's father, never manages to emerge as a distinct character from this form. The closest to this is the rather disconnected proclamation, 'But as I live! I am while I am!… I made the Northland smite them [the bowmen], I captured their inhabitants… ' (lines 94-95, p. 416); but from this experience no reflection emerges. Herein lies the difference: it is his narrative reference to experience that distinguishes Qoheleth's narration among ANE texts. The base that the autobiographical form creates for Qoheleth is, in this respect, fully exploited. Again, while a literary dependence can only be speculated among ancient texts, it is instructive to point out that Qoheleth's choice of narration does not appear to be random (or without serious import), but rather a choice which, as Isaksson remarks, 'perfectly fits his pretension to be a king of mighty deeds, great wisdom, and profound experiences' (*Studies in the Language of Qoheleth*, p. 49). Given the

narrative has prompted such labels as 'confessions', 'memoirs' or 'autobiography'. Like confessions or memoirs, autobiography is concerned with the events of the life of the primary narrator. The label 'autobiography', while seemingly anachronistic, is nonetheless appropriate.

The autobiographical form lends stable integrity to a narrative, for autobiography is concerned with the self of the narrator, and the narrator 'I' is the great adhesive quality of such a narrative. Such a strategy of discourse (on the subject of one's own experience) serves to free the narrator to touch on innumerable subjects, all of which are bound by the constant narrative presence of the autobiographer. While enabling Qoheleth to speak freely on a host of subjects (although even his subject matter is motif-ridden; see sec. 4, below), the integrity of his narrative has another, more ironic function: to fix his own image in a world that for him is transient, frustratingly repetitive and absurd. For, '[the autobiographer] believes it a useful and valuable thing to fix his own image so that he can be certain it will not disappear like all things in this world'.[65] Qoheleth reflects and juxtaposes the life he narrates to us against the transience and absurdity that he has observed and knows to be real. A generation comes and another goes, the earth will remain and Qoheleth has ensured his place under the sun. Ironically, *he* has been remembered and will doubtless continue to be.

This autobiographical integrity establishes a fixed point of reference

effects it engenders, through that chosen form Qoheleth's narrated experience is made difficult to forget.

65. G. Gusdorf, 'Conditions and Limits of Autobiography', in J. Olney (ed.), *Autobiography: Essays Theoretical and Critical* (Princeton, NJ: Princeton University Press, 1980), pp. 28-48 (30). W.P. Brown has, independently of myself, formulated part of this conclusion in arguing that Qoheleth immortalizes himself through the autobiographical form ('Character Reconstructed: Ecclesiastes', in *idem, Character in Crisis* [Grand Rapids: Eerdmans, 1996], pp. 120-50, esp. p. 122). Seow has made a different, related point in connection to Qoheleth's use of the royal guise: while Qoheleth imitates the style of other ANE inscriptions by listing deeds that should have had the effect of immortalizing him, his 'imitation of the genre is poignant in its irony. In the end the text makes the point that none of the deeds... really matters... The genre of a royal inscription is utilized to make the point about the ephemerality of wisdom and human accomplishments' ('Qohelet's Autobiography', pp. 283-84 [284]). Although by the act of telling Qoheleth immortalizes his own story, the content deconstructs that immortality. For more discussion on the function of autobiography in relation to the self, see Chapter 7.1 and 7.4.

for the reader, the ground for Qoheleth's consciousness. Without a constant 'I', Qoheleth's narration would lack the cohesive power that enables us to speak of Qoheleth as a unified, although multifaceted, persona.[66] 'How extraordinary it is', Robert Elliott remarks, 'that "I" somehow encompasses in a coherent way the thousand and one selves that constitute a "Self", and that the person whom one loves and the person one loathes also say "I".'[67] Thanks to the 'I', Qoheleth's thousand and one selves speak with a wonderfully coherent voice.

Some important rhetorical effects generated by Qoheleth's first-person narration are worth noting. For example, imagine a key text (7.29) with the more 'distant' narrative posture of a covert narrator:

> *First person:*
> See, this alone I have found: that God made humanity upright, but they have sought many devices.

> *Covert:*
> God made humanity upright, but they have sought many devices.

While the latter has the quality of a משל in isolation (at the most being connected thematically with other משלים), the former is bound unequivocally to Qoheleth's character as a narrator. The 'I' here is what marks this passage and makes it memorable as Qoheleth's own observation.

Similarly, intellectual assertion of many statements as they stand would be largely infeasible without the first-person stance. Take, for example, 3.10-11:

> I have observed the business that God has given human beings to be busy with. He has made everything beautiful in its time. Furthermore,

---

66. So Fox as well, who appropriately calls this autobiographical presence Qoheleth's 'organizing consciousness' (*Qohelet*, p. 159). He expands further: 'The pervasiveness of the teacher's consciousness in the book of Qohelet is the main source of its cohesiveness' (p. 160). Brown makes the same point, seeing literary cohesion emerging from the 'confessional or self-referential style' (citing W. Zimmerli; 'Character Reconstructed: Ecclesiastes', p. 120). Compare Crenshaw's comment: 'Repeated use of the personal pronoun ['I']... thrusts the ego of the speaker into prominence, leaving no doubt about his investment in what is being reported' (*Ecclesiastes* [OTL; London: SCM Press, 1988], p. 28). On the function of autobiography generally see, most recently, Sturrock, *The Language of Autobiography*; and see Longman, *The Book of Ecclesiastes*, p. 18 n. 68; Salyer, 'Vain Rhetoric', p. 246 n. 118.

67. *The Literary Persona* (Chicago: University of Chicago Press, 1982), p. 30.

> God has put eternity in their hearts so that humanity cannot discover the
> activity that God has done from beginning to end.

Unless one placed, 'Qoheleth observed that...' at 3.10a, how would the
sentiment of v. 10 otherwise be narrated as Qoheleth's own distinctive
words? The quality of observation would have to be extracted, leaving
the platitude of 3.11 to stand on its own. This would, by depersonaliz-
ing the narration, leave us with a completely different timbre, and
undermine the otherwise clearly narrative procedure of discovery at
hand.[68] We would hear not the disillusioned observer speaking in fiery
and critically unsure tones, but more likely the disembodied and sure
voice of the wisdom tradition, shaped inevitably from the context of a
body of maxims instead of through the 'I' of a fascinating thinker.

The form that first-person narration takes in English translations of
Ecclesiastes does not reflect very well the more entrenched Hebrew
form. The subject in English usually stands alone as an 'I',[69] whereas in
Hebrew it is conveyed in a host of first-person singular verb forms and
suffixes *as well as* the independent pronoun. In the case of Ecclesiastes,
the 'I' of English translation usually represents the Hebrew first-person
verb form. In Hebrew sometimes the verb is accompanied by the
pronoun, but the function of the pronoun is often ambiguous. It may
emphasize the sentence it occurs in or, more strictly, the speaking
subject. The self-referential function of Qoheleth's language, then, is
often subtle. I will here briefly review the presence of the Hebrew autobiographical form and touch on some of its potential interpretive consequences for reading.

---

68. Salyer argues in a similar vein, suggesting that Qoheleth's 'I' focuses the
reader's attention so strictly on *his* words that readers are effectively invited to
argue with his conclusions, which are set firmly in life's experiences (see 'Vain
Rhetoric', pp. 199-200, 227-28, 243, 275). However, it is worth heeding Crenshaw's correction of the notion that Qoheleth's conclusions are *always* subject to
the criterion of empirical experience: 'The simple truth is that Qoheleth accepted an
astonishing variety of transmitted teachings without submitting them to the test of
experience. Occasionally, he uses emphatic language, e.g., "I know", when asserting something that none can confirm (3,14-15 and 8,12-13)' ('Qoheleth's Understanding of Intellectual Enquiry', in A. Schoors [ed.], *Qohelet in the Context of
Wisdom* [BETL, 136; Leuven: Leuven University Press, 1998], pp. 205-24 [213]).
This said, even 'I know' shifts the balance of authority to Qoheleth's own experience, which the reader may rightly infer is empirical in nature.

69. Of course, very often the 'I' is implied, as in imperative statements.

The syntactical placement of the 29 occurrences of אֲנִי can be broken down as follows:

(A) immediately after a first-person singular preterite[70] (×21)[71]
(B) immediately before a verbal adjective (×2: 2.18; 4.8)
(C) immediately after a singular participle (×2: 7.26; 8.12)
(D) immediately after an infinitive (×1: 1.16)
(E) predicating a nomen (×1: 1.12)[72]
(F) immediately before a noun construct (×1: 8.2)
(G) immediately before a first-person singular imperfect (×1: 2.15)

Most of these occurrences cannot be properly represented in English and all the major translations duly ignore them. Every occurrence in A should be considered pleonastic in conveying the subject. That is, the presence of the first-person verbs in these examples render אֲנִי grammatically unnecessary. Categories D and G may be pleonastic as well.[73] Category F is, at the least, uncertain.[74] Categories B, C and E may be considered to be most like the English 'I' in translation:

(B)	2.18:	כָּל־עֲמָלִי שֶׁאֲנִי עָמֵל	(all of my toil at which *I* toiled ...)
	4.8:	וּלְמִי אֲנִי עָמֵל	(yet for whom am *I* toiling ...?)
(C)	7.26:	וּמוֹצֵא אֲנִי מַר מָמָּוֶת	(*I* found more bitter than death ...)
	8.12:	כִּי גַם־יוֹדֵעַ אֲנִי אֲשֶׁר	(yet *I* also know that ...)[75]
(E)	1.12:	אֲנִי קֹהֶלֶת הָיִיתִי	(*I* am Qoheleth. I was ...)

In these categories אֲנִי is wholly necessary to convey the subject.

70. By preterite I mean both the perfect, imperfect (non-conversive) and vav-conversive forms that have a past simple sense. The translation of some of these is a contentious issue (see Isaksson, *Studies in the Language of Qoheleth*, pp. 23-38). However, it is only the *presence* of the autobiographical form I am here concerned with and not the aspect of its narratorial level.

71. 1.16; 2.1, 11, 12, 13, 14 (with גַם), 15 (×2), 18, 20, 24; 3.17, 18; 4.1, 2, 4, 7; 5.18; 7.25; 8.15; 9.16.

72. See above, n. 34.

73. At 1.16 (D) אֲנִי, although syntactically different to category A, is rendered pleonastic by the proceeding הִנֵּה הִגְדַּלְתִּי. At 2.15 (G) אֲנִי emphasizes the reflexive nature of the מִקְרֶה that will also befall Qoheleth (יִקְרֵנִי). This occurrence is, again, pleonastic in English translation.

74. The אֲנִי of אֲנִי פִּי מֶלֶךְ (8.2) seems to have no purpose, and, not being represented in any of the ancient translations (although emendation theories abound) is likely a scribal error.

75. Without the pronoun in both of these occurrences little sense can be made of the participles in determining the subject. The LXX's modification in both cases of the participle to a first-person form (7.26 [7.27], εὑρίσκω ἐγώ; 8.12, γινώσκω ἐγώ) bears witness to the need for clarity here.

It is not clear in the other categories—bearing in mind that they are grammatically unnecessary—where the emphasis of אני lies. Usually in classical Hebrew the personal pronoun is placed before the verb for the sake of emphasizing the subject. But such verses as 1.16, where אני has two unusual placements, show a use of the pronoun largely peculiar to Qoheleth's style. Does אני in such instances emphasize something more than the speaking subject? Does it simply emphasize the presence of the speaker? Isaksson's detailed review of all occurrences of אני in Ecclesiastes shows convincingly that although the pronouns may be pleonastic in conveying the subject, they are 'added in instances of greater importance, where the narrative halts for a moment to make a conclusion or to introduce a new thought'.[76] In support of this, אני must have had a unique rhetorical effect on Hebrew readers when read aloud, stylistically marking instances of importance. There is another effect, however, which English translations necessarily fail to emulate.

The culminative effect of the sheer abundance of first-person reference, especially in chs. 1–2, is visually remarkable. The explicit self-referential quality of Qoheleth's language is visually depicted in a series of suffixed *yod*s which, for its density, is unprecedented in the Hebrew Bible. Take, for example, the ratio of suffixed *yod* words that are self-referential in the following sentences:

1.16:	8 out of 22 words
2.4:	6 out of 8 words
2.11a:	5 out of 9 words
2.9:	5 out of 10 words

The assonance and determining rhythm of the most impressive of these examples (2.4) is not only clear to the ear, but to the eye as well:

הגדלתי מעשי בניתי לי בתים נטעתי לי כרמים

I did great deeds. I built myself houses. I planted myself vineyards.

This may support Isaksson's thesis on another level. While the visual element may not emphasize the speaking subject per se, it does high-

---

76. *Studies in the Language of Qoheleth*, p. 171; and cf. pp. 166-71. Schoors appears to follow Isaksson on this point (*The Preacher Sought to Find Pleasing Words: A Study of the Language of Qoheleth* [OLA, 41; Leuven: Peeters, 1992], §1.2.1). Isaksson also points out that the syntactically similar placement of אני in Cant. 5.5, 6 signifies an emotional climax (p. 166). A similar point is made (with Qoheleth as an example) by B. Waltke and M. O'Connor in *An Introduction to Biblical Hebrew Syntax* (Winona Lake, IN: Eisenbrauns, 1990), p. 296.

light the intensity of that subject's experience by drawing attention to the grammar by which it is referred to. This partly reflects the duality that Qoheleth creates in the process of reflection. Through reflection the narrating speaking subject becomes separated from the earlier experiencing subject that is being reflected upon. From this disjunction arises the significance (the comprehension) of that experience.[77] The Hebrew first-person form, then, works to intensify the presence and significance of Qoheleth's experience in ways that English cannot hope to convey in translation.

In sum, first-person narration in Ecclesiastes is conveyed mostly through first-person singular verb forms, followed in frequency by אֲנִי (to the exclusion of אָנֹכִי), although this is often pleonastic in conveying the speaking subject. Together with first-person pronominal suffixes these all explicitly convey first-person narration. To demonstrate visually this remarkable presence of the first person, the following graph reflects each of the above forms I have mentioned (all first-person singular verb forms, pronouns and suffixes).[78]

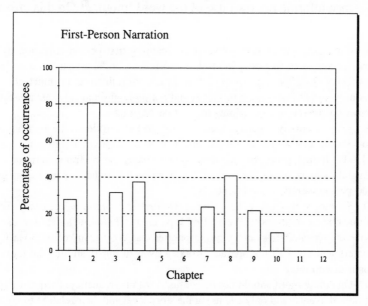

Figure 2

77. I explore this phenomenon of reflection in detail at Chapter 7.4.

78. In the graph I have omitted only the אֲנִי of 8.2 (see n. 74, above). I am assuming that the verses are of roughly equal length—at least enough so for my purposes here. The percentage of occurrences shown on the vertical axis is calcu-

What is most important about the first-person narrative stance, and
what this graph helps to demonstrate, is that it remains formally[79]
unchanged and unbroken from 1.12 to the frame narrator's appearance
at 12.8. That stance, which makes Ecclesiastes unique in the biblical
canon, contributes to the observational quality of Qoheleth's narration
and provides the anchor of his experience. Consequently, it is likewise
the anchor of his proleptic quest and the sense of mystery that it helps
to create. The narratorial voice is integral, therefore, to the functionality
of events and, as we have seen, to the coherence of the narrative as a
whole.

4. *Motif*

Motifs have a certain musical distinction. In fact, *Leitmotif* might be a
better word. *Leitmotif* (a term borrowed from music studies)[80] denotes a
phrase or idea, or (as with music) a figure or refrain that is repeated
throughout a single work having the effect of pronouncing a theme.
This sense informs my own use of the word 'motif'.[81] On this effect of

lated by dividing the number of verses containing first-person narration by the
number of verses in that chapter. Isaksson offers a similar graph (*Studies in the
Language of Qoheleth*, pp. 43-44) but it differs from this one in that Isaksson's
shows only verbal first-person instances and not pronouns and suffixes. My thanks
to Sonya J. Christianson for helping to produce the graph.

79. I say 'formally' because there remains to be considered the *implied* first-
person stance in the use of the second person of address; notably present in
chs. 11–12. In fact, given this element, nowhere except in the frame narrator's text
is Qoheleth's narrative stance broken. For more on this rather separate strategy of
second-person narration, see Chapter 8.5.

80. So Chris Baldick (*The Concise Oxford Dictionary of Literary Terms*
[Oxford: Oxford University Press, 1990], p. 121): '[*Leitmotif*] was first used to
describe the repeated musical themes or phrases that Wagner linked with particular
characters and ideas in his operatic works'. Even in music studies the narrative
notion is discernible.

81. One thing motif should not be confused with is frequency. Frequency is the
repetition of events (and only events) at the story level and their relation to the time
of the discourse or diegesis. This is the difference between story time and real time,
which is discerned in such devices as the telescoping or expansion of events (see
Genette, *Narrative Discourse*, Chapter 3; Chatman, *Story and Discourse*, pp. 78-
79). Motif, however, applies to words or phrases that recall previously mentioned
words or phrases by lexical or ideological semblance of some kind. Unlike motifs,
events can be phrased in completely different terms and still constitute frequency.

the motif critics seem agreed: it produces theme. Whether the reader is aware of it or not the motif will make its impact. E.M. Forster describes the effect of motif in the work of Marcel Proust thus:

> There are times when the little phrase—from its gloomy inception, through the sonata, into the sextet—means everything to the reader. There are times when it means nothing and is forgotten, and this seems to me to be the function of rhythm in fiction; not to be there all the time like a pattern, but by its lovely waxing and waning to fill us with surprise and freshness and hope.[82]

As Forster suggests, such 'rhythm' (although at times forgotten) forms a coherent theme or idea that through reading develops into a single fact of its own.

The real difficulty lies in determining just what constitutes a motif. Must a phrase have a certain percentage of lexical semblance to the phrase it is purported to resemble in some way? And once the location of the semblances (or 'repetitions') is decided, how many of them must occur before one can call their sum a 'motif'? For example, should 3.15a ('What was already is, and what is already was') be considered a reiteration of (or part of a motif with) 1.9a ('What was is what will be, and what has been done is what will be done')? Can one say of 1.9a that the quality of the existence of things is repetitious (or recurring)? I think so, particularly since the equivocation of 'what was' (שֶׁהָיָה) with 'what will be' (הוּא שֶׁיִּהְיֶה) places the scope of the statement in all existence at all times. And can one say of 3.15a that the quality of the existence of things is repetitious (or recurring)? Yes, although it is important to note that there is a development at hand. It is not only existence but activity at all times that is repetitious (or recurring). That recurrence of theme develops into an idea that is ascribable to the speaker (or one might prefer to say, 'work'): at all times the nature of events and happenstance is recurring. There is lexical semblance and ideological development and yet the subjectivity of the decision to call this a motif is clear. It is an ascription of meaning to the speaker. Motifs, unlike, for example, the analysis of the presence of the first person, are a purely subjective matter.

Even when we decide to call something a motif, its interpretation is problematic. The reader must, it seems, be aware of the haunting possibility that its significance runs only surface-deep. A comparison to

---

82. *Aspects of the Novel* (Harmondsworth: Penguin Books, 1962 [1927]), p. 168.

psychoanalysis may help to illuminate this problem. The analyst is often faced with the repetition of what Donald Spence calls the 'recursive operator'; that is, a recurring image or idea communicated by the patient, which *may* be polymorphous, the discovery and identification of which leads to the eradication of the problem that motivates it (e.g. a repeated image of anger towards someone, which is motivated by the fear of rejection). The temptation is great, argues Spence, to see in every recurrence of a given image or idea the presence of a recursive operator. Because psychoanalysis still operates in a largely Freudian context in which all such recurring phenomena must have a reasonable explanation, the possibility that there is no such explanation is unacceptable:

> [This problem] was never confronted during the Freudian age because of the belief that the answer could always be found, buried beneath layers of surface distortions...To begin to admit that...the surface of the world is frequently devoid of meaning is to come face to face with a terrible possibility...and the terror behind this challenge accounts for many of the more recent efforts to salvage the [Freudian theory of dreams].[83]

The answer to this problem, for Spence, lies in determining when a recurrence is worth pursuing. It is to be more willing to accept the terror of the unknown. The same may be said of the interpretation of motifs. The interpretation must be grounded in both a careful reading of the whole and a sensitivity to the fact that inscrutability of the significance of recurrence, and of events in general, is always a disturbing possibility, an idea that finds sympathy with Qoheleth's own thought (cf. 3.11; 7.14; 8.17).

If repetition so offends interpreters, Ecclesiastes is a chief offender. Qoheleth's is a book of themes—of key words and ideas—and the sensitive reader will no doubt notice the density of 'like words' that generate such motifs. Drawing on O. Loretz, R.E. Murphy has ably drawn our attention to them: 'Out of all the words appearing in chaps. 2–11 there is a variation of between 29.1 percent (chap. 2) and 14.1 percent (chap. 11) for the favorite words: "Among the 2643 words (Qoh 1,4–12,7) we count 562 favorite words, thus 21.2%."'[84] These often combine with other key words to make for phrased motifs. (This feature of Qoheleth's language accounts partly for how memorable the

83. 'Narrative Recursion', in S. Rimmon-Kenan (ed.), *Discourse in Psychoanalysis and Literature* (London: Methuen, 1987), pp. 188-210 (206).

84. *Ecclesiastes* (WBC, 23a; Dallas: Word Books, 1992), pp. xxix-xxx (xxix).

book is to many readers.) I would like to consider three of the simplest examples I could find: (1) all that is absurd;[85] (2) all that is under the sun;[86] and (3) all that is a pursuit of wind.[87]

Each of the motifs are distributed very similarly, particularly in the first six chapters. 75% of the first occurs in chs. 1–6; 70% of the second in 1–6; 100% of the third in 1–6. In ch. 2 the similarity is closer: the first occurs 33%; the second 23%; the third 33%. In other words, these all-encompassing judgments are concentrated in those parts of the text where Qoheleth is starting out on his test of wisdom. Each motif is developed and nuanced through repetition and altered through coupling with other phrases (e.g. the first is sometimes coupled with רע, 'evil', sometimes with 'a pursuit of wind'; see Excursus, sec. 3). The question, however, remains: do these merely bring again something darkly to the mind that found its inception in a forgotten nook, having the effect of mere tedium (if there is such a thing)? Or perhaps the particular place-ment of a motif serves to frame, or 'heighten' a certain passage?[88] Whatever effect each motif engenders, and however we are to interpret its significance, motifs are, collectively, a *stylistic* feature of Ecclesi-astes, and such stylized writing is sometimes a feature of narratives.

5. *The Structure of Narrative Discourse*

Since both of the narrators introduced in 1.1-2 go on to recount their own events, the consequent story-lines are, in at least one sense, neces-sarily separate. That is, when the frame narrator speaks at 1.1-2, the event of speaking is functional to the larger sequence of events; not so much to events in Qoheleth's story, but to those in his own: 'The words of Qoheleth, the son of David, king in Jerusalem. "Absurdity of

85. 1.2, 14; 2.1, 11, 15, 17, 19, 21, 23, 26; 3.19; 4.4, 7, 8, 16; 5.10; 6.2, 9; 7.6; 8.10, 14; 9.1; 11.8; 12.8.

86. 1.3, 9, 13, 14; 2.3, 11, 17, 18, 19, 20, 22; 3.1, 16; 4.1, 3, 7, 15; 5.13, 18; 6.1, 12; 8.9, 15, 17; 9.3, 6, 9, 11, 13; 10.5. As I pointed out above (n. 37), there is a syn-onymy between 'under the heavens' and 'under the sun' which suggests a lexical semblance.

87. 1.14, 17; 2.11, 17, 26; 4.4, 6, 16; 6.9.

88. So Wright ('The Riddle of the Sphinx Revisited', pp. 43-45), who sees a numerical significance and key to structure in the placement of the הבל judgments (he ambiguously uses the term *Leitmotiv*; p. 41). Note Mary Ann Caws's example taken from Virginia Woolf, in *Reading Frames in Modern Fiction* (Princeton, NJ: Princeton University Press, 1985), pp. 24-25.

absurdities", said Qoheleth, "Absurdity of absurdities; everything is absurd."' There are two implied events present here. The first (1.1) is that of the frame narrator presenting the words of Qoheleth. The second (1.2—located in Qoheleth's story as well) is the action of Qoheleth speaking. The events of speech are functionally related to the frame narrator's epilogue in which the reader learns who the addressee is (12.12a; his son/student) and is informed (albeit inadequately; see Chapters 4.2 and 8.3) as to the success of Qoheleth's quest (12.9-10). Like the functionality operative in Qoheleth's plot announcement, this propels the frame narrator's story forward and creates the possibility for change and choice, as well as the raising of narrative questions.

In the narrative set-up of Ecclesiastes, then, who is actually doing the talking? There is nothing after 1.2 that instructs the reader to forget that the frame narrator is doing so. We are subtly reminded of this structure at 7.27, where he gently intrudes, 'See, this is what I have found, *said Qoheleth*,[89] adding one to one to find the sum.' The reader is here reminded that it is still the frame narrator who is telling the story. Even the introductory passage of 1.3-11 (although its narrative form is, on the surface, impersonal) can only be the words of Qoheleth that were just introduced. And with the commencement of the first-person narrative of Qoheleth at 1.12 (although implicitly begun at 1.3 with a rhetorical question), the reader will inevitably forget (with the possible exception of 7.27) that these are reported words, and will assume that they are being narrated directly by Qoheleth throughout the rest of the book—until, that is, the epilogue, where the frame narrator appears again (12.8-14).[90]

It might be relatively simple to perceive who is speaking, but is there logical coherence in the narrative discourse? That is, is there any conflict in narrative stance or voice at any point? Also, how and where is the strength of the narrative line enforced to highlight the primacy of one speaker over the other, or to make the presence of the given

89. We should be in no doubt that this is the frame narrator's text. As Fox argues, the phrase is not an editorial insertion apart from the frame narrative since the grammar is too smoothly constructed for a later insertion to be plausible, nor is it a reference of Qoheleth's to himself in the third person: 'Even if we allow the third-person in 1:2 as a self-introduction [which Fox does not], such a switch of voice would be quite useless at 7:27 and 12:8' ('Frame-narrative', p. 84; and see pp. 85-87).

90. On this effect of diegetic levels, see Chapter 1.3 and 1.4.

narrator felt? The following outline of the syntactical forms that indicate person and voice, the flow of narration and the stance of the narrators—an overview of what is happening on the level of narrative discourse—will help to guide an attempt to answer such questions. It is based on the narrative form, not content, of the material; the discourse, not story.[91]

What does Figure 3 signify about the narrative structure? First, it shows that there is a logical confluence of narration. That is, the situation of each narrator in its respective setting is not in logical dissension with another narrator or narrative situation. When Qoheleth's narration is governing the text it is only altered by fluctuations in his own narrative stance. At the level of discourse, the two narrators do not compete or interfere with one another. That integrity of narration can be seen in Qoheleth's narration on its own as well. Qoheleth may seem to contradict himself at the story level, but he clearly does not at the discourse level. This means that even non-narrative material, such as the collections of proverbs in chs. 7 and 10, is located within the unbroken flow (in the medium and thickest lines) of Qoheleth's first-person narrative, and is therefore read in the context of the story's events.[92] Apart from 7.27, the frame narrator lets Qoheleth's words be spoken without interruption (although the *content* of the frame narrator's narrative, as we shall see, clashes dramatically with that of Qoheleth's).

91. The thickness of the lines represents the relative emphasis of the narrative flow—the medium and thickest widths are unbroken narration. There are other narrative asides besides those represented (e.g. the mini-parables in chs. 4 and 9) but the asides represented in the chart are those of specific narrative acts at the level of discourse.

92. Although I do not agree with Longman's attribution of 1.3-11 to the frame narrator (for three reasons: [1] the theology of the 'cosmos' poem is out of keeping with the frame narrator's theology as expressed in the epilogue [see Chapter 4]; [2] the announcement of Qoheleth's words is just that; [3] the inclusio [1.2; 12.8], which ends Qoheleth's words at 12.8, obviously starts them at 1.2), his outline of the narrative structure concurs with my own reading (*The Book of Ecclesiastes*, p. 20; cf. esp. Chapter 8.5, below):

1.1-11	Framework—Prologue
1.12–12.7	Qoheleth's Autobiographical Speech
1.12	Autobiographical Introduction
1.13–6.9	Autobiographical Narrative
6.10–12.7	Wisdom Admonitions
12.8-14	Framework—Epilogue

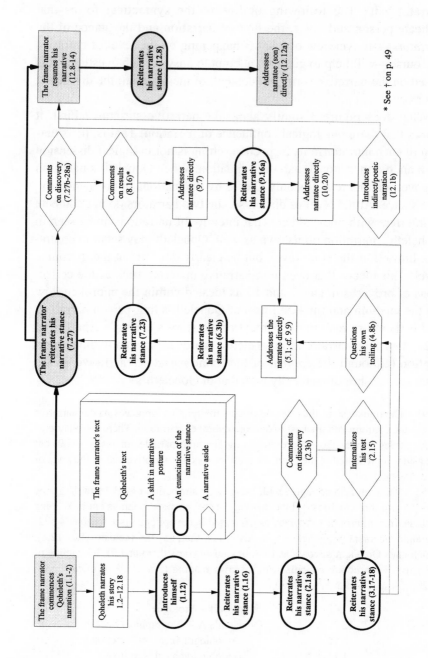

Figure 3. Outline of Narrative Discourse

* See † on p. 49

Second, the outline displays an attention to narrative technique. The narrative asides, for example, are always effective at complementing the strategy at hand. At 2.15 Qoheleth internalizes his test of wisdom: 'And I said in my heart, "As is the fate of the fool, so it will befall me. *Why then have I become exceedingly wise?*"'[93] The aside is not essential to Qoheleth's story. The question is whispered to himself *and* to the reader, and serves to accentuate the absurdity of his becoming wise while failing truly to understand why (cf. 1.18; 2.14, 16; 6.8; see below, Chapter 8.3 and 8.4).

Third, the outline shows that Qoheleth is active as a narrating character. The frame narrator's narrative apparatus (i.e. Qoheleth) is by no means static, but a dynamic character who is actively communicating with effective narrative strategies. The result of this narrating activity is that Qoheleth is able to emerge as a distinct character. The persona of Qoheleth is never lost in the often rhetorically powerful material it narrates.

The question posed at the beginning of this section, 'Is Ecclesiastes a narrative text?', may now be resumed. Certainly by Prince's definition ('the representation of real or fictive events or situations in a time sequence') the answer is yes. But this section has gone beyond this definition by sketching other indicators common to narratives. While motif, for example, is perhaps the most dubious of the narrative indicators I have suggested, the presence of motifs is something one might expect from a form of highly stylized literature. While it does not follow that all stylized literature is narrative, narrative literature is, by necessity, highly stylized. That is, it makes ample use of the types of narrative elements that I have so far reviewed (events, plot etc.).

---

93. The indirect quotation mark here could also appear after 'befall me' earlier. Regardless of where Qoheleth's indirect speech ends, the aside exists in the question being directed towards the reader.

† (See p. 48.) For MT's שנה בעיניו איננו ראה ('with his eyes he sees no sleep') read שנה בעיני אינני ראה ('with my eyes I see no sleep'). The subject for ראה could be indefinite (Murphy, *Ecclesiastes*, p. 81; RSV) or it could refer to the 'humanity' of the next verse (R. Gordis, *Koheleth—The Man and his World* [New York: Bloch Publishing, 1962], p. 288; Whybray, *Ecclesiastes*, pp. 138-39; this requires emendation as well). In the MT, ראה has no subject (LXX supplies αὐτοῦ). The emendation to first person makes the thought consistent with Qoheleth's other narrative asides in the first person where Qoheleth is racked with the vexation of his observations (2.15; 4.8b). Further, see Fox, *Qohelet*, p. 255.

Indeed, it may be that the mere presence of a frame narrative in Ecclesiastes is sufficient to qualify it as a narrative text, yet there is much more for the reader in store. There are more narrative strategies to be explored ahead. The only point I wish to emphasize at this juncture, however, is that those aspects of the text that I have chosen to survey so far suggest that Ecclesiastes can be viewed with confidence as a narrative text for the purpose of analysis.

Part I

THE FRAME NARRATOR'S STRATEGY

Chapter 1

PUTTING THE FRAME IN PLACE

Look here, upon this picture, and on this.

Shakespeare (*Hamlet*, act 3 sc. 4, l. 53)

1. *The Frame Proper*

Will you kindly tell me what width of frame the laws of the Medes allow?

Charles Dickens[1]

Of course, we borrow the rhetoric of the 'frame' from the physical frames that surround paintings. The interpretive potential of that physical type of frame is itself extensive, and interest in that potential is evidently on the rise in recent art criticism.[2] Frames demarcate the field of interpretation in decisive, non-negotiable terms that disturb (or otherwise influence) the flow of meaning between viewer and object, reader and text,[3] as Louis Marin suggests,

1.   Written to a friend about his portrait by Ary Scheffer, expressing some irritation regarding the strict regulations of the Royal Academy (cited in Jacob Simon, *The Art of the Picture Frame: Artists, Patrons and the Framing of Portraits in Britain* [London: National Portrait Gallery, 1996], p. 20).

2.   See especially the annotated bibliography in Simon, *The Art of the Picture Frame*, pp. 10-11, and the essays in P. Duro (ed.), *The Rhetoric of the Frame: Essays on the Boundary of the Artwork* (Cambridge: Cambridge University Press, 1996), and those in Eva Mendgen *et al.*, *In Perfect Harmony: Picture and Frame, 1850–1920* (Amsterdam: Van Gogh Museum, 1995). Interest in the topic was also evidenced by a generally successful exhibition entitled 'The Art of the Picture Frame', held November 1996–February 1997 at the National Portrait Gallery, London, for which Simon's book was an accompaniment.

3.   Compare Christine Traber's comments: 'The frame can be compared to a computer interface, determining the flow of information between the artwork and the viewer, but itself empty' ('In Perfect Harmony? Escaping the Frame in the Early Twentieth Century', in Mendgen *et al.*, *In Perfect Harmony*, pp. 221-47 [222]).

the mercurial play of palpable diversity, the stuff of perceptive syntheses
that the recognition of things articulates as difference, is transformed by
the frame into an opposition where the representation identifies itself as
such through an exclusion of any other object from the field of sight.[4]

And so by transforming what may have been only perceived borders (or
no borders) into actual physical borders, interpretive boundaries are put
into place.[5] Framing does not set limits on interpretation itself, but
rather on the canon in which the interpreter functions and has his or her
frame of reference. In fact, the frame can raise new questions by virtue
of its relationship to the material it frames.

Picture frames originated as a practical necessity to enable better
handling of paintings. Some even provided lids to protect the picture.[6]
Even early on, however, there was an eye towards the aesthetic. The
French painter Nicolas Poussin, when sending his *The Israelites Gathering the Manna* (1638–39), instructed its new owner to '*furnish* it with
a little "cornice", because *it needs it* so that, when looking at it from all
angles the eye is held by what is depicted, not distracted, its glance
muddled by the pell-mell intrusion of other neighboring objects'.[7] The
next phase was to take steps, via the frame, to integrate the picture into
its respective setting. By the seventeenth century, however, standard
rococo frames became so overpowering that they brought into question
the integrity of their relationship to the picture. Indeed, so burdensome
were the frames themselves that they became the object of ridicule.[8]
Framing became standardized as well. In Britain in the 1700s, frames

4. 'The Frame of Representation and Some of its Figures', in Duro (ed.),
Rhetoric of the Frame, pp. 79-95 (82).

5. As Mary Ann Caws says more directly, 'To frame is to privilege what is
contained within the borders of the picture' (*Reading Frames in Modern Fiction*,
p. 21).

6. N. Penny, 'Back to the Wall', *London Review of Books* 17.18 (21 September
1995), pp. 12-13 (12). Penny's article is partly a review of Mendgen *et al.*, *In
Perfect Harmony*. See the discussion of the construction of early frames in Simon,
The Art of the Picture Frame, Chapters 2 and 3.

7. As cited in Marin, 'The Frame of Representation', p. 82; italics Marin's. Cf.
the use of the same text in Caws, *Reading Frames in Modern Fiction*, p. 13.

8. See the cartoon by Bourdes in Simon, *The Art of the Picture Frame*, p. 19
(Fig. 7). Making analogy to the overpowering frames imposed on the Dutch masters, Penny wryly suggests that if 'the prim Dutch matron entered an opulent
Parisian hôtel she was divested of her dark suit and dressed for the ball' ('Back to
the Wall', p. 11).

often followed standard patterns 'rather than being specifically designed for each composition'.[9]

Certainly by the late 1800s, 'the artist-designed frame had become an art of the frame'.[10] Artists had responded to the institutionalization of frames by taking control of the whole object of interpretation and had become increasingly aware of the potential of the use of harmony and anti-harmony, mimesis and anti-mimesis, in the production of picture and frame. Some modern artists have consequently used frames as commentaries either on the painting itself or on some immediate social context. Pissaro was apparently one of the first to complement his painting by using the appropriate coloured frame and Picasso enjoyed using old Spanish frames for an ironic effect.[11] Taken to a further extreme, some curators of modern art museums have summarily rejected gilded frames and various period frames—even frames altogether—on the basis 'that the frame imparted unacceptable values or that it influenced perceptions in a way which distracted attention from the object itself'.[12]

Questions about relationships can be raised by considering the pictorial frame. Who is usually responsible for framing the painting? Some artists have had the luxury of choice. Some have even found it a form of rebellion to be 'against routine exhibition mouldings, against the opulence of dealers' frames, against mass-production, even against gilding'.[13] A choice of frame could be tantamount to resisting the pressure of dealers to conform. Indeed, artists unable to afford materials for painting, yet alone frames, may have had no choice but to accept frames that were not to their liking. In this context ideologies have clashed, which raises the question, Who is framing whom? One could also envisage situations where those who provided frames were attempting to give the paintings themselves as smooth and orthodox an

9.   Simon, *The Art of the Picture Frame*, p. 13.

10. Wolfgang Kemp, 'A Shelter for Paintings: Forms and Functions of Nineteenth-Century Frames', in Mendgen *et al.*, *In Perfect Harmony*, pp. 14-25 (19); cf. Penny, 'Back to the Wall', p. 12.

11. Both examples cited in Penny, 'Back to the Wall', p. 13. Simon laments the fact that few artists now are critically aware of (and exploit) the relationship between picture and frame (*The Art of the Picture Frame*, p. 109), although proportionately more give the matter *serious* attention (he cites Martin Rose, Humphrey Ocean and Hans Schwarz; p. 111).

12. Simon, *The Art of the Picture Frame*, p. 26.

13. Penny, 'Back to the Wall', p. 12.

inception into the gallery/public as possible. Or conversely, perhaps artists have made their own frames to protect their work with their own ideological shield, as it were. There is opportunity in this four-way relationship (painting/painter, frame/framer) for condescension and manipulation. Frames sometimes have such an overpowering, even garish effect that they are allotted the 'last say' regarding the observer's final impression.

Film provides another physical example of framing. In the technical construction of a film, the syntax of the filming frame (the position of the subject[s] in the frame) is of considerable importance. As James Monaco notes, 'The relationship between the movement within the frame and movement of the camera is one of the more sophisticated codes, and specifically cinematic.'[14] The physical act of framing a scene (composing what is *in* the film frame) merits our attention since its rhetorical effect is potentially extensive. Questions arise, such as, Are subjects free to leave the confines of the frame? Why? Who is responsible for the syntax of the frame? The actors? The ('real') director? The selection of material of the filmic frame is, as Chatman suggests, so 'totally discreet' that, as in the amnesia brought on by diegetic levels, we are quickly unaware of the frame's total control over the story space.[15]

As with models of interpretation, there are many types of framing that occur in the arts. Let me take an example from fiction: John Steinbeck's *Of Mice and Men*. George 'frames' his mentally ill companion, Lennie, by habitually speaking on his account and instilling a fear that causes Lennie to allow him to control his relation to the world (not always fairly, and usually for monetary motivation, which directs readerly sympathy to Lennie). From the beginning the two characters are cast in opposition: George having assuring, 'sharp, strong features', Lennie 'his opposite...dragging his feet a little, the way a bear drags his paws'.[16] George is quite obviously set up as Lennie's 'representative' in every form of social communication. When the reader, sympathetically aligned to Lennie's perspective, meets the outside world for

14. He further states that 'The masters of the Hollywood style of the thirties and forties tried never to allow the subject to leave the frame (it was considered daring even if the subject did not occupy the center of the 1.33 frame)' (*How to Read a Film* [Oxford: Oxford University Press, 1981], pp. 151-52; further, see pp. 152-54).

15. Chatman, *Coming to Terms*, p. 156.

16. John Steinbeck, *Of Mice and Men* (London: Heinemann, 1966 [1937]), p. 3.

the first time (in the form of the two men acquiring a job), the framing is clear:

> The boss licked his pencil. 'What's your name?'
>   'George Milton.'
>   'And what's yours?'
>   George said: 'His name's Lennie Small.'
>   The names were entered in the book...
> The boss pointed a playful finger at Lennie.
>   'He ain't much of a talker, is he?'
>   'No, he ain't, but he's sure a hell of a good worker.
> Strong as a bull.'[17]

The reader learns that the success of their gaining (and in particular, keeping) the job rests on George's skill (and Lennie's relative cooperation) in framing. This becomes a source of tension throughout the whole book—the tension between what the reader (via the narrator's access to thoughts etc.) knows of Lennie and George, and how the 'outside world' will perceive George's presentation of that shared knowledge. By thus 'normalizing' Lennie, his character is 'shown' to the outside world (outside, that is, of the two companions). This is potentially limiting, but the scope of those limitations depends, in this case, on the integrity of the one framing, George. It is by this same framing that Lennie's prospective relationships are left open, and George's integrity made known. By fashioning boundaries, then, this framing creates many possibilities.

Such is the importance of any type of framing: interpretive possibilities. I will return to the significance of the rhetoric of framing and the ideological and interpretive problems it raises in relation to Qoheleth in Chapter 5.

2. *Frame Narratives*

The 'list' of narrative framing techniques is potentially inexhaustible.[18] A frame *narrative*, however, is simply a more formally apparent type of

---

17. *Of Mice and Men*, pp. 32-33.

18. For example, 'delays and pauses to surround, with temporal and spatial borders, the central focused part, architectural surrounds to further mark them, repetitions and drastic contrasts to call attention either to the borders or to the dramatic quality of the scene pictured in them, an included picture to develop by non-verbal means the significance of the moral or psychological issues implied in the motifs thrown in relief... [etc. etc.]' (Caws, *Reading Frames in Modern Fiction*, p. 262).

framing than some of the examples I have been discussing. It is a text in which an external narrator narrates an inner story at its beginning and end, thereby framing (highlighting, privileging, delimiting etc.) the story that it narrates.

As with the physical relationship of pictorial frames and paintings, the relationship of the outer and inner stories varies immensely and determines the degree(s) of interpretive control allotted the frame narrative. The outer frame story can often dominate the entire text, in which case the less important inner story serves as a mere excuse for the outer, providing 'the material on which that [outer] plot feeds'.[19] Or, as with Ecclesiastes, the inner story dominates, allowing the outer story simply to highlight (usually to marked effect) the inner. However, shortness of length or a lack of complex events in the outer framing story does not necessarily diminish the frame's impact, and 'No matter how minimal or extensive the frame story may be...it forms a narrative in its own right.'[20] It is for this reason that in Ecclesiastes the frame narrator's brief introduction at 1.1-2 combines effectively with the epilogue to form, despite its brevity, a frame narrative that carries with it all the interpretive possibilities I have so far discussed.

It is widely recognized that granting the inner story a validation it could in no other way obtain is the most 'common' effect of framing.[21] That is, because a character is presented in the 'mouth' of another, usually more reliable character (i.e. an editor,[22] fictional author, person

19. L. Dittmar, 'Fashioning and Re-fashioning: Framing Narratives in the Novel and Film', *Mosaic* 16.1-2 (1983), pp. 189-203 (196). The detective novel is a good example of this type. The outer story in which the detective solves a crime frames the events that have led to the circumstances concurrent with the present narrating stance. Those events 'feed' the unfolding situation in which the detective works, thereby having the sole function of creating the drama necessary to demonstrate the detective's 'brilliance'.

20. Chatman, *Story and Discourse*, p. 255.

21. See Caws, *Reading Frames in Modern Fiction*, pp. 9-26; Fox, 'Frame-narrative', pp. 94-96, 100-106; Dittmar, 'Fashioning and Re-fashioning'; J.F. Summerfield, 'Framing Narratives', in T. Newkirk (ed.), *Only Connect: Uniting Reading and Writing* (Upper Montclair: Boynton/Cook, 1986), pp. 227-40; B. Romberg, *Studies in the Narrative Technique of the First-Person Novel* (Stockholm: Almqvist & Wiksell, 1962), esp. pp. 63-81.

22. For example, the occasional appearances of Rousseau as 'editor' in his *Julie, ou La Nouvelle Héloïse*... lend a 'guarantee of the editor's trust-worthiness and credibility' and 'an illusion of reality to the material presented by the editor' (Romberg, *Studies in the Narrative Technique*, p. 77).

of higher social status etc.), readers are more likely to suspend their disbelief and accept the 'fictional quality' of the work's premises.[23] Although the central 'framed' character may be difficult to accept on its own terms, with the respect tendered by the frame narrator, the reader may be enabled to hold that character in higher regard via the frame.

Michael Fox has adeptly scrutinized this effect in Ecclesiastes. He argues that the framing 'allows the author to maintain both a certain community of thought and feeling with the persona [of Qoheleth] as well as a certain distance'.[24] Hence the frame narrator is there as counsel to the reader to take Qoheleth seriously. In other words, readers are more willing to believe this kind of presentation, as opposed to 'These are stories by...'[25] The real author thereby hands over (via the introduction and epilogue) the actual presentation to the frame narrator. The distance created may be compared to hearing Qoheleth's tale told around the proverbial campfire, invariably shifting one's frame of reference to story-mode, thereby entering the narrative world of the teller. Through the frame narrator, then, an even greater illusion of reality (one distinct from a historical reality) is created,[26] with one foot in the camp of the real author and the other in Qoheleth's, each standing between 'reality and fiction'.[27]

23. This is not to claim that fictional works have any less a claim than non-fictional works on the 'real world'. It is not my concern to touch on this matter here. Suffice to say that I think the opposite is usually the case.

24. Fox, 'Frame-narrative', p. 95; cf. also pp. 96, 101. In the end he opts more for the distancing effect than that of a 'community of thought'.

25. Fox, 'Frame-narrative', p. 96.

26. That is, the force of the illusion strengthens the reality of Qoheleth as a character to the reader, and not necessarily the reality of a historical Qoheleth _who lived_.

27. So Romberg, discussing frame narratives in general (_Studies in the Narrative Technique_, p. 68). A more modern example of a frame narrative (again given by Romberg, pp. 69-70, _passim_, and used by Fox, 'Frame-narrative', pp. 100, 104) which strengthens the illusion of reality via the use of a fictional editor is that of _Gulliver's Travels_. The editor is a 'third man' between the real author and the implied (on the implied author see Chapter 6.4; on the implied reader see 8.5). The real author uses the editor to distance himself from the work, giving responsibility to him. That responsibility is grave, for it concerns the illusion of authenticity that the work either fails or succeeds to create. For the editor has only _collected_ the travels of Gulliver, and while he hopes that the reader will enjoy them, the author uses him to critique even the credibility of those tales (the credibility of the author

In creating an illusion of authenticity the frame set-up also creates a narrative setting in which to imagine the transmission of Qoheleth's words. Fox describes this setting as follows:

> ...the epic situation of the third-person voice in the epilogue and else-where is that of a man who is looking back and telling his son the story of the ancient wise-man Qohelet, passing on to him words he knew Qohelet to have said...[28]

Here we are prompted to envisage a dialogic interaction of characters on an epic level. The transmission of the story (Qoheleth's words) can be diagrammatically represented as follows:[29]

$$\textit{Text}$$

$$\textit{real author} \rightarrow \boxed{IA \rightarrow FN–(Q) \rightarrow narratee\text{-}(FN's\ son?) \rightarrow IR \rightarrow} \rightarrow \textit{real reader}$$

Figure 4

Although readers will often confuse the frame narrator with the real author and even with the character of Qoheleth himself (a problem I will discuss later), the basic frame provides a reference that enables one to perceive a sense of narrative direction, to place the characters in their appropriate narratorial positions relative to each other.

Although the frame allows readers effectively to 'enter' the story, there is often a more subversive element at play. As Linda Dittmar notes, 'frames actually subvert the reassuring function of bracketing. They encourage audiences to suspend disbelief but also force them to re-align the parts into new wholes.'[30] This is dependent, of course, on the subject matter of both the inner and outer stories. When there is

himself) and makes it clear that the editor is responsible for the final shape of the book.

28. 'Frame-narrative', p. 91.

29. In this figure, FN = the frame narrator, Q = Qoheleth, IA = the implied author and IR = the implied reader (the basic diagram appears in Chatman, *Story and Discourse*, p. 151). By 'real author' I am referring to the producer(s) of the text. As L. Eslinger argues, the term 'author' for biblical critics should include redactors, compilers, sources etc.; for to the text's final form all of these con-tribute ('Narratorial Situations in the Bible', in V.L. Tollers and J. Maier [eds.], *Mappings of the Biblical Terrain: The Bible as Text* [London: Bucknell University Press, 1990], pp. 72-91 [89]). For Fox, this 'author' is the frame narrator (or 'epilogist') himself.

30. 'Fashioning and Re-fashioning', p. 191.

incongruity (as the epilogue is often incongruous with the body of Qoheleth's narration; see Chapter 4.3) the frame narrator does more than foster a believable fiction. The framer sets up the suspension of disbelief *and* leaves space for the reader to question the inner story on its own terms. For the one framing is free to question that story fundamentally. Not to question whether it is a fiction or not, but to scrutinize the views it endorses. So, while readerly disbelief is enabled, so too are all the possibilities of a commentary that can do anything from ridicule to celebrate the inner story's hero.

Since each framing instance carries with it 'the significations it has acquired through usage and context',[31] it will be worthwhile to survey some biblical and ANE frame narratives that bear a formal resemblance to Ecclesiastes.[32] This survey is carried out not so much with the intention of in-depth comparison (although this occurs incidentally) as with that of encountering the variety of questions raised by frames, questions that are probably already familiar in terms of content (and with the biblical frames, in terms of ideology), cultural context and (although not so with all) structure.

a. *Biblical Frame Narratives*
The framing of stories is certainly not foreign to the Old Testament. Several examples are worth noting.

1. *Deuteronomy*. The story of the Israelites' journeys is retold to them

31. Dittmar, 'Fashioning and Re-fashioning', p. 190. This description of framing is in reference to the often metaphorical function of close-ups and montage in film.

32. Fox has already drawn a comparison between Ecclesiastes and the biblical frames of Deuteronomy and Tobit, as well as eight ANE frames; hence I refer the reader to his credible observations and will not add much to them ('Frame-narrative', pp. 92-94; reprinted in a shorter form although with additions to the number of texts compared in *Qohelet*, pp. 312-15). Irene Nowell has offered an insightful study of the narrative situation in Tobit but adds little to the understanding of the frame there ('The Narrator in the Book of Tobit', in D.J. Lull [ed.], *SBL 1988 Seminar Papers* [Atlanta: Scholars Press, 1988], pp. 27-38; esp. p. 29). Matt Wiebe has made an extensive analysis (more in-depth than Fox's, although to its detriment not compared in any way to Ecclesiastes) of 15 ANE (usually wisdom) frame narratives in comparison to the book of Proverbs ('The Wisdom in Proverbs: An Integrated Reading of the Book' [PhD dissertation; University of Sheffield, 1982], pp. 9-41). In addition to Wiebe's list, Fox includes the frames of *Neferti*, *Ipuwer* and *Duachety*. My analysis adds to both lists the frames of Job and Sirach.

by Moses. However, beyond Moses there is another, anonymous, external frame narrator.[33] At times this narrator invokes the 'additional' authority of Yahweh (29.1; 32.48). Throughout the book the levels of narration are complex, with 'examples of an utterance within an utterance within an utterance within an utterance'.[34] The introduction (1.1-5) clearly frames what is to happen: 'These are the words that Moses spoke *to all Israel* beyond [בעבר] the Jordan...in the land of Moab, Moses undertook to explain [באר] this law, saying...' (1.1, 5). The frame narrator is bridging the gap to the world of Moses' story, prompting the reader to (continue to?) imagine the dramatic scene of all the people gathered to hear Moses speak 'beyond the Jordan'.

Within the flow of narration the frame narrator intervenes to provide pertinent information. Note, for example, 4.41-43 (after Moses has been speaking): 'Then [אז] Moses set apart on the east side of the Jordan three cities to which a homicide could flee, someone who unintentionally kills another person...Bezer in the wilderness...[etc.]'. This allows the frame narrator to direct the attention of the reader periodically to data relevant to Moses' story.[35] But beyond this the frame narrator does not get 'involved' in Moses' story and certainly makes no attempt to interpret his words (as perhaps Qoheleth's framer is doing in the inclusio of 1.2 and 12.8).

The frame narrator does, however, exert control over the narrative perspective throughout while lending the book his own stamp of authority. In the epilogue Moses' life is appraised highly ('Never since has there arisen a prophet in Israel like Moses', 34.10a), which suggests that the frame narrator, as Polzin puts it, 'seems at great pains to impress upon his reader that it is Moses, and Moses alone, who possessed the type of reliable authority to convey accurately and authoritatively the direct words of God that form most of the book'.[36] It is the frame narrator who thereby gains the final word, and who is depicted as

---

33. Fox notes that 'in *Deuteronomy*...there is a voice telling *about* the chief character, looking back on him from an indefinite distance, while remaining itself well in the background' ('Frame-narrative', p. 93; italics Fox's).

34. So R. Polzin, *Moses and the Deuteronomist: A Literary Study of the Deuteronomistic History*. I. *Deuteronomy, Joshua, Judges* (Bloomington, IN: Indiana University Press, 1980), p. 25. All of this complexity, Polzin maintains, 'enables the book to be the repository of a plurality of viewpoints' (p. 26).

35. Cf. 27.1, 9, 11; 31.22-25; 32.44-45, 48; 33.1.

36. *Moses and the Deuteronomist*, p. 27.

having ultimate control not only over the canonical form,[37] but at least partly over the book's overall ideology.[38]

2. *Job*. The lengthy introduction (1.1–2.13) gives a narrative context for all the speeches that follow. Also, beyond the introduction, the frame narrator frequently offers clear markers of speech (e.g. 25.1; 26.1; 27.1; 29.1).[39] This frame set-up is much more stylized than that of Deuteronomy. All the relevant markings are clear, and sometimes interpretive by nature.

The problems that this frame raises for interpretation have been increasingly explored.[40] It seems clear enough that the prologue establishes first the reliability of retribution (Job is blameless and upright [1.1; cf. 1.22; 2.3], and after the implied *therefore*,[41] Job is materially blessed [1.2-3]), and then that same reliability is undermined (the Satan and Yahweh strike an inequitable deal upon which Job's character has no influence [1.6–2.13]). In the epilogue the principle of retribution is

37. Similarly, B.S. Childs: 'The new interpretation [in the form of the unique, edited narrative framework] seeks to actualize the traditions of the past for the new generation in such a way as to evoke a response of the will in a fresh commitment to the covenant. The present form of the book of Deuteronomy reflects a dominant editorial concern to reshape the material for its use by future generations of Israel' (*Introduction to the Old Testament as Literature* [Philadelphia: Fortress Press, 1989], p. 212).

38. This is Polzin's main area of interest: who controls the overarching ideology of the whole, the frame narrator (whom Polzin calls the 'narrator') or Moses? The frame of the presentation raises questions like these through such strategies as 'breaking frame' (distracting the reader from Moses' main message) and shifting the narrative audience so that the reader must decide for themselves with which ideology he or she will identify (Polzin eventually concludes that the competing ideologies form one monologic ideology; *Moses and the Deuteronomist*, p. 72; cf. esp. pp. 25-36).

39. For a precise narrative outline of the whole book, see D.J.A. Clines, *Job 1–20* (WBC, 17; Dallas: Word Books, 1989), pp. xxxvi-xxxvii.

40. See esp. A. Brenner, 'Job the Pious? The Characterization of Job in the Narrative Framework of the Book', *JSOT* 43 (1989), pp. 37-52; D.J.A. Clines, 'Deconstructing the Book of Job', in *idem, What Does Eve Do to Help? and Other Readerly Questions to the Old Testament* (JSOTSup, 94; JSOT Press, 1990), pp. 106-23; Y. Hoffman, *A Blemished Perfection: The Book of Job in Context* (JSOTSup, 213; Sheffield: Sheffield Academic Press, 1996), esp. pp. 267-76.

41. On the numerous implications readers draw from the vav-consecutive of Job 1.2a ('*And* there were born to him…'), see Clines, 'Deconstructing the Book of Job', p. 109.

again established (42.10-17). To make matters worse, the many voices that intervene between prologue and epilogue vary in the extent to which they support either ideology.

The question that we should ask of the frame is, What ideology are we enabled to believe? According to Athalya Brenner the narrator signals to the reader from the beginning that Job is only a parody of righteousness. Along with Y. Hoffman she suggests that the description of Job is purposely exaggerated to create an anti-mimetic effect.[42] As Hoffman puts it, 'the author deliberately wrote a story that declares of itself "I am not true", I am not an imitation of any reality';[43] and as Maimonides suggested of the first verse of the book, 'It is as if Scripture said to you: Meditate and reflect on this parable...'[44] Does this mean that we are not enabled to believe the frame narrator? Is David Clines's assertion that the 'epilogue deconstructs the book as a whole', in the end not enabling readers to believe anything about retribution or justice, able to be sustained?[45]

There is a great deal of potential interpretive control allotted to frame narrators and it is well exploited here. The infamous closing statement, 'And the Lord restored the fortunes of Job when he had prayed for his friends...' (42.10a), may, as we have seen, shape the theological message of the entire book. Is the reader meant to accept that the many speeches that confound the notion of a clear relation between deed and

42. Brenner discusses several elements that contribute to this effect: the cluster of superlatives describing Job; the use of such symbolically perfect numbers as 7 and 10 (7 + 3); the use of repetition; the unparalleled suggestion that Job offered pre-emptive sacrifices for his children ('Job the Pious?', pp. 300-306; for a similar view, cf. Hoffman, *A Blemished Perfection*, p. 271).

43. *A Blemished Perfection*, p. 271.

44. *Guide for the Perplexed* 3.22; cited in Hoffman, *A Blemished Perfection*, p. 272.

45. Clines, 'Deconstructing the Book of Job', p. 112. The closing lines of Hosea may also be noted: 'Those who are wise understand these things; those who are discerning know them. For the ways of the LORD are right, and the upright walk in them, but transgressors stumble in them. Who is wise, let them understand these things. And the discerning, let them know' (14.9). This final directive to the reader raises serious questions in relation to the content of the book and possibly 'deconstructs the possibility of a happy ending in which love triumphs, because curses linger subversively in the margins of the text' (Yvonne Sherwood, *The Prostitute and the Prophet: Hosea's Marriage in Literary-Theoretical Perspective* [JSOTSup, 212; GCT, 2; Sheffield: Sheffield Academic Press, 1996], p. 324; cf. Childs, *Introduction*, pp. 382-83).

consequence are now nullified? Is the world, after all the existential struggle of Job, so simple after all? As I will discuss in detail below, the frame narrator in Ecclesiastes likewise exploits such interpretive control and likewise forces us to ask, Whom are we enabled to believe?

3. *Proverbs.* Matt Wiebe has pointed out the resemblance of Proverbs to ANE frames. Wiebe acknowledges, however, that this is not so much a formal structural semblance as one of content. The presence of the frame is discerned mainly in the superscription (1.1), the narrative setting of a father instructing his son, the apologetic and instructional nature of the introductory material, and in the fact that 'the end of the introduction [9.17-18] and the start of the instruction [10.1-2] are marked by a change of focus'.[46] In many ANE frames (and in Ecclesiastes as well) the narrative situation is the same; that is, a father narrating to his son *about* wisdom or a hero of wisdom. Such a narrative situation is set up at Prov. 1.1-8a, and is unbroken until 10.1 where another proverb collection begins (משלי שלמה is repeated). At this point the audience seems to have been extended beyond the 'son' (בני is not used again until 19.20, 27). The son's position as audience is restored from 23.15 to the end of ch. 29 (with the second person of address from 22.17). Chapters 30 and 31, while not obviously structurally related to what precedes, may function as competing epilogues to the entire book.[47]

It is particularly the paternal narrative relationship (father–son) that frames the material in a narrative context, highlighting the way in which wisdom is acquired: through paternal transmission.

4. *Tobit.* Compare the opening words of Tobit to those of the Septuagint of Ecclesiastes:

---

46. 'The Wisdom in Proverbs', p. 56. Wiebe's classification of Proverbs rests on the widely held view that ANE instructional literature is characterized by a threefold form: (1) introduction, (2) instruction and (3) epilogue. Further, see below.

47. According to Wiebe, Agur (ch. 30) and Lemuel (ch. 31) represent two possible reactions to the presentation of Wisdom as Woman in Proverbs. While Agur chooses to reject it outwardly (30.3-4), Lemuel merely ignores it (his mother fears that his rejection will have repercussions [31.2-5]; 'The Wisdom in Proverbs', p. 218, *passim*).

Tobit 1.1:

Βίβλος λόγων Τωβὶτ, τοῦ Τωβιὴλ, τοῦ Ανανιὴλ...ἐκ τῆς φυλῆς Νεφθαλὶ.

Ecclesiastes 1.1:

'Ρήματα 'Εκκλησιαστοῦ, υἱοῦ Δαυὶδ, Βασιλέως 'Ισραὴλ ἐν 'Ιερουσαλήμ.

The identification of the book's content, lineage and location of the main characters each occurs in these traditional superscriptions from the frame narrators.[48]

In terms of framing there are other affinities with Ecclesiastes. For example, Tobit's frame narrator presents Tobit (even 'accompanies' him on his journey) while remaining at a distance from him. Also, in both Eccl. 1.12 and Tob. 1.3-4 the perspective of old age is introduced, which grants to the respective narrators a future stance for the telling *now* of their narratives.[49] Fox further notes that the sparsity of the frame narration at the introductions of both works accentuates their formal semblance.[50]

The epilogue of Tobit (14.11-15) merely provides biographical information and not so much an assessment of the main character as witnessed in other frames.

5. *Sirach.* The extensive prologue serves as an introduction that grants, as with other frames, a narrative setting for all that will follow. It is, as I have already mentioned, a form of analepsis. The frame narrator literally presents the book: 'I found a copy and...thought it absolutely necessary that I should devote diligence and labour...to the task of completing the book and publishing it.'[51] He also recommends that it be

---

48. The locale of Tobit's story is in and around Ninevah, which is where the tribe of Naphtali have been exiled (1.3ff.).

49. Further, see Fox, 'Frame-narrative', pp. 93-94, and above, Introduction, sec. 2. That there is nothing intervening between the introduction by Tobit's frame narrator and Tob. 1.3-4 may lend support to O. Loretz's theory of a primary Ich-Erzählung in Ecclesiastes, to which has been added 1.2-11 and other passages (see 'Ich-Erzählung', esp. p. 46). Without 1.2-11, Ecclesiastes' introduction formally resembles that of Tobit's. However, cf. the comparison of Ecclesiastes to Amen-emhet below.

50. 'Frame-narrative', p. 94.

51. Goodspeed's translation, *The Apocrypha*, pp. 223-24.

read. In so doing he assumes responsibility for the success of the
book's reception and readership.

   There is, however, no distinct epilogue to speak of. Instead is found
the interesting form of biographical summary by the primary narrator
himself (51.13-22), followed by an injunction to pursue wisdom in the
same fashion as he had: 'She [wisdom] is to be found close by. See
with your own eyes that I have worked but little, and yet have found
much rest for myself' (51.26b-27; see also 51.23-30). The narrative
shift (he now addresses himself to the 'untaught' [ἀπαιδευτοι] of
51.23, as opposed to 'my child' [τέκνον] from 2.1, *passim*) represents a
shift in concern for the way in which wisdom is to be attained, a
concern the narrator has grounded in his own experience (51.13-22).

b. *Ancient Near Eastern Frame Narratives*
In terms of their respective structures, many ANE instructional texts
invite comparison to Ecclesiastes. As noted above, I refer the reader to
Fox's study, and will here limit my comparison to three ANE works
that bear some of the most important likenesses to Ecclesiastes.

1. *Hardjedef.* The epilogue and most of the instruction no longer exist,
but it is credible to posit an epilogue due to the structural similarity of
what remains to other ANE frames. The opening lines make for a
noteworthy point of comparison:

> The beginning of the instruction which the prince and commander, the
> king's son Hardjedef made for his son whom he raised up, named
> Auibre. [He] says: Reprove yourself...[52]

It is clearly stated that the instruction was made by the prince for his
son. This differs from Ecclesiastes mainly in that no comparable origin
is offered. Since the story's source is less displaced (due to a more
precise description of its origin) it becomes easier to fix reasons for the
inner story's telling. The lack of such an origin in Ecclesiastes raises
questions as to the purpose of that frame altogether. Why was the
opportunity missed to anchor the words that follow with purpose and
context? How would Qoheleth's story read if it began instead, 'These
are the words of Qoheleth which he spoke for/to his son'? The narrative
situation as it stands in Ecclesiastes is less fixed, which in turn means

---

52. *LAE*, p. 340. This and a few more lines of instruction are all that is extant
from several ostraca of the Ramesside period.

that the reader is enabled to take the place of Qoheleth's audience in the story-world (on this see below, Chapter 8.5).

2. *Kagemni*. Only a little of the instruction and the whole epilogue remain, but, as with Hardjedef, it is reasonable to posit the rest of the structure. The epilogue runs as follows:

> The vizier had his children summoned, after he had understood the ways of men, their character having become clear to him. Then he said to them: 'All that is written in this book, heed it as I said it. Do not go beyond what has been set down.' Then they placed themselves on their bellies, they recited it as it was written. It seemed good to them beyond anything in the whole land. They stood and sat accordingly.
>
> Then the majesty of King Huni died; the majesty of King Snerfu was raised up as a beneficent king in this whole land. Then Kagemni was made mayor of the city and vizier.
>
> *Colophon*: It is finished (*AEL*, I, p. 60).

As with Eccl. 12.9-10, the frame narrator begins the epilogue with a summary of the main character's life's work (*he had understood the ways of men*), which, in Kagemni's case, authenticates what he relates to his children. The epilogue's function goes beyond that of Ecclesiastes, however, in its summary of a narrative context; one which may well have been more thoroughly sketched out at the introduction of the work. Finally, the epilogue of Kagemni, like Eccl. 12.11-12, implicitly emphasizes the importance of transmitted knowledge (*heed it as I said it*), an emphasis that is key to the tension in Qoheleth's relationship to the frame narrator (see Chapter 4.3).

3. *Amenemhet*. The introductory lines merit comparison to Ecclesiastes:

> The beginning of the instruction which the majesty of the King of Upper and Lower Egypt: Sehetep-ib-Re; the Son of Re: Amenemhet, the triumphant, made, when he spoke in a message of truth to his son, the All-Lord. He said:
>
> Thou that hast appeared as a god, hearken to what I have to say to thee...(*ANET*, p. 418).

As with other ANE frames, the introductory 'he said' sets up the narrative situation of the book. Indeed, as Wiebe points out, the introductory poetic stanzas that follow (1.2-11) set up a narrative situation in which Amenemhet will deliver his first-person narrative (from 1.12).[53] The

---

53. See Wiebe, 'The Wisdom in Proverbs', pp. 16, 70.

poetic introduction of Ecclesiastes (1.4-11) might be structurally comparable, with its setting the scene for the subject matter that will occupy Qoheleth's narration (1.3-11).[54]

Apart from the observations I have made in the course of the comparisons, the following structural features of ANE instructions also invite comparison to Ecclesiastes.

The frame narrator commonly introduces some king, courier or pharaoh in the opening sentences. As with biblical frames, the introductory lines usually identify the book itself, and the lineage and location of its main characters. All instructions have some form of introduction, some of them lengthy, providing a scenario in which to narrate the whole story (e.g. *Neferti*,[55] *Amenemope*,[56] *Ahiqar*,[57] *Satire of the Trades*;[58] cf. Job). After the introduction comes the main body of instruction. This often consists of iterative first-person narration (*Ankhsheshonqy*,[59] *Merikare*,[60] *Amenemhet*) that serves to ground the observations of the wise man or courier in experience. After the instruction, an epilogue usually completes the work. This often furthers the story of the outer frame (*Kagemni* [depending on extant material], *Ptahotep, Merikare, ANY*,[61] *Amenemope, Papyrus Lansing*;[62] cf. Job).

At this point it is interesting to note the conclusions of Katharine Gittes's thorough study of the history of frame narratives. She sees in the earliest (Arabic, Greek, mediaeval [*The Decameron* in particular]) some common organizing principles; in particular, the centrality of wisdom:

> Foremost among these organizing devices is the framing story itself... [and] various thematic motifs, most notably the wisdom theme, which often centers on secular knowledge and the importance of wit and intelligence as a means of survival in the world. No matter what topic

---

54. I.e. the cosmic setting of 'all that happens' and the pronouncement of such themes as weariness and frustration in 1.3-11. See R.N. Whybray, 'Ecclesiastes 1.5-7 and the Wonders of Nature', *JSOT* 41 (1988), pp. 105-12, esp. p. 110.
   55. *ANET*, pp. 444-46.
   56. *ANET*, pp. 421-27.
   57. *ANET*, pp. 427-30.
   58. *ANET*, pp. 432-34.
   59. *AEL*, III, pp. 159-84.
   60. *ANET*, pp. 414-18.
   61. *ANET*, pp. 420-21.
   62. *AEL*, II, pp. 167-75.

they discuss, most frame narratives [i.e. outer and inner story together] give a full, rounded view of that topic.[63]

Often, the inner stories that outer frames encompass are concerned with the quest or narrative journey of a particular hero or heroine of wisdom. Frame narrators, according to Gittes, came to embody a kind of corporate character in themselves. That is, the frame narrator became a stock type of character that authors only gradually came to exploit to a full extent. It is difficult to say whether or not the real author of Ecclesiastes was aware of the rich framing tradition of which he formed a part (this question is addressed in Chapter 5). Knowingly or not, however, there is a commonality of theme, purpose and rhetorical effect witnessed in even the most dissimilar of ancient frames.

3. *The Production of Narrative Levels*

For the sequential reader of Ecclesiastes the frame narration is primary. That is, until Qoheleth commences his own words, he exists only within the parameters that the frame narrator's description allows. But from his announcement at 1.1-2 emerges a narrative product: a story within a story. A person is telling a story in which a person is telling a story. Those stories have the same 'hero' (i.e. a central narrating character), Qoheleth. The frame narrator's Qoheleth is reflecting and looking back, reflecting on a younger Qoheleth; one who is experiencing and learning. Qoheleth is at once two characters: one experiencing, one reflecting.[64]

This *I now* and *I then* embedded in the narrative level was a strategy chosen by Virginia Woolf for her own memoirs. She described the reason for her choice as follows:

> I think ... I have discovered a possible form for my [memoirs]. That is, to make them include the present—at least enough of the present to serve as platform to stand upon. It would be interesting to make the two people

63. 'The Frame Narrative: History and Theory' (PhD dissertation; University of California, 1983), p. 188; cf. p. vii.

64. Fox discerns two levels of narration: level 1, the frame narrator, who tells us about level 2a, Qoheleth the reporter; who in turn is the narrating 'I' looking back from the vantage point of old age upon level 2b, Qoheleth the seeker; who is the experiencing 'I', the younger Qoheleth 'who made the fruitless investigation introduced in 1.12-13' ('Frame-narrative', p. 91).

I now, I then, come out in contrast. And further, this past is much
affected by the present moment.[65]

In her article on framing narratives, Judith Summerfield, after citing
this passage, goes on to flesh out the idea by discussing Richard
Wright's *Black Boy*:

> [Wright] constructed a text; he framed an event—from a vantage point
> years later, when he was a spectator of his past life. And the entire auto-
> biography moves between the I then and the I now; the 'participant' *in*
> things as they are happening; the spectator—*out*—looking back and
> reflecting upon, evaluating: the *in* and the *out* became the frame for the
> entire text.[66]

This framing by recollection occurs simultaneously in the told text and
the teller's text. In the same way the contrast is created with/by
Qoheleth. That is, the duality of his *now* and *then* allows him to include
his present while being acutely aware and critical of his past. It also
allows him to 'redeem' the folly of his youth from a more mature narrative stance (see Chapter 8.5). This effect of narrative level is partly due
to the structure of the frame narrative.

These levels may be precisely described in narratological terms. It
begins with the act of writing; the 'literary event' we attribute to the
author.[67] All events within the act of writing belong to the first
(diegetic) level of narration. The first level of narration in Ecclesiastes
is the frame narrator's. The frame narrator is external *to* Qoheleth as the
author is external *to* the frame narrator. Just as Qoheleth makes no reference to the frame narrator, the frame narrator makes no reference to
the author; that is, the person or group who is identified as writing. The
frame narrator's access to information, then, is unquestioned: there is
no source outside of his own story to be questioned (although we can
identify parts as borrowed from elsewhere, such as the Solomonic element etc.). The very effect of such levels is that readers easily forget
their presence.

4. *Narrative Level as a Cause of Amnesia*

Because of his position (in regard to narrative level) Qoheleth is made

---

65. Summerfield citing Woolf's *Moments of Being: Unpublished Writing*, 1976
('Framing Narratives', p. 231; italics Summerfield's).

66. 'Framing Narratives', p. 232 (italics Summerfield's).

67. See Genette, *Narrative Discourse*, pp. 247-48.

more accessible to the reader than is the frame narrator. That is, '[while the frame narrator is] existentially immune to conditions that will govern characters within the story-world and readers in the real',[68] Qoheleth is not so immune. He is what Lyle Eslinger calls 'epistemologically limited'. His *internal* position ensures that his story-world is limited to the narration of another character (Qoheleth has been framed!). As such, Qoheleth's world is easily entered. Not only is the frame narrator inviting the reader there, but he is providing the premises of a story-world, with all its epistemological limits. Qoheleth is thereby placed firmly *in* the story-world he narrates—within its 'spatial and temporal bounds'.[69] Everything said at that level becomes relevant to that narrator's 'ontological ties to the story world and his motivation to narrate is also conditioned by the bond'.[70] The relationship is not two-way, and this is why frame narrators are in such powerful interpretive positions. The frame narrator is essentially immune to the 'inhabitants' (actors) or events of Qoheleth's narrative level. Whether or not Qoheleth will succeed in his quest can be of no real consequence to the frame narrator's story.

The frame narrator's act of relating Qoheleth's words is easily forgotten as one reads (even the intrusion at 7.27 can pass unnoticed). Therefore, what is in reality an inner level of story (what Genette would term an intradiegetic level) 'becomes' a pseudo-primary level of story (pseudo-diegetic). Qoheleth as narrator 'takes over' the frame narrator's function as the primary (diegetic) narrator. This is one way in which Qoheleth is loosed from the epistemological bounds imposed by the frame narrator. This effect occurs in the much-quoted example of *Arabian Nights*. Scheherazade is threatened with death by her husband the king and occupies him with stories every night to preserve her life. Each of the stories has its own narrator/characters who in turn tell stories, until eight narrative levels are created. That the intradiegetic level(s) causes the king to forget this *shift* of level is crucial to Scheherazade's well-being, and therefore, to the outworking of her diegetic narrative.[71] While the diegetic level of Ecclesiastes is not bound to its intradiegetic level to such an extent, the 'forgetfulness' of

---

68. Eslinger, discussing biblical narrative situations in general ('Narratorial Situations in the Bible', p. 80).

69. Eslinger, 'Narratorial Situations in the Bible', p. 79.

70. Eslinger, 'Narratorial Situations in the Bible', p. 79.

71. See Bal, *Narratology*, pp. 143-44.

the reader is analogous. It is because we are drawn into Qoheleth's narrative that we forget the previous level of narration. Note Genette's comments about the pseudo-diegetic narrator of Proust's *Jeunes filles en fleurs*:

> ...the evocation forgets its memory-elicited pretext and to the last line unfolds on its own account as direct narrative, so that many readers do not notice the spatio-temporal detour that gave rise to it and think it a simple isodiegetic [of the same narrative level] 'return backward' without a change in narrative level.[72]

Until Qoheleth's narrative has reached its end, readers may either forget the frame narrator altogether or see him *and* Qoheleth as equally diegetic. In this way, Qoheleth, by loosing his epistemological bounds, becomes as 'free' (and hence enigmatic) a character as the frame narrator. Just as Scheherazade is set free by the king's forgetfulness, so Qoheleth is liberated by the reader's.

---

72. *Narrative Discourse*, p. 240.

Chapter 2

THE OUTER BORDERS: I

1. *The Superscription (1.1)*

The words of Qoheleth, son of David, king in Jerusalem.

This verse is often referred to as the 'title' of Ecclesiastes. It conforms to a common Old Testament rhetorical device[1] that might more properly be called a superscription. Superscriptions have a function analogous to that of titles. They are often descriptive and/or an abstraction of the content of the text they are heading. Often, a title contains pertinent biographical information, offering the reader a context of identity and place. In modern fiction, for example, the function of the title is potentially considerable. As Wayne Booth remarks, titles 'are often the only explicit commentary the reader is given: *The Portrait of the Artist as a Young Man, The Sun Also Rises*' and so on.[2] A superscription may do this and more. To 'superscribe' is to write *over* or *above*, and by extension, outside of. All of the frame narrator's text is, in this sense, a superscription. A title is a name. A superscription is a description that, at least in this case, lends a certain bias. While the frame narrator obviously supplies more elaborate commentary at 12.9-14, he makes it clear here that what follows has the 'stamp' of authenticity (rendered by the act of presentation) and of kingship.

a. *Whose Superscription Is It Anyway?*
The set of constructs at 1.1 does, of course, belong to a narrative voice, but 'whose'? Qoheleth's? One of many redactors? The frame narrator's? The first suggestion (Qoheleth) is ruled out by 1.2. That is, since the reference to Qoheleth in the third person at 1.2 is not self-referential[3] it is likely that the same holds for 1.1. The second suggestion

---

1. Eg. Jer. 1.1; Amos 1.1; Zeph. 1.1.
2. *Rhetoric of Fiction*, p. 198 n. 25.
3. Clearly, 1.2 is the frame narrator's voice with Qoheleth's only in indirect

(redactors) is not likely since there is nothing to suggest any editing beyond that of the frame narrator's own activity at this stage.[4] That is, there is no reason to posit *another* voice. Given the correlation of 1.1 to 12.10 (see below), and the lack of any narrative contradiction in voice, temporal stance or level between 1.1 and 1.2, I suggest that 1.1-2 is narrated in one voice: the frame narrator's. To be precise, then, the superscription is not Qoheleth's text. Qoheleth is, as in the rest of the book, an actor. In all but the frame narrator's text he is also a narrator. But here he is only an actor in another narrator's text. This makes 'his' words here a narrative *act*. As Mieke Bal puts it, 'In the narrator's text the words of the actor are not represented as *text*, but as an *act*.'[5]

What kind of 'actor' is Qoheleth? The frame narrator's presentation of him in 1.1 is of a ready-made character, with limitations immediately set for the reader. As such, all his actions and observations are set in a restrictive context. They may or may not betray the conventional behaviour expected of the son of David, king in Jerusalem.[6] Like framing itself, this creates interpretive boundaries in which to read. If what we read violates our boundaries a certain meaning is created in that

speech. The other grammatical third-person references (7.27; 12.8) favour this. When Qoheleth wants to be self-referential he is more evidently so (cf. 1.16; 2.1, 2, 15; 3.17, 18; 6.3; 7.23; 8.14; 9.16—half of these 'speech' events are intensely personal: e.g. 'I said in my heart', 2.1, 15; 3.17, 18 [1.16, *with* my heart]; on such idioms that may denote self-reflection, see *DCH*, I, p. 324). Further, see Fox, 'Frame-narrative', pp. 84-87, and Chapter 7.4 below.

4. As Fox points out (contra Galling), there is no reason to limit the original superscription to 'Words of Qoheleth' (which would suggest that the rest of 1.2 was added by an editor to harmonize better with what was already functioning to identify Qoheleth [1.12, 16 etc.]). Fox argues that the royal fiction was too rooted in the text for this to be likely (*Qohelet*, pp. 166-67). We should also ask ourselves why we might be willing to grant such 'cleverness' to a redactor for his ability to harmonize and not to a 'single hand' (on the question of the composition of the whole in relation to the frame, see Chapter 5).

5. Bal, *Narratology*, p. 142 (italics Bal's).

6. This last qualification has been sorely overlooked as a geographical narrative backdrop for what follows. It creates a fictional *locale* in which to understand this narrative. The backdrop is reiterated throughout Ecclesiastes: 'Jerusalem' (1.12, 16; 2.7, 9). Possible allusions to Jerusalem as a narrative backdrop are 5.1 (house of God = the temple?); 5.8 (*the* province = Judaea?); 5.9 (a land with a king = Israel/Jerusalem?); 8.10 (holy place = temple?; *the* city = Jerusalem?); 10.16-17 (a land with a king = Israel/Jerusalem?). Note that there is no other *explicit* geographical reference but Jerusalem.

process. Not only does the frame narrator, in a quasi-physical sense, limit what the reader 'sees' of Qoheleth, he sets the initial boundaries for his character (e.g. Qoheleth cannot *become* anything other than a king). These are boundaries that the reader may or may not choose to expand (or narrow even further) as a result of his or her sequential reading and/or previous conceptions of king, son of David and so forth.

As a character, no more need be said in the form of explicit commentary *about* Qoheleth. It is when the content of this story has passed, and the final depiction of Qoheleth in the epilogue (12.9-10) is given, that the elements of his character manifested collide and collage to form a unique picture. At this stage the frame narrator's Qoheleth is flat. That is, it lacks the 'ability' to deviate from a given set of characteristics or particular expectations.

b. *Eventual Implication*
As I have already noted, the superscription utilizes a common formula. Compare Prov. 1.1:

> The proverbs of Solomon, son of David, king of Israel.[7]

As in Proverbs, the descriptions of Qoheleth in the frame narrator's superscription are all static and not actantial. That is, while in this conventional mode of Hebrew syntax there is no explicit verbal form, there is a sense in which actions are implied. The activity of ruling is implied by the phrase בירושלם מלך (king in Jerusalem). An act of speech is implied in the construct דברי־קהלת (words of Qoheleth), and refers forward to the event of communicating in his narrative. This particular activity finds its functional counterpart in 12.10a:

> בקש קהלת למצא דברי־חפץ וכתוב ישר דברי אמת

> Qoheleth sought to find words of delight, and with integrity he wrote words of truth.

At 1.1 the narrative act is implied, signified, but at 12.10a the active quality of Qoheleth's communication is stressed and the means of it (being only implicit at 1.1) are made explicit. One could amplify 1.1: 'These are the words that Qoheleth, son of David, king in Jerusalem, communicated.' A wood engraving by Stefan Martin illustrates this declaratory aspect well.[8] It shows Qoheleth (as King Solomon) holding

---

7. Cf. Cant. 1.1 for another Solomonic ascription.
8. From Blumenthal (designer), *Ecclesiastes, or The Preacher*.

a Hebrew 'book' with the words of 1.1-2a written on it:

Figure 5

In his sketch Martin has recognized the allusion to activity in linguistically static constructions. In his reading he has taken words as signifiers of activity and enlarged their meaning. To take an example, the signified of דברי־קהלת (words of Qoheleth) is concise and of a particular nature. The phrase is comparable to what Barthes calls a 'cover word':

> ...the closing logic which structures a sequence [of activity] is inextricably linked to its name [i.e. the 'cover word' which signifies that sequence]; any function which initiates [for example] a seduction *prescribes*, from the moment it appears, *in the name to which it gives rise, the entire process of seduction* such as we have learned it from all the narratives which have fashioned in us the language of narrative.[9]

9.   R. Barthes, 'Introduction to the Structural Analysis of Narratives', in *idem, Image, Music, Text* (ed. and trans. S. Heath; London: Fontana Press, 1977), pp. 79-

In a similar way, דברי־קהלת signifies a sequence of events. As an act that initiates the communication to follow, it signifies the 'entire process of [communicating]...such as we have learned it from all the narratives which have fashioned in us the language of narrative'.[10]

2. *Plot and Desire (1.1-2)*

Published authors cannot escape the reality that they, in some sense, 'have the reader in mind'. That is, by the act of publishing the author in effect says, 'I desire to communicate'. No matter how 'pure' (i.e. devoid of explicit indications of the desire to communicate) or avant garde the work is, every published literary work is evidenced by a common denominator: the desire of its author to be read.[11] In Ecclesiastes, that desire to communicate is more explicit than not. The frame narrator's narrative act is a focal point by nature of its location and his implicit desire is to communicate Qoheleth's words and not his own per se. This is integral to another feature of the narrative movement, the plot.

The narrative act of 1.1 plainly suggests that the *content* of the words of Qoheleth are to follow. This prepares the sequential reader for the later events of Qoheleth's narrated experience. As such, that narrated experience is *made possible* (at least in the frame narrator's story-world) by the kernel narrative act of 1.1. The frame narrator's quotation of Qoheleth at 1.2 is part of this kernel as well. As Edwin Good, in his careful reading of Eccl. 1.2-11, observes,

> The sententious 'says Qoheleth', followed by the repetition of *hăbēl hăbālîm* not only underscores the phrase's importance but also makes us

124 (102) (italics mine).

10. It is particularly tempting at this juncture to suggest that דברי־קהלת may signify more than speech; i.e. *acts* in general. Elsewhere, דברי in a noun construct often signifies what a character *did* (so of Solomon, 1 Kgs 11.41; Jerobo'am, 1 Kgs 14.19; Rehobo'am, 1 Kgs 14.29; cf. 1 Kgs 15.7, 23, 31; 16.5, 14, 20, 27; 22.39). Yet the constructs found at Prov. 30.1 and 31.1 suggest that, however tempting this may be for my own argument, it is unlikely that the construct signifies acts in Eccl. 1.1. The idea particularly collapses in lieu of both Qoheleth's use of דבר (5.2-3, 7; 9.17; 10.12 etc.; however, cf. the ambiguity of 1.8, 10; 8.1) and the frame narrator's later description of Qoheleth as one who sought to find דברי־חפץ (12.10).

11. That this is a common denominator of literary works is argued convincingly by Wayne Booth, 'True Art Ignores the Audience', in *idem, Rhetoric of Fiction*, pp. 89-116.

> wonder what is going to be said about it and to what it will be attributed. The repetition of the phrase... intensifies the expectation that it will be applied to something...[12]

The first action of Qoheleth's referred to is the narrative speech-act of 1.2. By means of this and the superscription it becomes clear that Qoheleth's character (i.e. the evolution and manifestation of it in his 'own' words) is to be the principal concern of what follows. This is a thrust behind much modern fiction—to break away from the traditional notions of the beginning-middle-end procedure of the novel, not relying on the 'primitive' desire to know 'what happens next'.[13] Instead, a plot may have as the centre of its narrative logic the revelation of character. Hence the expectancy aroused concerns a character's development through what it says and/or does and not necessarily how it interacts and develops in relation to others.

This is not to say that there cannot emerge from such a plot the more traditional qualities of narratives such as suspense and resolution. The expectancy created here is not immediately fulfilled, and is certainly not fulfilled, as Good points out, in 1.3-11.[14] Indeed, it creates a gap that can only be filled by the subsequent development of Qoheleth's character in both the frame narrator's and Qoheleth's mainly independent narratives. The way in which that character-oriented plot develops will be discussed in detail in Chapters 7 and 8. The point for now is that such a plot commences in the full narrative movement of the frame narrator at 1.1-2.

---

12. 'The Unfilled Sea', p. 63. Good further defines the notion of expectancy he works with (and that I imply), which is worth quoting: 'something in the work first sets up in the reader a tendency to respond, arouses the expectation of a consequent, then inhibits the tendency, and finally brings the (or an) expected consequent' (p. 62). While Good applies this principle only to the reading of 1.2-11, it can easily be extended to an expectancy aroused concerning the entire narrative strategy of Ecclesiastes.

13. E.M. Forster has humorously depicted this 'primitive' desire: 'A ["modern"] plot cannot be told to a gaping audience of cavemen or to a tyrannical sultan or to their modern descendant the movie-public. They can only be kept awake by "and then—and then—" they can only supply curiosity. But a plot demands intelligence and memory also' (*Aspects of the Novel*, p. 94).

14. 'The Unfilled Sea', pp. 71-72.

Excursus

הבל AND QOHELETH'S NARRATED LIFE

> What shall I do with this absurdity—
> O heart, O troubled heart—this caricature,
> Decrepit age that has been tied to me
> As to a dog's tail?
>
> W.B. Yeats ('The Tower', pt 1)

Before discussing the main passage in which the frame narrator appears, it would be wise to address the likely meaning(s) of הבל, the most critical (and meaningful) word for both Qoheleth *and* the frame narrator (in 1.2, for example, הבל, in singular or plural form, constitutes five of its eight words). This brief excursus will aid both the narrative investigation at hand (in that it brings the content of what is narrated into sharper definition) and the investigation as a whole. The aim is not so much to establish some relationship between intent and meaning, but rather to establish the biblical semantic range within which הבל likely operates, particularly as a signifier of judgment.

1. הבל *outside Ecclesiastes*

In the Old Testament, excluding Ecclesiastes, at least eight distinct connotations of הבל may be found. They are, in descending order of frequency:

(A) breath/vapour (×8)[1]
(B) idols (×8)[2]

---

1. Pss. 39.6[5], 7[6], 12[11]; 62.10[9]; 94.11; 144.4; Prov. 21.6; Isa. 57.13. This meaning, according to D. Seybold, is attested by 'later Aramaic dialects that were influenced partly by the Old Testament', and might suggest an onomatopoeic word formation in the Hebrew ('*hebhel; hābhal*', *TDOT*, III, pp. 313-20 [313]).
2. Deut. 32.21; 1 Kgs 16.13, 26; Ps. 31.8; Jer. 8.19; 10.8; 14.22; Jon. 2.9[8].

(C)   worthless/false (×7)[3]
(D)   no purpose/useless (×6)[4]
(E)   futile (×4)[5]
(F)   nothing/empty (×3)[6]
(G)   fleeting (×1: Job 7.16)
(H)   deceptive in appearance (×1: Prov. 31.30)

Although there are some borderline cases in the distinctions I have made,[7] each occurrence constitutes a judgment or is integral to one. In each case something is usually judged *to be* הבל.[8] Take, for example, Jer. 16.19: 'The nations will come and say, "Our Fathers inherited lies, nothing! [הבל], and there is no profit in them [i.e. lies, שקר]."' Here it is lies that are associated with הבל (which I take to mean, in this context, 'false' or 'worthless'). And in all of the biblical occurrences something obviously false or futile, empty etc., is likened to or actually *named* הבל (e.g. Ps. 94.11). The judgments are both explicit (e.g. Jer. 16.19) and implicit (e.g. Jer. 10.15; Zech. 10.2).

In each of its occurrences, הבל is negative in connotation; that is, negative in a literal sense—denouncing something as negative in contrast to that which is potentially positive (e.g. true versus false [Jer. 16.19; 23.16]; useful versus useless [Isa. 30.7]; consoling words versus empty words [Job 21.34; cf. Zech. 10.2]; substantial versus insubstantial [Ps. 94.11; Prov. 21.6]). The opposites are, of course, usually implied. Take, for example, Prov. 31.30a:

שקר החן והבל היפי

Charm is deceitful and beauty deceptive.

Here charm (החן) is on a par with beauty (היפי). Both were (in the author's opinion) sought after by the women of his day. This is borne

---

3.   Jer. 16.19; 23.16; derivative (הבליעל): 1 Sam. 25.25; 2 Sam. 16.7; 1 Kgs 21.13; noun and verb constructs (ההבל ויהבלו): 2 Kgs 17.15; Jer. 2.5.

4.   Job 27.12; Isa. 49.4; Jer. 10.3; 10.15; Lam. 4.17; Zech. 10.2.

5.   Job 9.29; Pss. 62.10[11]; 78.33; Isa. 30.7.

6.   Job 21.34; 35.16; Prov. 13.11.

7.   For example, Ps. 78.33 could connote either 'futility' or 'vapour', and it is unclear to me whether Lam. 4.17 suggests 'having no purpose' or 'futility'.

8.   So also, Seybold: 'the term expresses an evaluation of people or things ...[and usually] accomplishes a (negative) qualification' ('*hebhel; hābhal*', p. 314). It is worth noting in relation to this that a הבל ('idol') may itself be judged הבל (Jer. 2.5; furthermore, see below) and any association with idols judged disobedient (Deut. 32.21).

out by the next contrasting stich: 'But a woman who fears Yahweh is to be praised' (31.30b). While some women might seek הבל (in the form of beauty) they are, it is implied, to be abhorred, for it is the woman who fears Yahweh who is to be praised. Both הבל and שׁקר are negative 'opposites' of the fear of Yahweh.

There is often a textual link between what is הבל and what is idolatrous (such as customs etc.).[9] The connection is apparent when the הבלים ('idols') themselves are considered futile or worthless. At 2 Kgs 17.15 this is especially evident:

וילכו אחרי ההבל ויהבלו

> ...and they went after idols and became false [or '...after worthlessness and became worthless'] (cf. Jer. 2.5).

Any association here with the הבלים *is* הבל.

Perhaps what is most striking (in relation to Ecclesiastes) is the sheer and consistent quality of negation in each occurrence of the word regardless of dissimilar contexts and referentiality. If we grant that words acquire multifarious colourings through usage, and all the import of their former contexts (albeit only those known to the author and/or reader), then the biblical use of הבל formed a paradoxically rich while bleak background, a blackboard of negativity on which Qoheleth could sketch his own nuances of his key word.[10]

2. הבל *in Ecclesiastes*

As I have noted, all the uses of הבל outside Ecclesiastes constitute a judgment or are integral to one. The same holds true in Ecclesiastes. There is, however, a major difference. None of the *hebbel* judgments outside of Ecclesiastes claim that since something is, for example, useless, it is therefore הבל. While beauty may *be* הבל (Prov. 31.30a), the fact that something is beautiful is not (necessarily) הבל. Only things, not situations, are הבל. The signifieds of הבל outside of Ecclesiastes do *not* include states of affairs within their scope of judgment,[11] nor do

---

9.   See Jer. 10.1-15 in which הבל occurs three times.

10.   Compare T. Polk's comments: 'Words do not work [as empty ciphers] at all... Everywhere the connotation of *hebel* is thoroughly negative' ('The Wisdom of Irony: A Study of *Hebel* and its Relation to Joy and Fear of God in Ecclesiastes', *SBTh* 6.1 [1976], pp. 3-17 [8]).

11.   As Fox argues, הבל in Ecclesiastes is used to report 'facts' about the world

they include, globally, 'everything'. It seems, then, that Qoheleth used the term quite unconventionally, for 21 of the 38 occurrences in his book are judgments on situations.[12] As such readers are invited to consider הבל in relation to the disclosure of Qoheleth's narrative, the situation of which falls under the *hebbel* judgment.

Those 21 occurrences can be classified into 2 types: (1) it is הבל that there is a divorce between deed and consequence in a certain situation (×14),[13] and (2) it is הבל that a situation is the way it is (×7).[14] Here is an example of the first type, a divorce between deed and consequence (2.15): 'And I said in my heart, "As is the fate of the fool, so it will befall me. Why then have I become exceedingly wise?" So I said in my heart that this too was הבל.' There is a disparity here. Qoheleth has become wise and he (as the reader is invited to) assumes that his fate should be different from the fool. There is no apparent logical relationship between (i.e. there is a 'divorce' between) deed (becoming wise) and consequence (having the same fate as the fool: death [2.16b]). The divorce itself is הבל.

Here is an example of the second type, that a situation is the way it is (4.4): 'And I observed that all toil and all skilful activity is the result of[15] one man's envy of another [קנאת־איש]. This too is הבל and a pursuit of wind.' The situation is stated plainly: toil and activity are the result of envy. This is הבל. In texts demonstrating this second type, Qoheleth literally calls things as he sees them, and this helps to form

---

at large, and outside of Ecclesiastes it is the lamentation psalms that come closest to this, but even these are very personal in nature and their scope does not extend to the world (*Qohelet*, p. 93). Similarly, see G. Ogden, '"Vanity" It Certainly Is Not', *BT* 38.3 (1987), pp. 301-307 (302-304, 306-307).

12. I include neither the judgments with הכל as referent (see below, sec. 3) nor the strictly adjectival qualification of nouns or noun groups (5.7; 6.11, 12; 9.9; 11.10). While 7.15 could arguably belong to the latter category, I extend its scope to that of an implied judgment (i.e. of the situation that immediately follows it—see below). It is worth noting that the semantic usage of הבל adjectivally in Ecclesiastes is similar to the more 'common' usage of הבל elsewhere (cf. Job 7.16; Pss. 39.6[7]; 94.11; Isa. 30.7). As in the Psalter, these adjectival usages are not concerned with situations.

13. 2.15, 19, 21, 26; 4.7-8a (×2), 16; 5.10; 6.2; 7.15-16 (implied); 8.12a, 14 (×2); 9.1-3.

14. 2.23; 4.4, 8b; 3.19; 6.9; 7.6; 8.11.

15. I take the particle כי here to have this resultant force (so Murphy, *Ecclesiastes*, p. 38; cf. Prov. 14.30: 'The bones rot [רקב] *as the result of* [כי] envy [קנא]').

the core of the book's indisputable observational quality. He rarely if ever offers a response to such comments; his point instead is simply to elucidate the realities observed. And here lies the difference between the two types: while the first is *demonstrated* by a 'divorce', the second is simply stated. In the second type, the divorce is assumed and not shown.

What English word might therefore best encapsulate הבל in Ecclesiastes? One clue comes from a uniquely existential quality of Qoheleth's use of the word. Qoheleth describes his most intensely personal experiences and yet relates them to a much wider scope of judgment, implying that there is something amiss about the created order. Such a bare confrontation with personal experience is not a little comparable to the key tenets of existentialism.[16] Drawing on the work of Albert Camus, Fox defines existential absurdity thus:

> The essence of the absurd is a disparity between two phenomena that are supposed to be joined by a link of harmony or causality but are actually disjunct or even conflicting...[quoting Camus:] L'absurde est essentiellement un divorce. Il n'est ni dans l'un ni dans l'autre des éléments comparés. Il naît de leur confrontation.[17]

The severance of deed from consequence, Fox argues, is explicit in other elements of Qoheleth's story as well:

> What is crooked [מעות] cannot be made straight
>   and what is lacking cannot be counted (1.15).

> Consider the activity of God:
> For who is able to make straight
>   what he has made crooked [עותו]? (7.13).

In this twisting (עות, 'to twist, pervert') 'is the severance of deed from consequence, which severance strips human deeds of their significance'.[18]

This definition works well with the 14 occurrences of the first type.

---

16. See my Postscript, esp. sec. 1, for a full discussion of those tenets.

17. *Qohelet*, p. 31 (Camus quote from *Le mythe de Sisyphe*). C.B. Peter has offered a far less convincing comparison than Fox's of Camus to Qoheleth, although he does manage to create some ground for analogy between what he calls 'Camusian Absurdity' and 'Ecclesiastesan Vanity' ('In Defence of Existence: A Comparison between Ecclesiastes and Albert Camus', *BTF* 12 [1980], pp. 26-43; esp. p. 40).

18. Fox, *Qohelet*, p. 47.

However, the 7 occurrences of the second type might best be translated 'futile'. In the example of 4.4 it is surely futile (or 'of no purpose', 'in vain') that all toil is the result of envy. The reader can only *assume* that Qoheleth thought it absurd as well. This is because the relation of deed and consequence can only *be* assumed, for there are no real deeds mentioned (no history, no events). Rather, the reader is expected to accept Qoheleth's opinion that all toil and all skilful activity have questionable motives. Furthermore, the reader is expected to assume that the deed (or 'work'?) of envy (for Qoheleth an unquestioned reality) should not have toil as a consequence. Indeed, it is the consequence itself that is judged to be הבל.

There are related considerations that affect the choice of translation. For example, הבל is closely connected to several other words or phrases that colour its meaning at particular points.[19] The proximity has led most scholars to assume a degree of semantic overlap between הבל and such phrases as 'a grievous ill'[20] and 'an evil [wretched?] occupation'.[21] The most important of these phrases are רעות רוח[22] and רוח רעיון.[23] Both רעות and רעיון occur only in Ecclesiastes and are probably derived from the same root, רעה. What that root means, however, is the problem. I will not rehearse all the options here,[24] suffice to say that I am in agreement with the wide consensus (as witnessed by some modern translations: RSV, NIV, NRSV, NASB) and some linguistic

---

19. It is important to note, however, that when הבל is coupled with a phrase such as 'a great evil' (e.g. 2.21, גם־זה הבל ורעה רבה) the *culminative* effect is metaphorical and *not* a strict equation of the two phrases. That is, one phrase is not used to qualify the other, but they are used together as a kind of collective metaphor to describe something else. For example, in 2.21 the two phrases together qualify the lamentable situation of leaving one's portion to someone who did not toil for it (2.21a). The phrases there clearly do not qualify each other. This frees the semantic field of הבל to be defined by its referents (situations, concepts etc.) and not by other concrete phrases (furthermore, see Seybold, '*hebhel; hābhal*', p. 315).

20. רע עלי; חלי רע—2.17; 5.13, 15; 6.2.

21. ענין רע—2.21; 4.8; 6.1-2; cf. 1.13; 4.3-4; 9.3; 10.5.

22. Appearing with הבל at 1.14; 2.11, 17, 26; 4.4; 6.9. It occurs once on its own as a רוח 'judgment' at 4.6.

23. Appearing with הבל at 4.16, and on its own in a רוח 'judgment' at 1.17.

24. For this see the commentaries, particularly that of G.A. Barton for the translation tradition (*The Book of Ecclesiastes* [ICC; Edinburgh: T. & T. Clark, 1959 [1908]), pp. 85-86).

testimony,[25] to translate 'pursuit'. More simply, I take רוח, when used with הבל, to mean 'wind'.[26] The proposed translation of רעות and רעיון, if correct, supports this translation of רוח (the idea of *pursuing* one's 'breath', for example, is difficult to imagine).[27] In relation to הבל, a 'pursuit of wind', implying as it does a vexatious chore,[28] can have no positive import and complements the sheer negativity of הבל.[29]

The notion of 'absurdity' to which I have thus far made reference is strictly intellectual. A divorce within the logical process is just that and nothing more. Yet couplings of הבל with phrases such as 'a grievous ill' and so on, carry a moral aspect (an aspect shared with uses outside Ecclesiastes). Obviously, רע has moral overtones, and situations that are denounced as הבל Qoheleth often clearly regards to be evil or unjust in themselves.[30] Can the notion of absurdity therefore be extended to include the moral aspect? Yes, but this entails a choice. While it is probable that most readers consider what is absurd to be not good (רע), the word's intellectual sense allows the reader to choose to ignore its moral aspect.

The choice to render הבל by 'absurd' (as with nearly every other

25. Admittedly this form could either derive from a verb common in Aramaic meaning 'to desire' or from רעה ('to shepherd' etc., the participle of which denotes 'shepherd' at 12.11). The latter word is used specifically of tending animals (Gen. 4.2; 37.2 etc.) and more generally of grazing and pasture (Gen. 41.2; Job 24.2; Isa. 5.17 etc.). In any case it is plausible that an ironic sense lies dormant in the morphological assonance of both רעיון and רעות with the biblical רעה (other possible forms include רעום, רעות, רעו). Compare LXX's rendering of רעה in Ecclesiastes, προαίρεσις, which suggests an action involving a deliberate choice and, by extension, striving or pursuit.

26. A related word such as 'vapour', however, might work as well and would not take away from the inherent negativity of the phrase that I will suggest.

27. For other meanings of רוח in Ecclesiastes, see Chapter 7.4c.

28. Qoheleth significantly tags the phrase to an observation on the futility of labour: 'Better a handful with rest than two handfuls with toil and a pursuit of wind' (4.6; cf. 1.6).

29. A good reason not to accept John E. McKenna's positive gloss on הבל, relating the word, without critical discussion of *any* text, to Qoheleth's supposed theology of trust in his creator ('The Concept of *hebel* in the Book of Ecclesiastes', *SJT* 45 [1992], pp. 19-28 [esp. pp. 24, 27]). McKenna also rejects any philosophized understanding of הבל on the erroneous understanding that existential absurdity signifies nothingness (Longman follows McKenna on this point [*The Book of Ecclesiastes*, pp. 64-65 n. 29]).

30. So esp. 1.13-14; 2.23; 8.14; cf. 7.6-7.

rendering of הבל) has been contested. For example, Daniel Fredericks (who opts for 'breath'), after surveying Fox's arguments, writes that

> we should not settle too soon for such despairing attempts to explain the complexities of a Qoheleth; rather perhaps there is a biblical meaning to *hebel*, contemporary with its composition, that would explain Qoheleth with greater coherency.[31]

Fredericks's objections are puzzling. Why can we not presume that the philosophical notion of absurdity was 'contemporary' with Qoheleth's experience? What reason is there to nullify the use of 'absurd' outside of its explication in, for example, Camus? There is none. Camus had sought to explicate an experience that he saw common to everyone. He (like Qoheleth) did not limit his own observations to a historical setting or movement.[32]

What of other suggested meanings and translations for הבל? One of the most interesting, coming from Edwin Good (followed notably by T. Polk), is that הבל has a fully ironic sense. Irony, it is argued, is aware of incongruity and smiles wryly at it. Like absurdity, it recognizes the disparity between human deed and consequence but goes further than absurdity *within* the reading experience: 'Having observed an incongruity, irony pricks the bubble of illusion into which one has blown his life's breath.'[33] While absurdity ceases at the point of observation, irony interprets that observation, choosing to believe that its overall purpose is to heal and not to destroy: 'the basis of irony...aims at amendment of the incongruous rather than its annihilation... Wherever Qoheleth uses *hebel*...the subject is treated ironically.'[34] While some element of irony is surely entrenched in Qoheleth's use of הבל, a substantial interpretive measure must be taken to perceive it. This is why

31. D. Fredericks, *Coping with Transience: Ecclesiastes on Brevity in Life* (TBS, 18; Sheffield: JSOT Press, 1993), p. 18.

32. Furthermore, compare Fox's citation of the Camus scholar Cruickshank: 'Whatever the special character of Camus's conclusions, the absurd itself remains a contemporary manifestation of a skepticism as old at least as the Book of Ecclesiastes' (cited in *Qohelet*, p. 32). It is worth noting (as C.B. Peter does) that Camus actually bracketed himself from the existential movement, choosing to disassociate himself with Sartre rather early on and focus on the particularly moral aspects of philosophy ('In Defence of Existence', p. 36).

33. Polk, 'The Wisdom of Irony', p. 7.

34. E. Good, *Irony in the Old Testament* (Sheffield: Almond Press, 1981 [1965]), pp. 27, 182.

'irony' or 'ironic' would be inappropriate as a translation. Indeed, translating 'irony' would ironically rob the given referent (situation) of its inherent irony! For the joy of reading irony lies in the unearthing of its subtlety.

Clearly a word is needed that best represents the majority of the instances. 'Meaningless' (NIV), for example, does not accomplish this. There is meaning even if a character's experience is meaningless (it would be impossible, I think, to show that Qoheleth ever regarded his experience as meaningless). The *fact* that experience is meaningless is meaningful. As Wayne Booth puts it, 'to be caught in a meaningless predicament is a bad thing, in which case there *is* meaning'.[35] There have been other more amusing, if inappropriate, suggestions such as Frank Crüsemann's of 'shit'[36] and F.C. Burkitt's of 'bubble'.[37] Other suggestions such as 'vanity' (KJV, RSV *et al.*) or 'futility' (TLB *et al.*) suffer from the same problem as 'meaningless': they cannot express the *hebbel*-ness of a situation over and above that of a specified object (and in Ecclesiastes, remember, the situation judgment is more common than the calling-it-as-it-is judgment). Perhaps ironically, to preserve some semblance of *meaning* (albeit one that may leave a bitter taste), 'absurd' is the best expression of Qoheleth's use of הבל. All said, 'absurd' remains the best choice throughout, if for no other reason than that the reader is enabled to perceive the thematic unity of the judgments.[38]

There is no other word connected more firmly to Qoheleth's experience than הבל. The word functions to judge the experience of his narrated (younger) life as a whole, for Qoheleth observes the following to be הבל in relation to his experience: all that he observes (1.14); the test that he made of wisdom and folly (2.1); all the deeds he had done (2.11, 17); his fate in comparison to the fool (2.14-15); the fate of his

---

35. Booth, *Rhetoric of Fiction*, p. 298 (italics Booth's). In support, G. Ogden argues that the *hebbel* judgments do not imply that life is vacuous or meaningless, but rather that the situations Qoheleth observed are in themselves anomalous, and that *that* is what is הבל ('"Vanity" It Certainly Is Not', pp. 302-304).

36. 'The Unchangeable World: The "Crisis of Wisdom" in Koheleth', in W. Schottroff and W. Stegemann (eds.), *God of the Lowly: Socio-Historical Interpretations of the Bible* (Maryknoll, NY: Orbis Books, 1979), pp. 57-77 (57).

37. *Ecclesiastes: Rendered into English Verse by F. Crawford Burkitt*, p. 9, *passim*.

38. Fox makes the same point (*Qohelet*, p. 44).

inheritance (2.18-19, 21; cf. 2.26; 4.7-8); the days of his life (7.15); everything (1.2; 3.19; 9.1; 12.8). All that he does is coloured by הבל and there is no better way to encapsulate his story, as the frame narrator recognized in 1.2 and 12.8.

3. הכל *and* הבל

Outside of Ecclesiastes, הכל always has an immediate referent in its own story-world. Here is a good example: 'Nothing was missing, whether small or great... David brought back *everything*' (1 Sam. 30.19). In all other biblical texts הכל refers to concrete nouns that act as simple referents. A *lack* of referent would therefore tell us something informative in that in such instances הכל must take on a unique, abstract definition/use. And, as we might expect, Ecclesiastes is again atypical in this respect. Of the 18 occurrences of הכל 8 stand in (sometimes ambiguous) relation to הבל,[39] and only 1 of these appears to have a clear referent.[40]

The lack of antecedent is obvious with 1.2 and 12.8 (cf. 11.8, כל־שבא הבל, 'all that comes is absurd'). There could, however, possibly be a referent for הכל at 3.19 if we take it there to mean 'everyone' (all animals and humans; so 3.20, ×3). It seems more likely, however, that Qoheleth reflected that (כי) everything is absurd (הכל הבל, 3.19b) *as a result* of comparing the circumstance of animals to that of humans (3.18-21) and that הכל at 3.19 is therefore more generalized and abstract. The referents of the other three (1.14; 2.11, 17) are less evident. It is worth noting, however, that all three verses are remarkably similar in content. At 1.14 Qoheleth observes (ראה) 'all the deeds that have been done under the sun' and concludes (הנה) that everything is absurd (הכל הבל) and a pursuit of wind. At 2.11 he considers (פנה) 'all

39. 1.2, 14; 2.11, 17; 3.19; 7.15; 9.1; 12.8. Eccl. 7.15 is the only verse in which the words occur yet are separated from each other, which creates an interesting ambiguity in itself ('in my absurd life I have observed everything...'; further, see below). John Jarick has suggested to me in conversation that the choice of placing הכל and הבל together may be purposefully to portray a visual word-play. They occur together only in Ecclesiastes and the only visual (and minimal) difference between them is a serif-mark.

40. 9.1, if we allow for emendation, is the only of these with an antecedent. By reading הבל at 9.2a for MT's הכל and placing it immediately after the הכל לפניהם of 9.1b, Qoheleth appears to say concerning the righteous and the wise that 'everything before them [i.e. their deeds and love and hate] is הבל'.

the deeds my hands had done [בכל־מעשׂי שׁעשׂו ידי] and the toil in which I toiled to do it', and concludes (הנה) that everything is absurd (הבל הכל) and a pursuit of wind and that there is no profit (יתרון) under the heavens. Of these three, however, 2.17 is the most informative example:

> And I hated life, for the work that was done under the sun was grievous to me. Indeed, everything is absurd and a pursuit of wind [כי הכל הבל ורעות רוח].

Here Qoheleth does not 'consider' or 'observe' work and *then* conclude that everything is absurd. Instead, the language of the judgment itself is more personal. It was grievous to him (רע עלי). At 1.14 and 2.11, 'everything' might exclusively refer to the work (or 'activity') done under the sun. However, at 2.17 it might also include every*thing*; that is, every material thing, including the agents that do the activity. This fits well with uses of הבל outside of Ecclesiastes that always connote material things, including agents (e.g. Ps. 119.91).[41] Furthermore, some of the *hebbel* judgments refer directly to *things* and not to general situations,[42] serving fully to demonstrate the dictum at 1.2: everything is absurd. Because of the all-encompassing referents for הכל, הבל must, it seems, be applied to all things without exception, including knowledge, wisdom and even the frame narrator's quite different epistemological priorities (see Chapter 4.3).

Of the other uses of הכל in Ecclesiastes, two are too vague to be of value in this survey (10.19; 11.5), four refer to 'everyone' and as such do not inform the abstract sense (3.20 [×3]; 6.6) and one clearly has a specific referent (12.13). The remaining three are instructive and may be summarized as follows: in the days to come הכל will be forgotten (2.16); God has made הכל beautiful (or 'appropriate', יפה) in its time (3.11); Qoheleth has observed הכל (*all* that happens to the righteous and the wicked?, 7.15b) in his absurd days. Each of these references broadens the scope of הכל immensely. הכל is here not simply limited to human activity or things under the sun, but to the very activity of God. Although Qoheleth specifies that it is everything under the sun (תחת השׁמשׁ)—all that God created—which falls under the scrutiny of his eye, by implication God himself is included. The incomprehensibility of the

---

41. Contra Fox (*Qohelet*, p. 37) who argues that the judgments refer only to activity.

42. So 5.7; 6.11, 12; 7.15; 9.9 (×2); 11.10; cf. 1.4-7.

world is, to Qoheleth's thinking, linked to the inability to understand God's works. These factors are one and the same. God's activity is at once יפה and הבל (3.11). The *human* aspect of activity (and by implication the human understanding of God's activity) will be forgotten (2.16). Here is an absurdity manifest in the text itself without Qoheleth drawing our attention to it as such. God has made everything pleasing—fitting in a pleasant order[43]—and yet it is unknowable, undiscoverable and absurd (3.11). For Qoheleth, this absurdity prevents him from being truly wise (7.23-24). Indeed, Qoheleth reports elsewhere that to attempt to understand all that is done—all that is absurd—is futile (8.17):

> I observed all the activity of God. For humanity is not able to discover all the activity that has been done under the sun. Therefore, [although] humanity toils to seek it, still they will not discover it. Although the sage claims to know it he will not discover it.[44]

In this text the principal referent of הכל is the activity of discovery, failed and futile. הכל is, quite simply, everything under the sun that Qoheleth observed and about which he sought to discover the inner working. When the inner and outer logic of that immense quantity of matter and events eluded him, he declared it הבל.

There are two particular effects that emerge from the linking of הכל to הבל. One is the emergence of a thread that links each of the *hebbel* judgments. That conjunction, Fox argues, 'implies that there is some meaning common to the various occurrences of the term [הבל, which]...infects the entire system [of Qoheleth's epistemology], making "everything" absurd'.[45] That link creates the second of these effects: the ability of הכל to encapsulate the great variety of situations to which the *hebbel* judgments refer.[46] The phrase הכל הבל enlarges the field of the definition of הבל and thereby creates ample range for Qoheleth to usher in his *hebbel* judgments. It is the generalization by abstraction of the

---

43. Cf. the use of יפה at 5.18.

44. Cf. 11.5. Further on Qoheleth's indictment of God in the inscrutability of the world, see Chapter 8.3.

45. Fox, *Qohelet*, pp. 35, 47; cf. p. 108.

46. Furthermore, cf. T. Polk: 'there is scarcely a topic in the book to which *hebel* is not applied' ('The Wisdom of Irony', p. 7); and note Douglas B. Miller's recent suggestion that הבל functions metaphorically to 'symbolize the human experience in its entirety' ('Qoheleth's Symbolic Use of הבל', *JBL* 117.3 [1998], pp. 437-54 [453]).

entire text (הכל הבל being the ultimate abstraction). As such it works as what Bal calls a 'mirror text': a phrase that comes to signify the whole scheme of a story and that 'lifts the whole narrative onto another level...[and] serves as directions for use'.[47] Qoheleth's paramount judgment, then, is a standard by which all of his consequent experience shall be judged. There can be no challenge laid against it. For Qoheleth, there is no one who can say, 'This is *not* הבל' concerning any activity or any *thing* judged so by way of his narrated life.

47. Bal, *Narratology*, p. 147.

Chapter 3

THE INNER BORDERS

1. הבל הבלים *in the Frame (1.2; 12.8)*

'Absurdity of absurdities', said Qoheleth, 'Absurdity of absurdities.'
'Everything is absurd' (1.2).

'Absurdity of absurdities', said Qoheleth. 'Everything is absurd' (12.8).

These verses are unique in several respects. The initial superlative construct in each verse, הבל הבלים, is peculiar to Ecclesiastes. The two verses together form what is widely agreed to be the most emphatic inclusio in the Old Testament. The final phrase in each verse (הכל הבל) is also peculiar to Ecclesiastes and occurs six other times in the book (1.14; 2.11, 17; 3.19; 9.1;[1] 12.8) forming one of the most concise and wide-sweeping judgments within the biblical literature.

The superlative expresses the uttermost of what is absurd: 'Absurdity of absurdities'. Like 'Holy of holies' (Exod. 26.33) and 'Song of songs' (Cant. 1.1), that phrase simply signifies the uttermost of the quality expressed. But unlike its biblical counterparts, that phrase is also used as a generalized expression reminiscent of a lament, having no other proper subject but the experience of the speaker himself. But there is a referent. The lone proclamation, 'Absurdity of absurdities', begs the question, 'What is this absurdity?' This absurdity, the sequential reader learns, is הכל, 'everything'.

As discussed above, the definition of הכל is made complete as the sequential reader progresses through the text. It is fully developed by the time the epilogue is reached, for it is at that point that the superlative appears again. Its occurrence at 12.8 lends the construct a finality. It is the alpha and omega of Qoheleth's judgments. The superlative phrase is limited to the frame narrator's text and the narrative

---

1.   Read הכל לפניהם הבל; see p. 88 n. 40.

representation suggests that the frame narrator has employed it in order to summarize the majority of Qoheleth's observations.

While הכל הבל also functions summarily, it appears in Qoheleth's text[2] as well as the frame narrator's and therefore does not carry with it the same uniqueness or level of judgment as הבל הבלים at 1.2 and 12.8.[3] This uniqueness is hard to overestimate. It suggests that not only is the frame narrator's understanding of Qoheleth himself seemingly complete, but also his understanding of Qoheleth's most crucial operating idea, הבל—the 'mental image which affects his thinking'.[4] The frame narrator is wholly aware, and makes explicit use, of this organizing principle of Qoheleth's story.

In sum, the elements of 1.1-2 that create a readerly impact have now been discussed: the commencement of a narrative frame, shift in narrative level and voice, commencement of desire and plot, and the significance of הבל to the frame narrator. All of these aspects can be seen to form the framing strategy. While this strategy is not limited to passages in which the frame narrator 'appears' (for its strategy is to be an ever-present indicator), it is fitting to see in those passages both a *formal* structural strategy and springboards for discussion.

2. *A Momentary Intrusion (7.27)*

Structurally speaking, the frame of Ecclesiastes is not so much a picture frame as a window frame with a thin partition in its centre. The frame narrator's intrusion at that centre serves to remind the reader that the frame narrator is still telling (on a level outside of the flow of narration) Qoheleth's story. The intrusion is found in the midst of one of Qoheleth's most immoderate observations, which begins at 7.23-24: 'All this I have tested with wisdom. I said, "I will become wise", but it was far from me. What has been is far off and deep, surely deep. Who

---

2.   1.14; 2.11, 17; 3.19. Also, see p. 88 n. 39.

3.   Seybold also recognizes the way in which הבל הבלים necessarily surpasses the level of the other *hebbel* judgments: 'The framework verses, 1.12 and 12.8, display indeed an expansion into the universal and a heightening of emotional interest that cannot be demonstrated in the maxims. In this way the catchword and battlecry of Qoheleth is elevated to a summary ideological conclusion, the expression of a nihilistic judgement on the world and its values' ('*hebhel; hābhal*', p. 320).

4.   Seybold, '*hebhel; hābhal*', p. 320.

can discover it?'[5] While the 'all this' (כל־זה) of v. 23 most likely refers to all that he has observed until that point,[6] it may likewise look ahead to the following observation, as a sort of thematic preparation. And yet Qoheleth establishes this by looking back, suggesting that his ambition lay firmly behind him. As with a Greek tragedy, the reader knows (by Qoheleth's rhetorical question [v. 24b], suggesting his own ironic awareness of the situation) that Qoheleth will fail in becoming wise. He establishes his own demise and the anticipation builds (7.25-26):

> I turned, with all my being, to understand, to search out and to seek wisdom and the sum of things; and to understand evil, folly and the folly of madness. And I found more bitter than death the woman who is traps, her heart nets, her hands chains. He with whom God is pleased will be delivered from her, but he who sins will be taken by her.[7]

He claims that he turned (סבותי אני) to know (לדעת), to explore (ולתור) and seek (ובקש) wisdom and the sum of things: to *understand* the antitheses of conventional wisdom's rewards, folly and madness (7.25b). This grouping of 'quest' verbs suggests that the forthcoming conclusion is paramount, for Qoheleth has enlisted all of his powers of observation to discover it.[8] But this is not yet the most important of his conclusions.

---

5. Cf. Job 11.7-8, where Zophar asks Job if he can find out (תמצא) the deep soundings of God (החקר אלוה) that are deeper than Sheol (עמקה משאול). Like Job's deep soundings, Qoheleth cannot discover that which has been. This is the subject of his discourse here: what he can*not* discover. Qoheleth addresses the issue similarly at 1.17; 2.12; 8.16-17.

6. Or at least to the section that precedes it (7.19-22). Further, see p. 209 n. 108.

7. For a full discussion of this difficult text (including history of interpretation, translation difficulties, overall theme), see Eric S. Christianson, 'Qoheleth the "Old Boy" and Qoheleth the "New Man": Misogynism, the Womb and a Paradox in Ecclesiastes', in A. Brenner and C. Fontaine (eds.), *Wisdom and Psalms: A Feminist Companion to the Bible (Second Series)* (FCB [Second Series], 2; Sheffield: Sheffield Academic Press, 1998), pp. 109-36; esp. pp. 110-21.

8. The בקש/מצא coupling, as M.V. Fox and B. Porten ('Unsought Discoveries: Qohelet 7.23–8.1a', *HS* 19 [1978], pp. 26-38) have pointed out, is unique and effective here, highlighting Qoheleth's own experiential ground (heightened further by the varying uses of חכם at 7.23; 'Unsought Discoveries', pp. 27-29). Each occurrence of one generates occurrences of the other, and the word-play is often rich or ironic (as in Qoheleth's *discovery* [מצא] that there is too much *seeking* [בקש], 7.29; 'Unsought Discoveries', pp. 37-38).

See, this I have found, said Qoheleth[9] ([adding] one to one to find the sum, which my soul has sought continually but I have not found): one man among a thousand I have found, but a woman among all of these I have not found. See, this alone I have found: that God made humanity upright, but they have sought many devices (7.27-29).

Rather, in 7.27 the greater emphasis arrives: '*See, this* I have found...' (adding the emphatic ראה זה to the lone verb of discovery at 7.26a), and the emphasis continues ('*said Qoheleth*') as Qoheleth informs the reader of his process of discovery, something which *until now* he was unable to discover. Finally (adding לבד to the already heightened formula of 7.27a), Qoheleth offers an observation that is integrally related to the first in this section (understanding is unattainable). The fact that he found a man among a thousand (even though we cannot know exactly what is meant by this),[10] but among the same amount of people he found no woman, is presented as a kind of evidence that humanity was first upright, but they now have sought many devices ('reasonings' that lead them astray). And this is how a thoroughly negative tone is conveyed: failure to discover, regardless the object of discovery, is Qoheleth's vexation in life.

The framing here is multilayered. It is at the heart of this key passage that the frame narrator has chosen to remind the reader that he is still remembering and recounting Qoheleth's story. Furthermore, by heightening this particular observation syntactically and by employing the guise of Solomon possibly more distinctly than usual (see Chapter 6.1), this passage is made inevitably memorable. The frame narrator's insertion here supplements the overall strategy of 'setting aside', marking its importance for Qoheleth's narrative.[11]

9. That this is the frame narrator's text and neither Qoheleth's self-reference nor a later editorial insertion, see p. 46 n. 89.

10. Whybray indicates the important fact (widely overlooked) that Qoheleth does not inform the reader either just what it was he was seeking in this instance or precisely what is meant by the hyperbolic 'one man among a thousand' (*Ecclesiastes*, p. 127). Further, see my discussion of this problem in 'Qoheleth the "Old Boy" and Qoheleth the "New Man"', pp. 113-16.

11. Lohfink agrees that the frame narrator's intrusion here serves to highlight his observation in contradistinction to others (as cited disapprovingly in Whybray, *Ecclesiastes*, p. 126).

Chapter 4

THE OUTER BORDERS: II

> So, naturalists observe, a flea
> Hath smaller fleas that on him prey;
> And these have smaller fleas to bite 'em,
> And so proceed *ad infinitum*.
> Thus every poet, in his kind,
> Is bit by him that comes behind.
>
> Jonathan Swift ('On Poetry', l. 337)

The epilogue[1] may be divided into four sections based both on form and content: (1) the narrative inclusio (12.8, the counterpart to 1.2); (2) the final description of Qoheleth (12.9-10); (3) the warnings to the frame narrator's son (12.10-11); and (4) the final word of advice to the reader (12.13-14). Of course, it is in the epilogue that the frame narrator comes to life as a character in his own right. In the first section he recalls Qoheleth's ultimate observation, laying claim again to a complete understanding of Qoheleth's story. In the second he offers an *individual* view of Qoheleth's activity (cf. 12.10—'words of delight' and 'with integrity he wrote words of truth'). In the third he makes clear his epic setting (of speaking to his son) and upholds what he regards to be the ideal epistemological process (see below). In the fourth he brings everything ('all that has been heard', 12.13) to an orthodox conclusion.

Unlike the superscription, there are not many exact structural parallels to the epilogue in other ANE frames.[2] G. Wilson has pointed out a

---

1. Whether or not this section is the work of one or more epilogists or redactors is not pertinent here. However, some argue that the epilogue does not begin until 12.9 (e.g. Murphy, Whybray). But 12.8 is the frame narrator's progression from 1.2, in which one must admit at least the presence of both Qoheleth *and* the frame narrator, if not the frame narrator alone. The fact that it is only at 1.2 and 12.8 that the phrase הבל הבלים occurs sets these texts sharply apart from Qoheleth; further, see above, Chapter 2.1a.

2. See Chapter 1.2. Some ANE frames, for example, further the inner narrative

structural similarity between this epilogue and the prologue to Proverbs. However, the connections he makes are strained.[3] While comparisons to overall structures and framing strategies are useful, it is best to treat this epilogue within the limited context of the story it frames.[4]

The epilogue has brought to the fore some interesting interpretive issues. Many commentators have seen in this passage a clue to the process of canonization *within* the Bible.[5] Also, the relationship of this passage's composition to that of the body of the book has merited much discussion and has been connected to the issue of canonization as well. While I will touch on these issues where relevant, my own discussion

more than Eccl. 12.8-14 does (e.g. *Kagemni*).

3.   Wanting to stress a thematic connection of the collections of Proverbs to Ecclesiastes, Wilson argues that the 'common elements' in Prov. 1.1-8 and Eccl. 12.9-14 serve to 'bind all between more closely together' ('"The Words of the Wise": The Intent and Significance of Qohelet 12.9-14', *JBL* 103.2 [1984], pp. 175-92 [183]). The evidence offered is that both the prologue to Prov. 1.1-7 and Eccl. 12.9-14 emphasize the importance of justice (מׁשפּט, Prov. 1.3; Eccl. 12.14; cf. Eccl. 3.17; 8.5-6) and (making a connection between Deuteronomic notions of justice and wisdom) that the 'fear God and keep his commands' of Eccl. 12.14 served to link the late near-canonical forms of both books together (pp. 189-92). Therefore, the 'canonical editors' of both works added all the superscriptions and Eccl. 12.9-14, 'making explicit the connections implied in Proverbs 1–9' (p. 190). The analysis fails on three accounts: (1) the material, which is indeed comparable, is, as Wilson admits, fairly stock wisdom material (justice, fearing God etc.; p. 181); (2) Wilson does not sufficiently deal with the content of Qoheleth's narration, thereby overlooking the immediate function of the frame narrator; and (3) if the connection was made as arbitrarily as Wilson suggests then it need not be taken as seriously as he suggests (e.g. 'This movement [of editing] so binds these two works together that now each must be read in the larger context of the other and in the light of the hermeneutical principle [fearing Yahweh/God] laid down in prologue and epilogue', p. 190).

4.   This said, I accept the opinion of Wilson and others that in 12.11-14 the emphasis of the frame narrator moves beyond (while still including) the subject of Qoheleth.

5.   See Chapter 6.3 below and, in particular, Childs, *Introduction*, pp. 584-89; J. Goldin, 'The End of Ecclesiastes: Literal Exegesis and its Transformation', in A. Altmann (ed.), *Biblical Motifs: Origins and Transformations* (Cambridge, MA: Harvard University Press, 1966), pp. 135-58 (Goldin deals mostly with the epilogue in relation to the Jewish canon, which includes the Talmud); G. Sheppard, 'The Epilogue to Qoheleth as Theological Commentary', *CBQ* 39 (1977), pp. 182-89; Wilson, 'Intent and Significance'.

will focus largely on the questions raised by the unique and tense relationship between the one framing and the one framed.

1. *The Inclusio (12.8)*

'Absurdity of absurdities', said Qoheleth. 'Everything is absurd.'

I have already noted the correlation of this verse to the superscription, and that it is identical except for the lack of repetition of the phrase 'absurdity of absurdities'. What has yet to be discussed is the *strategy* of inclusion at hand. Inclusion is a well-known device in nearly all forms of literature. It is a kind of framing, a formal mark of structure with an emphatic rhetorical function. The inclusio serves to mark off a specified section of text. In this case it surrounds precisely Qoheleth's narration and nothing else. Thinking in different terms, one might compare the inclusio to two identical doors at either end of the same room—serving as the only entrance and exit respectively—or perhaps the ornate covers of a book, which serve to create a unique sign, a feature of separateness. Just as book covers give the most obvious appearance that the book is physically stable (even though its real stability comes from the binding of the loose leaves inside), so the inclusio is the most obvious structural marker and thematic sign in Ecclesiastes.[6]

It is worth noting that the content of this inclusion is itself inclusive. That is, its content (the superlative in particular) is a summary, taking into account all that it frames, reckoning everything. This type of abstract reckoning creates the first notable incongruity between the frame narrator and the one framed. By being overtly aphoristic, the frame narrator flies in the face of Qoheleth's more open style of reasoning. As such, Michael Payne remarks, the frame narrator is 'at odds' with Qoheleth, who is

---

6.   So also, Viviano, 'The Book of Ecclesiastes', p. 80. Wright has suggested that the location of this structural marker is numerically significant: 'it is quite clear that the editor does take a carefully counted book of 216 verses...and he does in fact build that book to a total of 222 verses by the addition of six verses of epilogue and thus bring the book into perfect balance (111/111). It seems beyond reasonable doubt that he was aware of the numbers 111 and 216 and that the production of a perfectly balanced book is not something that he blundered into' ('The Riddle of the Sphinx Revisited', p. 44; see also pp. 43, 45 on the significance of the הבל phrases in the inclusio). Of course, Wright admits that the Masoretic versification may flaw his argument, but considers it 'consistent enough' for his purposes.

antiaphoristic, complexly dialectical, and thoroughly dramatic...It is not so much that Koheleth rejects [for example, the orthodox ideas expressed in 12.13-14]...as it is that he holds a larger, more comprehensive view, his meditations requiring the orthodox views to which they are a dialectical response.[7]

It is at the inclusion that this anti-dialectic finds its beginning.

What about the relation of 12.8 to the rest of the epilogue? Fox has offered an interesting paraphrase of 12.8: 'Utterly absurd! (*as the Qohelet used to say*). Everything is absurd!'[8] By rendering the perfect, אמר, as a frequentative simple past, Fox highlights the frame narrator's interpretive presence that is about to unfold fully. Although it is the imperfect (or vav-conversive) and not the perfect which usually suggests such a sense,[9] the story aspect is justifiably amplified as a paraphrase. The frame narrator is about to commence something of a biographical nature.

2. *The Final Portrait (12.9-10)*

Furthermore, Qoheleth was a sage. He continually taught the people knowledge, and he listened,[10] and studied [and] composed[11] many proverbs.[12] Qoheleth sought to find words of delight and with integrity he wrote words of truth.

While the other, latter texts of the epilogue (such phrases as עשׂות ספרים at 12.12 etc.) have received much attention, this section has received surprisingly little. In terms of Qoheleth as the frame narrator saw him, it is the most informative text in Ecclesiastes and presents the

7.   'The Voices of Ecclesiastes', p. 264.

8.   *Qohelet*, p. 347 (italics mine).

9.   See A.B. Davidson, *An Introductory Hebrew Grammar* (New York: Charles Scribner's Sons, 24th edn, 1932), §46.II.2. Compare the frequentative aspect found, for example, in Job 1.4: '[Job's sons] *used to go* (והלכו) to feast...and *they would invite* (ושלחו וקראו) their sisters...'

10.   Reading וְאִזֵּן at 12.9 as the piel perf. of אזן ('to hear'—supported by ancient versions; cf. Prov. 1.5-6; 12.15; 18.15—listening is an activity of the wise) and not as a derivative of the ill-attested מאזנים (weights, scales; so RSV and a few commentators). See Fox, *Qohelet*, p. 323.

11.   On these verbs (חקר and תקן) see below, n. 18.

12.   For examples of the semantic range of משׁל see M. Eaton, *Ecclesiastes* (TOTC; Downer's Grove, IL: InterVarsity Press, 1983), p. 153. Because a משׁל could include such 'genres' as parables and allegories, it is perhaps an apt nomen for the diverse quality of devices Qoheleth employed in his narration.

reader with a well-defined final portrait. While the effects of the frame narrator describing Qoheleth as if he lived (lifting him, in a sense, out of a fictive context) have already been touched on above, the content of that description remains to be explored.

This commencement proper of the epilogue reiterates the authority of the frame narrator as Qoheleth's foremost interpreter. First, his 'historical' existence is (albeit modally) insisted upon: Qoheleth *was* (שהיה). Second, his activity is described: Qoheleth *did* such and such. The existent and actantial modes together suggest a complete description. The frame narrator begins that description with something that should not take us by surprise: Qoheleth was a sage (חכם).

Much ink has been spilled over the meaning of חכם. Some have endowed it with a political sense; that is, one successfully dealing with powerful people, knowing how to get what he or she wants.[13] Or R.E. Murphy, for example, sees a חכם as one who is concerned with the things of the wise (the question of 'what is good', 'profitable' etc.) and argues against the notion that there was a professional class of 'the wise'.[14] Among the plethora of Old Testament passages concerning wisdom, Job 15.2-6 and Prov. 1.5-6 are particularly instructive regarding the *activity* of the חכם. The former passage suggests, by negation, that it is the responsibility of the wise to speak words of substance that end in profit (v. 3), are rooted in the fear of God (v. 4a), promote meditation (v. 4b) and testify to the integrity of the speaker (v. 6). (This last aspect is echoed in the frame narrator's description of the manner in which Qoheleth wrote: ישר; cf. Prov. 22.20-21.) Proverbs 1.5-6 suggests that the purpose of wisdom is both to gain skill (v. 5) and to make one cunning with words (v. 6). One common Old Testament idea (developed particularly in Proverbs) is that the ability of the wise derives from learning, or from the presumably self-induced action of fearing Yahweh (e.g. Prov. 1.7; 15.33). However, in passages such as Exod. 36.1-2, 4, 8; Deut. 1.13, 15, the wise are so because Yahweh has enabled them. And according to Sir. 38.24ff., wisdom is something acquired only if one has the luxury of time to pursue it.

13. For example, R.N. Whybray, 'Prophecy and Wisdom', in R. Coggins *et al.* (eds.), *Israel's Prophetic Tradition* (Cambridge: Cambridge University Press, 1982), pp. 181-99 (187, *passim*).

14. 'The Sage in Ecclesiastes and Qoheleth the Sage', in J.G. Gammie (ed.), *The Sage in Israel and the Ancient Near East* (Winona Lake, IN: Eisenbrauns, 1990), pp. 263-71 (265-67).

Qoheleth's own views on wisdom are varied. Wisdom itself is surely good (2.13, 26; 7.11-12, 19; 8.1-2; 9.13-18) and is clearly helpful for his own task at hand (1.13; 2.3, 9; 7.23). Yet wisdom is under the scrutiny of Qoheleth's eye as something to be wary of (1.17; 2.12; 7.25; 8.16-17) and is even in itself a vexation (1.18; also, cf. 2.16b; 6.8a; 7.7; 8.17; 9.11 [bread does not come to the wise]). In light of this, Murphy is certainly correct to point out that Qoheleth the sage *is* one who concerns himself with the question of what is good for humanity (2.3, 24-25; *passim*; cf. 4.9-12)[15] and, of course, of what is advantageous (having יתרון; 1.3; 2.13; 3.9; *passim*). The description, then, that Qoheleth is a חכם (given Murphy's bend to the interpretation), comes as no surprise to the reader.

Against such a semantic background the frame narrator (who was at least, it is implied, familiar with the 'words of the wise') claims that Qoheleth was a חכם. Qoheleth's myriad character fits well the varied hues of what it meant to be a sage. It would be difficult to claim, then, that the frame narrator has added anything new to the reader's understanding of Qoheleth at this point, except perhaps that by regulating him to this particular nomen Qoheleth is, once again, to whatever limited extent possible, 'normalized' by the one who frames him. In fact, by stating that Qoheleth was a חכם the tension between the kind of wisdom Qoheleth employed and the 'being wise' that he searched for (see Chapter 8.3) is glossed over.

What, then, does the frame narrator add to the portrait of Qoheleth? In what follows does he begin to inform the reader beyond what can be adduced from the body of Qoheleth's narration? Is there a tension? Are the activities described really manifest, or even implied, in Qoheleth's story? And what can we learn from differences between Qoheleth's self-understanding and the understanding the frame narrator has of him?

From Qoheleth's narration the reader may assume that he was

15. Whereas Qoheleth makes it a point to test what is good (טוב) for humanity, the narrator of Proverbs is very much in the habit of *telling* the reader what *is* good (Prov. 13.2, 4, 21; 19.8 [wisdom leads to what is good]; 28.10; *passim*). Interestingly, one finds a middle position in Job. At the outset Job piously asks if he can rightly receive what is good while rejecting what is bad (הרע, 2.10). However, later he complains that he will see no more good (7.7), and that when he sought what was good, evil (רע) came (30.26). Also, compare Elihu's statement concerning the 'case' of Job—that they should consider together among themselves 'what is good' (34.4; NRSV).

A Time to Tell

certainly qualified to teach about the subject of knowledge, a concept that, for him, worked as a matrix of interpretation by which to observe the world. However, that he actually engaged in teaching is not so clear. Or indeed, that he had an association with 'the people'[16] is a difficult concept to reconcile to his narration. He speaks early on of 'the people of old', and how they will or will not be remembered (1.11). In a parabolic proverb he speaks of a king of whom there was no end to 'the people' who followed him (4.16). This gap in Qoheleth's story creates, as it were, a gap for the frame narrator to fill. But the Solomonic connection becomes particularly relevant here in that Solomon's prayer at 1 Kgs 3.8-9 could function as a necessary pretext:

> And your servant is in the midst of your people whom you have chosen; a great people [עם־רב]…Then give to your servant a discerning heart [לב שמע] to judge your people and be able to discern between what is good and evil...

There are plenty of examples in the Old Testament of leaders explicitly teaching 'the people' and often in a sustained role, and the request of Solomon, that he might judge Yahweh's people 'in the midst' of them, suggests that he desired a *continual* role of instruction in Israel (cf. 1 Kgs 4.33-34 [5.13-14]). Qoheleth's own connection to Solomon (see Chapter 6) might fill in the gap and show that the reader has again gained relatively little additional knowledge. In fact, the very notion of teaching in the Old Testament is so diverse and ambiguous[17] that the

---

16. העם from Exodus to Joshua often *refers* to Israel (Exod. 1.20; 3.12; 4.16 etc.). This is usually due to the Israelites being the contextual antecedents of the word, but the word comes to *mean* Israel in later use (1 Chron. 13.4; cf. Ezra 3.1; Pss. 106.48; 144.15). There is a more general meaning found elsewhere that might denote 'humanity' (Isa. 42.5 [לעם]; cf. Prov. 29.2 and LXX's ἄνθρωπον for העם at Eccl. 12.9) or 'the public/community' (Jer. 39.8; Sir. 7.16 [7]). Because of the Solomonic context (see below), העם at Eccl. 12.9 probably refers to Israel—i.e. whatever that had come to mean in Qoheleth's location in history.

17. Moses taught Israel (or at least thought he should—Deut. 4.14; 6.1), but we are never told what that entailed. The *subject* of the piel of למד is sometimes indirectly conveyed by commands to parents to teach their children (Deut. 4.10; 11.19; cf. Jer. 9.14[13], 20[19]), or God himself is the subject (Ps. 25.4-5; Jer. 32.33). We do not know who the 'teachers' of the narrator of Ps. 119 are (v. 99). Daniel was presumably taught by court officials of some kind (Dan. 1.4). Among many other words that suggest teaching (ידע, hiph.; שכל; אלף, hiph.), compare some diverse examples—ירה: an idol can 'teach' lies (hiph.; Hab. 2.18); Job will 'teach' Bildad about the hand of God (Job 27.11)—בין: 'teachers' (hiph. part.) served in David's

frame narrator's description is perhaps insufficient to fill in the gap of Qoheleth's narrative.

The following three delineations of Qoheleth's character in v. 9b (וְאֹזֶן וְחִקֵּר תִּקֵּן [18] מְשָׁלִים הַרְבֵּה) taken together might, as M. Fishbane has argued, relate directly to the composition of Ecclesiastes. Drawing on examples of cognate verb forms in Assyrian and Babylonian colophons, Fishbane concludes that the epilogist wrote a similar kind of colophon, borrowing widely from the 'professional' language of his cultural milieu, creating a 'stylized variation of conventional scribal tasks well known in ancient Israel'.[19] Fishbane offers three examples of colophonic phrases grouped together which suggest scribal activity and concludes that the epilogue of Ecclesiastes was written consciously in a similar pattern. There are some difficulties with Fishbane's reading. Besides some weaknesses in his linguistic assumptions,[20] there is no evidence, beyond the description of Qoheleth, that the epilogue refers to any tasks or processes beyond those that are present. The main problem, however, is that the frame narrator's immediate concern is not so much to shed light on the scribal activity of a sage as to offer a very personal assessment of Qoheleth that adumbrates his character profile (hence such qualitative, value-laden adjectives as חֵפֶץ, יֹשֶׁר and אֱמֶת; see below).

entourage (1 Chron. 25.8) and the Levites 'taught' all Israel, being holy to the Lord (2 Chron. 35.3). For other examples (and on the other activities the frame narrator ascribes to Qoheleth), see Crenshaw, 'Qoheleth's Understanding of Intellectual Enquiry', pp. 215-21.

18. On the first of these three verbs (אֹזֶן) see above, n. 10. The second (חָקַר, 'to search out', 'examine thoroughly', 'investigate' [hence by extension, 'to study']; sometimes of land [Judg. 18.2]; sometimes in contradistinction to the 'unsearchability' of God [Job 28.27; Prov. 25.2; cf. Job 5.27]) certainly resonates with Qoheleth's descriptions of himself in passages where he proclaims that he intended to search out and discover the nature of wisdom and the world (chs. 2 and 7 esp.). The third verb (תָּקַן, 'to set in order', 'make straight'; Eccl. 1.15; 7.13; cf. Dan. 4.36[33]) is not well attested in the Old Testament. The sense of composition, which is likely meant at Eccl. 12.9, finds a parallel in Sir. (Heb.) 47.9, of singers 'composing' music. Murphy has made the attractive suggestion that these latter two verbs might echo Qoheleth's critical faculty as illustrated in Eccl. 7 and 8, in which case they suggest praise (*Ecclesiastes*, p. 125).

19. *Biblical Interpretation in Ancient Israel* (Oxford: Clarendon Press, 1985), p. 31. Fishbane reads the three verbs as 'ordered', 'examined' and 'fixed' respectively.

20. See Fox, *Qoheleth*, p. 323.

That Qoheleth composed or arranged 'many proverbs'[21] echoes the superscriptions found in Proverbs, and as a description the effect is surely to mollify some of the 'solipsistic or elitist' elements of Qoheleth's text.[22] That is, if any reader be tempted to think that Qoheleth was not involved in the more traditional activities of such sages or scribes as the 'men of Hezekiah' (Prov. 25.1), they need not doubt. With this and the previous three verbs associated with the activity of the wise, the frame narrator is perhaps at odds with Qoheleth's Solomonic guise. While kings might have discovered and even 'composed' proverbs, it is doubtful that they actually 'wrote' them down; such was the task of the scribe. Furthermore, Qoheleth's actions in his own narrative seem to fit more the picture of a king who is not so much concerned with teaching, study and proverbs, as with the political acumen by which he amassed his great wealth[23] and the issues that arose from his consequent failures. Qoheleth's self-depiction is again at odds with the frame narrator's.

Such incongruence is admittedly less clear, however, in v. 10. The shift here to a more personal description resonates more clearly with the body of Qoheleth's narration. In one way, this description anaclactically expands the plot; for Qoheleth sought, but the question may be raised, Did he *find*? As Fox points out, the frame narrator does not 'commit himself as to the success of this attempt [at seeking out words of delight]'.[24] But even more to the point is the tension in contrasting descriptions concerning what Qoheleth actually did. As to whether there is incongruence, the issue rests largely, I think, on the phrase 'delightful words' (דברי־חפץ). It is likely that the phrase refers to what G.A. Barton termed an 'elegance of form'[25]—Qoheleth sought to write in a pleasing and elegant manner.[26] First, there is a potentially harmonic

21. As is widely noted in the commentaries, 'many proverbs' does not necessarily suggest the book of Proverbs, but more likely refers to the specific sayings of Qoheleth (particularly in chs. 7 and 10).

22. So Sheppard, 'The Epilogue to Qoheleth', p. 184.

23. This is particularly evident in ch. 2, esp. v. 8; cf. 1 Kgs 4.20-28.

24. Fox, 'Frame-narrative', p. 101.

25. *Ecclesiastes*, p. 199.

26. In Ecclesiastes the word has two senses: (1) the usual Old Testament meaning, 'delight', 'pleasure' (5.3; 8.3—the king does 'whatever he pleases [= freedom]'; 12.1—'having pleasure in' [without vexation or pain; cf. the phrase before it: 'Before the days of misery [ימי הרעה] come...', which are days in which you cannot take delight]); (2) the more obscure Old Testament meaning, 'matter',

point to make. Perhaps Qoheleth found words that brought pleasure to a life that was otherwise vexatious and unbearable. Such well-chosen words might have escaped the הבל judgment of 5.2-7: 'For with many dreams and absurdities [there are] many words—but fear God' (5.7). But as a *summary* the description is seriously flawed. In Qoheleth's own terms he sought not 'delightful', elegant words, but the very existence and quality of all that is under the sun. He sought what was deep and far off (7.23-29; 8.17). What Qoheleth sought was substantially more than what his interpreter would have us believe and, according to Qoheleth's own estimation, he failed in discovering it (see Chapter 8.3).

It is significant that the frame narrator's description of Qoheleth remains at a comfortable distance from him. Besides the broad descriptive term חכם, he does not really tell us anything *about* Qoheleth. Was Qoheleth difficult to get along with? Did he love and serve his God all his days? He sought to write uprightly, but was he, like Job, truly ישׁר? Although there are reasons for (careful) readers to disbelieve (at the story-level) the frame narrator's description, that description is made with confidence. The activities described are not exactly radical or surprising, but he is nonetheless an explicit biographer, leaving us with his own disciplined glimpse of a bewildering character. Any more specific questions about Qoheleth are left for readers to engage.

3. *Admonitions to a Preferred Epistemology (12.11-12)*

The words of sages are as oxgoads, and as implanted nails[27] are [the] collected sayings[28] given by one shepherd.[29] Yet beyond these, my son,

'thing' (3.1, 17; 5.8; 8.6). The usual sense (1) at 12.1, borne out by the poem that follows it with its contrasting themes of delight and misery (12.1-7), likely colours what is found here at 12.9.

27. משׁמרות; 'nails'—generally something that keeps something else fixed (cf. Isa. 41.7; Jer. 10.4).

28. בעלי אספות, 'the owners [or masters] of collections [of sayings?]'. בעל at Eccl. 5.13 and 10.20 undoubtedly means 'owner'. There is a figurative use of בעל found at Eccl. 10.11: a בעל לשׁון (lit. 'owner of a tongue') could mean 'one skilled in speech', or one who controls a snake's tongue and who therefore 'charms' a snake (cf. Ps. 58.4-5[5-6]; Jer. 8.17; Sir. 12.13; also, see Whybray, *Ecclesiastes*, p. 154). Joseph, for example, is a בעל החלמות—a 'dreamer'; a maker or craftsman of dreams; a 'specialist' (Gen. 37.19). Although בעל usually refers to people, it is unlikely that 'people' would be given by a shepherd, even in a figurative sense. The sense should be extended to that which *represents* people; i.e. their writing, hence

take heed:[30] [of the] making[31] of many[32] books there is no end, and much study wearies the body.

The translation and general sense of this section present one of the most difficult tasks to Qoheleth studies. In v. 11 the metaphors at work are arranged in a difficult syntax. There are several rare idioms including the *hapax leg.*, בעלי אספות (v. 11c), the precise meaning of which would be enormously instructive as regards the process of any kind of 'professional' wisdom in ancient Israel. In v. 12 the antecedents/referents to 'these', 'the making of many books' and 'much study' are unclear. This is likely a text full of the jargon of a closed community.[33]

To help to untangle the metaphors in v. 11, a close reading of a kind is necessary. The first parallel seems clear:

complementing the preceding parallel, 'the words of sages'—hence 'the collected sayings [of the sages]'.

29. 'Shepherd' is often a metaphor for God (Gen. 49.24; Pss. 23.1; 80.1; Isa. 40.11; Jer. 31.10; Ezek. 34.12 etc.). It could refer to Solomon as a patron of wisdom or to Qoheleth himself. All that is clear is that since the shepherd here is the subject of נתן, 'it' is the source of the collected sayings just referred to and therefore plays a part in the dual parallelism at play. Since this shepherd is clearly the *source* of the sayings one might rule out a human referent, although such figures as David and Moses come to mind as sources of psalmody and law respectively. Solomon (or Qoheleth/Solomon?), then, should not be ruled out here (contra Gordis and Fox). Whether or not אחד is an enumerator (RSV *et al.*) or an indefinite article (Fox) affects the sense little.

30. הזהר; cf. 4.13, where it is used of an old and foolish king who, no longer 'taking heed', is thought worse off than a poor but wise youth (cf. Ezek. 33.4-6). It is associated with teaching (hiph.) at Exod. 18.20.

31. עשות ספרים has received much attention. There is wide agreement that עשה here denotes composition of some sort; that is, the physical making of books. P.A.H. De Boer makes the suggestion that עשה refers to 'working at' books. This can be rendered by metonymy as 'book learning' (R.B.Y. Scott), or 'use of books' (NEB; see De Boer, 'A Note on Ecclesiastes 12.12a', in R. Fischer [ed.], *A Tribute to Arthur Vööbus* [Chicago: Lutheran School of Theology, 1977], pp. 85-88). Since De Boer's suggestion does not exclude, for example, copying or transcribing books (p. 86), something at the level of composition may still be allowed for.

32. That הרבה should be understood as 'many' as opposed to the adverbial 'endless' (hence '*endless* making of books'; so H.L. Ginsberg) see Goldin, 'The End of Ecclesiastes', pp. 145-46. Also, cf. Eccl. 12.9b.

33. Compare Sheppard's comment: '[the frame narrator] speaks of "these" [12.12a] as though he can assume a recognition of their identity by his readers' ('The Epilogue to Qoheleth', p. 188).

words of sages = oxgoads

The words of the wise direct and prod one as a goad prods an ox. The recipient of those words plays a passive role while the role of the sages themselves is a hybrid between active and passive.[34] But this metaphor must be reconciled with the verb 'to give' at the end of the sentence. If the oxgoads and nails are both given by a shepherd then the following parallel is possible:

giving/use of oxgoads and nails by shepherd = use of words by sages

Just as a shepherd uses goads and nails to prod and fix, so sages use their words to inflict; the metaphorical sense breaks down somewhat and the parallel becomes more analogical. The words themselves are just as 'dangerous' to human recipients (who now function metaphorically with animals that are prodded) as goads are to animals.[35]

A more widespread understanding of the verse (presuming a more natural flow in the Hebrew) sees the 'collections of sayings' (as opposed to oxgoads and nails) as being given by the shepherd and creates the following dual parallelism:

words of sages = goads   //   *implanted nails = collected sayings*
                                   (that are given by a shepherd)

In this sense the words of sages and the collected sayings are each analogous to a 'fixing', shepherding image. Words and collections are both able to inflict, correct and so forth.

Both readings reveal something similar about the frame narrator. The less metaphorical sense, suggesting that the *giving* of words is painful

---

34. The limits of the metaphor can be explored further. The ox works and is therefore not passive, but is the very engine of the work of which it is a part. The ox, however, does not decide where it goes; this is the nature of its passivity. Its direction is determined by the prodding of the goad. In the same way, the student studies much (the student provides impetus) and the way (דרך) of wisdom must be kept to at all costs. Yet the direction must be determined by the teacher (passivity) and the (force of the?) teacher's words (12.11c). Furthermore, an ox must be goaded to pull the cart and keep it on the road (דרך), yet Qoheleth says to his reader, 'Walk in the ways of your heart [בדרכי לבך]'. C.D. Ginsburg, although still recognizing motion as the operative image, understood the function of the goads quite differently, as 'a striking metaphor to express what *urges forward*, and tends to the opening of new spheres' (*Coheleth (Commonly Called the Book of Ecclesiastes)* [London: Longman, 1861], p. 474; italics Ginsburg's).

35. So Fox, *Qohelet*, pp. 325-26.

in its correction, implies that the one framing views the method of conveying wisdom (the use of the shepherds' goads and nails *is like* the use of words *by* the wise) as a framing process itself. With the process expressed by two 'fixing' images (goads and nails) it propounds a forceful impression of the transition of wisdom and knowledge. The recipient of wisdom is forced (as the direction of the ox is forced) to *fix* his or her attention (and indeed, intellectual enterprise)[36] on the giving of wisdom. The other, more common reading suggests that the words themselves (those of Qoheleth are first to come to mind) and the collected sayings (Qoheleth is included inasmuch as he is part of the economy of wisdom as a sage) are somehow endowed with the ability to correct and keep one on the 'straight and narrow'. The overall strategy of framing is evident in both readings. The one who frames prescribes the boundaries of interpretation *and* adumbrates this with the metaphors. The frame narrator, as Qoheleth's presenter, fits his own partial description of the process of the wisdom tradition more closely than does Qoheleth himself. This is even more apparent from the following verse.

The thrust of v. 12 is one of admonition and warning, but the precise content of that warning is difficult to discern. If the antecedent for 'these' (מהמה) is the 'collected sayings' just mentioned, then the admonition to the son (the frame narrator's student) is not to 'go beyond'[37] the 'collections of the masters' (Qoheleth being one of them). However, if the antecedent is the story of Qoheleth (hence,

36. Compare G.L. Burns's comments on the midrashic understanding of Eccl. 12.11-12: 'In the midrashic texts themselves...[there is] a relentless preoccupation with the *force* of interpretation..."The Words of the wise are like goads", and so on—is a favourite of the rabbis because it concerns the point of midrash, its practical as against purely academic context...The words of the wise are *situated*; their meaning is embedded in their situation' ('The Hermeneutics of Midrash', in R. Schwartz [ed.], *The Book and the Text* [Oxford: Basil Blackwell, 1990], pp. 189-213 [203, 205]; italics Burns's). Torah (the fixed collections) and sage (the words of the wise) enjoy a relationship of appropriation. That is, the words of the wise, like goads, force an application, an appropriation of meaning, onto the life of the community.

37. יתר; cf. Eccl. 12.9: '*Furthermore* ['besides what you have just read'], Qoheleth was a sage.' Compare Est. 6.6—Haman says to the king, 'Whom would the king wish to honour *besides me*? [יותר ממני, *beyond, more than*]'. The phrase suggests an exceeding of the subject it qualifies in a manner that has already been carried out. Hence, the student has been instructed, by implication, about what is good, but studying or 'composing' more than this is not recommended.

'these [words just related]'), then the epilogist seems to be offering
veiled praise of Qoheleth's wisdom. In any case, some literary content
is being referred to, beyond which the frame narrator does not wish his
audience to extend any intellectual endeavour. Perhaps even a fixed
canon of literature is in mind.[38]

As the verse progresses, the warning is elaborated. The warning suggests that if one were to go beyond the fixed literature, the composition
(or 'working at' in general) of a great number of books would result
and the hapless victim drawn into much study. The picture is of the
student becoming weary with labour and the sentiment is perhaps surprisingly congruous with some of Qoheleth's own notions of absurdity:

> For the dream comes with much concern [ענין],
>> and the voice of a fool with many words (5.3; cf. 1.8).

> For with many dreams and absurdities [there are] many words—
>> but fear God (5.7).

For Qoheleth, too, the sheer quantity of things is a mechanism of the
absurd (cf. 1.18; 5.11; 6.3, 11). (It is interesting to note that the frame
narrator did not use הבל to describe what was 'no end' and 'a weariness
to the body'. Qoheleth undoubtedly would have.)

The congruity in this passage, however, ironically contributes to its
incongruity. Qoheleth does not suggest himself that there is a fixed
body of knowledge to which one must adhere, without which dire consequences would follow. For Qoheleth, the answer to what is 'no end'
and a 'weariness of the flesh' (what is absurd) lies not in the wisdom

---

38. For Sheppard the antecedent of 'these' is 'a set of extant collections or
books inclusive of, but larger than, Qoheleth' ('The Epilogue to Qoheleth', p. 188).
Goldin points to the *Anshe Keneset Ha-Gedolah* of the *Abot* which is taken to be
representative of the mishnaic understanding of Eccl. 12.12 as an admonition to
maintain the integrity of the Torah ('The End of Ecclesiastes', p. 156; *passim*).
Hence 'these' are the 'collections' of Torah. Therefore it was said, 'The Torah is
sufficient', even, 'preserve instead the more carefully edited readings provided'
('The End of Ecclesiastes', p. 149). Even the דברי חכמים at the beginning of this
section might refer to a 'knowable body of knowledge', although there is little
evidence to suggest that it refers exclusively to the books of Proverbs and Ecclesiastes (contra Wilson and, partly, Sheppard; see Wilson, 'Intent and Significance',
pp. 176-77). Goldin's arguments might be supported by the Deuteronomic admonitions to not 'add to' (לא תספו) the commands that the Lord has given, lest things
not go well (Deut. 4.2; 12.32). Also, see Roger Beckwith (*The Old Testament
Canon of the New Testament Church* [Grand Rapids: Eerdmans, 1985], pp. 319-
20), who argues that 12.12 refers to work outside of Ecclesiastes.

tradition—for wisdom itself has failed in liberating him from the incongruity of the world he has observed—but rather in the enjoyment with which God empowers people to escape absurdity. The answer rests with God. Even more incongruent is the fact that Qoheleth often suggests that for him such an absurd situation could only be observed[39] and not, as the frame narrator implies, overcome by mere resistance.

Do the warnings of 12.11-12 reveal a preference, then, for the frame narrator's own epistemological outlook?[40] To approach this question I would like to pick up on the phrase 'limits of knowledge'. First it should be clarified what kind of knowledge is meant. The distinction offered some time ago by Michael Polanyi, of two types of knowledge, will serve my purpose here.[41]

The first type is *tacit* knowledge, which is inarticulate in form and is received. Like a map that fixes one's location in relation to the recognizable features of a landscape, this kind of knowledge is *a-critical* in nature and is formed from 'systematically collected observations'.[42] The crucial point in relation to my analysis is that it is received essentially unaltered. (Tacit 'ability' is most apparent in the acquisition of language skills, as in the general observation that children learn a new language more quickly than adults.)

39. 4.1-3 is the best example of this; further, see the Postscript.

40. Epistemology is perhaps the most basic of philosophical inquiries and is therefore beyond anything like a thorough treatment here. I refer the reader to Fox's superb treatment of the subject in Chapter 3 of *Qohelet*, 'The Way to Wisdom: Qohelet's Epistemology'. Fox emphasizes Qoheleth's personal acquisition of knowledge. His conclusions are summed up well in his own words: 'The sages prided themselves not on having created knowledge but on having taken it to themselves. Whereas Qohelet's favorite verb of perception is "seeing", theirs is "hearing"' (*Qohelet*, p. 98). It is worth noting, however, the warning offered by J. Ellul, that most philosophical 'labels' foisted on Qoheleth are undeserved: 'At most we could concede that the "subjects treated" by Qohelet are also philosophers' favourite subjects—subjects that metaphysics has dealt with. But nothing more... Let us leave metaphysics to the metaphysicians, then, so that we can listen to Qohelet speak without metaphysicians' discourse interfering. This way we will see that he speaks differently from them' (*Reason for Being: A Meditation on Ecclesiastes* [trans. J.M. Hanks; Grand Rapids: Eerdmans, 1990], p. 27; see also pp. 26-30).

41. As elaborated in *The Study of Man* (Chicago: University of Chicago Press, 1959), pp. 11-40, which is the introduction to his longer works, *Personal Knowledge* and *The Liberty of Logic*.

42. Polanyi, *The Study of Man*, p. 17.

The second type is *explicit* knowledge. As the word implies, this knowledge can only be acquired through a process of discovery. The content of explicit knowledge is, in fact, tacit knowledge. That is, in the example of the map, the formulated knowledge that makes it up is expressed through a process of discovery that uses many forms of tacit knowledge (notes, surveys etc.). Such a process is doubtless evident in Qoheleth's text, in that it is his *explicit* reformulation of the tacit knowledge of wisdom that allows for his seemingly distinct brand of critical observation.[43] For example, in 3.16-17 Qoheleth observes some 'stock' elements of wisdom—elements that could be considered the fabric of tacit knowledge:

> But still I observed under the sun that in the place of justice there was wickedness, and in the place of righteousness there was wickedness. I said in my heart, 'God will judge the righteous and the wicked'; for [there is] a time for every matter and for every deed.

It is the intensely personal narrative element ('I said in my heart') that marks Qoheleth's sentiment as a reformulation, a judgment, an *explicit* idea about common human experience. Qoheleth thinks *about* wisdom. To 'go beyond', in such a way, the established parameters of tacit knowledge might well be seen as futile or perhaps something more threatening. Polanyi, while stating a hypothetical case, makes the following surprisingly applicable comment:

> ...the establishment of a completely precise and strictly logical representation of knowledge...might be championed as an ideal [and] any personal participation in our scientific account of the universe [is] a residual flaw which should be completely eliminated at once.[44]

While one cannot, of course, strictly equate Polanyi's notion of 'scientific account' with the frame narrator's notion of fixed learning and knowledge, the point remains relevant: moving beyond what is

43. It should be noted that the comparison being made here is *not* to the kinds of processes of discovery found in Job, Proverbs or any other wisdom literature. As has been widely noted (most especially by G. von Rad), similarities abound in the way in which sages acquired knowledge in the ancient world (cf. Crenshaw's comments on Qoheleth's 'examination of personal experience' in his review of Fox's *Qohelet*, in *JBL* 109 [1990], pp. 712-15 [715]). The comparison is strictly limited to the fixed notions of knowledge as found in the epilogue.

44. *The Study of Man*, p. 18. Polanyi goes on to refute this position as self-contradictory in that the 'most distinguished act of thought consists in *producing* such knowledge' (*The Study of Man*, p. 18; italics Polanyi's).

fixed is always a threat to the establishment that fixes it. In the case of the biblical wisdom literature, such conservatizing elements as the frame narrator's text may well have buttressed the establishment of power—political and social.[45]

It is Qoheleth's narrative setting that creates his epistemological foundation. He knows by experience. It is through the narrating 'I' that he sets out his own limits of what he knows of and in the world.[46] The frame narrator, it appears, has attempted to override that method of knowing with his own tacit preference. But it should be remembered that the frame narrator's epistemological 'preference' is only that. It is clear that his own priorities (what *his* student should heed) differ from Qoheleth's, but the reader has always had the option of choosing his or her own limits of interpretation. The force reflected in the midrashic readings of this passage, for example, was *chosen* by those readers. Indeed, the option always remains open to readers—the epilogue simply makes the options clear.

The epistemological tension can be illustrated further by Qoheleth's use of the language of shepherding, which is reversely paralleled in the epilogue. Both of the frame narrator's shepherding images (the goads that prod animals and the shepherd figure who is perhaps the source of something *like* implanted nails) serve to depict that which is fixed, even trustworthy (not departing from 'these' will guard the student from weariness of the body; 12.12b). The knowledge within which the student is to stay (presumably a knowledge with which the frame narrator was well acquainted) is tacit and is sure. For Qoheleth, however, the language of shepherding is suited to a contrary purpose: to depict that which is *not* fixed. So the refrain, 'Everything is absurd and a pursuit of wind'. 'Pursuit of wind' suggests, among other things surely, that the object considered is not under control.[47] This is particularly significant

45. So W. Brueggemann, 'The Social Significance of Solomon as a Patron of Wisdom', in Gammie (ed.), *The Sage in Israel and the Ancient Near East*, pp. 117-32 (126-27). Although Brueggemann does not mention Qoheleth's frame narrator, he speaks of the 'proverbial wisdom' of ancient Israel that assumed of the world a 'studiable system [with] constancy and durability, experienced as regularity and predictability' (p. 127). This is a perceived order that 'is not questioned or criticised...[and] *outside of which* questions are not raised' ('The Social Significance', p. 127; italics mine).

46. Of course, it is disputed as to whether 'I', as a literary device, is a viable entity capable of representing anything like a unified 'self'. Further, see Chapter 7.

47. The close association of הבל (as the name 'Abel') with the verb רעה at

when Qoheleth's ability to know is under consideration: 'And I set my heart to know wisdom and knowledge, madness and folly. I knew that this too is a pursuit [רעיון] of wind' (1.17). It should be noted that it is not wisdom and knowledge that are a pursuit of wind, but rather the fact that he set his heart to know them was *like* a pursuit of wind. Qoheleth's personal attempt at reaching true understanding is not fixed or able to be controlled. It is not something received and/or graspable. With Qoheleth the frame narrator's metaphor is reversed in that the acquisition of knowledge is most *un*like the activity of the shepherd.

Two illuminating examples of the play between the language of shepherding and of pursuit are worth noting. First, Prov. 15.14:

> The heart of the understanding seeks knowledge [יבקש־דעת],
> but the mouths of fools feed on [ירעה] folly.

Second, Hos. 12.1a [2a]:

> Ephraim herds the wind [רעה רוח] and pursues [רדף; cf. Eccl. 3.1] the east wind all day long...

As Crenshaw says of these two instances, 'both examples mock the behavior of shepherding, whether rounding up the wind or feeding on folly'.[48] Indeed, both examples show the capacity of Hebrew language and thought to suggest the ironic sense likely present in Qoheleth's narration, a sense that stands at odds with the frame narrator's more fixed usages of the terms.

The inherent irony in a warning against the composition of many books in the epilogue of a book can hardly be overstated. It is a clever deconstructive turn that one could imagine even Qoheleth would admire. Many times in my studies I have heard the phrase 'of the making... etc.' quoted jokingly in face of the stress of a large amount of work ahead. Likewise, I have often felt the absurdity of my own writing of a 'book' about a 'book' that denounces the activity involved in 'making' one. The frame narrator was surely aware of the simple irony, and that assumption by the reader (that he *was* aware of it) contributes further to the enjoyment of the irony. The irony serves to

---

Gen. 4.2 is interesting to note here: ויהי־הבל רעה צון ('Now Abel was a keeper of sheep'). The Lord was pleased with Abel (הבל) and his offering (4.4), and Cain states that he was not the keeper (שמר) of Abel (הבל, 4.9). Cain was unable either to account or be responsible for הבל. Of course if the author of Ecclesiastes was aware of the word association in Genesis it would be of some significance.

48. *Ecclesiastes*, p. 73.

alienate the frame narrator yet further from Qoheleth; for one can easily assume that the warning is an ill-concealed dissent from Qoheleth's own way of knowing. The creation of books might involve the creation of new knowledge, of thinking and of the critical reformulation of ideas to which the frame narrator seems opposed.[49]

To return to the phrase, '*limits* of knowledge', in this passage the language of fixing, guiding and shepherding abounds. This is the language of framing. The use of such language itself frames an alternative to Qoheleth's epistemology. After establishing the boundaries of Qoheleth's character in 12.9-10, the frame narrator goes beyond those boundaries to establish (prod and fix) his own epistemological preferences for his audience, thereby setting himself at odds with Qoheleth.

4. *The Final Word (12.13-14)*

[This is] the end of the matter—everything has been heard—fear God and keep his commandments; for this [applies to] everyone.[50] For God will bring every deed into judgment concerning all that is hidden, whether good or evil.

That the epilogue leaves the reader with a more conservative sentiment than Qoheleth would likely have offered (indeed, did offer [12.6-7]) has hugely shaped the overall understanding of the book. As Murphy remarks, 'The orientation provided by vv 12-14 exercised great influence in the history of the exegesis of Ecclesiastes.'[51] There is no conclusive evidence that the epilogue contributed to the acceptance of Ecclesiastes into the canon,[52] and there seems to be no other viable reason for this conservatism than that the frame narrator is again overriding Qoheleth's more radical message with his own more tacit priorities. This conservative emphasis is tied into the frame narrative set-up. Discussing this passage, Fox comments that the

49. Even the warning against much study carries this association. להג, a *hapax leg.*, is possibly related to the Arabic *lahija*, 'be devoted', 'apply oneself greatly' (see BDB, p. 529b). However, by following many commentators and taking this to be a defective form of הגה, suggesting an intense investigation (cf. Job 1.8, [*meditate* day and night]; Pss. 1.2; 63.6[7] [where it is synonymous with זכר]; 77.12[13] etc.), my thesis is supported even more strongly.

50. On this 'pregnant Hebrew phrase' (כי־זה כל־האדם), see the examples compiled by Gordis, *Koheleth*, p. 345.

51. *Ecclesiastes*, p. 126.

52. On this question see below, Chapter 6.2.

author blunts objections to the book as a whole by implying through use
of a frame-narrator that he is just reporting what Qohelet said, without
actually rejecting the latter's ideas. The epilogist thus allows the more
conservative reader to align himself with him, so that a reader need not
reject the *book*, even if he does reject the views of Qohelet.[53]

Many conservative readings of the book may be 'explained' this way.
To cite one example, because Ecclesiastes 'ends' this way, J.S. Wright
can say the following of the *book*:

> To summarize its contents, the book *constitutes an exhortation* to live a
> God-fearing life, realizing that one day account must be rendered to
> him.[54]

To be fair, it is not misleading to suggest that the frame narrator is in
fact offering a summary of the 'book' at 12.13-14. The phrase הכל
נשמע at 12.13a, in light of the narrative context (the epilogist has *told*
Qoheleth's story to his son), could be paraphrased, 'When Qoheleth's
story has been heard, what should be remembered is...' The fault of
such readings as the one I have just cited is that the summary of the
frame narrator is *a-critically* adopted as a *good* summary of Qoheleth's
thought, which it surely is not. (Even if we accept that הבל הבלים at 1.2
and 12.8 is a good summary of Qoheleth's thought, we cannot be sure
in what spirit it is written. In other words, the subtext could be: this is
the sum of what Qoheleth has to say, ultimate absurdity, and there can
come no good from saying that.) Worse yet, the verses are often mis-
construed as Qoheleth's own words when readers overlook the fact that
another voice is narrating at the epilogue. Critical misunderstandings
are then bound to occur. Take the example of L. Ryken:

> *The writer himself* [whom Ryken takes to be Qoheleth] signals the two
> types of passages that make up Ecclesiastes with a pair of metaphors
> near the end of *his collection*...The 'under the sun' passages are like
> goads that make us unable to settle down complacently with life lived on
> a purely earthly plane. The positive, God-centered passages are fixed
> points of reference.[55]

The frame narrator has allowed many generations the opportunity to

53. Fox, 'Frame-narrative', pp. 103-104 (italics Fox's).
54. 'The Book of Ecclesiastes', in J.D. Douglas *et al.* (eds.), *New Bible
Dictionary* (Leicester: Inter-Varsity Press, 2nd edn, 1982), pp. 295-96 (296) (italics
mine).
55. 'Ecclesiastes', in Ryken and Longman (eds.), *A Complete Literary Guide*,
p. 272 (italics mine).

misread and compress Qoheleth's inquiries, and the fact that the epilogue has engendered such assessments is yet more evidence that the frame narrator's epistemology is a tacit one.

Of course, Qoheleth offered his own conservative sentiments, but these can be accorded undue significance, for they are nearly always spoken in a critical context. The most cited example of his conservatism, for instance, has sharp critical undertones:

> Whenever you vow a vow to God do not delay to pay it, for there is no delight [taken] in fools. Pay what you vow! Better that you do not vow than that you vow and do not pay. Do not let your mouth cause your flesh to sin, and do not say to the messenger that it was an error. Why should God be angry at your voice and ruin the work of your hands? For with many dreams and absurdities [there are] many words—but fear God (5.4-7).

This could hardly be summarized as 'Fear God and keep his commands'. Indeed, this passage emits a strong 'aroma of paranoia'[56] out of keeping with the very positive effects that fearing God is meant to engender elsewhere, not the least of which is the beginning of knowledge (Prov. 1.7; cf. 1 Sam. 12.24; Prov. 3.7-8). Furthermore, in a celebrated passage, Qoheleth does in fact play havoc with one of the commandments of Torah:

> Rejoice, O young man, in your youth.
> And let your heart gladden you in the days of your youth.
> And walk in the ways [והלך בדרכי] of your heart,
> and in the sight of your eyes.
> And know for certain [that] concerning all of these things
> God will bring you into judgment (11.9).

In the Torah, the fringe that the Israelites were instructed to wear on the corner of their garments was there to *prod* them to

> remember all the commandments of the Lord and do them, and not to follow after [תתורו אחרי] your own heart and your own eyes, which you are inclined to go after (Num. 15.39; cf. Job 37.7-8).

In Qoheleth's variation on this text he has put a twist to the notion of keeping God's commands. He reformulates the commandment and

---

56. So Zimmermann (*Inner World*, pp. 37-41), who suggests that this passage is evidence that Qoheleth believed fiercely in what Zimmermann calls the 'omnipotence of thoughts' that contributed to his neurosis: 'Qohelet is so self-punishing [in 5.1-7] that no margin for error is allowed' (p. 40).

appropriates it to his own purposes. He certainly, in a sense, goes beyond it.

The frame narrator, however, is more cautious not to 'go beyond' anything. This is perhaps most evident in 12.13-14, which has been frequently compared to Sir. 43.27:[57]

עוד כאלה לא נוסף וקץ דבר הוא הכל

> More than this may not be concluded, the end of the matter, 'He is all in all.'[58]

While any literary relationship between Ecclesiastes and Sirach is rarely claimed, and while the position of this verse in Sirach is not 'epilogic', some comment is worth making. After a long description of the glory of the works of the Lord (42.15–43.26), the narrator in Sirach has reached a point where any more comment strikes him as superfluous. The end of such speech would be unreachable. Likewise, Qoheleth's frame narrator seems to say that there is no more that he wishes to (or can) say to his student. Such speech would 'go beyond' what is required. Perhaps Sirach felt, as did the frame narrator, that more words were unnecessary since the 'whole of humanity' lies elsewhere.

In his closing verse the frame narrator's views on judgment echo Qoheleth once more (cf. 3.17; 11.9b). The echo is ironic in light of all the discord the epilogue offers the reader. Yet even more ironic is, as Murphy notes, the frame narrator's idea that God will bring into judgment every מעשה ('deed, work'),

> which is used in the book to indicate the inscrutable divine action ('work of God'; 7:13; 8:17; 11:6; cf. 3:11), or events that transpire in this dreary human life (2:17; 4:3; etc.). Now the 'work' or 'deed' (human) is here associated too easily to divine judgment...The viewpoint of the epilogist...goes beyond the perspective of Qoheleth.[59]

In the final analysis, the frame narrator wishes to impose his tacit epistemology on 'everyone', that they might fear God and keep his commandments *without*, it seems, the kind of critical reformulation and expressive thinking that Qoheleth embodies.

---

57. See Gordis, *Koheleth*, p. 345.
58. Translation by Sheppard, 'The Epilogue to Qoheleth', p. 187.
59. Murphy, *Ecclesiastes*, p. 126.

Chapter 5

FRAMING THE FRAMER: FINAL REFLECTIONS ON *THIS* FRAME

> The prologues are over. It is a question, now,
> Of final belief. So, say that final belief
> Must be in a fiction. It is time to choose.
> Wallace Stevens ('Asides on the Oboe')

It might be contested that I have been unnecessarily hard on the frame narrator. Of course, some of the extent to which (and the manner in which) he summarized Qoheleth's story was necessary. The frame narrator was not at pains to write his own book and in this respect he was in keeping with his own views on the proliferation of knowledge. Indeed, the frame narrator kept relatively close to a common practice of ancient epilogues. As M. Wiebe notes of other ANE frames,

> The epilogues of [the genre of] Instruction all reflect back on the instruction [i.e. inner story of the frame] and sing its praises...The epilogues of *Kagemni, Ptahhotep, Merikare, ANY,* and *Amenemope* stress the importance of following the letter of the instruction presented and the continuance of the tradition of the 'sayings' or 'writings.' These epilogues refer to the instruction as the 'sayings of the past' and the 'words of the ancestors' and to the instruction itself as if it were a well-known written text.[1]

As in other ANE frames, the frame narrator reflected backward, sang Qoheleth's praises and likely referred inclusively to Qoheleth's work as 'words of the sages', while claiming that Qoheleth wrote 'sayings' himself. However, he differs from other ANE frame narrators in that his approval of Qoheleth's procedure of knowing is less evident. In no way did he 'stress the importance of following the letter *of the instruction presented*'. Why, then, as a narrative character, did the frame narrator bother to tell Qoheleth's story at all?[2]

1. Wiebe, 'The Wisdom in Proverbs', p. 42.
2. That is, in a fictional sense, for, historical considerations aside, the frame

In a way, I have obliged myself to answer this question. I offer the following, tentative, answer. The frame narrator did not demand anything like strict adhesion to Qoheleth's words. He did, however, stress that his (implied) audience should not go beyond a fixed body of knowledge, which *likely included* Qoheleth's story. It may be assumed, therefore, that his commitment to Qoheleth's story was only partial and that his duality of opposition and commitment to Qoheleth is to be explained by it. However, since the frame narrator lent such ample credence to Qoheleth's story by his act of framing, this seems unnatural. From the summary of the epilogue it is clear that the frame narrator *did not* agree with Qoheleth's approach to wisdom, God and tradition, bound, as they were, to his wholly different epistemology. Therefore, given the fiction of the presentation, the frame narrator comes across as a rather reluctant scribe who had to do what he could with what he had (knowing that he had the last say in any case), and this with evident respect to Qoheleth's words, which were, to his considerable annoyance, part of the wisdom tradition themselves.

To compare, again, frames of modern fiction, it is certainly not unusual for a fictitious frame to question purposefully the material it frames. Note Linda Dittmar's assertion about some fictitious frames:

> Faulkner and [film director] Kurasawa use their frame stories to question the very truth of the narrated materials they contain. Accounts [in the inner narrative] conflict with one another, yet each has a claim on us—the claim of the fictive come to life through acts of narration. The inner narratives reveal the extent to which subjectivity [like Qoheleth's 'I'] governs all knowledge...[and] a disjunction between story and frame puts into question the audience's relation to all accounts.[3]

This is one of the principal assets of framing: to put into question 'the audience's relation to all accounts'. A frame compels the reader to assess and evaluate the work at hand. By presenting his assessment, the frame narrator solicits the reader's own, personal assessment.

narrator *is* a character who, we are asked to believe, knew Qoheleth, was his foremost interpreter and told his story. On how the frame informs our understanding of the historical composition of Ecclesiastes, see below.

3. 'Fashioning and Re-fashioning', pp. 192-93, 199. Compare Mary Ann Caws's comments: '[inner narratives] can be expository, necessary to the [outer] plot, voluntary, or free in their function, and of the play-in-the-play sort; their relation to the frame is then of various kinds, but in every case the content is different from the content of the outer or framing text' (*Reading Frames in Modern Fiction*, p. 270 n. 16; italics mine; also, see pp. 269-71).

One reason the epilogue allows for such diversity of reading is that while the formal structure created by the frame around Qoheleth seems unbendable and unshiftable, the interpretive boundaries it sets are not strictly so. As Mary Ann Caws contends,

> the frame is valuable as a concept for the imagination, even in its strictest limits, as is the very act of 'trotting around' it occasions, plainly self-inclusive and self-framing...[Frames are,] above all, aids to perception...[and] *all frames are constantly open to shift and exchange.*[4]

That is, it is absurd to think that reading involves the *imagining* of polarized opposites that in no way share a flux of meaning between them. A frame involves both the interpretive borders that define itself and the content it frames to create its effects. In fact, there is open-endedness within the frame narrator's text itself. For example, the frame of Ecclesiastes raises the plot-oriented question of the audience's reception *within the story presented*: Will the 'son' accept what has been spoken about Qoheleth? Note Wiebe's comments:

> The presence of...[the] frame surrounding the instruction...[and the] progression within each Instruction...raises narratological questions such as, How will the son respond to the instruction?, and, Will the instructor witness a receptive audience for their instruction?...Answers to these questions are suspended until the Instruction returns to the narrative frame in the epilogue.[5]

Wiebe finds this concern present in only four of the Instructions, where all but one of the epilogues is lengthy: *Kagemni. Kagemni* (as noted above) bears a formal resemblance to Ecclesiastes, and the effect of the respective epilogues is comparable. According to Wiebe, in *Kagemni* the frame narrator 'answers any question[s] of the reception of this instruction by those instructed'.[6] Can the same be said of Ecclesiastes? Yes, but only to the extent that the frame narrator has made it relevant; and that happens to be minimal. That is, while the purpose of the epilogue of Ecclesiastes is to admonish the recipient of Qoheleth's story, the whole question of reception becomes overshadowed by the

---

4.   *Reading Frames in Modern Fiction*, pp. 4-5 (italics Caws's). That frames do not always lend themselves to neat division in the form of 'diagramming', see Brooks on Conrad's *Heart of Darkness* (*Reading for the Plot*, pp. 256-57 and p. 351 n. 8).

5.   Wiebe, 'The Wisdom in Proverbs', p. 43.

6.   'The Wisdom in Proverbs', p. 44.

opposition that the frame narrator has made to Qoheleth. The question is never answered.

Qoheleth's frame narrator does, however, 'close' at least one issue. Frames with symmetry provide the reader with a sense of origin and ending. For frames

> validate the interpretive act by foregrounding the story-telling context at least in the beginning and end of the text...Thus, once we realize that Alice's adventures are a dream framed by her falling asleep and waking up, the puzzle falls into place; we may continue to wonder about that Cheshire cat, but we trust the frame as a guide to the narrative within it...[For] frames normalize their content by attributing to it an origin and a context.[7]

This is precisely what Qoheleth's frame narrator does. By giving us an origin (from the mouth of the king) and a context (geographical,[8] of speech and of character), the frame narrator wins our trust and summons our attention, however much we may still wonder about Qoheleth, that Cheshire cat.[9]

To conclude this discussion an inclusio is in order. I will therefore finish where the discussion of the frame began: the rhetoric of the picture frame. Consider, then, the examples of two paintings. In both of my comparisons I will assume that my argument that Qoheleth's and the frame narrator's texts clash at the level of ideology is correct.

The first is Picasso's *Pipe and Sheet of Music* (1914).[10] Within the physical frame is a cubist still life surrounded by the artist's rendition of a frame, which imitates themes in the physical frame (namely the punched floral ornament design). At the centre of the bottom panel of the painted frame is the artist's name, 'PICASSO', in comic lettering.

7. Dittmar, 'Fashioning and Re-fashioning', p. 195.

8. I.e. Jerusalem; see p. 74 n. 6. However, see Zimmermann, *Inner World*, pp. 123-31.

9. The context of origin also contributes further to the work's authentication. This is done through allusions to historical figures and to an authorial presence. So K. Gittes: 'The "real" world of the framing story (and sometimes the less real world of the tales themselves) is usually authenticated by historical figures and by the authorial presence. Such authenticating makes the often unreal and fantastic events in the enclosed tales appear more credible' ('The Frame Narrative', p. 189). The 'historical figures' in the epilogue are Qoheleth/Solomon and the sages, while an authorial presence is discerned in the act of transference, the very telling of Qoheleth's tale.

10. It is found in Traber, 'In Perfect Harmony?', p. 230.

The artist's rendition mimics the physical frame as well as the act of presentation. Picasso's purpose was to raise questions about how we view frame and picture, but also to caricature traditional exhibition practices. He sought to raise the question of what was real, making it difficult for viewers to commit to any one ideology: 'We all know that art is not truth', he wrote. 'Art is a lie that teaches us the truth, at least as much truth as mankind can ever know.'[11]

Let us assume that the frame of Ecclesiastes is comparable to this example. We will therefore assume that the whole product came from one hand. If this is the case we may also assume that this author *intended* to raise questions about the relationship of the frame to the words of Qoheleth. Perhaps the epilogue could then be seen to caricature traditional wisdom practices. The artifice of the whole intends to teach us a truth that does not rest on the surface of either the words of Qoheleth or of the frame narrator.[12] We could support this with the argument that Qoheleth would not have chosen an unsuitable frame *unless* he was employing an aesthetic or subversive strategy of presentation. Thus we could grant, as does Fox,[13] that a hyper-self-conscious real author, in a vein of Romantic Irony, wrote the entire text, knowingly manipulating the literary conventions of the frame.

The second example is the 'Chandos Portrait' of Shakespeare (John Taylor, c. 1610) in the National Portrait Gallery, London.[14] The portrait was the museum's first acquisition (in 1856) and has been reframed

11. Cited in Traber, 'In Perfect Harmony?', p. 230.

12. That the frame and picture depict a whole entity is an illusion the frame itself creates. As Paul Duro notes, 'We should construe the work/frame [combination of painting and frame] as the indissociable/indefinable unity *through which* our notions of reality and truth, our expectations and desires, are given an (illusory) coherence' ('Introduction', in *idem* [ed.], *Rhetoric of the Frame*, pp. 1-10 [8; italics mine]). Compare the comments of D. Ananth: 'the frame is both necessary and supplementary, absent and present, an indispensable (if volatile) supplement to an entity that attempts to deny it needs one' (paraphrasing Derrida, cited in 'Introduction', p. 8).

13. Fox clearly intends more than a 'final-form' study of Ecclesiastes, rather, 'The author has given him [the frame narrator] a conventional—and fictional—epic situation' ('Frame-narrative', p. 104). Throughout his article, Fox maintains this assumption. It is particularly evident in his effective defence of 'single-handed' authorship (pp. 85-91).

14. The painting, in three different frames, is found in Simon, *The Art of the Picture Frame*, p. 28. The two frames for the painting I discuss are Figures 15 and 16.

several times since. The gallery owns two of the previous frames. According to Simon, painting and frame were grossly mismatched when, in 1864, a mock seventeenth-century frame was fitted to the picture. The new match, a wide black and gilded frame, focused 'attention on the frame at the expense of the picture', with the 'dark background [giving] the frame a rather eerie feel', out of keeping with the reddish colour scheme of the picture and making for a 'horrific result'.[15] The latest match (1983), with a narrower tortoiseshell frame of black and red, though not a period frame, enhances 'the scale of the picture and its sense of colour'.[16] The mismatch of frame and picture was due, according to Simon, to the imposition of the tastes of the trustees and curator, who simply misunderstood the painting.

Let us assume that the frame of Ecclesiastes is comparable to the mismatched frame of 1864. We therefore assume that there is no hidden agenda, no subversive strategy of presentation at hand. Those responsible for Qoheleth's frame simply misunderstood Qoheleth's story. The book, then, does not come from one hand but has at least two authors for Qoheleth's words and for the frame, each driven by wholly different visions of wisdom and ways of knowing. If this be the case, was the one who chose the frame intending to give Qoheleth's words as smooth and orthodox an inception into the public ('gallery') as possible? The 1864 Chandos Portrait frame, albeit mismatched, was made with the viewer in mind. It was the opinion of the trustees that the portrait at the time was 'seen to disadvantage in its present frame'.[17] Yet the frame was, as noted, so overpowering that appreciation of the picture was disadvantaged. We have seen this to be the case with conservative readings of Qoheleth based, as they are, on the frame and not the picture. Like the average gallery-goer up until the end of the nineteenth century ('Viewers…needed the gilt frame as legitimation'),[18] some readers need affirmation of a more conservative view than that represented by the framed material.[19]

15. Simon, *The Art of the Picture Frame*, pp. 29, 179.

16. Simon, *The Art of the Picture Frame*, p. 29.

17. Cited in Simon, *The Art of the Picture Frame*, p. 179.

18. So Traber, 'In Perfect Harmony?', p. 226.

19. One particularly striking example comes from Longman, who identifies the theology of the frame (which Longman argues, like myself, is contrary to Qoheleth's) as the book's overall normative theology. While Longman (unlike many authors) rightly distinguishes the two separate strategies of Qoheleth and the frame narrator, he allows the theology of the latter to dictate the interpretation of

There are balances to maintain in all of this. With the first option (Picasso) one might be suspected of anachronistically foisting on the author literary circumstances and conditions that should, at the least, be considered circumspect. To take the second option, if one grants that author what Romberg calls an 'unconscious infringement of point of view',[20] the risk runs in the opposite direction. That is, in assuming that the author took no conscious effort to depict the frame, the reader is likely to overlook the multifarious effects it creates, thereby implying that ancient writers and readers were not in fact capable of literary sophistication (i.e. the chronological fallacy).[21]

In recent years, the incongruity of the epilogue to the body of the book has been underplayed or the relationship ignored altogether.[22] The discrepancies are, however, evident and informative, and analysis of the relationship helps to unpack Qoheleth's own strategies. Just as some art critics are beginning to protest the practice of depicting paintings in books without the frame, a caution can be sounded in relation to Qoheleth. Ecclesiastes must be read as a whole, frame included, so that we might explore the differences ourselves. This is why, although I do not agree with his ultimate approach, I applaud the seriousness with which Longman regards the frame narrative (see above, n. 19).

Qoheleth's words. For example, in order to deal with the difficult words of Qoheleth at 7.26-29, 'it must be remembered that Qohelet is filled with tensions and contradictions since he is a confused wise man. For those concerned that a biblical book appears to support the views of a misogynist, it must also be remembered that the views of Qohelet are not the teachings of the book of Ecclesiastes any more than the speeches of the three friends constitute the normative teaching of the book of Job' (*The Book of Ecclesiastes*, p. 204). This is because 'the theology of the frame narrator...is the normative theology of the book as a whole' (p. 32).

20. *Studies in the Narrative Technique*, p. 335 (in reference to Rousseau's problematic application of his name to the fictional editor in *La nouvelle Héloïse...*).

21. It should be noted that although the frame of Ecclesiastes may not have been created *for the purpose* of effecting the strategies I have been discussing, this does not alter the persuasive force of those strategies over the reader.

22. For example, among modern commentators some virtually ignore the relationship (Crenshaw, Eaton, Fredericks, Wilson [who is concerned more with the epilogue's relation to Proverbs]) or see the tension the frame narrative creates as a 'corrective' of Qoheleth's thought (Childs). Some see the tension as essentially positive, laudatory (Murphy, Ogden) or essentially at odds with Qoheleth in purpose (Fox [although see *Qohelet*, pp. 315-16], Gordis [in part], Longman, Sheppard).

With whose ideology, then, does/should the reader identify? And whose ideology is actually present in the frame? Who frames whom? Of course I cannot refute anyone's belief that Qoheleth (i.e. an author) achieved a subversive literary sophistication by creating the whole, but I suggest rather that someone chose the frame for him, so to speak. Indeed, were I forced to speculate on matters of history, I would be inclined to imagine that the frame narrator was himself a sage of a more moderate temperament than Qoheleth, who was obliged (to his annoyance?—or perhaps with 'the reader in mind'?) to present Qoheleth's largely pre-formed story in his own garish, 'establishment-issue' frame. I hasten to add that, if that helped Qoheleth's words into the canon, I for one am glad he did so.

Now, finding a suitable point of departure to discuss Qoheleth's narrative strategy is a daunting task. The rubric *narrative* can easily include such aspects as characterization (of narrators, implied authors and audiences etc.), setting, voice, point of view (focus), fictive versus historical assumptions and so forth. Here is where the tone of the work must determine the questions brought and the approach(es) taken. Because Qoheleth's character is so intimately constructed and conveyed in the first person, his narration lends itself naturally to questions of identity, selfhood and implied authorship, which lead to questions, as shall become evident, of the *subject* and of the narrative intentions of the subject. I begin with probably the most empirically graspable (in the sense that it lends itself to analysis most forthrightly) of Qoheleth's narrative strategies, and yet perhaps the most playful and elusive.

Part II

THE NARRATIVE STRATEGY OF QOHELETH

Chapter 6

THE SOLOMONIC GUISE

> He played the King as though under momentary apprehension that
> someone else was about to play the ace.
> > Eugene Field (critiquing a performance of King Lear,
> > *Denver Tribune*, c. 1880)

Ecclesiastes was written in a sometimes elusive Solomonic guise.[1]
However, the employment of it is not, as shall be seen, as simple a
strategy as has been widely assumed. Its presence suggests some pertinent questions. What strategies are ascertainable in the use of the guise?
What problems has the half-hearted presence of the guise created for
reading the book of Ecclesiastes as a whole? What motivation(s) might
be suggested, if any, for the creation of such a guise by the real author
(i.e. why is it there?)? And in what ways do the real author, implied
author,[2] Qoheleth and the frame narrator relate to one another in terms
of the guise? In order to address such questions the guise itself will
need some delineation.

1. *Scope and Strategy*

Many of Qoheleth's interpreters insist that his Solomonic guise (or
royal fiction, as it is often called) is strictly 'contained' in the first two
chapters, after which the guise is, for all intents and purposes, dropped.[3]
There follows no more allusion to Solomon nor is any rhetorical
function of the guise apparent after ch. 2. Most also agree that the
superscription (1.1) commences both the book and the Solomonic guise

---

1.   Implied by 1.1; 1.12–2.26 and other verses, as will be argued below.
2.   The definition of these terms will be fleshed out below. Suffice to say that I
am relying substantially on the distinctions of Wayne Booth in *Rhetoric of Fiction*.
3.   The list includes A. Barucq, B.S. Childs, J. Crenshaw, F. Ellermeier,
K. Galling, H.L. Ginsberg, R. Gordis, T. Longman III, R.B. Salters, C.-L. Seow,
G.T. Sheppard and W. Zimmerli. I will make reference to most of their positions
specifically below.

proper (1.1 and 1.12–2.26—or 1.1; 1.12–2.17, according to some).

From its beginning the guise reveals its ambiguous quality. The phrase 'king in Jerusalem' (מלך בירושלם, 1.1), for example, is peculiar to Ecclesiastes and could refer to David (although 1.12 suggests Qoheleth). 'Jerusalem' is difficult since when referring to an Israelite king in the Old Testament, 'Israel' is usually the place of power. Bearing in mind the ambiguity, what connection to Solomon might be signified? The issue rests mainly on the phrase, בן־דוד, 'son of David'. Crenshaw has suggested that this phrase 'in Hebrew usage…can refer to grandchildren or simply to a remote member of the Davidic dynasty'.[4] While there is some evidence that בן can, as Crenshaw also suggests, denote a 'close relationship of mind and spirit'[5] or simply affection (e.g. 1 Sam. 24.16), nowhere in the Old Testament does בן־דוד mean anything other than a biological son of David and only once is it other than Solomon (2 Chron. 11.18). Admittedly, '*sons* of David' can be used of people other than Solomon,[6] but the point remains that the singular nomen 'son of David' does not seem to carry any figurative meaning. There is nothing to suggest that Eccl. 1.1 is an exception to this usage. It is therefore likely that the title makes implicit reference to King Solomon, to whom was ascribed Proverbs 1–29.

As is widely noted, the name Qoheleth (1.1, 2, 12; 7.27; 12.8, 9, 10) can be understood in reference to Solomon. The verb קהל (of which *qōhelet* is a participle), 'to assemble' or 'gather', is only used of people being assembled, and particularly of Solomon's assembling the elders of Israel for the Temple's dedication (1 Kgs 8.1-2).[7] In that narrative, the derivative כל־קהל (1 Kgs 8.14, 22, 55, 65) is used to denote '*all of the assembly* of Israel', which Solomon has gathered and speaks to. It is well known that participles were often used to denote the activity or profession of a person (e.g. in Ezra 2.55, 57, הספרת [scribe] and פכרת הצבײם [one who tends gazelles] are used as masculine names). Conceivably, 'Qoheleth' has a similar function. It is not the 'concrete' Solomon we are to picture but rather a facet of his traditional persona/

---

4.   Crenshaw, *Ecclesiastes*, p. 56.
5.   *Ecclesiastes*, p. 56.
6.   2 Chron. 13.8 = various kings ruling Israel; 23.3 = Davidic line of kings (cf. 32.33); Ezra 8.2 = David's descendants returning from Babylonia.
7.   Crenshaw rightly points out that this does not necessarily imply that 'Qoheleth' denotes an 'Assembler' of the משלים of the epilogue (12.9; *Ecclesiastes*, pp. 33-34).

profession as king and wise man—assembler of the people.[8] Already both the 'concrete' and the ambiguous forms of the persona of Solomon are present. I will turn to the unique problems this creates below.

Just to clarify that Qoheleth was an Israelite king (as opposed to another, e.g. Persian) the *place* of Qoheleth's kingship is explicitly stated in what has been called the book's 'second title' (1.12): 'I am Qoheleth. I was king over Israel in Jerusalem.'[9] Here Qoheleth makes his first introduction and, as if mercilessly to amuse himself at the reader's expense, suggests by the use of הייתי not that he *is* a king, but that he *was* a king. This has been a serious problem for those holding Solomonic authorship dear, since Solomon reigned until his death (1 Kgs 11; 2 Chron. 10). For example, Ibn Ezra felt compelled to suggest that 'Solomon wrote it [Ecclesiastes] in his old age, and appeals...to the new or rising generations, and tells them such and such things I tried in my lifetime.'[10] T.A. Perry suggests that the statement is to be understood figuratively:

> ...the retired king is introduced less for autobiographical purposes than to bring to the center of debate the question and value of withdrawal from public affairs and, by extension, worldly involvement...[the] withdrawal is not a philosophical one...he has come to the conclusion, through the frustrations of experience, that life is simply not worth the bother.[11]

8. There has been no shortage of suggestions for understanding the significance of the name 'Qoheleth'. Jacques Ellul has made the interesting suggestion that 'Qoheleth' be understood 'in terms of the book's content rather than etymologically'. For Ellul, 'Qoheleth' may function as an antonym to the rest of the book: a feminine form in a text that is anti-feminine (*Reason for Being*, pp. 17-18). It is difficult to imagine, however, that the kind of obscure literary environment necessary for such an antonym was even available to the author. On the ambiguity fostered by the use of the name, see Salyer, 'Vain Rhetoric', pp. 281-83. Most accept that 'Qoheleth' is a proper name (see O. Eissfeldt, *The Old Testament: An Introduction* [trans. P.R. Ackroyd; Oxford: Basil Blackwell, 1974], p. 492).

9. For the term 'king over Israel', cf. 2 Sam. 19.22 and 1 Kgs 4.1 (of Solomon). H.L. Ginsberg's thesis that מֶלֶךְ should here be pointed מֹלֵךְ, denoting a land owner, requires the unlikely corruption of על (among other problems) and has received little acceptance (H.L. Ginsberg, *Studies in Koheleth* [New York: Jewish Theological Seminary of America, 1950], pp. 12-15).

10. As cited and translated by Ginsburg (*Coheleth*, p. 268). The problem may be imaginary if, as Seow suggests, הייתי may be translated '*I have been* king' (*Ecclesiastes*, p. 119).

11. *Dialogues with Kohelet: The Book of Ecclesiastes* (University Park, PA:

Whether figurative or literal, the textual ambiguity here does not seem to diminish the effect of the guise, for the real effect is not so much to fasten Qoheleth's persona immovably to that of the historical Solomon as to create a unique interpretive freedom (indeed, one that might have been exploited in the way Perry suggests).

The next likely allusion to Solomon occurs at 1.16:

> I spoke to myself in my heart, saying, 'Behold, I have increased greatly
> in wisdom, more than all who were before me over Jerusalem.'

By the description, the wise king meant here is surely Solomon,[12] but the 'all who were before' him could be either (the house of?) David or a long line of Jebusite kings (more strange ambiguities).[13] What is more to the point, however, is Qoheleth's self-depiction. By it he sets himself up to conduct his tests and observations in a mode that is radical. He is not just conducting them as a wise man but as the wisest king. This suggests that the conclusions he reaches are to be considered absolute. Yet it also implies that if he fails it is that same absolute wisdom that fails with him, and such constitutes a critical indictment of Solomon's wisdom and all for which it might have stood. And royal wisdom such as Solomon's wisdom, it has been suggested, may not have been a signifier of a time of peace as much as a time of turmoil and exploitation.[14]

Pennsylvania State University Press, 1993), pp. 39-40. Perry is the only scholar I have read who has made any attempt to read the guise as present through the whole work: 'on inspection, the royal fiction is both pervasive in extent and remarkably complex. It portrays ambivalence less about the king's political status than about his psychological commitments and reservations' (p. 40; cf. p. 38). Perry sees a literal dialogue at play throughout the book and briefly explores the relationship between the kingship of one and the critical attitude towards the kingship of the other.

12. This verse likely draws on such tradition as 1 Kgs 3.12-13; 4.29-30; 10.23. See esp. 1 Chron. 29.25: 'Now King Solomon was greater than all the kings of the land with regard to riches and wisdom' (RSV).

13. Cf. Gen. 14.18; Josh. 10. Given the absence of David's God Yahweh, the latter may be preferable. But this is made unlikely since it is difficult to imagine that the author envisages any other way of being 'over' Jerusalem than the way of Solomon—i.e. *as* a tribal descendant of Israel.

14. So Frank Spina who argues that Qoheleth's use of Solomon constituted a repudiation of the manipulation of people and events for the strictly political ends that such royal wisdom affected: 'for the theology and ethic of Qoheleth is virtually opposite to that of Solomon, the king who made paganism fashionable, normative

The motif is picked up again at 2.9: 'And I became great and surpassed all who were before me in Jerusalem; also, my wisdom
remained with me.' As in 1.16, only David is a candidate for the 'all
who were before' Qoheleth. What would be a crucial error now appears
purposeful because of its recurrence. Qoheleth has hereby caused
problems, again, for interpreters relying on Solomonic authorship. For
example, *Targum Qohelet* solves the problem by suggesting a creative
referent for 'all': 'I am the one who multiplied and increased wisdom
more than all *the sages* who preceded me in Jerusalem...'[15] The ambiguity in Qoheleth's text again suggests that his association with
Solomon, while undeniably present, is purposefully nebulous, allowing
Qoheleth to preserve his individuality with congruity to his association
with Solomon. In ch. 2 the linking of Qoheleth's character to King
Solomon becomes progressively less ambiguous.

The chapter is a relatively undisputed unit (which properly begins at
1.12) that relates Qoheleth's experience as a king, and his consequent
'considering' (2.11) and 'observing' (2.12, 13, 24) that led him to hate
(שׂנא, 2.17, 18; cf. 3.8a) and to despair (יאשׁ, 2.20). It can be broken
down into three stages: (1) consideration of pleasure/success (2.1-11);
(2) consideration of wisdom and folly (2.12-17); (3) consideration of
toil (2.18-26). For each particular item listed in the first stage of
Qoheleth's experiment (particularly in 2.4-8), a parallel exists in
the biblical narratives about King Solomon.[16] And there are other

and even enviable, paving the way for all those "wise" fools who followed in his
footsteps and instituted policies that resulted in the ashes in the midst of which
Qoheleth composed his eloquent rebuttal' ('Qoheleth and the Reformation of
Wisdom', in H.B. Huffmon *et al.* [eds.], *The Quest for the Kingdom of God:
Studies in Honor of George E. Mendenhall* [Winona Lake, IN: Eisenbrauns, 1983],
pp. 267-79 [279]). Spina quotes 2 Sam. 14.1-21 (Joab and the Tekoan woman),
16.20–17.23 (the deceitful counsel of Hushai) and other passages to support the
idea that royal wisdom was oppressive and ethically inimical to Israel's 'ancient
religious traditions' (see pp. 274-77).

15. P.S. Knobel (trans.), *The Targum of Qohelet* (The Aramaic Bible, 15; Edinburgh: T. & T. Clark, 1991), p. 22 (italics Knobel's); see Ginsburg, *Coheleth*, p.
273. The LXX simply drops the problematic preposition 'over' of 1.16 and reads ἐν
Ἰερουσαλήμ instead—presumably to denote all of the wise as opposed to a ruler?

16. Especially 'silver and gold' (2.8); cf. 2 Chron. 1.15: 'Solomon made silver
and gold as common as stone, gathering them from provinces' (RSV). There is,
however, one major defect in the list. Solomon's most celebrated achievements are
missing: the widespread use of chariots and horses and the Temple. With its meandering 'historical' references, there is a sense in which this passage reads, as Salyer

similarities to King Solomon's story. Qoheleth's taking of whatever his eyes desired (2.10), for example, echoes the motif in 1 Kings that Solomon took (or was given) all that he desired.[17] Clearly, the affinity with Solomonic tradition is too established to conclude from this section that it is only a fiction of 'general kingship'.[18] It is more likely that the author was simply exercising a freedom that is witnessed in such roughly concurrent 'Solomonic' texts as the Song of Songs, which offers an imaginative, if inaccurate, description of Solomon's vineyards (Cant. 4.12–5.1; 6.2, 11; 8.11-12).

Although there may be a practical strategy at hand,[19] Qoheleth has linked himself to Solomon for the purpose of critique. By first citing lists of improbable items and amounts ('concubines and concubines!', 2.8) and imaging to his younger self an omnipotence of imposing skill, know-how and entrepreneurialism, and then concluding that

> I considered all the deeds my hands had done and the toil in which I had toiled to do it. And behold, everything was absurd and a pursuit of wind, and there is no profit under the heavens (2.11),

his point is made in binary opposition: material profit versus true profit. Material profit in the light of considering where it actually gets you (the fate of the fool and the sage—the unsuccessful as well as the successful—is the same nonetheless)[20] becomes immaterial. Indeed, if Walter Brueggemann is correct in suggesting that wisdom in the context of such power and riches usually becomes 'trivialized', then Qoheleth, in ch. 2 at least, trivializes Solomon's wisdom *in the context* of his (i.e.

suggests, 'almost like a fairy-tale' ('Vain Rhetoric', p. 219).

17. See 1 Kgs 5.7-12; 9.1, 11. For other linguistic parallels (even in word order) compare 1 Kgs 4.11 to Eccl. 2.24; 3.13; 5.18; 8.15. For more examples of echoes of the Solomon narratives, see Seow, 'Qohelet's Autobiography', p. 277. Zimmermann also suggests that such textual echoes augment Qoheleth's association with Solomon (*Inner World*, p. 83).

18. So Crenshaw, *Ecclesiastes*, p. 71.

19. The Solomonic perspective helps to make sense, for example, of Qoheleth's lament at 2.21 that one must leave his reward to someone who did not toil for it; presumably his son. Normally it would be good to leave an inheritance for a son (Prov. 13.22; 19.14 etc.), but in Qoheleth/Solomon's case it is הבל that Rehobo'am should receive it (cf. *Targ. Qoh.* 1.1-2, which sets up the whole book as an exposition of the loss of Solomon's kingdom).

20. A recurring idea in 2.13-23. Further, see my application of the actantial model in Chapter 8.3, particularly the discussion of wisdom as Helper.

Solomon's and, by implication, Qoheleth's own feigned?) power and riches.[21]

The assertion that the guise ceases after ch. 2 is usually founded on the (legitimate) claim that such obviously Solomonic allusion no longer occurs after this point. The following related question, however, has not been (but should be) asked: Why cannot the Solomonic guise be admitted as an interpretive strategy intended to encompass the whole of Qoheleth's narration? I suggest that the guise is not wholly turned from; indeed, at times it is subtly reinforced.

One of the reasons proffered to limit the extent of the guise is that the perspective of the narrating Qoheleth has changed from that of ruler to subject after ch. 2. It is also argued that particular passages (3.16-17; 4.1-3; 5.8; 8.2-9; 10.5-7, 16-17) undermine Qoheleth's 'royal' character since they are the opinions of one who 'writes as an outsider to the court',[22] 'lacks power to correct human oppression'[23] (and to correct human oppression was to be expected of an Israelite king)[24] or is 'a commoner who fears royal authority'.[25] Most of the scholars listed in n. 3 above at one point or another list the above texts in marshalling their arguments but do not actually exegete those texts in relation to the guise. Note the recent example of O. Kaiser: 'the viewpoint in iv 13ff., vii 19, viii 2ff. and x 16ff. is clearly that of a subject, not a ruler [case closed]'.[26] This 'argument' is typical of those who limit the scope of the Solomonic guise and then often go on to make an issue out of Qoheleth's rejection of the guise as either ironic cleverness or evidence of a redactional layer.

---

21. 'The Social Significance', p. 131. The recent observations of Seow and Kamano support this view. For Seow's view that Qoheleth deconstructs the traditional ANE notion of the king's immortality, see above, p. 36 n. 65. Kamano's position, drawing on Seow's work, is similar: 'Qoheleth presents himself as king, only in order to deconstruct the unchallenged, authoritative position that kingship represents' ('Character and Cosmology', p. 424).

22. Seow, *Ecclesiastes*, p. 98.

23. J. Crenshaw, *Old Testament Wisdom: An Introduction* (London: SCM Press, 1982), p. 146.

24. An imperative forcefully expressed in Ps. 72 (esp. vv. 4, 14); Prov. 29 etc.

25. So R.B. Salters, 'Qoheleth and the Canon', *ExpTim* 86 (1974–75), pp. 339-42 (341).

26. 'Qoheleth', in J. Day, R.P. Gordon and H.G.M. Williamson (eds.), *Wisdom in Ancient Israel: Essays in Honour of J.A. Emerton* (Cambridge: Cambridge University Press, 1995), pp. 83-93 (84).

One of the disputed passages[27] suggests that Qoheleth was a keen observer of oppression:

> Again I saw all the oppressions[28] that are done under the sun.
> And behold, the tears of the oppressed;
>> and there was no comforter for them.
> Yet from the hand of their oppressors [עשׁקיהם] was power—
>> and there was no comforter for them (4.1).

This is an observation, a calling to attention. Quite simply, the whole question of intervention is absent. There is no injunction to act positively and Qoheleth's concern, it seems, is only to make the reader aware. Admittedly, if Qoheleth is counting himself among the 'upper class', as Gordis suggests,[29] his position is morally bankrupt according to wisdom tradition and the connection to Solomon is thereby unlikely, for to relieve the suffering of the poor is to correct injustice (cf. Ps. 146.7; Prov. 14.31; 22.16; 29.13 etc.). But in one respect this is not the point. That particular moral concern is secondary here, for Qoheleth observes that although the oppressors had power it remained that there was none to comfort their victims. The real atrocity, for Qoheleth, is not so much the oppressions themselves but the very existence of both the oppressors and the oppressed. It would be better if all had never been brought into being (so the force of his ensuing argument in vv. 2-3). If an 'anti-royalty' sentiment were really meant here it would have been far more effective for Qoheleth to count himself among the oppressed, but he counts himself among no one. And there *is* a moral aspect as well. Like a journalist, he reports his observations without 'taking sides', yet, as with some journalists, his compassion is implied in the rhetoric of his account and it is a compassion that could have been intended to inspire his readers to do justice. For Qoheleth's dramatic 'Behold!' (הנה) and his effective repetition of the lament, 'there

27. Longman says of the passage, '[Solomon] could easily have done more than bemoan the plight of the oppressed; he could have taken steps to alleviate it' (*The Book of Ecclesiastes*, p. 6). Strangely, for Longman this is a reason to suggest that Solomon is not the intended speaker ('these verses are awkward coming from the king', *The Book of Ecclesiastes*, p. 6). The biblical portrait of Solomon, however, as Longman suggests, implies that, like Qoheleth, Solomon would have done nothing.

28. 'Oppressions' (from עשׁק) may denote different types of oppression: political (Prov. 28.16; Eccl. 5.8), economic (Prov. 14.31; 22.16; Amos 4.1) or of labour (Mal. 3.5).

29. *Koheleth*, p. 77.

was no comforter for them', may suggest that his observation, while not explicitly commanding action, was intended to stir it.[30] To push the analogy a little further, when journalists in 'closed' countries such as China and Saudi Arabia risk their lives to observe *and then relate* injustice and oppression, they take a profound moral stance.

There is no reason why the observational quality witnessed here and the narratorial voice of kingship in general, or even of Solomon, cannot validly coexist. In fact, if anything it is *imperative* to regard Qoheleth's voice as the king's, here and in any text that even remotely hints at the limits of the king's power, precisely because by doing so Qoheleth is seen to question the potency of the king and continues, if Seow and Kamano are correct (see above, n. 21), his strategy of deconstructing the socially unquestioned power and authority of the king.

Again, Qoheleth observes oppression (5.8-9):

> If you see oppression of the poor and the plundering of justice and rights[31] in the province, do not be amazed at the matter;
> for a high one is watched over by a higher,
>   and the highest is over them.
>
> Here is something which, on the whole, benefits the land:
>   a king, for the sake of agriculture.[32]

Do not be surprised at oppression and injustice (says Qoheleth), for the hierarchical system is such that there are no safeguards.[33] This verse

---

30. מנחם at 4.1 ('comforter') does not suggest passivity but rather decisive action (cf. Pss. 23.4; 71.21; 86.17; also, see Whybray, *Ecclesiastes*, p. 81). Eccl. 4.1 is strikingly similar to some of Isaiah's and Jeremiah's laments in the course of judgments on Jerusalem. Cf. Isa. 51.19, where the prophet says to Jerusalem, 'These two things have befallen you—who will grieve with you?—devastation and destruction, famine and sword—who will comfort you?' (here the NRSV follows variants ['Gk, Syr, Vg'] where the MT offers, 'how may I comfort you?' [מי אנחמך]; the basic effect of the rhetorical question, however, is the same in both cases in that the plight is highlighted); cf. Jer. 4.23-26 (where observation plays a similar, emotive role) and 15.5.

31. וצדק; see Prov. 31.9 (King Lemuel's mother to him): 'Open your mouth, judge righteously [שפט־צדק], maintain the rights of the poor and needy [ודין עני ואביון]' (RSV); cf. Prov. 8.15 and Isa. 32.1 also on this sense of צדק as the duty of kings.

32. On this translation see D. Garrett, 'Qoheleth on the Use and Abuse of Political Power', *TrinJ* 8 (1987), pp. 159-77 (164). Garrett extends 'tilled field' (נעבד לשדה) to 'agriculture' by metonymy.

33. Hence the meaning of כי גבה מעל גבה שמר וגבהים עליהם. The consecutive

comes at the end of a small but potent critique of religious activity (5.1-7) and is in sharp contrast to the seriousness with which the addressee's relationship to God is to be taken. Do fear God, says Qoheleth (5.7), but this will not shield you from seeing oppression. Indeed, if God is the highest one who watches over the whole justice system (reading the divine plural), there is nothing you can do; for God is in heaven and you are on the earth (5.2). As in 4.1, Qoheleth is standing apart from the system, perhaps as a king (as the positive assertion of 5.9 might support), to comment critically on it.[34] But again there is perhaps a positive aspect to Qoheleth's critical, even cynical outlook, which makes the royal perspective feasible (if not, at least, not unlikely). Compare Garrett's slightly overstated but still sound conclusion:

> [Qoheleth] is far from naive and will not be shocked at the existence of corruption in high places when he sees it... he does not, in self-righteous arrogance, avoid the dirty world of politics... The *Sitz im Leben* of a large portion of Ecclesiastes is the power struggle in the royal court.[35]

It could even be that Qoheleth observed injustice with such clarity and intensity, embittered by the idea that nothing (actually, wisdom and success in particular) can change the fate of the poor, of the worker, of the sinner or of the sage (indeed of anyone; cf. 9.1-3), that his words of advice had to be, Do not be shocked at what you see (cf. 7.16-17). Even a king and a wise man can do nothing to alter the absurd, which includes everything. This need not imply that Qoheleth did not accept

adjectives of comparison (גבה, 'high') reflect increasingly higher persons of rank (cf. Ezek. 21.26 [21.31]) and a system that in essence traps people at the bottom (so Whybray, *Ecclesiastes*, p. 97). Note that the *BHS* margin offers וְגֹבַהּ מֵעֲלֵיהֶם for וּגְבֹהִים עֲלֵיהֶם (v. 8 [7]), making the final official singular and possibly making clear a reference to God (the plural could accomplish this as well, although not as clearly), fitting more appropriately with 5.1-7, which calls for the fear of God. Qoheleth may here be invoking God as judge over the entire schema of activity (as he does at 3.16-17 where he declares God to be judge over the righteous and the wicked, himself standing as observer—one who sees [רֹאֶה]—a motif woven substantially throughout Qoheleth's narrative [2.3, 13, 24; 3.2, 16, 22; 4.4, 7, 15; 8.10, 16, 17; 9.11]).

34. Contra Ginsberg (*Studies in Koheleth*, p. 13). Even if Qoheleth is criticizing the monarchy, it is ludicrous to assume (as Ginsberg does) that a king cannot (according to some unspoken principle?) be self-critical of the system of which he is a part. This assumption is basic to most scholars who deny any presence of the guise after ch. 2. I will return to this faulty assumption below.

35. 'Qoheleth on the Use and Abuse of Political Power', pp. 176-77.

the possibility of change at a more personal level (cf. 4.9-12, esp. v. 12 where empowerment in community can overcome oppression), for this observation concerns the *system* of justice (higher and higher authorities, not 'lower and lower', where one-to-one change is accessible), which for Qoheleth was what had been made crooked and was never to become straight (cf. 1.15; 3.16-17; 7.13).

It has been suggested that another passage reveals Qoheleth's incongruity with royal authority (8.2-5):

> Keep[36] the command of the king, because of [*or:* in the same manner as you would] an oath of God. Do not leave in a hurry from his presence. Do not stand your ground about an unpleasant matter,[37] for he takes delight in all that he does.[38] The word of the king is supreme, and who can say to him, 'What are you doing?' One who keeps a command will know no harm, and the heart of the wise will know the time and procedure of a matter. Indeed, for every matter there is a time and a procedure; but [even still] humanity's misery lies heavy upon them.

Is there a 'sense of fear of royal authority' here?[39] Certainly, in 8.2 the king's command is not to be questioned. But why is that? The answer rests on the translation of ועל דברת (8.2b). It could be translated 'in the same manner as'.[40] Obeying the king's word in the 'same manner' as you would obey God's fits well with the word of the king being שלטון, 'supreme' (8.4; from שלט, to rule). That is, the supremacy of the king's word places it on a par with a divine oath. The phrase could also be translated 'because of'. This presumes the commitment of the implied reader to an oath. Is it an oath made *by* the implied reader (a courtier? sage?) to God, or is it an oath made by the king to God? The latter hardly makes sense (how could the king's oath bind him to a sage or

36. The אני ('I') at the beginning of this verse is probably a scribal error. It makes little sense in this context and is not represented in any ancient versions.

37. That is, 'Do not persistently champion an idea which the king opposes' (see Garrett, 'Qoheleth on the Use and Abuse of Political Power', p. 169).

38. כי כל־אשר יחפץ (lit. 'for all in which he delights') functions as the object of עשה here.

39. Thus Gordis (*Koheleth*, p. 41). For further evidence (besides 8.2-5) Gordis points out that there is a noticeable lack of any 'national motif' throughout Ecclesiastes, but the consequences of this lack, and why such a motif should be present in the first place, are not made clear. Childs also relies on this passage to support the limitation of the guise to the first two chapters (*Introduction*, p. 584).

40. Cf. Ps. 110.4 for the same meaning ('You are a priest forever, *in the same manner* as Melchizedek'), and see Seow, *Ecclesiastes*, p. 279.

courtier except in unusual circumstances?). Translations are therefore probably correct to add 'your' to 'oath' or translate 'you made an oath' (e.g. NIV, NRSV, RSV, TLB). 'Because of' finds support from Qoheleth's own seriousness on the issue of the reader's behaviour before God (5.1-7). The oath once made is tantamount to 'an offer you can't refuse'. In either case Qoheleth is offering friendly advice to the court sage to prevent potential embarrassment incurred by confronting the king.[41]

At any rate, all we can ascertain from such counsel is that Qoheleth knew well the workings of the court, knew how sages came to be embarrassed and, being a sage himself, appreciated the task of dealing with a difficult king, who in any case should take heed of the words of the wise ('Better is a poor but wise youth than an old but foolish king who no longer knows to heed advice', 4.13). After establishing this counsel (vv. 2-4), Qoheleth brings wisdom itself into the equation. The sage will know the best time and way to escape tyrannical harm (v. 5). If the king is sinister or inexperienced (cf. 4.13; 10.16-17) then this becomes particularly relevant: obey the king's command with shrewdness. Even so, Qoheleth continues, *no one* can retain the spirit, nor escape the ultimate tyranny of death or war (8.6-8). Qoheleth hereby proceeds beyond the sphere of obedience and disobedience and seeks to contrast disobedience to the king with matters on a much larger scale. (He does so in the kingly mode of wisdom after having praised wisdom at 8.1; cf. Prov. 16.15.) Wisdom may change one's fate at the person-to-person level, but it cannot deliver from those larger hazards in life that are connected to systems and institutions (war) or to God (death). Yes, Qoheleth is contemplating the misuse of authority (v. 9) and there is perhaps a latent attack on despotism, but to say that Qoheleth is himself *fearing* authority is mere speculation.

Two other texts have been cited as examples of the perspective of a subject, as opposed to that of a ruler or king: 10.5-7[42] and 10.16-17.

> There is an evil I have seen under the sun, as it were an error that proceeds from the ruler:
>> fools are set in many high places
>> and the rich dwell in a low place.
> I have seen servants on horses
>> and princes travelling as servants do, on foot (10.5-7).

41. See Murphy's comments, *Ecclesiastes*, pp. 82-83.

42. In particular by Salters, who labels it a criticism of 'corrupt leadership' ('Qoheleth and the Canon', p. 341).

Woe to you, O land, when your king is a child,
    and your princes eat in the morning!
Happy are you, O land, when your king is the son of nobles,
    and your princes eat at the proper time—
        for strength and not for drunkenness (10.16-17).

The first example is preceded by a word of caution: 'If the anger of the ruler rises against you, do not leave your place, for calmness will quell great offences.' Like the knowledge of 'court practice' demonstrated in ch. 8, this word of caution makes best sense coming from one who has had opportunity to grant forgiveness for an offence against a king (i.e. a king!),[43] and such a construct of the speaker (as king) works nicely in the verses that follow as well (vv. 5-7). These verses are just as likely a lament from one who has known the place of power (and who regards this situation as an evil of direct consequence) as they are the reflections of the monarch's subject. However, given the presence of the guise we have so far seen and the absence of a change in that narratorial voice (as king), the former must be preferred. The same can be said of 10.16-17, where Qoheleth simply grieves the fact that, in some lands, power is not in the proper hands. Again, we might expect such words from someone in a position of power.[44]

What else does Qoheleth have to say about kings? There are two pericopes (4.13-16; 9.13-16) that, while mentioning kings, merely use the idea of kingship to contrast the poor man's praiseworthy wisdom. Their significance is marginal. Ecclesiastes 4.13-16 is best summed by its first verse: 'Better is a poor and wise youth than an old and foolish king who no longer knows to heed advice' (4.13). The poor youth

---

43. Compare Prov. 16.14: 'A king's wrath is a messenger of death, and a wise man will appease it' (RSV); or, 'My son, fear the Lord and the king, and do not disobey either of them' (Prov. 24.21 [RSV]; also, cf. Prov. 16.15; 25.6). The theme of 10.4 (proper behaviour towards a ruler) is reiterated at 10.20 in which Qoheleth simply praises wise demeanour towards a king: 'Even in your thought, do not curse the king...for a bird of the air will carry your voice' (contra Longman, who sees here the king depicted as a 'suspicious bully'; *The Book of Ecclesiastes*, p. 6). This is in keeping with other proverbial conventions on the matter: 'He who loves purity of heart, and whose speech is gracious, will have the king as his friend' (Prov. 22.11, RSV).

44. Prov. 19.10 offers a similar charge: 'It is not fitting for a fool to live in luxury, much less for a slave to rule over princes' (RSV). Whybray suggests that 10.16-17 may reflect a reaction against Hellenistic attitudes towards kingship at a time when child kings were becoming more common (*Ecclesiastes*, p. 156).

became king, and it is הבל that none who come later will rejoice in him (4.16; cf. 1.11).[45] The latter (9.13-16) is a more complicated narrative in which the poor man (although not a king) delivers a city from a *great king* by wisdom. From this Qoheleth draws a clear conclusion:

> And I said, 'Better wisdom than might.'
> But the wisdom of the poor man is despised,
>   and his words are not heeded.
> The calm words of the wise are heeded
>   more than the shouting of a ruler among fools (9.16-17).

In these passages there is neither criticism nor praise of kingship, but kings are the stratagem by which Qoheleth brings the wisdom of the poor into sharp relief. Perhaps ironically he thereby fulfils a mandate to be concerned for the poor—for he has 'opened his mouth' in their favour (recalling the instruction of King Lemuel's mother at Prov. 31.9).

We have seen that there is an assumption in Qoheleth studies that runs something like this: 'Monarchs cannot be self-critical, or critical of the monarchy of which they are a part.'[46] There is one ancient work about a monarch, a Roman emperor to be precise, which should cast doubt on such an assumption: *The Meditations of Marcus Aurelius*. In this semi-autobiographical work, Aurelius offers some reflections on

---

45. G. Ogden has argued that this pericope is a thesis (the *Tôb-Spruch* of 4.13) with an observation that verifies it (4.14-16), and that the youth who went on to become 'counsellor' (Ogden's reading of למלך at 4.14a) may be a veiled historical allusion to Joseph or David. While I accept that some kind of allusion may be present, in order for Joseph to be a candidate Ogden is forced to argue for a rather ill-attested reading of מלך and to ignore the contrast of the youth *becoming* king to an old king, which contrast gives full breadth to the point made in the *Tôb-Spruch* ('Historical Allusion in Qoheleth iv 13-16?', *VT* 30 [1980], pp. 309-15 [311, 312-13]).

46. Obviously, I am generalizing the nature of the assumptions. J.A. Loader is one scholar who objects more thoroughly to what I am suggesting than most. His only objection that I have not yet dealt with, however, is that 'If the whole book were royal fiction, one would have expected it to occur in the first pericope [1.3-11], which is not the case' (making reference to Ellermeier in *Polar Structures in the Book of Qohelet* [BZAW, 152; Berlin: W. de Gruyter, 1979], p. 19). The problem with this objection is that the word 'occur' begs definition. Why is it that the distinct identification of the narrator at 1.1-2, as well as its subsequent development (1.12, 16 etc.), cannot continue to hold sway without its (unnecessary?) explicit reiteration?

the state of concurrent political structure. I have chosen four examples that, given the assumption I have just mentioned, could not have come from the mouth of a ruler or king:

> Be not Caesarified [i.e. a courtier], be not dipped in the purple dye; for it can happen (6.30).

> ...envy, tricking, and dissimulation are the character and consequences of tyranny (1.11).

> Be neither slave nor tyrant to anybody (1.31).

> Consider...how many tyrants, who managed the power of life and death with as much insolence as if themselves had been immortal...and here you will find one man closing another's eyes (4.48; cf. esp. Eccl. 4.1; 5.8).[47]

The work was written c. 175 CE and shares some affinities with Ecclesiastes.[48] The narrator is a monarch who reflects on the mismanagement of political power structures. Like Ecclesiastes, the narrative of the *Meditations* is veiled in an obscure genre. As B. Rutherford puts it, the *Meditations* has no real literary counterpart, and 'the absence of a familiar generic background' proves a hindrance to study, for 'no single genre will provide the master key'.[49] Here is an individual expression of criticism of corrupt power structures coming from one in power. As with Aurelius, if Qoheleth was critical of the monarchical (or other) power structure of his day (as I believe is likely in Eccl. 5.8; 8.2-9; and perhaps 4.1), it need not in any way preclude his consistent and mischievous reference to Solomon.[50] To strike a modern analogy, there are

47. All translations are taken from *The Meditations of Marcus Aurelius* (trans. J. Collier; rev. A. Zimmern; London: Walter Scott, 1887), except for the first (6.30), which is from B. Rutherford's *The Meditations of Marcus Aurelius: A Study* (Oxford: Clarendon Press, 1989), p. 65. Rutherford comments that the tyranny (τυραννική) in question may often have been self-referential (*Meditations*, p. 65).

48. I note here that the only other significant comparison of Ecclesiastes to Aurelius's *Meditations* I have come across is that of O. Loretz (following W. Rudolph), who suggests that both works employ a journal-keeping method ('Tagebuchaufzeichnungen'); 'Ich-Erzählung', p. 52. H. Fisch does, however, make a brief comparison of Qoheleth's notion of circularity to Aurelius's of the same ('Qohelet: A Hebrew Ironist', p. 194 nn. 15-17).

49. Rutherford, *Meditations*, p. 7.

50. It is interesting to note on this score that Jewish rabbis of the Middle Ages were not afraid to associate kings with 'anti-royal' sentiments. In 4.1-3 of *Targ. Qoh.* there is no attempt made to enhance any moral aspect, and sometimes even

a large number of lecturers in North America and Britain who are often more than self-critical of the educational systems in which they participate! The assumption is erroneous.

Thus far I conclude that it is unfair to suggest that a royal fiction is either undermined or forgotten after ch. 2. But what else suggests that Solomon is alluded to? Besides 1.12–2.17 (2.26?) there are two other traces of a particularly *Solomonic* guise. It is a tradition of Solomon as a recognizable individual who had experiences peculiar to himself upon which the first passage, 7.25-29,[51] conceivably draws.[52]

> I turned, with all my being, to understand, to search out and to seek wisdom and the sum of things; and to understand evil, folly and the folly of madness. And I found more bitter than death the woman who is traps, her heart nets, her hands chains. He with whom God is pleased will be delivered from her, but he who sins will be taken by her. See, this I have found, said Qoheleth ([adding] one to one to find the sum, which my soul has sought continually but I have not found): one man among a thousand I have found, but a woman among all of these I have not found. See, this alone I have found: that God made humanity upright, but they have sought many devices.

Solomonic tradition portrays an exorbitantly xenophilic man, at least when it came to women:

David was implicated in 'anti-royal' sentiment (e.g. *Qoh. Rab.* 10.4). One may also compare some remarks in the ANE text, *The Instruction for King Merikare* (*ANET*, pp. 414-18). In the mouth of the king who is father of Merikare we find such advice as 'impair no officials at their *posts*' (l. 48; italics in *ANET*), and 'there is no one free from a foe' (ll. 114-15). It would clearly be spurious to suggest that since in these verses (decontextualized as they are) there is no explicit, glowing reference to the king, or anything to suggest clearly that the speaker is *not* a subject of the king, that the narrating perspective is therefore *not* that of a king.

51. For a full discussion of the passage see my essay, 'Qoheleth the "Old Boy" and Qoheleth the "New Man"', esp. pp. 110-21.

52. That tradition is a cohesive one from which a very particular character emerges. On this point (concerning 1 Kgs 1–11 in particular) see B. Porten, 'The Structure and Theme of the Solomon Narrative', *HUCA* 38 (1967), pp. 93-128. Porten argues that from 1 Kgs 1–11 emerges a recognizable pattern of promise and fulfilment, which created an unambiguous Solomonic tradition (see esp. pp. 94-102, 113-14, 124). Zimmermann assumes such a cohesive Solomonic tradition in his psychoanalytic treatment of Solomon in relation to Qoheleth, in *Inner World*, Chapter 10. I am not suggesting that the case cannot, particularly in this instance, be stated more loosely, as, for example, Brueggemann's remark that the author of Ecclesiastes 'appealed to some abiding memory of the connection between Solomon and wisdom' ('The Social Significance', p. 119).

> Now King Solomon loved many foreign women…from the nations con-
> cerning which the Lord had said to Israel, 'You shall not enter into mar-
> riage with them…for surely they will turn away your heart after their
> gods'; Solomon clung to these in love. He had seven hundred wives,
> princesses, and three hundred concubines; and his wives turned away his
> heart…and his heart was not wholly true to the Lord his God… So
> Solomon did what was evil in the sight of the Lord… Then Solomon
> built a high place for Chemosh… And so he did for all his foreign
> wives…(1 Kgs 11.1-8, RSV).

It seems that in order to make some sense of this flaw in Israel's great
wisdom teacher the 'historian' turned to a seemingly simple and time-
honoured solution: ascribe the problem to women. There is already a
hint of this at 1 Kgs 11.3b, but only a hint. At Neh. 13.25-26 the excuse
theme is picked up more clearly:

> …I made them take an oath in the name of God, saying, 'You shall not
> give your daughters to their sons, or take their daughters for your sons,
> or yourselves. Did not Solomon king of Israel sin on account of such
> women? Among the many nations there was no king like him, and he
> was beloved by his God, and God made him king over all Israel; never-
> theless foreign women made even him to sin' (RSV).[53]

God's displeasure ('Solomon did what was evil *in the sight* of the
Lord') has been miraculously transformed into God's beneficence ('and
he was beloved by his God'), and Solomon's shame ('his heart was not
wholly true') to his exaltation ('there was no king like him'). This character make-over may have reached new heights in Eccl. 7.25-29. First
we need to remember that nothing stops the reader from reading with
the same Solomonic context that is well established in the first two
chapters. Furthermore, this passage is in no way an isolated text. It is
entrenched in the course of narration (particularly, as we have seen, in
that of the frame narrator's), couched in the language of experiment
that is such a distinctive mark of the guise 'proper' (see n. 61 below)

---

53. The editorial cleansing of bad character traits is a well-known feature of the
biblical historical books. One immoderate example is that of Manasseh who,
according to 2 Kgs 21.1-17, was irredeemably evil; and only by his own accord
(21.16b). His evil activities result in a judgment from 'the Lord's prophets' (21.10-
15) and the final summary of his life is *not* good (21.17). However, the Chronicler
(2 Chron. 33.1-20) apparently thought that Manasseh's image needed a good wash.
Not only is the Lord's judgment replaced with a story of Manasseh's repentance
(33.10-17), but the final summary has been redeemed (even presented as an example of repentance worthy of emulation! 33.18-19).

and comprises *an experience*, alluded to by the narrator: 'I found more bitter than death...' (v. 26).

And in what context did Qoheleth search for one woman? Perhaps he searched in the numerical context of Solomon's experience: one woman among a thousand (of Solomon's wives? [1 Kgs 11.3]) he could not find. Solomonic tradition would be an ideal backdrop for his experiment. (R. David Ibn Zimra suggested this context for the whole book.)[54] 'Woman' (note, not a particular woman or 'women') in 7.26 is likely a generic term meaning women in general (as אדם is so often used generically to refer to men; cf. 2.8; 7.29). Just as Solomon 'fell victim' to women, 'woman' is the accident waiting to happen to our unsuspecting Qoheleth/Solomon (the military imagery of traps and hunting reflects this; cf. 9.12). By offering such a hapless picture, however, Solomon may here be criticized for being too willing a 'victim', and Solomonic tradition may thereby be under scrutiny.[55]

It has been suggested that the frame narrator, in the epilogue, ignores the guise of Solomon.[56] But does the description, for example, of Qoheleth as a sage suggest an image incongruous with that of 'king'?

54. 'According to those who rule that *Ecclesiastes* was written when Solomon was elderly, [it is recorded] that his [Gentile] wives turned away his heart; thus the Bible witnesses "So built Solomon". Since he did not rebuke his wives [for worshipping idols] the Bible considers him as if he himself worshipped idols and *the ruach hakodesh [divine presence] left him and his wisdom was reduced from being above the sun* [very great]. Thus he states many times in *Ecclesiastes* that he is "under the sun"' (Responsa 2.722, cited in Michael J. Broyde, 'Defilement of the Hands, Canonization of the Bible, and the Special Status of Esther, Ecclesiastes, and the Song of Songs', *Judaism* 44.1 [Winter 1995], pp. 65-79 [70; italics in Broyde]).

55. Ellul makes the same point, but for very different reasons (*Reason for Being*, p. 20). Ellul notes that in the mouth of Qoheleth/Solomon the passage becomes a challenge to Solomon himself. But for Ellul the challenge consists of the idea that this is what Solomon would have said 'were he truly wise' (p. 202). Both Zimmermann (*Inner World*, p. 86) and Barton (*Ecclesiastes*, p. 147) suggest a general Solomonic context as well. Interestingly, Elizabeth Cady Stanton, writing at a time when Solomonic authorship was still widely accepted, remarked of 7.26-29 that 'Solomon must have had a sad experience in his relations with women. Such an opinion is a group reflection on his own mother, who was so devoted to his success in the world. But for her ambition he would never have been crowned King of Israel' (*The Woman's Bible* [2 vols.; Edinburgh: Polygon Books, 1985 (1898)], II, pp. 99-100).

56. Notably Crenshaw (*Ecclesiastes*, p. 29).

While the *association* of sage with king is not explicit in the epilogue, it is possible that the epilogue allows the already established image of Qoheleth as king in his narrative to merge with that of a celebrated image of sage.[57] Such Solomonic tradition as the following may be compared:

> [Solomon] was wiser than all others...and he uttered three thousand proverbs [מָשָׁל]...And they came from all peoples to hear the wisdom of Solomon, and from all the kings of the earth, who had heard of his wisdom (1 Kgs 4.31-34 [5.11-14]).

As I argued in Chapter 4.2, the epilogue implies that there are מֹשׁלִים not included that the epilogist could have selected (12.9) and may therefore draw on such tradition as this concerning Solomon's great literary activity.[58] Further, the use of 'shepherd' (מרעה, 12.11) may have found its prototype in such tradition as 1 Sam. 25.7, in which shepherds are likened to Israelite kings, possibly presuming Qoheleth's association with royalty.[59] Finally, if 'shepherd' refers to God (see p. 106 n. 29), the divine origin both of Ecclesiastes and of Proverbs may here be asserted, and hence the putative author of *both* (Solomon) indirectly referred to.

One could easily imagine that the wise Qoheleth of the epilogue is a king. The association brings the proverb to mind, 'It is the glory of God to conceal things, but the glory of kings is to search things out' (Prov. 25.2, RSV). And the idea that King Solomon is alluded to in v. 9[60] is

57. In rabbinic literature, מלך was sometimes substituted for חכם at 12.9. Again, no quandary was found in associating the two (e.g. *Targ. Qoh.* 12.8-10). One MS (110 of the Bibliothèque nationale, Paris) reads at 12.9, 'King Qoheleth was wiser than all the people...' (cited in Knobel, 'The Targum of Qohelet', p. 54).

58. See also, Fox, 'Frame-narrative', p. 100. It was this tradition of Solomon having encyclopaedic knowledge and being a prolific writer that the frame narrator may have seized upon. Hezekiah (reigned c. 716–687 BCE) may have been responsible for fostering hugely popular legends of Solomon's great literary reputation (so R.B.Y. Scott, 'Solomon and the Beginnings of Wisdom', in M. Noth and D.W. Thomas [eds.], *Wisdom in Israel and in the Ancient Near East* [VTSup, 3; Leiden: E.J. Brill, 1955], pp. 262-79 [271, 272-79]), and perhaps this vibrant tradition is alluded to in the epilogue.

59. Crenshaw has suggested a possible association with Egyptian literature that likens shepherds to pharaohs (*Ecclesiastes*, pp. 32-33). Further, see Chapter 4.2, where I argue that in 12.9 it is Qoheleth's connection to Solomon that fills in an alluring gap—i.e. Who is the teacher? and How did he teach?

60. Thus also, Michael Eaton: 'The epilogue portraying Qoheleth has all the

supported by the frame narrative's incongruity with Qoheleth's narrative. In other words, by connecting Qoheleth to Solomon without any of the apparently subversive strategies that Qoheleth evidences in *his* use of the guise, the frame narrator evidences an orthodox, Solomonic summary of Qoheleth's life that serves to marginalize Qoheleth/Solomon's bitter-sweet cynicism.

The Solomonic guise is not simply a matter of a text here and there that 'supports' it or remains silent about it. Besides what I have already touched on, the guise, which all admit is present in the first two chapters, is entrenched via the repetition of certain motifs that have their origin in the Solomonic guise 'proper' of 1.1 and 1.12–2.26.[61] The fact that those motifs have their origin *there* suggests that the Solomonic guise is deeply embedded in Ecclesiastes. Also, it follows that the guise proper is likely *not*, as has been suggested,[62] a product of redaction. Attributions that are the product of redaction might more resemble that found at Prov. 10.1, where (unlike Ecclesiastes) what follows is not narrated strictly in the first person (as if the person introduced at the title continued to speak in that same person), but is a series of relatively isolated proverbs.[63]

appearances of referring to an actual historical character: a wise man, a collector of proverbs, a teacher and writer. Who else but Solomon?' (*Ecclesiastes*, p. 23).

61. These 'throwbacks' to the guise proper are numerous. There are such recurring phrases as 'absurd and a pursuit of wind' and 'What is crooked cannot be made straight' (cf. 1.15 at the commencement of the king's reflection to 7.13), which both can be found in the Solomonic guise 'proper'. Also, the experimental quality of the guise proper is felt throughout Ecclesiastes. Take, for example, sayings that suggest that Qoheleth is testing: 'I observed' (2.12, 24; 3.16, 22; 4.1, 4, 7, 15; 8.17; 9.11); 'I gave my heart over'—i.e. 'I applied myself' (1.13, 17; 8.16); 'I tested' (2.1; 7.23); or in which Qoheleth is concluding: 'I said in my heart' or 'I said to myself concerning' (1.16; 2.1, 2, 15; 3.17, 18; 7.23; 8.14); or the הבל judgments (1.2, 14; 2.1, 11, 15, 17, 19, 21, 23, 26; 3.19; 4.4 etc.). All are a natural validation of Qoheleth's narrative springing from the guise proper of chs. 1–2. As Whybray says of the relation of ch. 2 to the rest of Ecclesiastes, 'The reflections attributed to Qoheleth-Solomon are not peculiar to him but are echoed throughout the book; and since the whole book is expressed in the first person singular, it is impossible to be certain at what point the "I" of Solomon gives place to the "I" of Qoheleth himself' (*Ecclesiastes*, p. 46).

62. E.g. Crenshaw, *Ecclesiastes*, pp. 28-29, 56-57.

63. Compare D. Dimant's comments on the Wisdom of Solomon: '[The association with Solomon is] organic to the original framework [...Wis.] does not state

In some sense I agree with Fox that 'the king fiction is a rhetorical device, not an attempt to assert Solomonic authorship for the whole book'.[64] At times the narrator is an intensely personal 'I' that is unconventionally non-historical. But the guise continually reasserts itself. That is why Fox's statement cannot be agreed to in principal. The Solomonic guise is more complex than that. It provides for the reader an ever-present, if sometimes elusive, sometimes insinuated context in which to grasp the experiments of Qoheleth.

2. *The Guise, the Canon and the Rabbis*

It is widely held that Ecclesiastes was received into the Jewish canon due mainly to its association with Solomon.[65] We know that rabbinic debate about the book in general was abundant. Ecclesiastes and Esther were perhaps the most frequently discussed books. The real issues of those discussions are, however, difficult to determine.

Not only is the word 'canon' itself problematic,[66] but what it meant in practice. After an exhaustive analysis of the subject, Sid Leiman suggests that only books used in teaching and disputes by the rabbis

explicitly the pseudonymic author, nor the *precise* circumstances of his life. Instead, it employs a complete system of biblical allusions in order to indicate the pseudonymic author' ('Pseudonymity in the Wisdom of Solomon', in N.F. Marcos [ed.], *La Septuaginta (V Congreso de la IOSCS)* [Madrid: CSIC, 1985], pp. 243-55 [245]; italics mine). The same can, I believe, be said of Ecclesiastes.

64. Fox, 'Frame-narrative', p. 86.

65. This view seems to have been 'traditionally' accepted in biblical scholarship; recently advocated by Svend Holm-Nielsen ('The Book of Ecclesiastes and the Interpretation of It in Jewish and Christian Theology', *ASTI* 10 [1976], pp. 38-96 [55]), Salters ('Qoheleth and the Canon', pp. 340-42) and Whybray (*Ecclesiastes*, p. 3), although Whybray is hesitant. Others suggest that the association with Solomon was only likely to have formed part of the reason for Qoheleth's acceptance in the canon (e.g. Longman, *The Book of Ecclesiastes*, p. 28; Seow, *Ecclesiastes*, p. 4).

66. As I.H. Eybers reminds us, the terms 'canonical' and 'canonization' are relatively new (fourth century CE) and do not appear in the discussions of the rabbis before this time ('The "Canonization" of Song of Solomon, Ecclesiastes and Esther', in W.C. van Wyk [ed.], *Aspects of the Exegetical Process* [OTWSA, 20; Pretoria West: NHW Press, 1977], pp. 33-52 [33]). I use the word for convenience because of its acquired usage and the specific definition I take on board should become clear.

were considered canonical; that is, part of a group of books accepted and recognized as Scripture that a given community uses to establish ethical and religious practice and ideology. In other words, a *canonical* book became such because it was used pragmatically and frequently in rabbinic circles. This is why talmudic discussions reveal indifference towards the question of a book's 'use', for its canonical status was already assumed in any such discussion.[67] Instead, according to Leiman, the discussions give greater weight to a book's ability/inability to 'defile the hands',[68] or to its inspirational status in general.[69] Take, for example, *t. Yad.* 3.5:

67. Broyde has, however, recently cast doubt on some of Leiman's conclusions, namely that *all* of the rabbinic literature worked with this notion of canon: 'the fact that Rabbi Shimon ben Menassiah expounds a law from the book of Ecclesiastes does not automatically prove it to be canonical in his opinion, as Sanhedrin 100b and Bava Kama 9128 expounds on a verse in Ben-Sira, a clearly noncanonical work' ('Defilement of the Hands', pp. 68-69). More often than Leiman would allow, Broyde suggests, disputes were indeed about the canon.

68. That a book is capable of defiling the hands shows that it is holy or inspired. This notion was 'a protective measure which the rabbis enacted in order to keep sacred literature from being mishandled' (S.Z. Leiman, *The Canonization of Hebrew Scripture: The Talmudic and Midrashic Evidence* [Hamden, CT: Archon Books, 1976], p. 116; see also pp. 104-20; for the origins of the phrase in practice—as a measure to keep scrolls from being stored with sacred food, thus leading to mice and rats(!)—see Broyde, 'Defilement of the Hands', p. 66]). Some books were considered both uninspired *and* canonical (e.g. *Meg. Ta'an.*; Leiman, *Canonization*, p. 112), including, at least for some rabbis, Ecclesiastes. Leiman argues that the definition of canonical as that which is used pragmatically (instead of only inspired) corrects a misunderstanding in biblical scholarship with a long history. In opposition to Leiman, D. Kraemer argues that Leiman falsely assumes that 'the challenge to... [the] inspiration [of the books in question] could have been divorced from the question of their inclusion in the canon' ('The Formation of Rabbinic Canon: Authority and Boundaries', *JBL* 110.4 [1991], pp. 613-30 [628-29]). But Leiman does not attempt to 'divorce' these questions as much as to show the lack of evidence for their causal relationship. Besides, it may be that the question of the defilement of hands was not one of inspiration per se. As James Barr comments, 'the question is a truly ritual one: the discussion is not, whether this or that book is canonical, but whether it, canonical or not, had certain ritual effects' (*Holy Scripture: Canon, Authority, Criticism* [Philadelphia: Westminster Press, 1983], p. 51; see also, pp. 49ff.).

69. E.g. *t. Yad.* 2.14 (see below).

All the holy writings defile the hands [כל־כתבי הקדש מטמאין את־הידים].
The Song of Songs defiles the hands, but there is a dispute about Ecclesiastes. R. Jose says: Ecclesiastes does not defile the hands, but there is a
dispute about the Song of Songs.[70]

Meg. 7a is similar: 'As learned "Rabbi Shimon ben Mennasiah states:
Ecclesiastes does not defile the hands since it is the wisdom of
Solomon."'[71] The degree to which a book defiled the hands was a measure of its holiness. Ecclesiastes, Esther and Song of Songs were all
disputed as to the extent to which they defiled the hands. Broyde suggests, in convincing fashion, that these books could not defile the hands
because, unlike all other books of the Hebrew Bible, none of them
contains the tetragrammaton.[72]

Discussions at the so-called Council of Jamnia (c. 90 CE) suggest that
Ecclesiastes was in danger of being deemed גנז—'that which is stored
away'—since it fostered heretical ideas. But the reported debate likely
served to confirm its canonical status early on, since only problematic
canonical books were at risk of being 'stored away'.[73] In this respect
the Solomonic connection faded to the background. In none of the discussions at Jamnia was Solomonic authorship even mentioned, and in
the end no books discussed at Jamnia were withdrawn from canonical
use anyway.[74] Ecclesiastes was spared גנז, but not because of any association with Solomon.[75]

70. Translation from *The Babylonian Talmud* (trans. I. Fishman; London: Soncino Press, 1948). See also, *t. Yad.* 2.14; *'Ed.* 5.3; *Meg.* 7a; *Lev. R.* 28.1.

71. Cited in Broyde, 'Defilement of the Hands', p. 67.

72. Broyde, 'Defilement of the Hands', esp. pp. 66, 73.

73. So Leiman, *Canonization*, pp. 79-80, 86, 104-109.

74. Indeed, Jamnia may have been only an 'academic discussion' that made no
'authoritative' decisions (so Beckwith, *The Old Testament Canon*, pp. 276-77).

75. Contra R.B. Salters, G.A. Barton and R. Gordis. It is more likely that Ecclesiastes survived a selection process by which it was finally deemed orthodox (late
third century CE?) because it 'begins and ends with Torah' (*b. Šab.* 30b. As *Qoh.
Rab.* at 1.3 reads, 'Is it possible that the words might be applied to man's labour in
the Torah?' (taken from 'Midrash Rabbah Koheleth', in *The Midrash*, VII [trans. A.
Cohen; London: Soncino Press, 1939]; all citations of *Qoh. Rab.* are taken from this
edition). That is, one should not toil for one's own material need but for and in the
Torah (and, according to *Qoh. Rab.*, Ecclesiastes ends with the Torah at 12.13).
This might have been appealing at a time when wisdom and religion were at a low
ebb (so Salters, who suggests this tentatively as an alternative; 'Qoheleth and the
Canon', p. 341). According to some talmudim, it was only because the men of
Hezekiah had copied and examined Ecclesiastes, finding it acceptable, that it was

Furthermore, as early as the second century there were rabbis who were unwilling to divulge (or who were truly ignorant about) the origin of uneasiness about the inspiration of Ecclesiastes (and, at the time, the Song of Solomon). They believed that 'their uneasiness went back to their predecessors'.[76] This forms, again, an ironical reflection of Ecclesiastes' long-standing canonical status. Its canonicity may never have been disputed. As Roger Beckwith puts it,

> Is it not possible that the disputes [i.e. rabbinic disputes in general] were about books long acknowledged as canonical... and all of them privately studied as Scripture, before and during the period of the disputes, no less than afterwards?[77]

This may explain why the Shammaites, who argued that Ecclesiastes did not 'defile the hands', nevertheless expounded verses from the book publicly, treating it, according to Leiman, canonically. In their infamous dispute on this topic with the school of Hillel, Solomonic authorship was not brought into play.[78] Indeed, reference to Solomon may not

---

saved from גנז (along with the Song of Songs; cf. David Halperin, 'The Book of Remedies, the Canonization of the Solomonic Writings, and the Riddle of Pseudo-Eusebius', *JQR* 72 [1982], pp. 269-92 [277-78, 281]; cf. Prov. 25.1). L. Ginzberg (*The Legends of the Jews* [7 vols.; Philadelphia: The Jewish Publication Society of America, 1968], VI, p. 368) notes another 'legend' concerning the men of Hezekiah in which Ecclesiastes was withdrawn by them from public use because of its 'unholy nature'. In the end, it is difficult if not impossible to determine just how Ecclesiastes escaped גנז.

76. Halperin, 'The Book of Remedies', p. 277. Halperin also argues that discrepancies between *Yad.* 3.5 and *Meg.* 7a concerning the Ushan authorities cited, 'add to the impression of uncertainty in traditions'.

77. Beckwith, *The Old Testament Canon*, p. 276. Evidence outside the rabbinic disputes may further substantiate this claim. I.H. Eybers lists several possible allusions to Ecclesiastes from the Thanksgiving Hymns at Qumran (fragments dated 150 BCE). In my opinion, only the following allusion seems plausible: compare 1QS 6.7 to Eccl. 11.9, both of which employ the rare biblical idiom, 'the way of thy heart' (I.H. Eybers, 'Some Light on the Canon of the Qumran Sect', in S.Z. Leiman [ed.], *The Canon and Masorah of the Hebrew Bible: An Introductory Reader* [New York: Ktav, 1974], pp. 23-36 [26]). The New Testament betrays no sure knowledge of Ecclesiastes, which tips the scale of judgment in neither direction. Additionally, although any substantial use of Ecclesiastes was slow-coming among the early Christian church (see below), there is no evidence among the fathers of dispute over its use.

78. *T. Yad.* 3.5; *'Ed.* 5.3.

have been effectual anyway. Witness the early third-century CE
reported opinion of R. Simeon ben Menasya:

> The Song of songs defiles the hands, because it was spoken through
> Divine inspiration; Ecclesiastes does not defile the hands, because it is
> [only] Solomon's wisdom. They replied: Did he write this alone? Scrip-
> ture says, 'He spoke three thousand parables, and his songs were a thou-
> sand and five' (1 Kgs 5.12), and 'Do not add to [God's] words, lest He
> rebuke you and you be found a liar' (Prov. 30.6).[79]

And again from Jerome:

> ...the Hebrews say that, among other writings of Solomon which are
> obsolete and forgotten, this book [Eccl.] ought to be obliterated
> [*oblitterandus*], because it asserts that all the creatures of God are in
> vain.[80]

In both examples any correlation to Solomon was irrelevant (or even
damaging) to Ecclesiastes' canonical status. This is compounded by the
notion, evident in the first quote, that the phrase 'the wisdom of
Solomon' 'indicates that [the words in question] are not written with
complete divine inspiration'.[81]

Usually debates focused instead on some of the acknowledged contradictions of the book (even the 'defiling of hands' debate may have
had this problem at its centre). *Qoh. Rab.* 11.9 records what was perhaps the most serious of debates on Ecclesiastes:

> The Sages sought to suppress the Book of Koheleth because they dis-
> covered therein words which tend toward heresy. They declared, 'This is
> the wisdom of Solomon that he said, "Rejoice, O young man, in thy
> youth!"' (Eccl. 11.9). Now Moses said, *that ye go not about after your
> own heart* (Num. 15.39)... Is restraint to be abolished? Is there no
> judgement and no Judge? But since he continued, 'But know thou, that
> for all these things God will bring thee into judgement', they exclaimed,
> 'Well has Solomon spoken'.

The first tractate of the Mishnah states the case in general terms.
R. Tanhum of Nave is quoted as saying, 'O Solomon, where is your
wisdom, where is your intelligence? Not only do your words contradict
the words of your father, David, they even contradict themselves.'[82] It

---

79. *T. Yad.* 2.14 (with variations); *b. Meg.* 7a (trans. by Halperin, 'The Book of
Remedies', p. 277).
80. As cited by Ginsburg (*Coheleth*, p. 15).
81. So Broyde, 'Defilement of the Hands', p. 78 n. 53.
82. *Šab.* 3, cited in Longman, *The Book of Ecclesiastes*, p. 27.

seems natural to assume that in order to solve such dilemmas as Qoheleth's perceived heresy, rabbis would have turned to the argument that Solomon was incapable of heterodoxy, and that since he wrote Ecclesiastes there must be some other explanation (i.e. other than that 'Qoheleth' was in fact a heretic) to account for its heterodoxy.[83] However, there is no evidence to suggest that this critical line was ever taken up. In the example above, it is only what can at best be called a contrived reading of Eccl. 11.9b that 'redeemed' the text, thus giving Qoheleth's words an orthodox edge.[84]

Most debates of the ancient readers are concerned mainly with the content of Ecclesiastes. In fact, the references to the use of the book seem to act as a ruse to discuss what is in it and how that affects one's reading of it.[85] Ancient readers did not seem to be bothered with the much asked modern question, Why is Ecclesiastes in the canon? And we cannot come up with a satisfactory answer anyway. We have seen that there is no evidence to suggest that any association with Solomon was responsible for it.[86] Other suggestions, however, have been offered. For example, John Jarick suggests that, in the end, this 'little scroll...was simply too attractive to be surrendered'.[87] S. Schloesser suggests that the profoundly moral stance of Qoheleth's scepticism (a more honest and authentic expression of experience than the older schools of wisdom) is what granted it a place in the canon.[88] While

83. So, for example, Gordis, *Koheleth*, p. 42.

84. This is not to suggest that the question of orthodoxy did not come into play (it undoubtedly did, particularly in relation to the increasing emphasis on torah, as K.J. Dell maintains in 'Ecclesiastes as Wisdom: Consulting Early Interpreters', *VT* 44 [1994], pp. 301-29), but simply that the connection to Solomon in no way favoured an orthodox reading.

85. Compare Eybers's statement: 'the discussion surrounding these books [Cant., Eccl., Est.] were more of an academic exercise, based on certain objections which could be raised against these books' ('Canonization', p. 34).

86. J. Barton makes the same point (*Oracles of God: Perceptions of Ancient Prophecy in Israel after the Exile* [London: Darton, Longman & Todd, 1986], p. 62); and similarly, see Dell, 'Ecclesiastes as Wisdom', pp. 320-22, 327-28.

87. Jarick further suggests that Solomonic authorship was relevant to the extent that it would have placed the writing of Ecclesiastes before the time when, traditionally, 'the Holy Spirit ceased out of Israel' (*Gregory Thaumaturgos' Paraphrase of Ecclesiastes* [SBLSCS, 29; Atlanta: Scholars Press, 1990], pp. 288, 317-18).

88. '"A King is Held Captive in her Tresses": The Liberating Deconstruction of the Search for Wisdom from Proverbs through Ecclesiastes', in J. Morgan (ed.), *Church Divinity* (Bristol: Cloverdale Corporation, 1989–90), pp. 205-28 (228).

these suggestions are more feasible to me than the Solomonic connection, in this case, of the making of many speculations there is no end, regardless how well informed. Ancient readers did not seem to question the fact that for one reason or another Ecclesiastes was there. The connection with Solomon was assumed but did not raise any significant interpretive issues (compare sec. 5 below). As Perry suggests, the more interesting question than 'How did Ecclesiastes get into the canon?', is 'What is the nature of a canon that includes such books?'[89] To the reader who would demand a seamless cohesion of ideology, its nature is strange and potentially graceful.

3. *The Guise and Pseudonymity*

Putting a label on the device that I have until now for the sake of convenience called the Solomonic guise is made difficult by the fact that there is little concurrent with Ecclesiastes that is like it: the ruminations of a 'Qoheleth' (of any kind) who playfully, elusively and problematically sets his words in the mouth of a king.[90] A host of appellations have been offered: 'organ of himself', 'abstraction of the historical', 'Pseudo-Solomon', 'effective foil', '*nom de plume*', 'putative author' and so forth.

Is the guise a pseudonym? Strictly speaking, no. The name of Solomon appears nowhere in the book. However, this may be attributed to the fact that, in a culture whose notion of authorship was much more fluid than our own,[91] the association with Solomon may not have

Salyer suggests similarly that Qoheleth's discourse entered the canon due to its superior 'intellectual prowess' ('Vain Rhetoric', p. 423).

89. *Dialogues with Kohelet*, p. 48.

90. Compare Hengel: 'The semi-pseudonymity of the work is unique' (*Judaism and Hellenism*, I, p. 129). Hengel goes on to compare Ecclesiastes to other roughly concurrent pseudonymous works—e.g. Wisdom of Solomon (he dates this about 200 years later than Ecclesiastes) and the final recension of Proverbs.

91. For example, schoolchildren in the Hellenistic empire of the third to second century BCE were expected to write a χρεία (fable) as part of their secondary school literary studies, and attribute it either to Aesop or 'some sage of antiquity'. It is possible that Ecclesiastes was written in a culture whose populace was at least familiar with a loosely structured form of pseudonymity from an early age (see H.I. Marrou, *A History of Education in Antiquity* [trans. G. Lamb; London: Sheed and Ward, 1956], p. 174). Furthermore, Barton argues that within the biblical tradition itself existed a very fluid concept of authorship, i.e. as to the 'historicity' of authors (*Oracles of God*, p. 61). Modern readers have been uncomfortable with the notion

required the name. Such fluidity may have meant, in the end, that Qoheleth's readers found only a blurred distinction between Solomon and Qoheleth/Solomon. The fictitious beginning by the frame narrator coupled with Qoheleth's imaginative use of Solomon and first-person narration suggests a seemingly conscious effort to achieve pseudonymity.[92] That is, it seems that there is an effort, to whatever degree, to achieve a suspension of disbelief that involves believing that 'Solomon' is the primary narrator and therefore the 'author' of the framed material. To speak in such a guise, then, is partly analogous to pseudonymity.[93]

The use of this 'semi-pseudonym', it is widely recognized, did not likely create moral problems for readers.[94] The 'voice' of Solomon in Ecclesiastes was simply an amoral strategy of communication, one that

of pseudonymity or anonymity. As Foucault comments, 'We cannot tolerate literary anonymity. We do not welcome its enigmatic quality' ('What Is an Author?', *PrtRev* 42 [1975], pp. 603-14 [609]). Indeed, according to Foucault, we apply principles that reach back to the time of Jerome to determine whether a text was written by the author it is purported to be written by and thereby rubber-stamp its 'authenticity' ('What Is an Author?', pp. 609-10).

92. J. Geyer, contrasting Ecclesiastes to the Wisdom of Solomon, argues that the nature of the guise had the effect of *anonymity*; i.e. the book deceived no one and was hence rendered anonymous (*The Wisdom of Solomon* [London: SCM Press, 1963], p. 18; E. Bickerman also suggests that Ecclesiastes was essentially anonymous ['Koheleth (Ecclesiastes) *or* The Philosophy of an Acquisitive Society', in *idem*, *Four Strange Books of the Bible* (New York: Schocken Books, 1967), pp. 139-67 (142)]). This is only partly true. While the theory of anonymity does justice to Qoheleth's individuality it leaves no room for the rather complex relationship Qoheleth undeniably has, as a character, to Solomonic tradition.

93. Compare the comments of David Meade, who suggests that the authoritative stamp of revelation embodied in the tradition of God revealing himself to Solomon is 'passed on', as it were, to Ecclesiastes through the use of the Solomonic guise. Says Meade, 'Authorship [in the Israelite wisdom tradition] is more concerned with authoritative tradition than literary origins [and Ecclesiastes represents] an entirely new work issued under the authority of another... [If] this is not the essence of pseudonymity, what is?' (*Pseudonymity and Canon* [WUNT, 39; Tübingen: J.C.B. Mohr, 1986], p. 59).

94. C.H.H. Wright stated the case eloquently: 'There are... passages to be found in the Book of Koheleth itself in which the author lifts up his visor in such a manner as to show the intelligent reader that the character and name of Solomon were simply assumed, not for any purpose of deception, nor as "a pious fraud", but by a perfectly allowable literary device' (cited in Longman, *The Book of Ecclesiastes*, p. 4).

ancient readers would likely have recognized as such.[95] Readers were
neither fooled into thinking this was Solomon nor were they concerned
about the issue anyway.[96] This said, to what *extent* did readers come
from Ecclesiastes with the impression that this, as Michael Eaton comments, is 'what Solomon would have said had he addressed himself to
the subject of pessimism'?[97] To answer that in historical terms is
impossible, but we can conjecture three good reasons for the author of
Ecclesiastes to have wanted people to read with Eaton's convictions.

First, in an odd way, Solomon's 'presence' in the book protects
Qoheleth from himself. As Brevard Childs puts it, since the book functions as an 'official corrective' to/against more traditional wisdom
texts, the Solomonic guise was necessary to guard it from 'interpretations which would derive Koheleth's views from his changing moods
or pessimistic disposition rather than to see them as playing a critical
role within Israel's corpus of wisdom literature'.[98] If this is at all true
then the guise is, as the frame narrative, analogous to the modern picture frame. Just as some producers of frames used more socially
acceptable frames in order, in Childs's terms, to guard the picture from
'interpretations which would derive [the painter's] views from his
changing moods or pessimistic disposition', so the guise enables

95. However, that pseudonymity was not so readily 'amorally' accepted in
antiquity, see S. Robinson, 'Lying for God: The Uses of Apocrypha', in G. Gillum
and C. Criggs (eds.), *Apocryphal Writings and the Latter-Day Saints* (Religious
Studies Monograph Series, 13; Provo, UT: Religious Studies Center, Brigham
Young University, 1986), pp. 133-54 (138-40).

96. This is widely accepted and impossible to refute, but I cannot account for
the fact that, even before the time of Jerome (cf. Foucault's comments above, n.
91), no one questioned the idea of Solomon as author until Luther. Further, see sec.
5b below.

97. Eaton, *Ecclesiastes*, p. 24.

98. Childs, *Introduction*, pp. 584, 588. To evaluate Childs's claim that Ecclesiastes functioned as a 'corrective' against a particular school of wisdom it would be
necessary to discern Qoheleth's alleged counterparts with at least some degree of
definitude. While this is beyond the scope of this book, Childs's point (that the
guise would have functioned as a distraction from Qoheleth's overall tone in order
for his readers to better focus on the content of his thought) can be readily accepted.
This would also grant Qoheleth's unorthodox wisdom (as troubled the rabbis) a
graver tone in Solomon's mouth. Crenshaw agrees (ironically, in light of his frac-
tured view of the Solomonic guise) that the connection to Solomon was made in
order to keep the book's authority from being questioned (*Ecclesiastes*, p. 28; similarly, see Meade, *Pseudonymity and Canon*, pp. 49, 56).

Qoheleth's words a 'smoother' entry into a dialogue with other works (in a larger, better-attended 'gallery') that would not have been otherwise possible.

Second, it may be that the power of Solomon's 'voice' was not limited only to the immediate Jewish culture, but that it earned Ecclesiastes a hearing in a wider Hellenistic culture. The garb of Israel's skilful orator of wisdom, Eissfeldt suggested, was conceivably respected among Greeks who prized rhetoric.[99] Indeed, any of the pseudo-Solomonic works at the time may have intended to demonstrate, says Hengel, 'the great age and...superiority of the national wisdom over against that of Greece'.[100] This was the natural outworking of hero worship and it may have struck critical chords in the traditions that surrounded it. Similarly, D. Dimant has suggested that the Wisdom of Solomon was written in a vein much like that of concurrent Hellenistic literature (e.g. Pythagorean treatises on kingship, Jewish apocrypha such as the *Letter of Aristeas* [second or first century BCE] etc.). For Dimant, the author of the Wisdom of Solomon utilized Solomon's persona partly because Solomon was a character who traditionally had enough of something like stoic virtue and could meet the stoic and Platonic criterion of 'proof from example' ($\pi\alpha\rho\acute{\alpha}\delta\epsilon\iota\gamma\mu\alpha$); hence its 'teaching' would receive a hearing.[101] If Ecclesiastes is at all connected with a Hellenistic culture (as Hengel and others suggest),[102] then a similar background is possible. In this regard, as Christopher Rowland has argued concerning the biblical prophets, the pseudonym may have been used to communicate, in effect, with more authority.[103]

---

99. *Introduction*, pp. 429-30.

100. So Hengel, *Judaism and Hellenism*, I, p. 129. Hengel supports his argument with other plausible suggestions: 'The riches and the wisdom of Solomon form a pendant to the splendour of the Ptolemaic kings [who, like Solomon, were] the richest and most learned of their time' (p. 130).

101. Dimant, 'Pseudonymity', pp. 249-50, 254-55.

102. For a recent discussion of Qoheleth's historical milieu see C.R. Harrison, 'Qoheleth among the Sociologists', *BibInt* 5.2 (1997), pp. 160-80 (esp. pp. 171, 178-80). Although Harrison is reticent to identify, as Hengel does, 'Qoheleth's individualism with Greek thought' (pp. 170-71), he allows that the third-century context of Judaea (for which he argues) had to 'withstand the pressures of the Hellenistic Age' (p. 171).

103. This function of pseudonymity, C. Rowland argues, was commonplace in the prophetic tradition, and there is no reason to suggest that it was foreign to the wisdom tradition either (although Qoheleth does not make any prophetic claims—

Third, with the guise Qoheleth may have been enabled to turn conventional notions of *general* kingship (as particularly expressed in Prov. 16–22.16) on their heads, particularly the idea, as W. Lee Humphreys describes it, that 'Yahweh's powers and judgement and his ultimate incomprehensibility' place the king 'in a sphere above other human beings'.[104] If it can be accepted that the king was placed on a level above human understanding (often equating the king with Yahweh) then it must be said that Qoheleth, because he is a king and because he is unable to discover the nature of things (see Chapter 8.3), makes the king thoroughly human, and has, in a sense, derobed him of his heavenly powers of discernment.

I have still not considered a question the rabbis *did* ask about the guise: Why Solomon? There is one obvious answer: the association with Solomon was determined by the nature of the book. Wisdom literature is attracted to the name of Solomon as the Psalms are to David, or nomic texts to Moses. David was a 'psalmist', Solomon a 'wise man'.[105] The choice was natural. But this is likely only a fraction of the answer.

Qoheleth does not lose his identity in Solomon's. He enjoys the

i.e. as one 'speaking for' God; the closest Ecclesiastes comes to this is the frame narrator's comments at 12.10-11). To speak (even partly) in the voice of a great figure of the past would have lent a greater credibility to Qoheleth's conclusions (see *The Open Heaven* [London: SPCK, 1982], pp. 61-70). J. Barton argues similarly concerning the prophetic tradition (*Oracles of God*, p. 210). Interestingly, *Targ. Qoh.* begins, 'The words of prophecy…' (again at 3.11; 4.15; 9.7; 10.7; cf. *Qoh. Rab.* 1.1-2).

104. 'The Motif of the Wise Courier in the Book of Proverbs', in Gammie *et al.* (eds.), *Israelite Wisdom*, pp. 177-90 (182). Humphreys is not suggesting that the king and Yahweh are 'interchangeable' nomens, but that the king was more divine than human, and that that interchange could *sometimes* be made without significantly altering the meaning of the text.

105. Porten concludes thus from a study of Psalm ascriptions ('The Structure and Theme', p. 117). While it is doubtful that לדוד (the 'ascription' at the beginning of each of the Davidic psalms) was an attempt to claim Davidic authorship, the slight nature of the ascription may be similar to what we have in Ecclesiastes (see Peter Craigie, 'Psalms and the Problem of Authorship', in *idem, Psalms 1–50* [WBC, 19; Waco, TX: Word Books, 1983], pp. 33-35). This said, that ל sometimes suggests actual authorship has recently been argued convincingly by Hebraist Bruce Waltke ('Superscriptions, Postscripts, or Both', *JBL* 110.4 [1991], pp. 583-96 [586-88]). His most illuminating biblical examples of such a use of ל are Isa. 38.9-10 and Hab. 3.1.

unique opportunity of being 'Solomon the Qoheleth', or simply the more elusive 'Qoheleth'—at times a wholly separate identity. Ultimately, one must answer the question 'Why Solomon?' with the question 'Who else but Solomon could have spoken with such vehement denunciation on the vanity of riches, wealth, and even human existence?' As Rabbi Eleazar is reputed to have so aptly noted, 'but for Solomon…I might have said that this man who had never owned two farthings in his life makes light of the wealth of the world'.[106] But historically, Qoheleth is an unknown man to us, whose 'pretentiousness would have amused Rabbi Eleazar'.[107]

To summarize so far, Solomon's lurking presence in Ecclesiastes is obviously multifaceted. Solomon's authority (for all it is worth) is present in the text on its own terms. That there are no 'apologies' from the editor or the narrator, or any appeal to superlative virtues (i.e. apart from the Solomonic), suggests that the authority already imbued in the figure of Solomon rendered redundant any appeal to further authority by the author of Ecclesiastes. It was already present in the Solomonic tradition. Only a Qoheleth with the meandering aid of Solomon could deliver a critique on the רדד of wisdom that would be received earnestly, even if, in the end, he delivered to Solomon in return a crushing, deconstructive blow. However, in the next two sections I will turn to those issues that my exploration of the questions raised by canon and pseudonymity has not dealt with satisfactorily; namely the problems that the guise presents to reading.

4. *The Implied Author and/as Qoheleth/Solomon*

['Mythologized' writing is] a transposition of the person into symbolic figures, references, etc., which may be taken from events private in the [real author's]…experiences and therefore not known to the reader (unless the writer explains them), or may be taken from external sources—from books, other men's experiences, and so forth…even if the reader manages to identify them, he cannot know their points of contact with the writer's person, which gave them their potency for [the author].

Patrick Cruttwell[108]

---

106. *Qoh. Rab.* 3.11.
107. So Bickerman, *Four Strange Books*, p. 142.
108. 'Makers and Persons', *HudR* 12 (1959–60), pp. 487-507 (493).

It was Wayne Booth who first coined the phrase, now frequently found
in biblical and literary studies, 'implied author'. Booth argued throughout his ground-breaking *The Rhetoric of Fiction* that the implied author
is a 'solid' existent, which has its own moral codes and is an implied
version of the author's self. Booth's ideas have since been modified in
the field of narratology. Shlomith Rimmon-Kenan criticizes Booth's
'second-self', qualifying it more carefully as a 'construct based on the
text'. Instead of being a 'voice' or 'speaker', the implied author is a set
of implicit norms.[109] In *Coming to Terms*, Chatman has recently
brought the discussion up to date (see pp. 74-89 and the bibliography in
n. 1, p. 215) and defended the use of the phrase with several
modifications, particularly as regards any remnants of authorial intention. For example, he critiques Booth's notion that the values of the
implied author represent the '"*choosing, evaluating person*" *who produces the work*' (p. 81, italics Chatman's). For Chatman such authorial
intentions remain with the author. The text can only be a 'record of
textual invention' and does not so much represent the choices and
commitments of the real author as the intention of the text as a separate
entity. Expressed another way, anti-intentionalists such as Chatman
suggest not 'that the artist's statement of intention should be discounted
in interpretation. They argue only against the relevance of [for exam-
ple] the sounds Bach might have heard in his own *head...*' (p. 78,
italics Chatman's). 'Upon publication, the implied author supersedes
the real author' (p. 81). The issue of intentionality will be explored
further in the next chapter, suffice it to say that even such a committed anti-intentionalist as Chatman cannot escape using language
that betrays that commitment.[110] The degree to which the real author

109. *Narrative Fiction*, p. 87. Chatman similarly points out, for example, that the
codes of the implied author may not only be moral, but cultural and aesthetic as
well (*Story and Discourse*, p. 149).

110. For example, after arguing that *interpreters* should not speculate on the
author's intention (specifically, what, e.g., Milton was *planning* when he wrote
Paradise Lost), Chatman states further that 'there is no suggestion that biographers
and historians may not do so' (*Coming to Terms*, p. 78). But why the distinction?
The notion that historians are in fact interpreters is surely undisputed by now. Even
the notion that the implied author 'supersedes the real author' (p. 81) is perilously
close to what he refutes, such as the practice of referring to the implied author as a
'human surrogate or image of the real author' (p. 82). In fact in Chatman's discussion one could sometimes replace 'implied' with 'real' without a change in meaning (a feature of Booth's writing that Chatman criticizes). For example, the implied

transforms his or her values in the construct 'implied author' is, like most areas of literary theory, unquantifiable (and hence unable to be proven, but more importantly, unable to be disproved) and it is therefore appropriate to speculate on the matter.

All said, the basic notion of this 'second self' has proven valuable as a model for thinking about the writing process and enables consideration of the relationship between the narratorial 'voice' and the overall commitments and ideology *as expressed in* the text. It is a creation (conscious or not) of any and every real author. But authors are capable of presenting many different implied authors in various works (e.g. we present different implied versions of ourselves as we write letters to different people for different reasons). To speculate for a moment, it may well be that the immediate success of Ecclesiastes depended upon the extent to which the real author lurked safely *behind* the implied author. The identity of the real author has been so well hidden that very little can be said about him or her as a historical character; as 'one who lived'. The complexity of the guise, and its relation to Qoheleth as an individual character in the text, is the main contributor to our lack of surety on this score.[111] Through this use of 'Qoheleth', the Solomonic guise may be an attempt to cast off 'ego-ridden private symbols' and transform the text's vision into 'something that is essentially public'.[112] But that is as far as I dare speculate about the real author's strategy in this regard.

Of what, then, does the implied author consist? First, as we shall see,

author is 'the inventor' who assigns to the narrator its words (p. 84) and 'dictates the elaborate network of tellings' in Conrad's *The Nigger of the Narcissus* (pp. 85-86). As Chatman forgives Booth for the confusion so we could forgive Chatman. Precision is nigh impossible here.

111. This is because the Qoheleth that can be 'known' is strictly the Qoheleth of Ecclesiastes; there is no other *authorial* referent. As Chatman rightly comments, 'the speaker of a literary work cannot be identified with the author'. That is, unless we are given a 'pragmatic context' by the real author we may only reconstruct the 'character and condition of the speaker … by internal evidence alone' (Chatman citing M. Beardsley, *Story and Discourse*, p. 147). In this sense it is by virtue both of Ecclesiastes' being written after the time of Solomon and of the displacement of origins that the frame narrator has effected, that there is no such 'pragmatic context' concerning the real author. Qoheleth is a truly separate existent from the real author and from the tradition of Solomon.

112. Booth's description of the real author's use of the implied author (*Rhetoric of Fiction*, p. 395).

the implied author is more than the Solomonic elements of Qoheleth.[113] In fact, the investigation of the implied author yields the '*totality* of meanings that can be inferred from a text'.[114] This means that the cultural and moral values that both Qoheleth and the frame narrator on the whole express must be taken into account. Although Qoheleth and the frame narrator both vie to be the implied author,[115] by my theory (see Chapter 5) I must discount the frame narrator's bid. In other words, as a reader I have chosen to cast my lot with Qoheleth's implied author. With this in mind, the important distinction now to keep is between the implied author (the overall values expressed in *Qoheleth's* text, 1.3–12.7) and the (contextual) narratorial voice.

The implied author as a construct is most useful when there is some incongruity between the text's overall values and the opinion of its narrator and/or its particular characters. While Ecclesiastes was probably not written as fiction per se, its narrator is used to 'persuade the reader to accept [the work within which it functions] as living oracles'.[116] Qoheleth as a narrator is complex. His language is teeming with self-referentiality, which arises particularly from the elements of autobiography. With the further complication of the Solomonic guise, he is sometimes masked, and we are not sure who lies 'behind' the mask or for what expressed commitments that character is responsible.[117] An example should help to unpack the complexity.

Even when Qoheleth is more Solomon than Qoheleth he is not heavy-handed. This is evidenced, for example, in his test of pleasure (שׂמחה) at 2.1-11. The subtlety of Solomon's presence allows Qoheleth

---

113. In the same way, it should be noted, Qoheleth and Solomon do not merge seamlessly into one character but remain somehow separate. As P. Höffken remarks, 'Qohelet sagt zwar auf eine individuelle Weise "ich", aber so, dass diesses Ich sich in der Rolle der Salomo artikuliert' (cited in Isaksson, *Studies in the Language of Qoheleth*, pp. 41-42).

114. Bal, *Narratology*, pp. 119-20 (italics mine). Similarly, Booth: 'the implied author includes…the intuitive apprehension of a completed artistic whole; the chief value to which *this* implied author is committed, regardless of what party his creator belongs to in real life' (*Rhetoric of Fiction*, pp. 73-74; italics Booth's).

115. So Fox, 'Frame-narrative', p. 105.

116. Booth, *Rhetoric of Fiction*, pp. 218-21; cf. p. 86.

117. For an engrossing discussion of the Solomonic guise as a mask, and the manner in which it confounds issues of identity and responsibility, see Rüdiger Lux, ' "Ich, Kohelet, Bin König…" Die Fiktion als Schlüssel zur Wirklichkeit in Kohelet 1:12–2:26', *EvT* 50 (1990), pp. 331-42 (esp. p. 335).

to be more effective. Thus, as Qoheleth reflects on his experiment, the values of the implied author are not ponderous. As the sequential reader will know even by this point, this is a view that Qoheleth's text on the whole expresses (the judgment of הבל on the experience expressed in his early, narrated life). The implied author's views are being voiced, but to what degree is that voice Solomon's? The identity has shifted, if imperceptibly. In fact the views expressed by the narrator (esp. the boasts of 2.4-8) are, in the end, subjected to the views of the implied author, who circumscribes 'Solomon' in 2.1-2 (this test is absurd, laughter is 'mad', pleasure 'useless'), 2.11 (all [of this] was absurd) and, in a comprehensive manner, throughout Qoheleth's narration.

Consider another example. In 3.10-11 Qoheleth gathers several of his themes together (the question of what is profitable, toil, the activity of God) and puts an unexpected theological twist to them:

> What profit has the worker from that at which he toils? I observed the business that God has given to human beings to be busy with. He has made everything beautiful in its time. Furthermore, *he has placed eternity in their hearts* so that humanity cannot discover the activity that God has done from beginning to end.

Although the sentiment is, perhaps atypically, overtly theological, there is no reason to suspect that the narrator is here contradicting the implied author, that is, the values expressed in the text as a whole. But what would be the effect of acknowledging the presence of Solomon in the narrator's voice here? It was said of Solomon that 'The whole earth sought the presence of Solomon to hear his wisdom, *which God had placed in his heart*' (1 Kgs 10.24; 2 Chron. 9.23). This would not merit any comparison were it not for the fact that the idea that God places *anything* in the heart is rarefied in itself. When God (or Yahweh) is the subject, 'give' (נתן) the verb, and the heart (לב) the indirect object (as in Eccl. 3.11), the sense is usually, 'God put it in my/your/their heart to do such and such'.[118] The only examples that come close to Qoheleth's idea here (particularly in terms of the grammatical conditions) are: Yahweh places wisdom in human hearts (Exod. 36.1-2) and Yahweh will place (and write) his law in the hearts of the house of Israel (Jer. 31.33). The Solomonic element is made even more significant by its prominence in 1 Kings 1–11 (the idea is repeated in 1 Kgs 3.12; cf. 3.9;

---

118. 2 Chron. 30.12; Ezra 7.27; Neh. 2.12; 7.5; Jer. 24.7; cf. Deut. 29.4; Ps. 86.11; Dan. 10.12. Note that Qoheleth 'applies' (נתן) his heart to his deeds (1.13, 17; 8.9, 16; cf. 7.2, 21; 9.1).

4.29). God's purpose in placing wisdom in Solomon's heart was that he might govern his people and 'discern between good and evil' (1 Kgs 3.9), but most importantly, the result[119] was that 'Solomon's wisdom surpassed the wisdom of all the people of the east, and all the wisdom of Egypt. He was wiser than anyone else…his fame spread throughout all the surrounding nations' (1 Kgs 4.30-31 [5.10-11]). In other words, the very (Solomonic) results of wisdom that Qoheleth deconstructs (1.16-17; 2.9) were linked explicitly to God in the traditions about Solomon. For Qoheleth, God places eternity (העלם) in the human heart for a contrary reason: 'so that [מבלי אשר, for the reason that] humanity cannot discover [לא־ימצא] the activity that God has done from beginning to end' (3.11).

This touches on the function of wisdom for the king. Qoheleth is still speaking as Solomon and as such presents Solomon's loss of wisdom not only in the royal fiction proper, but in a text such as this (and, as we have seen above, perhaps 4.1). What God once did for King Solomon, with positive results, he now does for humanity, with results that Solomon himself could not have understood ('although the wise claim to understand it [i.e. the observable activity of God 'under the sun'] they will not discover it', 8.17b). It is not wisdom (or great understanding), but rather (a sense of?) endlessness that he has put in the human heart, which will have the directly opposite result that wisdom had for Solomon. The king now receives nothing while humanity receives something that is indicative of the crookedness of the moral order (cf. 1.13, 15; 7.13 and the discussion in Chapter 7.3).

I have chosen to look for the Solomonic element in 3.10-11 and I am not certain enough of the findings to be insistent about its overall significance. It is neither as clear nor as significant as the first example (2.1-11). However, in ch. 3 Qoheleth is in fact still speaking, in a sense, as Solomon, the presence of whom in the implied author possibly creates a conflict with the narrator. But in the end, the implied author is more than Solomon. In fact, the Solomonic perspective (and all for which it stands?) is made to comply to the critical, world-weary stance expressed in no uncertain terms by the implied author.

119. That is, after informing us that God gave Solomon great wisdom (1 Kgs 4.29), the next verse informs us that his wisdom surpassed the wisdom of the east etc. NRSV picks up on this causal link by inserting 'so that' at the beginning of v. 31.

5. *Solomonic Readings and Readers*

Before proceeding I will clarify what I mean by a 'reading'. I do not refer to the sense associated with reader-response criticism, where a 'reading' may entail an entire vision of reality that shapes the whole interpretation of a literary work. A *feminist* reading, for example, would require that the reader reads as a woman. This is not merely a matter of assuming sexual and 'gender inflections', but seeks to encapsulate 'the way in which the *hypothesis* of a female reader changes our apprehension of a given text'.[120] Instead, my notion of 'reading' is more text-based. By a 'reading' I mean any given comment, interpretation and so forth, *as to* the nature of the book in question. By Solomonic reading I mean any such expression by a reader who reads in the belief that Solomon was the *real* author of Ecclesiastes.

a. *History of Solomonic Readings*
The most substantial biblical narrative about the eventual dispersement of Solomon's kingdom (1 Kgs 11.9-40) is sparse, even ambiguous. Ambiguity leads to a proliferation of explanations, and this particular ambiguity may have been the impetus for a number of legends about Solomon.[121] In those books attributed to him (including Ecclesiastes) early Jewish tradition sometimes made attempts to understand the particular circumstances of Solomon's writing. The most fascinating example is that of Solomon and the demon Asmodeus. According to the legend,[122] when Solomon gained too many wives for himself and desired too many horses and too much gold, the Book of Deuteronomy (i.e. the Law) stepped before the Lord and requested that Solomon be

120. Jonathan Culler citing E. Showalter in *On Deconstruction: Theory and Criticism after Structuralism* (repr.; London: Routledge, 1989 [1983]), p. 50 (italics Culler's). I am oversimplifying in order to illustrate the essential difference present.

121. The same holds true in regard to the process of 'character-cleansing'. For example, since Israel's hero is reputed to have followed after foreign women there is an attempt via legend to make sense of his flaws (see Holm-Nielsen, 'The Book of Ecclesiastes', p. 71). That this attempt is present in biblical accounts as well, see above, sec. 1.

122. Knobel ('The Targum of Qohelet', pp. 22-23) discusses the presence of the legend in the Targum and concludes that although *Targum Qoheleth* is dated to the seventh century CE, this version is known among other Babylonian and Palestinian talmudim and the source for them is not known. This tradition possibly pre-dates those talmudim (as early as 200 CE).

chastised. The chastisement was Solomon's dethronement. While Solomon was dethroned the demon Asmodeus assumed his likeness and took his place. During that time Solomon experienced the life of a beggar and consequently returned to his throne in Jerusalem, a repentant king.[123] *Targum Qoheleth* says that Asmodeus was sent because Solomon became too proud. Solomon went about the world weeping during his dethronement, saying, 'I am Qoheleth, who was previously named Solomon', and it was in this time of dethronement that Solomon wrote Ecclesiastes.

A midrash tradition of authorship relates to Solomon's whole life. In his youthful lusts, it says, he wrote the Song of Songs, while Proverbs contained 'the ripe fruit of a man who knows life [middle-age]; but when he became old he composed Ecclesiastes'.[124] And another states that 'Solomon wrote Qoheleth in his old age, when weary of life "to expose the emptiness and vanity of all worldly pursuits..."'[125] While the Solomonic connection in such readings is not exploited in order to colour the meaning of specific texts, such readings do attempt to understand the whole book in *the context of Solomonic authorship*. To say, for example, that Solomon wrote Ecclesiastes in a time of dethronement is a commentary on the nature of the book as a whole. It implies that the content of the book is necessarily bitter and cynical (being written before Solomon's repentance and specifically during his weeping). It makes sense of the content of Ecclesiastes by ascribing to Solomon a disposition at the time of writing.

Targum Qoheleth drives home the notion that Solomon not only wrote Ecclesiastes, but did so by the Holy Spirit:

> When Solomon king of Israel saw through the holy spirit that the kingdom of Rehoboam his son would be divided with Jeroboam the son of Nebat and that Jerusalem and the Temple would be destroyed and the

123. As cited in Ginzberg, *Legends of the Jews*, IV, pp. 165ff. Of course, this is wildly different from the biblical account of Solomon's punishment, which was that the kingdom was to be torn away from him. But this with two consolations 'for David's sake': (1) the kingdom would be torn away from his son *after* his death, and (2) his son would have one tribe to rule, 'that David may always have a light before [the Lord] in Jerusalem' (1 Kgs 11.13). And then an adversary, Hadad the Edomite, was raised against him (v. 14; and even more adversaries later, vv. 23-25).

124. Cited in Ginzberg, *Legends of the Jews*, IV, pp. 301-302.

125. As cited by Barton, *Ecclesiastes*, p. 19.

people of the household of Israel would go into exile, he said to himself, 'Vanity of vanities...of everything for which I and David my father laboured' (1.1-2, 4).

Here we are told to read Ecclesiastes as an exposition of the vanity that is the loss of Solomon's kingdom.[126] The Targum continues (1.13), 'And I set my mind to seek instruction from the Lord at the time when he revealed himself to me at Gibeon' (cf. Eccl. 1.13; 1 Kgs 3.5-9). This link with Solomon is subtle. It is not to support a particular rabbinic argument or (as far as we can tell) to correct some previous misunderstanding of Eccl. 1.13, but rather it is to underscore the presence of Solomon as the primary narrator/author of these words. The perspective of Solomonic authorship is kept throughout the Targum.[127]

What of early Christian readings? On the whole it seems that there was little value attached to the idea that Solomon actually wrote Ecclesiastes. Origen began the Christian tradition of a 'Solomonic corpus', which included Ecclesiastes, and, as R.E. Murphy states, this 'context created a way of looking at the book'.[128] There were some Church Fathers who explicitly indicated and/or made significant use of Solomonic authorship in their paraphrases or commentaries, such as Clement of Alexandria, Origen, Gregory Thaumaturgos, Cyril, Chrysostom, Jerome and Augustine.

From Gregory (a student of Origen) onwards it seems that the significance of the Solomonic context went beyond the formulaic 'Solomon said...' As Gregory's paraphrase begins we are left in little doubt as to the importance of Solomonic authorship:

> Solomon (the son of the king and prophet David), a king more honoured and a prophet wiser than anyone else, speaks to the whole assembly of God...(1.1).[129]

---

126. Svend Holm-Nielsen argues that in *Targum Qoheleth* there are instances in which 'the verity of the words [of Qoheleth] is not denied, but their validity is restricted to certain situations to be found in the history of Israel' ('The Book of Ecclesiastes', p. 64; here commenting on 1.2). See also R.E. Murphy, 'Qohelet Interpreted: The Bearing of the Past on the Present', *VT* 32 (1982), pp. 331-37 (335).

127. In fact, such emphases are not limited to the 'royal fiction' section (1.12–2.17); e.g. *Targ. Qoh.* 3.12; 4.15; 7.27; 9.7.

128. Cf. Murphy, 'Qohelet Interpreted', pp. 331-32.

129. Translation by Jarick, in *idem, Gregory Thaumaturgos' Paraphrase*, p. 7.

John Jarick, in his study of the paraphrase, states at length the influence
of Solomon throughout the work:

> This presumption of Solomonic authorship gives rise to certain motifs in
> Gregory's interpretation. One idea referred to throughout...is that
> Solomon lost and subsequently regained wisdom—he had received
> wisdom from God but had afterwards rejected it... And since Gregory
> sees Solomon as being...a prophet, a number of statements are treated
> as speaking in a somewhat visionary way of the cosmic battle between
> the forces of good and evil...this apocalyptic motif reaches its climax in
> an ingenious paraphrase of the final chapter's 'Allegory of Old Age' as a
> prophecy of the end of the world.[130]

And Gregory was not alone in finding Solomon's presence worthy of
note. Augustine, for example, stated (c. 410 CE) that 'Solomon, the
wisest king of Israel, who reigned in Jerusalem, thus commences the
book called Ecclesiastes, which the Jews number among their canonical
Scriptures: "Vanity of vanities, said Ecclesiastes..."'[131] More importantly, however, he rejected Origen's interpretation of Eccl. 1.9-10 (that
it suggested the cyclical nature of all things until they returned to their
original state): 'At all events, far be it from any true believer to suppose
that by these *words of Solomon* those cycles are meant.'[132] It may be
that the appeal to Solomon was an attempt to clinch the argument.

Chrysostom (c. 370 CE) has unusually high praise for the *words of
Solomon* in Ecclesiastes when he says, in the flow of another topic of
discussion altogether, '[Solomon] who enjoyed much security...that
very sentiment of Solomon...so marvellous and pregnant with divine
wisdom—"Vanity of vanities."'[133] However, it is Jerome (c. 400 CE)
who is the first of the Christians to have written substantially *about*
Ecclesiastes. He grouped it with Proverbs and the Song of Songs, each
representing successive stages of Christian growth. He often used the
'fact' that Solomon wrote Ecclesiastes to make sense of certain texts.
Following the rabbis, at Eccl. 2.18-19, where Qoheleth lamented the
fact that he must bequeath the reward of his toil to a fool, the fool
becomes Solomon's son.[134]

130. *Gregory Thaumaturgos' Paraphrase*, pp. 314-15.
131. *City of God* 20.3.
132. Augustine, *City of God* 12.13; Origen, *de Princ.* 3.5.3.
133. *Concerning the Statues* (from the Nicene and Post-Nicene Fathers edition,
IX [New York: Christian Literature Co., 1889], pp. 439-40).
134. *Ad loc.*, *Commentarius in Ecclesiasten*. See Holm-Nielsen, 'The Book of
Ecclesiastes', p. 70.

These examples reflect a secure standing in the early church of both the status of the book (Solomon's words are safe) and the notion of Solomonic authorship in general. This notion of authorship among the early Christians is, on the whole, only assumed and not really exploited. This is most evident where allegorical interpretation held sway. With allegory the character of Solomon eventually became lost among other concerns. While with midrashic interpreters there is a concern for 'earthly' matters (e.g. expositing the history of Israel), it was more the habit of the early Christians, with their 'Jesus is the Ecclesiast' approach, to allegorize to the extent that a Solomonic framework was rendered unnecessary.[135] For example, Gregory of Nyssa identified the 'Ecclesiast' with the true king of Israel, Jesus.[136] The basis for the typology 'Ecclesiast' could have come from any figure. And it should be pointed out that the inconsequence of Solomon's presence is not found only in the Christian texts. In *Qoheleth Rabbah* authorship becomes a non-question early on since the more pressing concern is to have a forum for rabbinic discussion on an unbelievably vast array of topics. The Solomonic context was only faintly kept.

While the relative importance of the 'fact' of the Solomonic authorship of Ecclesiastes seems to have been either constant or diminished only slightly through the centuries, in Jewish and Christian readings it is not until Luther that the 'fact' itself is challenged.

b. *The Consequences of (Not) Reading Solomonically*
The Solomonic guise is stylistically comparable to the frame narrative of Ecclesiastes. Both help to create suspensions of disbelief that enable the reader to focus the reading process through interpretive frames. For inasmuch as Qoheleth and the frame narrator are made believable as characters, so the Solomonic codes they each employ are made credible tenets.[137] But what about when Solomonic authorship is considered more critically by readers? That is, what happens when the reader *reads*

135. So M. Hirshman, 'The Greek Fathers and the Aggada on Ecclesiastes: Formats of Exegesis in Late Antiquity', *HUCA* 59 (1958), pp. 137-65 (155-57).

136. Referring to Jn 1.49. See Hirshman, 'The Greek Fathers', p. 147.

137. That is, the (implied) reader 'pretends' that Qoheleth is Solomon and helps to create the 'Teller of this tale' and believes it 'as if' it happened. The Solomonic illusion is created by the reading of Solomonic allusion. See Booth, *Rhetoric of Fiction*, p. 430.

against that strategy and refuses to suspend his or her disbelief?
In Luther's *Table Talk* he is reported to have said that

> Solomon himself did not write Ecclesiastes, but it was produced by
> Sirach at the time of the Maccabees... It is a sort of Talmud, compiled
> from many books, probably from the library of King Ptolemy Euergetes
> of Egypt.[138]

He was followed by Hugo Grotius in 1644 who wrote that Ecclesiastes
was a collection of opinions of different sages 'written in the name of
this King Solomon, as being led by repentance to do it' (he goes on to
cite Ezra, Daniel and the 'Chaldee paraphrasts' as the sources).[139] After
Grotius, critical, non-Solomonic readings escalated in Germany,
reaching a plateau of sorts in the nineteenth century.[140] Today, that critical stance is universally held even by the most conservative of
scholars.

Relatively suddenly, commentators were free to speak about the dis-
unity of Ecclesiastes as a manifestation of its non-Solomonic authorship. For example, Paul Haupt in 1894 wrote, '[Ecclesiastes] reminds
me of the remains of a daring explorer, who has met with some terrible
accident, leaving his shattered form exposed to the encroachments of
all sorts of foul vermin'.[141] Or take Elias Bickerman's more recent,
simple observation that '[Qoheleth is] a scholar turned haranguer'.[142]
Both are 'random' selections yet are representative of a prevailing attitude since Luther's ground-breaking observation. This general shift in

138. Cited in Barton, *Ecclesiastes*, p. 21. Either this is unreliable or it represents
a change of opinion after Luther's *Commentary on Ecclesiastes* (1532), for in the
commentary he is emphatically of the opposite opinion: '[Solomon spoke these
things] after dinner, or even during dinner to some great and prominent men... and
afterwards what he said was put down and assembled... This is then a public
sermon which they heard from Solomon' ('Notes on Ecclesiastes', in J. Pelikan
[gen. ed.], *Luther's Works. XV. Notes on Ecclesiastes, Lectures on the Song of
Solomon, Treatise...* [St Louis: Concordia Publishing House, 1972], pp. 1-187 [12];
cf. also pp. 22, 28, 38, 144, where Luther appeals to the notion of Solomonic
authorship to make sense of what is happening in the text).

139. Cited in Barton, *Ecclesiastes*, p. 21.

140. Barton lists five from the eighteenth century and reports many more in the
nineteenth century, when, apparently, only a few scholars argued seriously for
Solomonic authorship—notably, Wangemann in 1856 (Barton, *Ecclesiastes*, pp.
21-22).

141. Cited in Barton, *Ecclesiastes*, pp. 27-28.

142. Bickerman, *Four Strange Books*, p. 143.

view of Ecclesiastes' overall meaning reflects a shift in the 'consensus' perception of the implied author. Of course, there may be much to commend both the new and the old perceptions. One inescapable result, however, is that Qoheleth is no longer sitting comfortably behind any Solomonic mask. That whole conglomerate of protection, criticism and commentary became quite suddenly vacant in readings. Because of the new vision of authorship with which scholars operated, the 'remains' of the (oddly unified) implied author, *as* Solomon *as* Qoheleth, were much more scattered. Consider, then, two examples of readerly consequences.

The early Christian paraphrast Gregory Thaumaturgos understood Qoheleth's (read Solomon's) quest for wisdom to be motivated by his (Solomon's) historical loss of a wisdom that was once divinely imparted. As I outline in Chapter 8.3 below, Qoheleth *did* seek wisdom and his search was thwarted. If we read Ecclesiastes, as Gregory, with the idea that Qoheleth, as Solomon, *once had* true wisdom and understanding, his consequent need to find it becomes indicative of the divine punishment inflicted on him, instead of becoming an example of, or even metaphor for, the human condition. To state the case more generally, Qoheleth as just Qoheleth is able to be owned by anyone. He is able to be placed in our own historical contexts because he is context-less. Reading Qoheleth as *not* Solomon enables readers to appropriate his experience of wisdom and the world and the text becomes, in a way, more open. Now I offer a more modern example.

There is an anonymous work from 1880 (now known to be written by D. Johnston) entitled, *A Treatise on the Authorship of Ecclesiastes.*[143] It is a 557-page scathing attack on the arguments of Ginsburg, Bleek, Hengstenberg, Grotius and Delitzsch who each represented fairly well-received 'non-Solomonic' approaches of the author's day. One half of the book is an impressive compilation of grammatical analysis. But the author proceeds a posteriori in his thesis, for anything approaching the appearance of pseudonymity in a biblical book is by definition blasphemous and therefore undermines that book's general trustworthiness (see esp. pp. 413-18). While the work does not appear to have achieved acceptance, it remains an interesting example of one author's dilemma about authorship. Any incongruity between what Johnston saw to be the implied author (the sum of the Solomonic codes and norms Johnston believed Ecclesiastes to express) and the (nineteenth-century constructed) real author of Ecclesiastes (i.e. *not* Solomon) was entirely

143. London: MacMillan and Co., anonymous edn, 1880.

unacceptable. (And yet by writing anonymously he refused to take responsibility for how readers might understand his own work in this respect.)

In sum, perhaps the biggest obstacle to the approaches of canon and pseudonymity, in terms of exegetically unpacking the guise, is the relationship of the effects of the guise I have suggested to historical constructs of milieus that are largely intangible (such as a reading audience's given understanding of pseudonymity). The model of implied authorship is useful for a text that generates such complicated constructs of authorship as Ecclesiastes, which constructs solicit decisions from readers. We are free to choose, for example, whether the implied author of Ecclesiastes is 'in agreement with' the frame narrator. The complexity of the implied author, I believe, suggests that 'he' was not always in agreement with the real author. This was the real author's way of cluing the reader in on the character of Qoheleth's discourse—not of Solomon's, but of Qoheleth's, who sometimes speaks as, sometimes evokes the authority of, Israel's King of wisdom.

Chapter 7

QOHELETH AND THE SELF*

For words, like Nature, half reveal
  And half conceal the Soul within
    Tennyson ('In Memoriam A.H.H.', Canto 5 [1850])

Run my name through your computer
Mention me in passing to your college tutor
Check my records, check my facts...
Pore over everything in my C.V.
You'll still know nothing 'bout me

Sting[1]

This chapter addresses the fact that readers of Ecclesiastes often gain the impression that they somehow 'know' Qoheleth. It seems that an interaction takes place, one in which the reader feels the concern of identity and of the formation of Qoheleth's character. That transaction is not likely superficial, for if there is any intimation of Qoheleth's 'self' it refers to something embedded deeply in his narrative. I refer to a transference of identity, the reader's to the narrator's, whereby a self is recognized whose experience is identifiable and able to be appropriated. The readerly experience this entails is difficult to grasp. Elizabeth Stone makes the following poignant remark that reflects the experience well:

> Like a candleflame in mist, we cannot see him or touch him or name him, and yet he is there. And as surely as food gives a fragrance and drums resound, Koheleth gives us his own particular light, whether he is one or many men, whether the page has felt the point of one or many pens.[2]

* Large sections of this chapter have appeared in my 'Qoheleth and the/his Self among the Deconstructed', in A. Schoors (ed.), *Qohelet in the Context of Wisdom* (BETL, 136; Leuven: Leuven University Press, 1998), pp. 425-33.

1. 'Epilogue (Nothing 'bout me)', from the album, *Ten Summoner's Tales* (A & M Records, 1993).

2. 'Old Man Koheleth', p. 98.

How do we get at that candleflame in mist? What makes it shine at all? How can a reader say with such confidence that Qoheleth 'is there', as sure as the fragrance of a good meal to the nose and the tenor of music to the ear? Most importantly, how, if at all, does Qoheleth's narrative form a way of accounting for human experience?

1. *Self-Presence?*

> You could not discover the limits of the self,
> even by travelling along every path:
> so deep a *logos* does it have.
>
> Heraclitus (frag. 45)

> The self...is infinitely difficult to get at, to encompass, to know how to deal with: it bears no definition; it squirts like mercury away from our observation; it is not known except privately and intuitively; it is, for each of us, only itself, unlike anything else experienced or experience-able. And yet, the man who commits himself to the whole task of the autobiographer intends to make this self the subject of his book and to impart some sense of it to the reader.
>
> James Olney[3]

The self is not a modern invention, but it has relatively recently under-gone something of an ideological transmutation. It has transformed from something of which we could be certain, or of which we at least spoke confidently, to something diverse and impossible to define. As Olney remarks in the epigraph above, 'it squirts like mercury away from our observation'. The problem is culturally evident. In the early 1970s American popular culture suffered a 'minor crisis' when the notion was put about that the real Paul McCartney of the Beatles had died a few years previously and been replaced by the winner of a Paul McCartney look-alike contest. The furore ceased when people came to accept that as long as the face and the voice were essentially the same, it mattered little who the flesh-and-blood person actually was. The veracity of Paul McCartney's self was reduced to the quality of an audio-visual image.[4] A more recent indication comes from a spate of television series such as BBC's *Reputations*, which examines inexplicable (or perhaps disturbingly explicable?) paradoxes between the

---

3.   *Metaphors of Self: The Meaning of Autobiography* (Princeton, NJ: Princeton University Press, 1972), p. 23.

4.   So Michael Sprinker, 'Fictions of the Self: The End of Autobiography', in Olney (ed.), *Autobiography*, pp. 321-42 (322).

private and public personas of such complex characters ranging from Bertrand Russell to John Wayne. The judgments such programmes deliver challenge cherished ideas. Errol Flynn, that swashbuckling cinematic heartthrob of the '30s and '40s, pronounced impotent. Walt Disney, the supposed genius behind the early animated 'Disney' characters, could not draw Mickey Mouse to save his life. The series is just one example of how traditional ways of talking about and defining the self—ways in which we understand a public or private persona, a visual[5] or textual persona—are being questioned and overturned. The image of the self, whether text or media-based, is elusive and virtually unknowable by its signs.

As already discussed (Introduction, sec. 3), readers of autobiography naturally *expect* the source of its cohesion to be the author's self, and Qoheleth's 'chosen' form of narration, whether we like it or not, is that of autobiography. His narrative is primarily concerned with his experience. And so, as with all autobiography, Qoheleth's form of narration allows him his loose approach to his subjects. This, as I have already noted, forms the literary integrity of Ecclesiastes. It does so because the reader is enabled to follow the lexical signs that indicate that the character who is speaking and experiencing throughout the narrative is one and the same. Yet while the autobiographical form intimates self, it leaves largely open the question of that self's essence and substance. In other words, the autobiographical form gives it a name, a history and a foundation for its action, but its principal function is to be only the arena *through which* the narrator may discourse all the past of its life in a particular interpretive light.

It is because the first-person form at least intimates self that we are prone to see something more imbedded *in* it—Stone's candleflame in mist. As Ian Michael remarks, 'It is easy to regard the first person as more than a grammatical category, it seems to contain the speaker's

---

5. Jonathan Alter, in an incisive piece on the O.J. Simpson case (the athletic superstar charged with murder in the US in the spring of 1994) in *Newsweek International* ('Television's False Intimacy', 27 June 1994, p. 25), argued that the public at large fell victim to the false intimacy created by television. The Janus face of the television personality given to the world is at one time friendly, yet born of violence. The visual image elicits judgments. We are invited to decide for ourselves who is speaking the truth. The frame of reference that people in the US made use of in their time of disillusionment was that of Simpson's media character which, while familiar, was unknowable.

conception of himself as being distinct from other people.'[6] Michael is alluding, of course, to a reading experience. Likewise, the density of the autobiographical form in Ecclesiastes gives one the impression, as Elizabeth Stone expressed, of brushing with the narrator's person, a self that is somehow more than a grammatical category.

Qoheleth also raises distinctly 'modern' questions of sincerity such as those we put to our John Waynes and Walt Disneys. The formidable presence of the self solicits from the reader a query, an invitation to question its sincerity. The combination of the autobiographical form and the frame narrator's historical presentation contribute to this invitation. Is this a believable self? Does not 'I' beg the question of sincerity? When we read 'I' we want to know if the author of that 'I' is telling the truth. If there is only 'I', the witness to what the 'I' asserts becomes nothing less than the very integrity of that speaker, and this becomes an issue. Because the author speaks about him- or herself (however indirectly) the question is raised: does he or she offer a true reflection of (narrated) experience? The frame narrator reflects this concern when he finds it necessary to assert that Qoheleth did in fact write words of truth with integrity (12.10—and how can he know that Qoheleth was, like Job, ישר?). This is a question of character, and character is a question of identity. With what kind of person are we dealing? And because what this person says is so individualized and affecting, how do we judge it to be true?

(The 'I' that we question does not necessarily belong to the historical author. The distinction can become blurred. This is true in the case of Ecclesiastes due in part to the fictional premises of the frame narrative. I sometimes use the word 'author' to denote the character who says 'I' because Ecclesiastes, despite its fictional premise, is autobiography, and assumes the telling of someone's life. The 'I' therefore makes the kind of claim to truth I am here discussing. It is not a claim to history. Even if we were searching for documentary evidence, autobiography is not necessarily the best place to look.[7] This is why the conclusions of,

---

6. Cited in Elliott, *The Literary Persona*, p. 30.

7. Note John Sturrock's insightful remarks: 'historians who go to autobiography for documentary evidence about the past are in no better case than the literary theorist... They would do well moreover to heed the warning of the theorist and question to what extent artifice and literary convention may have determined the "historical" evidence they assume they have found' (*The Language of Autobiography*, p. 12).

for example, A. Lauha about the degree to which Qoheleth's wisdom reflects real events is not relevant in this regard.[8] That question is unquantifiable at any rate and the issue is different from what I am discussing—that is, the experience of sensing a self when reading Qoheleth's autobiography. I am considering a literary strategy that, as we shall see, *does* raise questions about the self as subject.)

In Qoheleth studies scholars have often made assumptions concerning our ability to 'know' Qoheleth's self through referential signs. For example, Frank Zimmermann sees in Ecclesiastes 'a mirror of the chain of neuroses that afflicted [Qoheleth]'.[9] This is because Zimmermann, like Leon Edel, views the semiology operative in a literary text as 'symbols of...[the author's] self, signature of his inner being'.[10] Also, Michael Fox is able to perceive in Ecclesiastes a 'single brooding consciousness' through which all of Qoheleth's observations are filtered.[11] Why? Of course, Fox presents his evidence (mostly concerning Qoheleth's epistemological procedure), but is what Fox sees so obvious that we shouldn't even ask why? Kurt Galling recognized that Qoheleth's autobiographical style was necessary to depict his 'prevailing inner posture'.[12] Michael Eaton feels confident enough to say of Ecclesiastes that 'Within its pages there is a *person* who unobtrusively appears in the words "says the Preacher".'[13] Is Eaton recognizing the signified of a linguistic sign? Harold Fisch regards so seriously the density of first-person forms in Ecclesiastes that he is confident to remark that 'Qohelet could have said with Montaigne, "It

8. Lauha suggests that in several passages Qoheleth may not be drawing on specific personal experiences, but rather has formed his opinion in relation to anyone's experience (*Kohelet* [BKAT, 19; Neukirchen–Vluyn: Neukirchener Verlag, 1978], p. 56, on Eccl. 2.20). We therefore cannot make judgments on Qoheleth's private life history (*Private Lebensgeschichte*, p. 88, on Eccl. 4.7-12), for his observations are drawn from the general circumstances of people in the world he has observed (cf. pp. 140-41).

9. *Inner World*, p. ix.

10. Zimmermann, *Inner World*, p. xiii. He then aligns himself with an even more emphatic expression: 'Anatole France has said that it makes no difference whether a man writes about a fly or Julius Caesar, he is not writing so much about his subject as about himself' (p. xiv).

11. *Qohelet*, p. 159.

12. His 'jeweiligen inneren Haltung' ('Kohelet-Studien', *ZAW* 50 [1932], pp. 276-99 [281]).

13. *Ecclesiastes*, p. 21 (italics mine). Ironically, the words he refers to are the frame narrator's.

is my portrait I draw... I am myself the subject of my book."'[14] How or why aside, all of these scholars have in some way or another felt the weight of Qoheleth's self in his narration.

Of course, in literary criticism authorial presence has been a nearly constant point of contention. For example, a committed notion of authorial self-representation was expressed in John Frey's 1948 article, 'Author-Intrusion in the Narrative.' He summarizes the 'objective' view thus: 'Self-presentation *occurs* when the author actually appears as a character in his story, as in some novels of the Romanticists', and this is *prima facie* observable.[15] But this position is rarely, if at all, to be found today. Towards the more popular and subjective end of the spectrum, Judith Fishman suggests that authors enjoy a richness of choice in how they represent themselves (or selves) as characters:

> The insight into self as character... within the narrative, both of self and others, opens further still the complexity and richness of choice... [and] writers of autobiography must first know 'how much fiction is implicit in the idea of a "self"'.[16]

Whether the essence of its narrator is made purely of symbolic signatures or embedded in the rich fictive choices of character open to authors, autobiographical literature will always be approached with some notion of the self in mind. As in popular culture, however, we are faced with the problem first that the self seems virtually unknowable by its signs, and second, as we shall now observe, that we cannot even be sure what we mean by 'subject' or 'self'.[17] Are we dealing with a soulful or a soulless sign? And how can a review of Qoheleth's attitude both of *him*self and *the* self inform this discussion?

14. 'Qohelet: A Hebrew Ironist', p. 158.

15. 'Author-Intrusion in the Narrative: German Theory and Some Modern Examples', *GR* (1948), pp. 274-89 (278; italics mine). Frey himself argues that there are no pre-established tenets that determine exactly what the author's intrusion is (if any), but rather, the more significant question to ask of self-representation or intrusion is How?: 'how harmonious a constituent of the whole work is it made?' (p. 289).

16. 'Enclosures: The Narrative within Autobiography', *JAdC* 2 (1981), pp. 23-30 (27-28) (citing Elizabeth Bruss).

17. As Jim Kanaris remarks, 'Our systems of measurement [by which we attempt to define the subject] are... humbled by a forever elusive, experientially meaningful bull's-eye' ('Calculating Subjects: Lonergan, Derrida, and Foucault', *Method: Journal of Lonergan Studies* 15 [1977], pp. 135-50 [146]).

2. *The Deconstructed Subject*

Ours is the age of what Robert Elliott once termed 'the denigration of the subject'.[18] Cultural concerns about the self, such as those outlined above, are in turn reflected in our academic concerns. Questions of self are being raised in many quarters: cultural studies, history, literature, biblical studies.[19] Critics such as Barthes, Foucault and Derrida have argued (to a wide and receptive audience) that the subject (i.e. *ego*, self—see below) is a construct determined by its socio-linguistic context, whose only reference is itself and nothing more. The author, who had been thought for ages to lurk stealthily behind the text waiting to be unearthed with the appropriate tools, is now, quite simply, dead. As Barthes wrote in 1968, in his classic essay 'The Death of the Author', the linguistic subject 'I' is 'empty outside of the very enunciation which defines it',[20] and at least one critic has observed that the death of the author has heralded the death of the self.[21] Stephen Best and Douglas Kellner state the case harshly: postmodern criticism has gone as far as to 'valorize' the 'pulverization of the modern subject',[22] and we have thereby been 'thrown into apocalyptic doubt about all previous beliefs about humanness and all courses of actions that such beliefs sustained'.[23] The present impasse in speaking about the self, then, is coming to terms with its death.

To come to terms with the self or subject at least as an issue, an attempt at definition will help. The *Concise Oxford Dictionary* offers the following two (among 14!) definitions of 'subject': (1) *philosophy*—'a thinking or feeling entity; the conscious mind; the ego, esp. as opposed to anything external to the mind' ('the central substance or core of a thing as opposed to its attributes'); (2) *psychology*—'the ego

18. *The Literary Persona*, p. 119.

19. As Kanaris has remarked, 'The discourse on subjectivity...has never been more alive, nor more controversial' ('Calculating Subjects', p. 142).

20. Barthes, 'The Death of the Author', in *idem, Image, Music, Text*, pp. 142-48 (145).

21. So Sprinker, 'Fictions of the Self', pp. 324-25. See Kanaris, however, who refutes the practice of charging Derrida and Foucault with the death of the author or with nihilism in general ('Calculating Subjects', p. 141).

22. Steven Best and Douglas Kellner, cited in J. Richard Middleton and Brian J. Walsh, *Truth Is Stranger Than It Used to Be* (Gospel and Culture; London: SPCK, 1995), p. 51.

23. Middleton and Walsh, *Truth Is Stranger Than It Used to Be*, p. 51.

or self and the non-ego; consciousness, and that of which it is or may be conscious'. In both definitions the concept of difference is operative. Compare the same dictionary's first definition of 'self': 'a person or thing's own individuality or essence'. (The second definition is 'a person or thing as the object of introspection or reflexive action [*the consciousness of self*]'.) To be a subject in the sense that I have thus far used the word is to be a self (*ego*) *capable* of consciousness and able to be distinguished from *another*.[24]

The deconstructed view of self (which heralds the death of author and self) has difficulty maintaining that sense of difference and otherness. Where it differs from an older, Cartesian view is in its emphasis on the self's origin, and therefore its relationship to the text and the reader. In his recent book, *Narrative and the Self*, Anthony Paul Kerby neatly sums up the deconstructed position: 'self arises out of signifying practices rather than existing prior to them as an autonomous or Cartesian agent'.[25] This statement is key to Kerby's position and forces him into the unfortunate position of regarding the computer named HAL in Stanley Kubrick's film *2001* as more of a person than the preverbal child.[26] To be fair, as Kerby states, HAL is not, of course, a person by our 'societal definition', which entails embodiment, and the Cartesian as opposed to language-based subject, for Kerby, is only *a way* of accounting for the notion of self-identity, which, he admits, we all have, and which is expressed in our narratives (and what Kerby calls

24. In his book, *Oneself as Another* (trans. K. Blamey; Chicago: University of Chicago Press, 1994), Paul Ricoeur fills out the idea of otherness implicit in the idea of self. Commenting on the philosophical intention of his work, Ricoeur states that implicit in its title is the notion that 'otherness of oneself implies otherness to such an intimate degree that one cannot be thought of without the other...[and to] "as" I should like to attach a strong meaning, not only that of comparison (oneself similar to another) but indeed that of implication (oneself inasmuch as being another)' (p. 3). That is, for the self to exist it must be in relationship to the other as much as it *is* the other for another. Self and the other, for Ricoeur, enjoy a transferential relationship. My use of 'self' and 'subject' assumes this concept of otherness. This will become particularly relevant when discussing *Qoheleth's* concept of the self and its connection to the notion of otherness.

25. *Narrative and the Self* (SCT; Bloomington: Indiana University Press, 1991), p. 1. Kerby draws heavily on continental deconstructionist theory and his treatment of such issues relates specifically to the relationship between theories of the self and their expression in narratives.

26. *Narrative and the Self*, pp. 70-71, 123 n. 11.

our quasi-narratives—the constructs by which we attempt to understand the events that propel our whole lives). However, Kerby cannot escape the absurdity of his alarming admission that persons can only *exist* through acts of expression. We are all, in Kerby's world, soulless selves, hollow bodies except for the mental constructs of language. And, of course, the question that he never addresses, presumably because he cannot answer it, is What is the source of language itself (not only its genesis, but the determinism implied in its ongoing development) if it is not the (even preverbal?) self? Furthermore, how can any one self relate to another self with any real significance? Is the whole idea of communication between selves that are able to exist outside of the linguistic act absurd, since 'I' has no referent? Indeed, Kerby says of his own implied self as conveyed in the first person of *his* text that he can only live with the absurdity of its presence, for his own 'I' has no referent. The problem of referentiality is the most serious for the deconstructive theory of the subject, but most especially for Mr Kerby since he cannot exist.[27]

Other well-known implications of Kerby's position are worth restating. Because of the paradigm shift from Cartesian to deconstructed self, language is to be regarded as strictly material and no longer 'merely' the tool of a Cartesian self but rather the house of Being where

27. *Narrative and the Self*, p. 14. See also Michel Foucault's 'What Is an Author?', where he argues that the self (particularly as author) can no longer exist outside of its enunciation. Foucault's arguments suffer overall from the conflicting notions that writing refers only to itself, yet, in order for it to create the space through which the *subject* (does he mean author?) can continually disappear (which 'transference' is, for Foucault, the 'true' function of authorship) it must pass outside itself, by which is assumed a notion of self (see esp. pp. 604, 608). This is, in my view, the most potent critique *against* the deconstruction of the subject: that in order for meaning to occur, some kind of *referential* movement (not necessarily metaphysical!) must take place. See furthermore, B. Polka's comments on the paradoxical self-referentiality of Freud's critique of religion ('Freud, Science, and the Psychoanalytic Critique of Religion: The Paradox of Self-Referentiality', *JAAR* 62.1 [1994], pp. 59-81; esp. pp. 67-68, 74, 78-81). Polka sees in Freud's critique of religion the assumption that the neuroses of individuals and communities are indeed accessible to the critical psyche, and that in championing that assumption Freud commits what is his perception of religious illusion. As Sprinker comments, Freud's psychoanalytic approach as adopted by Jacques Lacan has been an important motivating force in the modern (particularly French intellectual) deconstruction of the self ('The End of Autobiography', pp. 324-25).

'meaning is only provided by a systematic arrangement of differences'.[28] Self, then, has become a product of language. Language can
no longer be regarded as 'a more or less neutral medium of communication for ideas'.[29] External reality requires language to be what it is.
Semiotics has overthrown the metaphysics of referent, for a referent
only IS in a closed system of signs. Kerby himself suggests that this
overthrowing of the self from its previously privileged place has
engendered a crisis; namely 'a loss of causal efficacy for the self and a
stress on the subject's social setting'.[30] (Such a loss is reflected in the
popular media crisis in identity discussed above.)

What can a study of the self in Qoheleth's narration contribute to this
discussion? How can different versions of the self, such as Qoheleth's
and the deconstructed, be viewed in light of each other? If the subject
(indeed, the language) of the self is so problem-ridden, why even
bother to bring it to bear on Ecclesiastes? The evidence we have seen
for readers (*others*) seeing a self (*subject*) in Ecclesiastes is essentially
credal and suggests that Ecclesiastes, perhaps more than any other biblical book, is a text that is self-attesting. And there may be plenty that
Qoheleth has to say about his own self and the self as subject, to the
extent that he perhaps 're-privileges' the self to the centre.

3. *The Biblical Self*

I have already discussed the way in which first-person narrators refer to
themselves in biblical Hebrew. The presence of the suffixed ׳ is the
most prominent feature of this self-referentiality. But how does the Old
Testament convey the self *as a subject*? In my own review of this
question, three words have consistently come to the forefront: נפש, לב
and רוח ('heart' or 'mind', 'soul' and 'spirit'). There is no Hebrew
word for 'self' or 'person' (נפש comes closest), but the idea is often
conveyed through the use of these words. The Old Testament authors
preferred both to speak indirectly of the self and to assume its palpable
(sometimes even tactile) existence. To grasp something of the composition of the human person in the Old Testament—the 'candleflame in

---

28. R. Coward and J. Ellis, *Language and Materialism: Developments in
Semiology and the Theory of the Subject* (London: Routledge & Kegan Paul, 1977),
p. 3.

29. Kerby, *Narrative and the Self*, p. 3.

30. *Narrative and the Self*, p. 5.

the mist'—I will explore some semantic possibilities of these words, and review two particularly informative passages (Job 10.8-11, 18-22 and Jer. 1.4-10).

a. לב—'Heart', 'Mind'

> The [Hebraic] heart is 'the very hearth of life's impulses—the supporter of the personal consciousness, combined with self determination and activity of the reason—the training place of all independent actions and conditions… In the heart are found the postulates of speech… and all by which בָּשָׂר [flesh] and נֶפֶשׁ is affected, comes in לב into the light of consciousness.'[31]

Obviously, the word 'heart' carries with it an impressive modern repertoire of images. By it we signify our romantic inclinations, our emotional disposition, our stamina and so forth. In the Old Testament, לב carries with it just as impressive a repertoire.[32] The word is used more than any other in the biblical literature to make reference to the metaphorical 'insides' of a person. It conveys a wide range of emotional, intellectual and physical experiences. It can be applied to an individual psalmist or to the whole nation of Israel whose heart melts in sight of the enemy. The semantic range is extraordinary, and a look at just a few informative examples will demonstrate why this can be said confidently.

One of the most memorable examples of the word shows its volitional connotations. The לב of Pharaoh is described in a series of *Leitmotifs* (in Exod. 4–14) as made heavy (כבד√)[33] or hardened (חזק√)[34] by Yahweh or by Pharaoh himself. By becoming 'heavy' the heart is, suggests Robert R. Wilson, simply no longer able to 'receive external stimuli in the normal way'.[35] When hardened the heart is made 'steadfast, unswerving in its purpose, unchanging and courageous… [all

---

31. I. Cohen, citing Beck, in 'The Heart in Biblical Psychology', in H.J. Zimmels, J. Rabbinowitz and I. Finestein (eds.), *Essays Presented to Chief Rabbi Israel Brodie* (2 vols.; London: Soncino Press, 1967), I, pp. 41-57 (47).

32. See the extraordinary survey of meanings in H.-J. Fabry, '*lēḇ; lēḇāḇ*', *TDOT*, VII, pp. 399-437. Compare also the survey of H.W. Wolff, who remarks that לב is 'The most important word in the vocabulary of Old Testament anthropology' (*Anthropology of the Old Testament* [trans. M. Kohl; London: SCM Press, 1974 (1973)], pp. 40-58 [40]).

33. Exod. 7.14; 8.15[11], 32[28]; 9.7, 34.

34. Exod. 4.21; 10.20, 27; or in 7.3, קשה.

35. 'The Hardening of Pharaoh's Heart', *CBQ* 41 (1979), pp. 18-36 (22).

of which] can be either positive or negative, depending on the point of view of the person using the description'.[36] The end of the means is always to control the outcome of Pharaoh's decision, and results in an inability on Pharaoh's part to listen.[37] The realm in which the word operates here is the will—it will change only according to the disposition/quality of the לב. Hardness or heaviness of heart reveals a degree of resolution against or with God's will. In a similar example, Ezekiel informs us that Yahweh will give Israel one heart and a sanctified spirit. He will remove their heart of stone (לב אבן) and replace it with a heart of flesh (לב בשר). The new heart, being now able to listen, will enable them to follow the statutes that he provides (Ezek. 11.19-20; 36.26). Elsewhere, it is the לב of the people itself (along with their נפש) that must seek Yahweh for the purpose of building a sanctuary (1 Chron. 22.19); that is, its ethical imperative is to seek the will of Yahweh.

The opposite volitional aspect is the pliability of the לב; that is, its 'ability' to become soft. With Job the softness results in his being terrified by Yahweh's presence (Job 23.16). Similarly, the לב may melt like wax and become utterly demoralized (Josh. 2.11; 5.1; 7.5; 14.8; 2 Sam. 17.10; Ps. 22.14), implying inversely that the לב may be a source of courage.[38] In the לב may be found the capacity to enjoy life (courageously?), as well. It can be gladdened with wine (Judg. 19.5, 6, 8, 9; Ps. 104.15; cf. Eccl. 2.3; 9.7; 10.19) and strengthened with nourishment (לחם) for the tasks ahead (e.g. Gen. 18.5). Fabry sums up the volitional aspect well: 'The *lēb* functions as the driving force behind the voluntative endeavours of the individual; it engages in performative conceiving and planning; it is the seat of courage and enterprise.'[39]

The לב can also be a source of moral judgment and conscience. David's heart smote him (violently struck him, נכה) after he counted Israel (2 Sam. 24.10). If a person has no integrity of speech they may be described as speaking with a double intention (בלב ולב, Ps. 12.3),[40]

---

36. Wilson, 'The Hardening of Pharaoh's Heart', p. 23.

37. E.g. Exod. 7.13. It is interesting to note, however, that despite the control exerted on Pharaoh, the hearts of his servants are able to change (14.4-5). Compare Prov. 21.1-2, in which Yahweh is said to control the hearts of kings as he does the flow of rivers.

38. See Fabry, '*lēb; lēbāb*', p. 425.

39. Fabry, '*lēb; lēbāb*', p. 423. Cf. also Wolff, *Anthropology of the Old Testament*, pp. 51-55.

40. Cf. the Ezekiel texts above that refer to the *one* heart that Israel should have.

reminiscent of the Hollywoodized Indian's indictment, 'White man speak with forked tongue!' And because the inner self (קרב) and the לב are deep (עמק), they are aloof, difficult to understand and potentially deceptive (Ps. 64.6; cf. Ps. 51.6). Connected to this moral sense is Israel's stated duty to love the Lord their God with *all* (כל; i.e. not doubly) their לב, נפש and strength (Deut. 6.5-6), as a result of which the words Yahweh speaks shall be inscribed upon their hearts.

The לב has an important intellectual aspect as well. It should be applied (נתן) to wisdom and truth (Prov. 22.17; 23.12; cf. Eccl. 1.13; Ezek. 44.5).[41] Also, to speak in one's heart (אמר בלב) suggests a kind of thinking or considering, an inner thought process. At 1 Kgs 12.26, for example, Jeroboam thought to himself (אמר...בלבו) that his actions might secure the kingdom. Such an insight into his inner plotting is key to the way in which that narrative unfolds. Shimon Bar-Efrat cites several examples of this phrase as an effective narrative device for referring directly to a character's inner thoughts and feelings.[42]

Some miscellaneous meanings are worth mentioning. It is the לב that reveals the true person.[43] The word itself can even signify wisdom or 'good sense', which quality protects its possessor from evil or foolishness (Prov. 19.8;[44] Hos. 7.11). Acquiring לב gives one the sense to carry out acceptable human behaviour. Hence when Nebuchadnezzar's heart was exchanged for that of an animal he lost his capacity to be human and became like an animal (Dan. 4.13). It may also seek truth through reflexive meditation (Ps. 77.6).

As I. Cohen has suggested, and as the intellectual nuance noted above especially implies, the לב is often the centre of consciousness, of thinking about something as a subject, revealing 'the states and

---

41. This said, the לב is only part of the whole learning enterprise. 'The primary responsibility of students was to observe and listen, eye and ear uniting to convey knowledge to the mind for storage in the belly until released through the mouth. Such corporal imagery underlined the belief that the act of cognition involved more than the mental faculty, the heart (לֵב)' (Crenshaw, 'Qoheleth's Understanding of Intellectual Enquiry', p. 218).

42. *Narrative Art in the Bible* (JSOTSup, 70; Sheffield: Almond Press, 1989), pp. 63-64. Further, see below.

43. So, for example, Prov. 18.2: 'The fool takes no delight in understanding, but only in expressing himself' (כי אם־בהתגלות לבו, the htp. of גלה meaning 'to become known', 'manifest'; cf. Gen. 9.21).

44. In this text the heart as a general noun actually benefits the נפש—for the one who loves their soul will gather לב, 'good sense'.

condition of the self as experienced in various circumstances'.[45] That is, it serves as an indicator through which *all* of the experience of the self is expressed.[46] Through it, in it and by it a person can experience an express change of will, fear, courage, pangs of conscience and the consciousness of intellectual enquiry. The heart thereby serves as a focal point for thought, will and strength.

b. נפשׁ—'*Soul*'[47]

This word is probably the closest Hebrew can come to the English 'person' (see Gen. 27.4; 49.6; Num. 31.19, 28, in which each occurrence signifies a whole physical person, an entity that acts).[48] Perhaps the most emphatic expression of the person as נפשׁ is found in the Yahwist creation narrative (Gen. 2.7). God forms the first human from the dust as a potter would form (יצר) a pot of clay. Although the first person is a composite creature[49] and we should be hesitant to call it a soul,[50] the final result is a נפשׁ חיה, a living being come to life by the breath of God. The physical created separateness of God and humanity (in contrast in particular to the physical affinity of humanity and the gods found in some ANE creation myths) is a fundamental tenet expressed by this text—the *imago dei*. Through creation, humanity has not become simply a part of the substance of the Other, but has become separate from the Other—the Another of the Other. I will take up this important point again below.

45. 'The Heart in Biblical Psychology', p. 43. He states elsewhere, citing M. Lazarus, that the heart 'is the most all-embracing expression which "comprises the whole world of psychic phenomena"' (p. 41).

46. As Fabry notes, the לב 'functions in all dimensions of human existence and is used as a term for all the aspects of a person: vital, affective, noetic, and voluntative' ('*lēḇ; lēḇāḇ*', p. 412).

47. 'Soul' is by no means always appropriate as a translation but works, on the whole, best in the instances I will consider.

48. See the examples suggesting '"person", "individual", "being"' discussed by Wolff, *Anthropology of the Old Testament*, pp. 21-22.

49. A point, James Barr maintains, widely overlooked by those who use this passage to argue for 'Hebrew totality thinking': 'the element which is closer to the soul is the "breath" that comes from God, which is quite distinct from the mass of mud out of which Adam was made... The passage is obviously dualistic: there are two ingredients in man, the mud and the breath' (*The Garden of Eden and the Hope of Immortality* [Minneapolis: Fortress Press, 1992], p. 37).

50. So the force of Barr's comments in the previous note, and cf. Wolff, *Anthropology in the Old Testament*, p. 10.

The word נֶפֶשׁ occurs several times in one particularly curious anthropological formulation, Lev. 17.10-11:

> If anyone of the house of Israel…eats any blood I will set my face against that person [נֶפֶשׁ] who eats blood… For the life [נֶפֶשׁ] of the flesh [בָּשָׂר] is in the blood; and I have given it to you to make atonement for your lives [נֶפֶשׁ] on the altar; for, as life [נֶפֶשׁ], it is the blood that makes atonement.

The person (נֶפֶשׁ) is judged for violating the life element (נֶפֶשׁ) of the physical body (that which makes the flesh live, God's breath) that is in the blood. Eating the blood is cannibalistic in that by consuming it one consumes the essence of Another, and the fundamental tenet of separateness is thereby defiled. Oneness of the body (בָּשָׂר) and the life element (נֶפֶשׁ) is central here, as it is in biblical formulations of human rights elsewhere (cf. esp. Gen. 9.4-6).

This said, נֶפֶשׁ also lends itself to the most dualistic notions of person in the Old Testament. Many passages imply that the soul is a separate entity from the body (e.g. Gen. 6.17; 7.15, 22; Josh. 11.11; Job 34.14-15; cf. Eccl. 12.7), and when that final separation occurs, human existence ceases (cf. Job 14.22; Eccl. 9.10). However, rather than concluding from these instances that the נֶפֶשׁ is only *part* of the whole self, we should understand them, suggests R. Laurin, 'as expressions of the life principle in specific functions of the organism'.[51] That is, since the נֶפֶשׁ appears often to be the motivating life-force of the body (that which causes and animates life), it cannot enjoy proper human existence outside of the body (as evidenced by the Leviticus text). On the whole, the נֶפֶשׁ can be understood as possessing a delicate balance of independent and dependent existence.[52]

Finally, the נֶפֶשׁ, like the לֵב, makes up that part of a person that interacts with God's grace and judgment.[53] It is encouraged to seek things out of its own accord (1 Chron. 22.19; cf. Deut. 6.5), and, as is particularly evident in the Psalms, the נֶפֶשׁ is capable of seeking Yahweh as an

---

51. 'The Concept of Man as a Soul', *ExpTim* 72 (1961), pp. 131-34 (132).

52. Barr offers examples of the נֶפֶשׁ being at the same time part of a 'psychosomatic unity' and yet being in a sense independent from the body (*The Garden of Eden*, pp. 39-40).

53. Compare Wolff's remarks in relation to the נֶפֶשׁ: 'the knowledge of Yahweh's saving acts makes the man of understanding free to turn his vital, emotional, needy and desirous [i.e. all the attributes the נֶפֶשׁ signifies] self to joyful praise' (*Anthropology of the Old Testament*, p. 25).

act of worship or of blessing (Pss. 42.1, 2; 103.1, 2; cf. 131.2), and yet it may very well experience painful bitterness towards Yahweh (Job 7.11). It is the centre in and from which God's grace can be experienced—affirmed or denied.

c. רוח—*'Spirit'*[54]

Although there are some informative examples elsewhere,[55] it is in the book of Job that רוח has its most significant nuances for this analysis.

At 7.11 Job remarks that he cannot restrain his speech. He is so overcome from the distress (צר) of his רוח that he must give vent to his speech and complain in the bitterness of his נפש. The idea occurs again, more forcefully, at 32.18-19, this time from Elihu:

> I am bursting with speech! My spirit within me constrains me. Behold,
> my insides are like wine with no vent, like new wineskins ready to burst!
> I must speak to find relief. I will open my lips and reply.

Elihu describes his insides (בטן) as a bursting wineskin, and his רוח is so overcome that it is in danger of restraining his speech. He is full of discourse (מלתי מלים; cf. Job 30.9). That is, his inner person is so full of experience waiting to be expressed that it must find release. Through speech he will find the space to relieve his pent up emotions.[56] We learn from 32.1-5 that he had become angry that Job had 'justified himself' and that his three friends had given no answer to him, and he had now waited as long as he could stand. In other words, his experience, which had become internalized, motivated his speech to the point where it could be controlled no longer. The disposition of both his physical (בטן) and spiritual (רוח) self so affected him that his actions became determined. This movement from the inner self to outward speech (i.e. the image of the self as source of speech) is apropos to the age of the semiotic and soulless self.

54. As discussed above (Excursus), רוח is one self-referential word to which Qoheleth put a fascinating twist. Here I will limit myself to the more narrow question of its significance to the Old Testament notion of the self.

55. A few significant examples: the psalmist's רוח, along with his נפש, is actively self-reflective (Ps. 77.6); God has a רוח active in creation (Gen. 1.2); at death, the רוח returns to God who gave it (Ps. 104.29; cf. Eccl. 12.7); the רוח has a moral aspect (as a 'place' of iniquity, Ps. 32.2).

56. The metaphor of wineskins makes the aspect of space come to life here. In that constrained amount of space, too much wine will press outwards in search of an expanse. Also, keeping in mind that רוח often means 'wind', it is worth noting that it is through the physical release of air that we speak as well as breathe.

Our term has an intellectual nuance in Job as well. At 20.3, Zophar states that 'a spirit [רוח] from my understanding [מבינתי] answers me' (here paralleled to a word of instruction [מוסר] that has just 'defamed' him). And, foreshadowing God's final speech, Elihu states that it is not so much the passing of days and years that teaches wisdom (the experience of growing old), but 'it is the spirit [רוח] in a person, and the breath of the Almighty, which causes understanding [תבינם]' (32.8). It may be (we can better judge after reviewing the evidence) that, in Qoheleth's case, the notion that the רוח in a person provides understanding above and beyond that of acquired wisdom or received instruction brings to the fore in even clearer terms the distinctions between Qoheleth's experientially grounded epistemological procedures and the frame narrator's received ones.

d. *Two Texts of Interest*
1. *Job 10.8-11, 18-22*. Well into the stride of his complaining, Job states that he will tell Yahweh that he has despised the work of his own hands. Job loathes his metaphysical predicament—he has been created intricately and wonderfully by Yahweh, yet the same creator, it now seems, has turned upon him to destroy him (10.8-11):

> Your hands fashioned and made me;
>> yet at the same time you turn and destroy me.
> Remember that you fashioned me like clay
>> and you will return me to dust.
> Did you not pour me out like milk
>> and curdle me like cheese?
> With skin and flesh you clothed me,
>> and with bones and sinews you knit me together.

Job somehow knows what God has done—how God has formed and fashioned him—and uses this argumentatively. His argument is expressed in highly stylized speech. In the first two strophes of vv. 8-11 the activity of God vacillates between first creating, then destroying, then creating, then destroying. In the final two strophes he is only creating, and this is where the emphasis lies. The materials for creation (skin, flesh and bones) and even their corresponding expressions (milk and cheese) are raw and tactile. Even the operative metaphors for creation itself are textile (clothing and knitting). This self, the existence and eventual destruction of which Job is lamenting, forms as tangible an experience for the sufferer as the covering of a coat on a windy day.

A little later in the same chapter Job asks Yahweh (10.18-22),

> Why have you taken me from the womb?
> O that I would expire—that no eye would have seen me;
>> that I would be as though I had never been,
>> carried straight from the womb to the grave!
> Are not my days few? Cease! and leave me alone!
> Let me find a little comfort before I go (and I shall not return!)
>> to the land of darkness and of deathly shadow.

Job wishes things were different, and the implied anthropology is striking. In the extraordinary statement of v. 19a (כאשר לא־הייתי אהיה), he wishes his very existence away. Existing itself has become the source of his misery (cf. Eccl. 4.3; 6.3-5). His existence consists in the absolute opposite of nothingness, and because God actively took him from the womb, Job could not have escaped the experience that his self now faces. The existential dilemma foregrounds the self as an experiencing subject.

2. *Jeremiah 1.4-9.*

> And the word of Yahweh came to me saying,
>> 'Before I formed you[57] in the womb, I knew you.
>> Before you came out of the womb, I sanctified you.
>> As a prophet for the nations I appointed you.'
> I said, 'Ah, Lord Yahweh, behold, I do not know how to speak,
>> for I am only a youth.'
> Yahweh replied to me, 'Do not say "I am only a youth",
>> for to all to whom I send you, you shall go,
>> and all that I command you, you shall speak.
>> Do not fear their presence, for I will be with you,
>> in order to deliver you', said Yahweh.
> Then Yahweh put out his hand and touched my mouth;
> And Yahweh said to me, 'Behold, I have set my words in your mouth.'

As Jeremiah is faced with Yahweh's call, an impotency of the human spirit freezes him—he is unable to speak.[58] For Jeremiah, this impotence is the critical problem that Yahweh is addressing, and he addresses it by affirming Jeremiah's created origin and the tangibility of his self. The substance of that self existed before birth and constituted, in some sense, a person—for Yahweh himself *knew* it. It could

---

57. From צור, the steel forger's word—cf. Exod. 32.4; 1 Kgs 7.15.

58. לא־ידעתי דבר (Jer. 1.6); cf. the strikingly similar phrase at Eccl. 1.8: לא־יוכל איש לדבר.

even be set apart, made separate; for his principal activity in life (his profession?) was/is determined. Jeremiah can face the conflict with the knowledge that Yahweh will be with him and will place his words in his mouth (cf. Isa. 49.1-3).

The prophet is concerned about the futility of his speech, impaired by his youth. The concern, then (if speech is so connected to the quality of being), is for the formation of his character. 'The most striking literary achievement of that chapter [Jer. 1]', Sean McEvenue suggests, 'is to render in words a most sensitive encounter of a divine self and a human self... Jeremiah presents an imposed upon and querulous and suffering self.'[59] The self that Yahweh knew before bringing it into being will now be affirmed by asserting (as in Job's case) the expression of its speech by which it will be self-empowered. Although the self is inner and not humanly graspable, it is affirmed in this encounter between Jeremiah and Yahweh—through the promise of its being sent (to the nations) and its empowerment (speech). Here speech finds its genesis in the creator and in turn has a determinative effect on the subject.

Of the very few studies of the Hebraic conception of the self, most seek to address the issue of Hebraic wholeness over against that of Western dualism (body/soul) which, some hold, finds expression in the New Testament.[60] My review confirms that stance against (any supposed) Western dualism, although it must be stressed that the self as expressed through the metaphors may be contrasted to other 'parts' of the self, especially those metaphors that are *organic*.[61] Other words that refer to the inner person are בטן (belly, womb), כליא (kidneys, Ps. 139.13)

---

59. In personal correspondence, January 1995.

60. See G. Whitlock, 'The Structure of Personality in Hebrew Psychology', *Int* 14 (1960), pp. 3-13 (10); Laurin, 'The Concept of Man as a Soul', pp. 131-32; Cohen, 'The Heart in Biblical Psychology', p. 41; E.W. Marter, 'The Hebrew Concept of "Soul" in Pre-Exilic Writings', *AUSS* 2 (1964), pp. 97-108 (106-107); M.J. Boivin, 'The Hebraic Model of the Person', *JPsT* 19.2 (1991), pp. 157-65 (159). Boivin argues that the duality that scholars have argued against has been oversimplified, but agrees with the basic assertion that the Hebrew notion of self is far more holistic than the more Platonic notions assumed in the New Testament.

61. I.e. of human organs. נפש may be related to cognate words meaning 'throat' or 'breath' (see BDB, p. 659a) or 'stomach' (see Marter, 'The Hebrew Concept of "Soul"', p. 103); רוח can mean 'breath'; לב can refer to the 'heart' as the physical organ (e.g. 2 Kgs 9.24) or in general the chest area (see Fabry, '*lēḇ; lēḇāḇ*', p. 411).

and simply קֶרֶב (that which is inner). The former two are obviously physical, while the latter can refer to the physical inside of a person as well as the emotional and intellectual psyche. The physical overtones constitute an intricate part of the portrait of the individual. As Edmund Jacob suggests, the person in the Old Testament 'is a psycho-physical being and physical functions are bound so closely to [its] physical nature that they are all localized in bodily organs which themselves only draw their life from the vital force which animates them'.[62] Or, as R. Gundry puts it, the Hebraic person doesn't *have* a body, it *is* a body.[63]

R. Murphy is surely right in suggesting that 'there is no logical consistency within the Old Testament regarding the terms used to convey the make-up of the human individual'.[64] Yet from this brief analysis a portrait, if incomplete and even partially fragmented, of the Hebraic understanding of the self has emerged. It is whole, physical, created by God, a centre of existence, of courage, of will, of worship, of meditation and of intellect. For most biblical writers the identity of self was individual, for the prophets in particular it was national. Yet there is an awareness in all of the biblical texts that God creates something fixed, solid—a self that is as substantial as the metaphors suggest. The idea of self, as far as can be implied from these examples, is not merely language-based. Indeed, in the Old Testament the self-construct pre-exists the process of speech. The language of self is referential, referring

62. As cited in Boivin, 'The Hebraic Model of the Person', p. 161. Mark S. Smith has recently suggested that 'Israelites associated emotions with the internal organs where the emotions were perceived to be felt physically'; emotions that prepare 'the self for action' ('The Heart and Innards in Israelite Emotional Expressions: Notes from Anthropology and Psychobiology', *JBL* 117.3 [1998], pp. 427-36 [431, 436]).

63. As cited in Boivin, 'The Hebraic Model of the Person', p. 161. Boivin goes on to relate the consequences of this understanding of the physical person to psychoanalysis: 'the essential aspects of personhood...extend to the actions performed by the flesh (behavior), as well as to the physiology which mediates those actions' (p. 161); and this, says Boivin, is just the sort of corrective psychoanalysis needs. Such a 'totality' approach is, however, rightly questioned by Barr: 'Is it even remotely plausible that ancient Hebrews...already had a picture of humanity which agreed so well with the modern esteem for a psychosomatic unity?' (*The Garden of Eden*, p. 36).

64. *Ecclesiastes*, p. 37. Cf. the similar comments of Barr in relation to the problem of speaking of any one 'concept' of נֶפֶשׁ (*The Garden of Eden*, p. 38).

beyond itself to Another. That Another (self) is an object of mystery which, like God, cannot be empirically known but is intuitively sensed—felt in the most extreme of circumstances (Job, Psalms, Jeremiah), yet assumed in everyday existence (Pentateuch, Proverbs). It is made up of the body (the heart, the breath, the guts) and what we might call the mind or heart, soul or spirit; yet each is bound to the other.

4. *Qoheleth on* the *Self and* his *Self*

How did Qoheleth assume (or not?) the kinds of constructs of the self we have so far seen? To what extent did the Hebraic portrait of the self figure in Qoheleth's own? What thoughts or themes echo between them? To determine this I will mimic the outline of the last section by reviewing in Ecclesiastes the three key biblical words of self-reference. After that I will discuss some key passages in which Qoheleth delineates not only the self as subject, but the centre of his own experiencing self. This will bring us back, at sec. 5, to the forum of our initial concerns about the self and to the manner in which Qoheleth attempts to account for the self.

Two of the three words of self-reference, לב and רוח, are among Qoheleth's favourite words, and while נפש is not a favourite word, its presence is still relevant to the topic at hand. The first two words occur with surprisingly high frequency. In fact, רוח has its highest relative frequency in the Old Testament in Ecclesiastes, at 5.36 occurrences per 1000 words (Haggai and Job have the second and third highest frequencies with 4.33 and 2.54 respectively). Also, לב has its second highest frequency in Ecclesiastes, with 9.15 occurrences[65] (Proverbs is just ahead of Ecclesiastes with 9.77, and Obadiah follows on with a paltry 4.57).

a. לב

In Ecclesiastes this word can be classified into seven aspects, with few borderline cases. They are as follows (in descending order of frequency):

---

65. Although these statistics show the relative frequency as against occurrences in other biblical books, it should be noted that לב, not רוח, has the highest absolute frequency in Ecclesiastes—×42 as opposed to ×23. נפש occurs seven times.

(A)	instrument[66] of searching and/or testing (×11)[67]
(B)	instrument of moral 'good sense' (or its opposite) or belief (×10)[68]
(C)	seat of reasoning, inner-dialogue (×6)[69]
(D)	seat of joy, gladness (×6)[70]
(E)	seat of vexation, striving (×4)[71]
(F)	instrument of knowledge (×3)[72]
(G)	instrument of speech (×1, 5.1)

Among the biblical connotations reviewed in the previous section, it is the intellectual that finds its fullest expression in Ecclesiastes. For example, when the word is used in connection with Qoheleth's procedure of discovery (A), it is the לב that is fated to advance along the lines of intellectual inquiry, to seek and to explore by wisdom all that is done under the sun. It is the instrument by which Qoheleth makes his observations, and in this capacity it appears to take on a life of its own. In fact, it is the לב itself that often does the observing. At 9.1 Qoheleth states, 'I set my mind[73] to all of this [i.e. all that he had just observed in

66. Most instances display an understanding of the לב as *instrumental* in human experience. That is, it is an instrument of (channel of, vehicle for) Qoheleth's experiences (and of humanity's or 'the wise'); experiences that primarily consist of testing the value of wisdom and coming to know its vexation.

67. 1.13, 16b, 17; 2.3 (×2); 2.10 (×2); 7.25; 8.9, 16; 9.1.

68. 7.2, 4, 7, 21, 26; 9.3 (×2); 10.2 (×2), 3. At 7.26, the לב of the woman that Qoheleth observes is *like* the nets of a hunter. Although the heart can be anthropomorphized (2.10; cf. 2.20, 22, 23), this is the only instance where Qoheleth uses another concept to illustrate the nature of the/a heart. The woman's heart, for Qoheleth, exhibits her moral essence/sense. For in v. 25 he states that he is determined to understand evil and he then states in v. 26 that the woman is more bitter than death and that the sinner is taken by her.

69. 1.16a; 2.1, 15 (×2); 3.17, 18.

70. 7.3; 9.7; 11.9a, 10. At 11.10 the removal of כעס, vexation, may be understood in relation to the previously mentioned 'gladdening' (יטב) of the heart.

71. 2.20, 22, 23; 8.11.

72. 3.11; 7.22; 8.5.

73. The MT margin reads נתתי אל־לבי for נתתי את־לבי. Either way the sense remains that Qoheleth's לב is being *applied to* the matter at hand. On the use of אל with לב, see n. 78, below. Also, most translations offer 'mind' as opposed to 'heart' for לב (although cf. LXX which, in typically literal fashion, opted for καρδία instead of, e.g., νοῦς, 'mind'). I shall discuss the distinction further below. See above on the intellectual nuance of לב, which is likely present here.

the previous section, the unit of 8.15-17[74]], and [my mind] observed it all—that the righteous…' By this he makes clear that his procedure of discovery revolves around the activity of the לב itself. For Qoheleth, this centre of consciousness is vital to the overall tone of his queries.

It is perhaps significant that the first occurrence of לב (both the first intellectual nuance and the first occurrence of לב in the book) coincides with Qoheleth's proper introduction of himself. At 1.13 he sets out clearly what arenas of the self he will be operating in—observation, knowledge and the mind:

> I set my לב to investigate and to search out by wisdom all that has been done under the heavens. It is an evil business that God has given to human beings to be busy with.

The duality present here has unique implications. Because Qoheleth invokes his לב as a *separate* entity, he invites the reader to explore and observe his inner person as he does, for Qoheleth is, as Fox contends, 'his own field of investigation'.[75] The לב enjoys this privileged place as Qoheleth's intellectual centre, and it is from here that all of his observations will flow. Is this centre therefore the same as the 'I'? Not always. Qoheleth would have us view his experiences as he does, through a diversified lens. For example, at 1.16b it is again his לב that does the actual observing, acting as a narrative focal point for the reader. And in the next verse Qoheleth applies (נתן) his לב *for the purpose of* knowing wisdom and folly (1.16-17):[76]

> I said to myself, 'Behold, I have become great and increased in wisdom more than all who were before me over Jerusalem'; and my mind observed much wisdom and knowledge. And I set my mind to know wisdom and knowledge, madness and folly. I knew that this too was a pursuit of wind.

His לב justifies its own private existence as a narrative character and,

74. See p. 209 n. 108.
75. *Qohelet*, p. 87. It is interesting to note in this regard that elsewhere in the Old Testament the לב signifies 'the inaccessibly unexplorable…anything that is quite simply impenetrably hidden' (Wolff, *Anthropology of the Old Testament*, p. 43).
76. This duality features in most of the occurrences in the intellectual categories (A, C, F), particularly when the לב is applied to something or does the actual observing. In fact, any usage in which the לב is *instrumental* (A, B, F, G) implies separateness. Note the duality implied between body and the self's intent in 5.6: 'do not let your mouth [i.e. what you say rashly] lead your body [בשרך] into sin…'

along with the 'I', the student and the frame narrator, serves to fill out Qoheleth's tale.

Another undertone that emerged from the biblical overview and that is present in Ecclesiastes is the capacity to employ 'good sense'; that is, 'sound judgment in practical behavior and practical affairs'.[77] For example, it is better to avoid the house of feasting, says Qoheleth, and the living will 'take this to heart' (יתן אל־לבו, 7.2).[78] Yet the same phrase has a subtly different implication in 7.21, where Qoheleth urges his student in a moral tone:

> To all things that are spoken do not *set your heart*, lest you hear your servant cursing you. Surely your heart knows that many times you your- self have cursed others (7.21-22).

While the subject matter is different, the imperative to 'not take to heart' (or better, 'not believe') remains a moral one, here ratified by the 'golden rule', 'Do unto others...'

At 9.3, the moral significance of the heart is again made clear. The לב of the children of humanity, Qoheleth laments, is full of evil and there is madness (הוללות) in their hearts[79] while they live—and after- wards, to death. The heart here is a moral *place*, a nexus of being as over against behaviour, and lies at the core of Qoheleth's reflections on the fate of humanity. Whether they are wise or foolish, whether they sacrifice or do not sacrifice, what matters is that their hearts are full of evil—or, as he says elsewhere (8.11), the heart of human beings is set on *doing* evil—and this bears witness to the fate that humanity will be unable to avoid in this life.[80] Compare Gen. 6.5:

> The Lord saw that the wickedness of humanity was great in the earth and that every imagination of the thoughts of their hearts [וכל־יצר מחשבת לבו] was only evil continually [רק רע כל־היום].

Here, as in Qoheleth's text, the concern is with the moral quality (רע)

77. M.V. Fox, 'Wisdom in Qoheleth', in L.G. Perdue *et al.* (eds.), *In Search of Wisdom* (Louisville, KY: Westminster/John Knox Press, 1993), pp. 115-31 (118).

78. Qoheleth uses the stock biblical idiom אל־לב. Compare, for example, Gen. 6.6 (God was grieved to his heart); 2 Sam. 13.33 (David believed [שׂים] in/to his heart that his sons were dead); 2 Sam. 19.19 (Shimea asks David not to remem- ber—not set [שׂים] to heart—what he has done); cf. Eccl. 9.1.

79. בלבבם—the only occurrence of the related form, לבב.

80. As Fabry comments in relation to this verse, in Ecclesiastes 'wickedness and folly are so fundamental to the *lēb* ("human nature") that they are the cause of human mortality (Eccl. 9:3; cf. Prov. 10:21)' (*'lēb; lēbāb'*, p. 423).

of inner life (the יֵצֶר—intent, imagination [cf. צוּר, from the same root, in the Jeremiah text above]—of the thoughts of the mind/heart). It is a question of *being* motivating behaviour. In fact, at Eccl. 9.3 and elsewhere, the only characteristic of people of which Qoheleth seems sure is that which comes within the sphere of being and involves the לב.[81] He is sure that it exists outside of the enunciation that defines it and that it is linked to behaviour.

When Qoheleth is thinking, or reasoning at an inner, dialogic level[82]—that is, in the form of his 'I spoke in my heart' sayings (אמר בלב—equivalent to the phrase, 'talking to oneself'? or not talking out loud?; cf. Gen. 24.45)—we are given a privileged glimpse *inside* his character. It is worth noting that אמר בלב is a frequently employed device used to demonstrate the inner processes of a character in a *narrative* fashion. As Bar-Efrat comments, after reviewing a host of examples, the phrase, 'said in my/his/her heart' usually suggests that 'characters wish to convince themselves that the action they are taking, rather than an alternative course, is the right one'.[83] That is, the phrase represents an inner struggle. At Eccl. 2.1, for example, the implication is that Qoheleth's struggle is/will be *with* himself, essentially as another:

> I said in my heart [אמרתי אני בלבי], 'Come, I will test you [my heart?] with mirth and enjoy good things.' But behold, that too was absurd.

Indeed, it is in ch. 2 that this inner dialogue culminates and the heart is established as Qoheleth's fixed position of reference for the experiences of his youth upon which he reflects, and yet the intense inner-dialogic language persists throughout Qoheleth's narration. His heart bears the brunt of his most vexatious and joyous experience (cf. 9.1a), and we are again left with the distinct impression of a palpable experiencing self.

---

81. We might note the function of the heart in 3.11 in this regard. God places a sense of eternity in the heart of humanity, thereby denoting, as Fabry puts it, 'in a unique way the existential nature of humanity' ('*lēb; lēbāb*', p. 421).

82. Reference may again be made to Perry, *Dialogues with Kohelet*. Perry pushes the notion of dialogue between two major characters (P, the presenter and K, Koheleth) throughout Ecclesiastes, with interesting if sometimes excessive results. Compare Seow's comments: 'If the book as a whole is any reflection of the author's inner struggles, his debates with himself, one should not be surprised that various perspectives are considered at once, even contradictory ones' (*Ecclesiastes*, p. 41), which, I might add, is one of the 'cohesive' effects of autobiography.

83. *Narrative Art in the Bible*, p. 63.

This leads us to another general biblical category of the word, the emotional.

In his לב Qoheleth *feels* despair, striving, even evil, ער: 'And I turned to despair my heart [ליאש את־לבי] concerning all the toil at which I toiled under the sun' (2.20; cf. 2.22, 23; 8.11). And it is this disposition of misery that will find its redemption in the same *place*. That is, the לב will also be the locus where one of Qoheleth's most important themes is realized: joy and gladness. The heart is the place of שמחה:

> Everyone to whom God has given riches and wealth and has enabled to partake of them, and to take their portion and rejoice in their toil—this is a gift of God. Indeed, they will rarely remember the days of their lives, for God answers them[84] in the joy of their heart [בשמחת לבו] (5.18-19).

Recent attempts to show the importance of joy to Qoheleth's narrative have relied heavily on this passage,[85] but little if any attention has been given to the function of the heart here. The noun in the construct state possibly shows that the לב is capable of *owning* joy. But can joy be owned or is it something experienced? Does such a construct suggest a consistent quality of heart or an *encounter* with joy (an event)? Other biblical occurrences of the construct suggest the latter.

At Cant. 3.11 the daughters of Zion are encouraged to

> Go forth!…and behold King Solomon, with the crown with which his mother crowned him on the day of his wedding, on the day of the gladness of his heart [וביום שמחת לבו] (RSV).

Solomon's heart knows joy on an appointed day. It is a singular event. At Isa. 30.29 the prophet informs Jerusalem (in contradistinction to Assyria) that they

---

84. The root ענה is usually taken to mean 'occupy' or 'be busy with' (as is more clearly the case in 1.13 and 3.10, where it plays off of ענין, 'occupation'). But cf. the convincing arguments of N. Lohfink ('Qoheleth 5:17-19—Revelation by Joy', *CBQ* 52 [1990], pp. 625-35; esp. pp. 626-29). Lohfink's article takes ענה here to mean 'answer' or 'reveal' ('God answers [reveals himself] by/in the joy of humanity's heart'). The consequence is the startling proposal that Qoheleth's theology is revelatory, being offset by his more cynical approach to God and wisdom, but not overcome by it. Lohfink suggests that 5.18-19 is representative of a theme that permeates the book via such key phrases as 'fear of God' (3.14-15; 5.6; 7.18; 8.12-13; 12.13) and the joy theme in other passages; all part of the 'divine gift' of the knowledge of God.

85. Particularly the influential articles of Lohfink ('Revelation by Joy') and Whybray ('Qoheleth, Preacher of Joy', *JSOT* 23 [1982], pp. 87-98).

shall have a song as in the night when a holy feast is kept; and gladness
of heart [ושׂמחת לבב], as when one sets out to the sound of the flute to go
to the mountain of the Lord, to the Rock of Israel (RSV).

At Jer. 15.16, in the course of seeking the reassurance of his position,
Jeremiah responds to the Lord:

Thy words were found, and I ate them, and thy words became to me a
joy and the delight of my heart [ולשׂמחת לבבי]; for I am called by thy
name, O Lord, God of hosts (RSV).

In the above examples the construct state suggests not that the heart is
to 'become' always joyful, but that it is to *experience* joy as sacrament
(Canticles), worship (Isaiah) and self-understanding (Jeremiah); that is,
as a unique event. Likewise, in Ecclesiastes the place of the heart is
partly to receive the reply of the divine to its own misery, enabling it
for a time to forget the toil of living.

Other texts, while just as important to realizing the overall theme,
relate the לב more indirectly to joy. For example,

Better vexation than laughter;
for with a downcast face the *heart is made glad* (7.3).

And in Qoheleth's celebratory passages:

Go! Eat your bread with joy,
and drink your wine *with a glad heart*;
For God has already approved your deeds.
At all times let your garments be white,
and let oil not be lacking on your head... (9.7-8).

Rejoice, O young man, in your youth.
And *let your heart gladden you* in the days of your youth.
And *walk in the ways of your heart*,
and in the sight of your eyes.
And know for certain that concerning all of these things
God will bring you into judgment.
Remove vexation from your heart,
and take away misery from your body;
For youth and the prime of life are fleeting (11.9-10).

The heart should be glad (טוב) and it should gladden (יטב). The reference to Num. 15.39, which states that the ways of the heart are not to
be followed after, is worth mentioning again (see the discussion at
Chapter 4.4). The heart is what inclines a person to act. It is a movement of the will, which for Qoheleth is a source of gladness. However,

following after this inclination, according to the Numbers text, is no less than outright disobedience. The heart must be dedicated wholly to the Lord, and any abberation is to be rejected. Qoheleth's reversal in theology is a reversal in anthropology as well. He has no fear of his experience, and affirms the episode of the heart to be authentic and human (cf. Prov. 13.12).

In discussing this last aspect I have used the word 'heart', since the emotional implications, I believe, cannot be rendered well by 'mind'. But 'mind' is surely the best rendering in those instances when the לב functions as a centre of consciousness—most clearly in the dialogic and intellectual instances. It is due to elements such as these that Qoheleth has earned himself his reputation as the Old Testament's foremost individual thinker. Indeed, it is the *intellectual* self that rules Qoheleth's realms of thinking, yet it is offset by his acceptance of the emotional. While for Job the intellectual heart dominates, in Qoheleth we find a more balanced integration.

b. נפש

This word occurs only seven times in Ecclesiastes. Three of those can be passed over briefly. The first instance signifies a receptacle of pleasure and occurs within one of Qoheleth's 'better than' sayings (2.24). The second occurs in a narrative aside in which Qoheleth asks rhetorically, 'Why have I deprived *my soul* of good things?' (4.8). By such usage he effectively demonstrates an *inner* turmoil, and draws readerly sympathies. The third also employs the traditional sense of 'person', and describes Qoheleth's procedure of discovery. It was his נפש that sought to know the sum but could not find it out (7.28). The remaining four occur in ch. 6, in a remarkable set of statements.

Qoheleth's discussion in 6.1-5 is preoccupied with the satisfaction that the נפש is able (or not able) to obtain in its existence. The implication is that although some people enjoy a wealth of material goods, their inner selves remain insatiable. The lament is tragic and poetic:

> There is an evil that I observed under the sun, and it prevails upon humanity: [There is] a man to whom God has given riches and wealth and honour [so that] he lacks nothing for his soul [נפש] from all that he desires; yet God does not enable him to partake of them. Instead, a stranger partakes of them. This is absurd and a grievous ill.
> If [that] man begets one hundred children and lives many years, though many be the days of his years, and his soul [נפש] is not satisfied by [these] good [things]—and indeed, there is no burial for him—I said,

'The stillborn child [הנפל] is better off than he is.' For in absurdity it comes and in darkness it goes, and in darkness its name is covered. Although it has neither seen the sun nor understood it, it finds rest rather than he (6.1-5).

Qoheleth is obviously not referring to himself, but to an example of absurdity and evil that he has observed. The tragic comparison of the stillborn (an 'untimely birth' [cf. Job 3.16]—'in absurdity it comes and in darkness it goes') to the lack that this man's נפש experiences, suggests that the consciousness of absurdity and evil—which the נפש knows from living/experience—is worse than having never come into consciousness. The נפש, then, is what participates in living. It is what separates the living from the stillborn—from those who cannot or will not be. If its name is covered it cannot be remembered and can never know existence. It has not been able to see or *know* the sun. (And remember that seeing the sun is, for Qoheleth, living, being conscious of existence—7.11; 11.7; 12.2 [inversely].) The stillborn has not been aware of—nor has it perceived—the life the נפש knows.

A few lines later Qoheleth twice puts a new twist to the word:

All the toil of humanity is for their mouths, but the appetite [נפש] is not satisfied.
What advantage has the sage over the fool?
What have the foolish in knowing [how] to conduct themselves among the living?
Better the sight of the eyes
    than the wandering of the soul [נפש].
This too is absurd and a pursuit of wind (6.7-9).

Verse 7 serves as a neat summary of what has gone immediately before. Consciousness of the נפש is a vexation, for it has embodied an insatiable desire (cf. 1.8). In v. 9 the 'sight of the eyes' probably suggests what is immediately obtainable and, by implication, desirable (cf. 2.10), keeping well within the present motif. However, the phrase 'wandering of the soul' (or 'desire'—מהלך־נפש) is the problem here. The phrase may be, as Whybray points out, a 'circumlocution for dying',[86] since the verb הלך, in Ecclesiastes and elsewhere, can mean to 'depart', as in 'return to God'. If this is so, then Qoheleth is rejecting death (not to be confused with Ecclesiastesan non-existence) as an alternative, even an alternative to the vexation of existence. This is a

---

86. *Ecclesiastes*, p. 109.

splendid example of the primacy of existence to Qoheleth's thought.[87]

Another divergence can be observed here between Qoheleth and the biblical tradition. Gone is any seeming duality between the נפשׁ and the body. It is not so much that the נפשׁ and the body are separate as that in Ecclesiastes they are not distinguished as such. The 'experiences' of each are affirmed equally by Qoheleth. Indeed, the נפשׁ desires substance (טוב) as the body desires food. But the otherness of the נפשׁ and its inherent quality in defining existence remain intact.

c. רוח

It is worth remembering that this word has its highest relative frequency in Ecclesiastes. I have already discussed the significance of the phrases רעות רוח and רעיון רוח (see the Excursus), which account for 9 of the 21 occurrences of רוח in Ecclesiastes. But more significant to Qoheleth's concept of self are the remaining instances. Outside of the couplings with רעה (in all of which רוח most likely means 'wind'), רוח designates one of two meanings of 'spirit': (1) a characteristic or trait,[88] or (2) a 'life-force' (of an animal or person).[89]

The first meaning has some significance for our discussion. Two of the four examples occur in constructs in one of Qoheleth's 'better than' sayings. A patient spirit (ארך־רוח), says Qoheleth in 7.8, is better than a proud spirit (גבה־רוח). (Note the spatial play: lit. a long spirit is better than a high one!) Such adjectival usage is common in the biblical literature as a means of delineating the expected behaviour of a person or group, or simply of stereotyping for rhetorical effect.[90] As in Qoheleth's usage, it is a means of easily 'understanding' one's relation to others and to the world. The next verse (7.9) further expands on the 'better than' saying: 'Do not let your spirit be quickly vexed [אל־תבהל ברוחך לכעוס], for vexation rests in the bosom [בחיק] of fools.' By assigning the quality of patience to the spirit,[91] Qoheleth offsets his own ontological experience, for early on he had described his own self as racked with despair and vexation (1.18; 2.17-23 etc.), and will

87. Further on 6.7-9 and the significance of הלך, see my discussion in Chapter 8.2.

88. 7.8 (× 2), 9; 10.4.

89. 3.19, 21 (× 2); 11.5; 12.7.

90. Cf. Exod. 6.9; Num. 21.4; Job 21.4; Mic. 2.7.

91. Qoheleth also associates the spirit with *anger* at 10.4, and prescribes calmness as its antidote: 'If the spirit of the ruler [המושׁל] rises against you, do not yield your place; for calmness [מרפא] will quell great offences.'

conclude in ch. 11 by admonishing the student to remove vexation from his heart (and pain from his body, 11.10).

Where it occurs, the second meaning has generated much discussion. More than any of the references reviewed in Qoheleth's narrative so far, these reflect a theological concept of person. The most elaborate formulation of this comes at 3.18-21:

> I said in my heart concerning human beings, 'God has set them apart[92] to show them that they themselves are animals.' For the fate of human beings and the fate of the animals is the same fate: as one dies, so dies the other, and all have the same spirit [ורוח אחד לכל]. Humanity has no advantage over the animals, for everything is absurd [כי הכל הבל]. Everyone goes to one place. Everyone is from the dust and returns to the dust. Who knows whether the spirit of human beings goes upwards, or whether the spirit of the animals goes down into the earth?

It is significant that this group of observations is set in terms of inner reflection ('I said in my heart'). Qoheleth's observation on what constitutes the human self and its fate is intensely personal. From the narrative structure that we are given we can only assume that this is what Qoheleth *said* as a result of his test of wisdom and pleasure 'just' experienced in the first two chapters. Its primary narration is *tunc* (*then* as opposed to *now*), and roots the saying firmly in the experiential. Qoheleth himself *knows* that just as it is fair to say that the fool and the sage die the same death (2.14, 16), so it is fair to equivocate the fate of human and animal. The experiential strain is kept in the foreground.

Qoheleth concludes that 'the way of all flesh' (their wandering and their demise) under the sun is inherently flawed. He ascribes no blame to anyone or anything. That the human spirit is like this is simply a fact. It is the way things are, and it is connected to the absurd. It is *due to*[93] הבל (i.e. as a principle observed in the world) that the spiritual fate of humanity is reduced to the same as that of the animals of the earth

92. לברם האלהים, 'God set them (humanity) apart'. 'Set apart' or 'separate' is the most clearly attested meaning for the root ברר, but does not agree with some commentators and most translations (RSV, NASB, NIV, NRSV), which opt for 'test'. But, as Fox argues, with the accompanying verb 'to show' (ולראות, '[in order] to show them'; so the sense of Peshitta and LXX, 'to separate' makes the most sense. It is by placing humanity below the heavens, to share mortality with the animals, that God shows them that they are like the animals, yet not (as made clear in Gen. 3) like God (*Qohelet*, p. 198).

93. Such is the causative force of כי in 3.19, as in, for example, 2.17; 4.10; 6.11; the second כי in 9.5; and 12.3.

(בהמה).[94] Qoheleth has already perceived that there is no logical relationship between deed and consequence, particularly as regards what he
can grasp of the human predicament of toil and fate, so this comes as
no surprise. It is inescapable, and the fact of it raises the question of
advantage.

This again sets Qoheleth apart from the rest of the biblical literature.
The virtual equation of the human 'life-breath' to that of the animal is
not necessarily a radical one (cf. Gen. 1.30; 2.7), but it is so rarely
expressed in the Old Testament that it may seem so. Also, Qoheleth
takes the Genesis formulation further; that is, to death. The prophets
and sages had not asked, as Qoheleth does, What profits humanity
given such a plight? If humanity is, like the beasts, so strictly isolated
from God (3.18b; and cf. 5.2: 'God is in the heavens and you are on the
earth'), even in death, what *does* set humanity apart? To push the case
further, what makes people human? What constitutes the other/self?
Whereas elsewhere in the Bible the constitution of the self is assumed,
Qoheleth raises questions about it.

Another occurrence of רוח also brings out this concern. At the conclusion of Qoheleth's elegant contemplation on old age, his final words
are as follows (and it is worth remembering that since the frame narrator commences his text in the next verse, these are *Qoheleth's* final
words to the reader):

> And the dust returns to the earth as it was,
> and the spirit returns to God who gave it (12.7).

Here he alludes to the question at 3.21, 'Who knows...?' But the narrative context is significant. In ch. 3 Qoheleth's *tunc* stance placed his
statement within an experiential context, which made his question a
rhetorical 'fact' based on his own empiricism. Here, however, Qoheleth
is at the story's end and he has shifted from observation to wise counsel. Indeed, the context of the poem itself forces the reader to allow
Qoheleth a certain laxity with his technicity of vocabulary. This is not a
formulaic statement, but a poetic climax imbued with a great deal of
rhetoric so that the reader—as the poem has rhythmically established—

94. As virtually all the commentaries point out, the force of the question is
negative and Qoheleth is likely refuting a concurrent notion that there was a difference between the fate of humans and of animals. In other words, people may claim
to know that humans go one way and animals another, but as far as what is observable (and we should expect this meaning from the Bible's chief empiricist), their
fate in death is the same.

should remember. Here is a lyrical affirmation of creation's link to God, insinuating its intrinsic worth: the self originated from its creator and will return to it.[95]

There is one borderline case that is worth considering. At 8.8a Qoheleth states that

> No one has authority over the spirit [שׁלִיט ברוח] to retain the spirit [לכלוא את־הרוח] and no one has authority over the day of death [שׁלטון ביום המות].

If רוח does mean 'spirit' here[96] then Qoheleth is reiterating human ignorance and impotence in the face of death. The spirit, its fate and movement, is not bound to the realm of human governance. The logical conclusion is that such fate rests in the hands of God.[97] Like the נפשׁ in the general biblical review, the prospects of the רוח are likely caught up in the divine will, and this affirms, more explicitly than 3.18-21, the value of the human spirit and its essential freedom (that is, from human governance, but not from what may befall humanity at any time).

While the Job texts reflect the idea that the רוח in a person provides understanding above and beyond that of acquired wisdom or received instruction, this aspect appears to be missing here. Also missing is Job's idea that the רוח is a provocation of speech. Instead, in Ecclesiastes, this favourite word of Qoheleth's[98] has more to do with the individual's relationship to the future unknown—death especially. More than in any other biblical texts dealing with the רוח, Qoheleth uses it to show a concern for the value of selfhood and the individual spirit and its freedom.

d. *Two Key Texts*
1. *1.12–2.26*. What can we learn about Qoheleth's attitude to the self

---

95. Barr notes that Qoheleth may have drawn on the language of Gen. 2.7 to make the distinction that although the flesh returned to dust (cf. Eccl. 3.20), the spirit 'went in a different direction' and returned to God (*The Garden of Eden*, p. 44).

96. So, for example, Gordis ('spirit of life', *Koheleth*, p. 280) and Murphy ('life-breath', *Ecclesiastes*, p. 80), who perhaps opt for such a translation over 'wind' on the grounds of the following paralleled thought concerning the 'day of death'.

97. Cf. 3.10, 18; 5.18; 7.14; 8.15; 9.1; 11.5; 12.7.

98. It appears sixteenth in Loretz's list of Qoheleth's 28 favourite words (cited in Murphy, *Ecclesiastes*, p. xxix).

from what he has to say about his own self? First of all, Qoheleth tells
us very little 'about' himself. Apart from the frame narrator's text most
of the relevant material comes from chs. 1–2. On its own that passage
reads like the beginning of a good story. It begins with Qoheleth's
poem on the circuity of the cosmos and proceeds with his list of
achievements (2.4-10), which continues the storytelling style of the
passage. There is, however, something odd about this passage that is
likely noticed only on reflection. The quest is not happening as we read.
We are reading about it as a past event. The tense fluctuates from past
narration to present and back and so forth. It begins with a clear past
tense (1.12-13a) and then returns to the present with a conclusion/
reflection (1.13b). It is a style that is found elsewhere in the book but is
particularly striking here. It is thoroughly engaging and continues
throughout the passage:

storytelling	1.12-13a
conclusion/reflection	1.13b
storytelling	1.14a
conclusion/reflection	1.14b-15
storytelling	1.16-17
conclusion/reflection	1.18
storytelling	2.1a-b
conclusion/reflection	2.1c
storytelling	2.2-3

The effect of the reflections is to engage the reader in the present of
narration/reading. It is to remind us that there is a critical distance being
kept. And although the interspersed reflections precipitate Qoheleth's
final attitude to the story being told, it is the storytelling parts that dominate here. This suggests that the most important thing for Qoheleth is
to *relate* his story. The narration is 'spoken' directly to the reader in
that there is no intermediary figure; Qoheleth, as elsewhere, stands
alone. This solitude is enhanced (if not caused completely) by the use
of the first-person preterite. The preterite sets the story in the past and
the narrator in the 'present' moment of telling/reading, and unless there
is a story-setting for the narrating moment, there is no audience but the
reader. Like Job (see above on Job 7.11), Qoheleth will only find relief
through this unhindered speech. His (remembered) experience is pent
up and in need of release. The experiencing subject is thus fore-
grounded as the quest begins.

He was a king (of sorts!), a builder of vineyards, of parks, of gardens;
a wealthy man. He made these things *for himself* (לי, 'for me', is the

operative word that frequently occurs in the references to building and acquiring). In other words, he virtually 'made' himself and leads us to believe that, as a result, he considered himself a man of great importance. His importance was both social and intellectual, for *he defined himself* in terms of status and material wealth.[99] His intellectual ability had even become part of that status ('I said...."Behold, I have become great and increased in wisdom more than all who were before me over Jerusalem"', 1.16). It was this 'definition' of himself that he set out to test at the beginning of ch. 2:

> I said in my heart, 'Come, I will test you with mirth and enjoy good things.' But behold, that too was absurd. 'To laugh', I said, 'is madness; and to be merry, what use is it?' I set out in my heart to cheer my flesh with wine (my heart conducting itself with wisdom), and to take hold of folly until I should see what was good for human beings to do under the heavens the few days of their lives (2.1-3).

Here is a full-blown interest in the constitution of his own self, and it results in a concern for action: What is the best humanity can do given their situation? In this regard, it is no coincidence that the majority of Qoheleth's advice to his reader occurs towards the end of his narration, after the majority of his experiences have been related.

As a result of the definition of self that Qoheleth chooses, he comes to despair his very life:

> I hated life, for the work that has been done under the sun was grievous to me. Indeed, everything was absurd and a pursuit of wind! And I hated all my toil at which I toiled under the sun, seeing that I must bequeath it to the man who comes after me; and who knows whether he will be a sage or a fool? Yet he will be master of all my toil at which I toiled and at which I was wise under the sun. This too is absurd.
>
> And I turned to despair my heart concerning all the toil at which I toiled under the sun (2.17-20).

His toil and reputation—that is, all by which he defined himself—will leave him in death and will probably go to a fool. Qoheleth found little satisfaction in what he regarded his own self to be, and such failure was a source of vexation.

This passage crystallizes the many subtle intimations to inner experience that Qoheleth makes throughout his narration. As Brown states,

---

99. Brown, in reference to the same texts, states the case well: 'In social means and stature, Qoheleth is one step beyond the biblical Job in the business of wisdom' ('Character Reconstructed: Ecclesiastes', p. 121).

'The bulk of this book...consists of a person who, like Job, shares his personal discoveries and bares his soul, but without dialogic partners.'[100] For example, because each הבל judgment emanates from Qoheleth's 'brooding consciousness' (Fox), an *individual* relationship to the absurd is evoked. The absurd is both defined by Qoheleth's experience and the self which that experience reflects.[101]

2. 7.23-24.

All this I tested with wisdom [בחכמה]. I said, 'I will become wise [אחכמה].' But it was far from me. What has been is far off and deep, surely deep. Who can discover it?

Commentators have long recognized the glaring problem here. Qoheleth has clearly stated that he did achieve wisdom (esp. in ch 2), and even here wisdom is the instrument by which he will explore,[102] but he then claims that becoming wise was far from him. To solve the dilemma it has been suggested that Qoheleth is employing two types of wisdom: the practical (by which he explores), and the elusive divine wisdom that he cannot attain.[103] What has been outrightly overlooked, however, and which also sheds light on the passage, is both the significance of the verb חכם and its narrative context.

What does Qoheleth mean by אחכמה? Of all 28 occurrences of the verb, חכם (be/become wise), in the Old Testament only 3 are first-person singular: Eccl. 2.15, 19 and 7.23.[104] Therefore, only in Ecclesiastes is the idea of becoming wise related so reflexively to the speaker. In the *tunc* of Qoheleth's story, becoming wise is within the grasp of the experience of his self. Unlike Job 28 and Proverbs 8, where the poet seeks wisdom itself, Qoheleth seeks to *be* wise—to *become* wise. There is, perhaps, an intimation towards a philosophized sense of becoming

100. 'Character Reconstructed: Ecclesiastes', p. 121.

101. Compare Brown's statement: '*Heḇel* is as much a description of the absurdity of the cosmic and human condition as it is an indication of *how the self is positioned in relation to the world in its totality*' ('Character Reconstructed: Ecclesiastes', p. 131; italics Brown's).

102. Note Fox: 'it is precisely *bĕhokmâ*—"by intellect"—that one inquires into such matters [as the frustration of inquiry]' ('Wisdom in Qoheleth', p. 119).

103. E.g. Gordis, *Koheleth*, p. 270. See the discussion in Murphy, *Ecclesiastes*, pp. 71-72. Also, see my discussion on wisdom as Helper, Chapter 8.3.

104. 7.23, as G.A. Barton noted, is the only instance of a cohortative verb in the book, and therefore 'expresses strong resolve' (*Ecclesiastes*, p. 147).

here, a becoming that is far off and deep. This would not be too rarefied an idea to attribute to Qoheleth, particularly considering that he recognized 'being' as an entity unto itself, including in the passage under consideration: 'What has been [שהיה] is far off.'[105] The notion of becoming supports the idea that there are degrees of wisdom at work here, for Qoheleth draws a sharp distinction between practical and spiritual wisdom: one a wisdom of action, the other of being.

The other instances of the first-person verb in ch. 2 refer to the past failed experiment. Eccl. 2.15 is especially notable:

> And I said in my heart [ואמרתי אני בלבי], 'As is the fate of the fool, so it will befall me.' Why, then, was I exceedingly wise? [ולמה חכמתי אני אז יותר] And I said in my heart [ודברתי בלבי], 'This too was absurd.'

The הבל judgment suggests that becoming wise should have been a successful enterprise, but, as in 7.23-24, it had clearly failed. To be sure, the language suggests that, if within the realm of possibility, becoming wise would involve the self in its entirety.[106] Furthermore, as with all the other 'I said in my heart' passages, Qoheleth is referring to past experience.[107] This puts a striking twist to the observation. Qoheleth is narrating from an enlightened perspective. Having observed its trappings, he concludes resolvedly (in his heart) the failure of the process of becoming wise. This is enhanced by the fact that in 7.23-24 he, in effect, concludes *from* the preceding observations, which have to do with wisdom's value.[108] The failure of this process is one thing of which Qoheleth can be sure, and the narrative device heightens this sense of resolution.

---

105. Other texts that reflect this recognition of 'being' are 1.9; 3.15; 6.10; 8.7; and 10.14.

106. Note the repetition of 'heart' and the emphatic אני.

107. 2.1, 2; 3.17, 18; 6.3. In each of these cases the narrative stance is clearly reflective. Take, for example, 3.16: 'But still I observed under the sun that in the place of justice there was wickedness, and in the place of righteousness there was wickedness.' Now consider the context of 3.17: '*I said in my heart*, "God will judge the righteous and the wicked"; for [there is] a time for every matter and for every deed.' Like the test just narrated in ch. 2, Qoheleth is *telling* the reader his thoughts, which result from self-reflection and experience.

108. That 'all this' refers to the preceding observations of ch. 7 as opposed to the proceeding section (vv. 25-29) is supported by the fact that what precedes is also concerned with the failure of wisdom, particularly the ambiguity of its value (7.15-19). Admittedly, 'all this' could serve as a link to what follows *as well* (cf. 7.28 esp.).

e. *Splitting Image*

Were we to imagine Jacques Lacan's question, 'Is the subject I speak of when I speak the same as the subject who speaks?',[109] delivered as a pensive, reflective aside in Qoheleth's narration, the result would be illuminating. The answer, as befitting Qoheleth's rhetorical style, would obviously be no. It cannot be yes since Qoheleth distances himself as a speaking subject, an observing subject. Both Fisch and Brown have observed this phenomenon in Ecclesiastes. For Brown it is because Qoheleth cites his 'accomplishments' as failures that he makes his narrated self a 'stranger', and therefore separates his 'reputation' (public image) from his individuality or essence. Qoheleth thereby 'steps out of himself' and creates a ghost.[110] Fisch sees in Qoheleth's 'self-duplication' an 'ironic mode', which, by its smiling awareness of what happens to itself, constitutes something 'near the very ground and origin of all irony'.[111]

As autobiographer, Qoheleth is capable of distinguishing himself from his (narratorial) past point of view. That is, because he is aware that he is narrating his own subjective past (the 'event of self-consciousness is inseparable from the history of saying "I"'),[112] he transcends it and creates two characters in the process: the one whom we envision writing or speaking—in real time—and the one about whom is written or spoken—in narrated time. As James Olney says of reflective autobiographical literature,

> while it is true to say that one can see with no other eyes than one's own, it is also true to say that one can, after a manner, see oneself seeing with those eyes: one can take a point of view on the point of view one has taken, and so...transcend the point of view through the point of view.[113]

Qoheleth sees himself seeing with the same eyes. He sees a youthful

---

109. Cited in Barthes, 'Introduction to the Structural Analysis of Narratives', p. 112.

110. 'Character Reconstructed: Ecclesiastes', pp. 130-33.

111. Fisch comments further that 'even as the philosopher contemplates himself as the passive *object* of a universal *process*, his active contemplation of this process in the language of philosophy detaches him from the process, affirms his freedom and independence as a *subject*... Irony brings together man as object, immersed in the world, and man as a subject, capable of rising superior to pains and pleasures' ('Qohelet: A Hebrew Ironist', p. 169; italics Fisch's).

112. Calvin Schrag, cited by Gusdorf, 'Conditions and Limits of Autobiography', p. 38.

113. *Metaphors of Self*, p. 43.

king who saw that his life was abhorrent. He sees a sensitive sage who saw that the oppressed had no comforter to comfort them. Qoheleth is thus a thinker in that he thinks/sees/observes *about* thinking/seeing/ observing. Qoheleth understands the process of (failed and, by implica- tion, successful) understanding. In such a way Qoheleth transcends himself. Through his continually self-conscious narration Qoheleth demonstrates awareness of his past. And so is established a focal point for readers: Does he smile wryly at his past? Does he frown at his folly? Does he weep? Both the self (*subject*) and Qoheleth's self, through his reflective redoubling, are brought into the sharpest relief.

5. *Accounting for the Self*

Qoheleth's way of accounting for the self offers an adequate measure of experience—a way of understanding what it means to be human— and we may consider/judge it in contradistinction to the deconstructive approach of accounting for the self outlined above. I do not claim to pass judgment by some objective standard but rather I offer my own subjective consideration. Mine is merely an attempt to question the adequacy of these distinctive world-views as a reader.

I began this chapter by outlining two elements for consideration. (1) Qoheleth is, like a candleflame in mist, 'there', in and through his narration. Readers reflect this experience of 'brushing with' Qoheleth the person in their responses to and renditions of his story. I answered the 'why' of this fact by suggesting that his narrative demonstrates a concern for character formation and reflection on experience through autobiography, cohesion, the splitting of image and so forth, through all of which Qoheleth leaves an indelible impression on readers. (2) The deconstructed notion of self heralds the death of the author and of the subject. The self is dead because we cannot find it. There is no referen- tial link available that enables interaction with Another—with a person. The most important implication from this is that since the self can only be a product of language (and not vice versa), self-existence is made difficult to affirm, establish and/or communicate.

These two positions are made incongruous by the fact that Qoheleth's involves a reading experience, while the deconstructive is a broad theory that, while encompassing reading, attempts to account for human communication in general. They are, however, able to be linked by three points. (1) The deconstructive is discussed and formulated through writing *and* reading. (2) Both positions are credal. The first is founded on a reading hunch and yet can be discussed critically, while the second asks us to believe that, contrary to our expectations, we do not exist outside of the enunciations that define us. (3) The positions are made 'conversable' in that Qoheleth's claims about his own self, as we have seen, amount to claims about the subject and the self in general. His treatment of the *subject* forces us to look hard at it—and 'What you look hard at', said Gerard M. Hopkins, 'seems to look hard at you.'[114]

To clarify the matter, in Qoheleth's concern for the formation of his own self is implied a wider view of the self. That is, his self-reflective language acts metaphorically as a way to understand the concept of self as a whole—it is a mirror text. His narrated experience is a way of observing the development of the self over the expanse of time. As autobiography it becomes a way for readers to examine the arenas in which the formation of the self might take place. We look hard at Qoheleth's self (he gives us no choice) and our gaze is returned, with the (frightening?) prospect that the quality of our own selves will be reflected (to be הבל?).

Qoheleth's view shares an interesting trait with the deconstructive. Qoheleth acknowledges that he cannot discover the reasons why things happen the way they do and in this he is sceptical of ideologies that he has received.[115] In fact, just as the deconstructive competes with the Cartesian, Qoheleth's way of accounting for experience, as has been widely noted, competes within its own canon by overturning received ideas. But the similarity ends here.

Qoheleth tests a way of accounting for his 'youthful' experience—one that is not unlike the deconstructive position—and is wholly dissatisfied by it. As the reader follows Qoheleth on his self-journeying (and this decidedly more intensely than in any other biblical book) the question of fate is a constant subtext. What will be the end result of testing wisdom *with* his heart? How will Qoheleth's self (part Qoheleth, part Solomon, part disillusioned, part full of life) fare in the face of the absurd world? For Qoheleth attempted first to define himself in terms of wealth and reputation, and this failed miserably. In this respect it was the media-based image of self (an image connected as we have seen to the death of self) that Qoheleth tried and tested. He did attempt to

---

114. Cited in Olney, *Metaphors of Self*, p. 33.

115. Further, see my discussion of his ideological differences with the frame narrator in Chapter 4.

define his own identity in reference to a public persona—based on material wealth and so forth—and this failed him. That failure was itself absurd. For Qoheleth, the self was in need of a more substantial base for definition than the experience of extreme folly and mirth could offer. In the end result, the self must be further defined by an honest confrontation with the absurd. There are also, beyond the test of wisdom (which was really a test of his own self), some germane observations: relationships do fail (many are based on envy, 4.4); the attempt to understand God fails (3.11; *passim*); and Qoheleth asks repeatedly of human striving and of toiling for good things, For what purpose—what advantage—are these? Qoheleth's is the failure of living, for not only is it better never to have been born (cf. esp. 4.1-3 and ch. 6) but the day of death is better than the day of birth (7.1). To put it another way, the failure of living is the failure of the self to achieve definition satisfactorily—otherwise life is not absurd but merely meaningless.

Ultimately Qoheleth's narrating stance sets apart his idea of the self from the nihilism of the deconstructed self in its assertion of what it means to be human. In Qoheleth's acknowledgment of the failure of living he affirms the reality of the experience of those who live. By saying that the stillborn is better off than the living he affirms that it is because there is a defining faculty in the individual that that person, while living, is prevented from being consigned to the designation, 'cipher of words'. By thinking, by reflecting on events, by centring the place of experience and by feeling the weight of absurdity so deeply he acknowledges that the self is not simply a mental peg on which to hang his ideas and observations. The self is at the centre. The movement of expression is from Qoheleth's mind/heart, soul and spirit *to* speech. Furthermore, each of these terms relates to *Another* and/or affirms the authenticity of the self. The לב is the place of שׂמחה where God answers and where the act of feeling life is not feared but is affirmed. Although not linked directly to God, the נפשׁ establishes the primacy of existence by rejecting death as an alternative to vexatious existence. The רוח returns to God who made it—the self's origin—and the (intellectual) comprehension of its experience is thereby asserted. In fact, Qoheleth exhibits the primacy of existence (see the Postscript)—and it is an existence not of words or the constructs of speech but of his self outside of the words that enunciate its presence, for those words are regardless הבל in the end and ultimately fail to express life's brightest and darkest experiences. God answers humanity not with words in the wind, but with joy in the heart, in the innermost and secret places.

The crisis in which the self has lost its privileged place, and in which we can find no more 'causal efficacy for the self', is alien to Qoheleth's world. In Qoheleth's world the causes, if absurd, for the failure of the self are brutally clear. The world and the self's relationship to it are not as they should be. This places every individual in Qoheleth's world (everything and everyone under the sun) under the vexatious curse of futile toil and circular existence. To state it another way, the concreteness of Qoheleth's experience is what defines his personhood. As Dietrich Bonhoeffer put it, 'the person, as a conscious person, is created in the moment when he is moved, when he is faced with responsibility, when he is passionately involved in a moral struggle, and confronted by a claim which overwhelms him. *Concrete personal being arises from the concrete situation.*'[116] There is redemption (and I will discuss that more extensively in the next chapter), but the point here is that the self cannot escape its very real existence.

Qoheleth's 'younger' self, split from his older, telling self, is remarkably like the postmodern self, one 'consumptive of images and experiences [a self that] will likely prove to be even more insatiable than its modern [colonial and imperial] ancestor'.[117] Like Qoheleth's media-based self, it is found wanting. Here is a qualitative popular appeal of Ecclesiastes and something that might even go towards explaining its inclusion in the canon: its truthfulness in describing the human condition, then as now. As Roger Lundin says of the cultural, postmodern self, 'There is no goal for [its] actions...save the fulfilment of its desires.'[118] And this is a driving force of Qoheleth's story: the fulfilment of desire and the inability to contain or achieve it; for Qoheleth and those he observes find לא־תשׂבע, no satisfaction, no fulfilment of desire (1.8; 4.8; 6.3; cf. 6.7 and the waning of desire in the closing poem).

At least one scholar has made a case for Qoheleth espousing elements of deconstruction, such as, for example, the undermining of

---

116. From Dietrich Bonhoeffer's doctoral thesis, *Sanctorum Communio (Communion of Saints)*, cited in J. de Gruchy (ed.), *Dietrich Bonhoeffer: Witness to Jesus Christ* (The Making of Modern Theology; London: Collins, 1988), p. 46 (italics mine).

117. Middleton and Walsh, *Truth Is Stranger Than It Used to Be*, p. 55.

118. Cited in Middleton and Walsh, *Truth Is Stranger Than It Used to Be*, p. 59.

traditional ways of knowing.[119] And I have heard people in the 'guild' of biblical studies refer to Qoheleth as a sort of bedfellow of postmodernity. While it is true that Qoheleth displays a subversive tendency to undermine what is generally 'accepted', he does not take the further step of carnivalizing the practice. That is a wholly new enterprise. Qoheleth did not 'play with the text' of his ancestors. He brought into question their ways of knowing by bitterly detracting the results and thereby heralded a wholly new set of values embodied in an honest confrontation with evil and injustice that found no easy answers.

119. See Schloesser, 'A King is Held Captive in her Tresses', pp. 210-11.

Chapter 8

QOHELETH'S QUEST

> Man is the shuttle, to whose winding quest
> And passage through these looms
> God ordered motion, but ordained no rest.
> > Henry Vaughan (*Silex Scintillans*, 'Man' [1650–55])

> But where shall wisdom be found?
> And where is the place of understanding?
> Mortals do not know the way to it,
> And it is not found in the land of the living.
> The deep says, 'It is not in me',
> And the sea says, 'It is not with me' ...
> It is hidden from the eyes of all living...
> Abaddon and Death say,
> 'We have heard a rumour of it with our ears'.
> > Job 28.12-14, 21-22 (NRSV)

Qoheleth's is not an aimless odyssey, for there is seemingly a definite goal at hand. It is not a trek, for there is no demanding physical journey (although, as we shall see, Qoheleth uses language that creates such an impression of motion). It is not an intense search for a material object. Qoheleth is embarked on a *quest*. His is the act of seeking or pursuing a goal, an object of intrinsic but immaterial value. That act touches every corner of Qoheleth's narrative, and its intensity causes readers to recognize in Qoheleth a sincere commitment[1] (although they might not always agree about what, precisely, Qoheleth is searching for).

What makes this a narrative feature? Any presentation of quest must involve a *proleptic* element of story. We have seen how prolepsis works to create an initial tension in Ecclesiastes—for Qoheleth begins

---

1. Take, for example, Ryken's comment that 'the writer of Ecclesiastes is a great organizer and stylist committed to the intellectual quest for truth' (*Words of Delight*, p. 320).

with knowledge and the reader is left to fill in the details as to how he attained it. We have also seen how the plot is propelled forward by the frame narrator's kernel event at 1.1-2. It creates the expectancy that Qoheleth's character will become rounded and full in the course of his narration. The plot concerns Qoheleth himself, for the outcome of his actions will only affect him. The whole notion of his quest, then, is related to the self, for it is the nature of his own self that Qoheleth tested and sought out, and part of what he *discovers* is just what he is 'made of'.[2]

Qoheleth's dramatic quest often creates strong reactions in readers. Perhaps it is because stories of explorers have a luminous quality. With great interest some read the exploits of explorers who dedicate themselves whole-heartedly to pushing boundaries that, to our own minds and to the canon of our culture's received ideas, are immovable barriers. Thinking analogically, Qoheleth's quest has its own reference points—its own boundaries and limitations that Qoheleth attempts to overcome. These are landmarks in a metaphysical terrain. And what is the purpose implied in his movement there? What are the recognizable features of that landscape of the heart and mind that Qoheleth travels in order to achieve his destination? What is it that readers seek to find in his exploits? Has he pushed beyond the constraints of some intellectual boundary that mirrors something more personal in our own intellectual experience? Has he found what he was looking for? Are his the remains, as Paul Haupt commented, 'of a daring explorer, who has met with some terrible accident, leaving his shattered form exposed to the encroachments of all sorts of foul vermin'?[3] And what is that elusive object he pursues? The concern of this chapter is to draw up a guide to that not necessarily tangible terrain.

1. *Success, Failure and Many Questions*

'Where is the rule then, and what hope can we have of success or profit?'
Pécuchet, Gustave Flaubert's *Bouvard et Pécuchet*[4]

2.   Compare Fisch's comment: 'What he [Qoheleth] mainly has to tell us of course in this extended discourse of the self is not the account of material achievements—we hear little of these after the sentences...from chapter 2—but the account of his mental voyaging, his self-discoveries in the region of "Wisdom"' ('Qohelet: A Hebrew Ironist', p. 158).

3.   Cited in Barton, *Ecclesiastes*, pp. 27-28.

4.   *Bouvard et Pécuchet* (trans. A.J. Krailsheimer; London: Penguin Books,

There is a popular conception that Qoheleth sought out what Fisch calls the 'aesthetic ideal',[5] and that this search forms the overall structure and meaning of the book. In discussing the meaning of Ecclesiastes with friends who generally have no critical background in biblical studies I often find that Qoheleth is likewise seen as a maverick of sorts who was able to achieve fame and fortune and reject it all in a grand swipe of bitter cynicism—often in the guise of King Solomon. I like to think that the comments of my grandmother, Helen Ross, in a letter she wrote upon learning that I would be studying Ecclesiastes (and not much else!) for four years, are representative of a great deal of readers:

> So, you're studying the beautiful Book of Ecclesiastes... But why so much time with one when there are 65 others that are beautiful too?... I have read and re-read it many times and I try to understand it as I believe it was meant to be understood... Solomon had the whole world at his feet, he drank deeply from the cup of life, monarchs came from every kingdom to marvel at his wisdom, wealth, temple, servants etc, he had 700 wives and 300 concubines (can you imagine?) but they did not satisfy his soul, for over and over he said 'All is Vanity' (29 October 1991).

The key to this reading is the notion of success and competing failure. Qoheleth/Solomon did succeed at reaching one state of affairs and failed at another. I think the reading is well on the mark. The popular conception of Qoheleth's story as having won his personal success at the onset (i.e. as his initial proleptic stance from an older age) is one that is confirmed by the conclusions of the above review of the Solomonic guise: Qoheleth's proclamations are about a doomed enterprise. Rabbi Harold Kushner states the reading in another way:

> In his book, he tells us the story of his life. He writes of his successes and his frustrations, of all the ways in which he tried to be successful and make something of his life, and of all the reasons why the question, What does it all mean in the long run? was never really answered... He is a man desperately afraid of dying before he has learned how to live.[6]

1976 [1881]), p. 56.

5. For Qoheleth, through חכמה, 'The aesthetic ideal is beheld, pursued, achieved, and also rejected' ('Qohelet: A Hebrew Ironist', pp. 160-61).

6. *When All You've Ever Wanted Isn't Enough* (Sydney: Pan Books, 1987), pp. 37-38. Compare Ryken's comment: '[Qoheleth's] quest is...a journey of the mind and soul. It is the most crucial of all quests—the quest to find satisfaction in life' (*Words of Delight*, p. 321).

Kushner rightly grasps the smallest component of this overall scheme of success and failure: the question. I will return to the notion of success and failure at the end of this chapter (again, the notion is on the mark, but will probably need some modification), but for now we can begin our own quest for Qoheleth's quest, and the function of the question is a good place to start.

Any question, any pursuit of fact, data, knowledge or human feeling, is part (indeed, the kernel) of the myriad expressions we use to signify the experience of human searching. A question itself is the leaving open of possibilities and the absence of closure. Without the proleptic element there is no sense of mystery, of quest or of the *questi*oning character who forms the book's tenor as a whole. In fact, prolepsis is about such absence of closure—the story is incomplete, unfinished.

Out of 222 verses in Ecclesiastes, 26 (11.7%) are or contain questions. All but two of these are seemingly addressed to the reader (2.2; 4.8). Instead of being questioned directly, like the audience of a doubting soliloquy we are invited frequently to seek to answer the questions *with* Qoheleth. And whether the question is stated indirectly or not there is always the possibility that the reader alone is being addressed.

Qoheleth's style of questioning at first glance seems to involve the opposite strategy of prolepsis; that is, while it is partly to let questions remain without any obvious answer, most of his questions are in fact rhetorical and therefore seemingly closed. In a rhetorical question, however, the answer is only apparent—there is an uncertain tone. The question is a test, as if to say, 'This is what is only apparent on the outside, but come test this theorem to see if things are actually as they appear.' And here is where the openness of the questions lie: in the potentiality of Qoheleth's final attitude. That is, in the end, his attitude towards the implied statements of his rhetorical questions will determine their ultimate function in the book. The opening rhetorical question (1.3), beginning his basic, programmatic enquiry into the value of toil, thus functions as a benchmark for all that follows: 'What profit has humanity in all their toil at which they toil under the sun?' Since no answer is given either Qoheleth genuinely does not know it or he relies on the absence of a readerly expectation for an answer. Of course we do not expect answers from rhetorical questions, yet we assume a living context between speaker and audience. If we create and sustain that assumption then the suggestion here is that there is and will be no profit.[7] A more direct answer comes later, as the result of Qoheleth's own experience:

> And I considered all the deeds my hands had done and the toil in which I had toiled to do it. And behold, everything was absurd and a pursuit of wind, *and there is no profit under the heavens* (2.11).

The theme of profit and advantage (√רי) occurs many times. Ogden refers to the query as Qoheleth's 'programmatic question', to which is made constant reference.[8] The question is not only general (What profit is there under the sun/heavens?), but specific: What profit is there from owning many goods? (5.11; cf. 5.16), from knowing wisdom and etiquette? (6.8) or from many words? (6.11). Yet his query is not conducted throughout the whole book (as Ogden would have it) but is limited to the first six chapters.

After the questioning of advantage falls silent a shift occurs, from What? to Who? Who knows the interpretation of a thing? (8.1); Who will tell humanity what will 'come after them'? (6.12; 7.24; 8.1; 10.14); Who can make straight what God has made crooked? (7.13; cf. 1.15). The question in 6.12, as A.G. Wright has shown,[9] works as a thematic link between the two halves of the book:

> For who knows what is good for humanity while they live the few days of their absurd lives that they pass as a shadow? And who will tell humanity what will be after them under the sun?

---

7.   Compare Murphy: '[the rhetorical question in Ecclesiastes] often tends, as here [1.3], to suggest a negation...there is no profit in one's hard lot' (*Ecclesiastes*, p. 7); and Whybray: '[1.3 is] a rhetorical question to which the expected answer is "None!"' (*Ecclesiastes*, p. 36). This is particularly significant for Whybray since he does not regard what follows (1.4-7, the poem on nature's circuity) as necessarily continuing the themes of *hebbel* and the futility of toil expressed in 1.3 (see *Ecclesiastes*, pp. 39-40; *idem*, 'Ecclesiastes 1.5-7', pp. 105-112). That is, it would work better for Whybray's argument if the answer to Qoheleth's question at 1.3 was not so clearly implied.

8.   *Qoheleth* (Readings; Sheffield: JSOT Press, 1987), p. 29.

9.   Wright suggests that for a number of reasons there is a clear structural marker between chs. 1–6 and 7–12. He argues that the continuity arrives from the theme of Qoheleth's evaluation of experience in 1.12–6.9, having to do primarily with the question 'What profit is there...?' ('The Riddle of the Sphinx', pp. 320-24) and that the second portion of Qoheleth's discourse (6.10–11.6) has to do with humanity's (Qoheleth included) inability to discover ('The Riddle of the Sphinx', pp. 324-25). The position of questions (which Wright touches on briefly) alone confirms Wright's thesis.

It begins with the question of profit and at the same time introduces the Who? motif. The symmetry is not perfect (cf. the 'Who' questions at 2.19; 3.21-22), but the balance weighs in favour of there being a structural strategy at work.

Also in favour of the strategy is the fact that in the latter half of the book, Qoheleth, after having reached a state of authentic ignorance, turns his attention to instructing the reader/audience directly, and his concern is more with the formation of the individual than with broader intellectual questions—a concern to which the 'Who' questions are well suited. What matters most here is that the types and positions of questions inform us as to the tone and inception of Qoheleth's quest, and that at this level of questioning, the smallest unit of human searching, the quest is purely intellectual. But how is the quest carried out? What linguistic clues are present to help us unpack the *means* by which Qoheleth searches?

2. 'And Move with the Moving Ships': Qoheleth's Physical Language

I shall sleep, and move with the moving ships,
Change as the winds change, veer in the tide.
> Algernon Charles Swinburne ('The Triumph of Time', 1866)

In the ironical play of consciousness the mind [of Qoheleth] is constantly in motion, trying different possibilities as it circles and seeks conclusions.
> Harold Fisch[10]

Although Qoheleth's quest is largely an intellectual one, there is a language element that suggests that we understand the quest, at least in part, as a physical journey, one which leaves the participant(s) exhausted and in dire need of rest. In this respect the language that suggests (or is closely related to—more on this below) movement/motion acts as a sign or signifier, affording a physical way of thinking about the quest. After listing the words that make up this language in Qoheleth's narrative (I exclude from consideration any occurrences in the frame narrator's text) I will discuss them in some detail. They are, in order of descending frequency:

---

10. 'Qohelet: A Hebrew Ironist', p. 173.

הלך	'go, walk' (×30)
בוא	'come in, arrive' (×15)
רעיון/רעות	'pursue, chase' (×10)
שוב	'return' (×10)
סביב/סבב	'encompass, surround' (×8)
יצא	'go out, flee' (×5)
דרך	'path, road' (×4)
תור	'reconnoitre' (×3)
פנה	'return' (×2)
רחוק/רחק	'distance, far off/away' (×3)
עמק	'deep' (×2)
שלח	'send, let loose' (×1)

In most cases, the manner in which the words relate to physical movement is obvious. The translations offered here (with the exception of פנה[11]) are the words' well-established primary English renderings. All of them have a connection of some kind to walking or running, some to journeying. The following are often used directly to describe such movement: הלך, בוא, שוב, סביב/סבב, יצא, תור, פנה and שלח. Others have a less direct connection: דרך (what is travelled on), רחוק/רחק and עמק (terms of geographical distance).[12] Some of these words, however, can have a figurative or metaphorical sense (e.g. הלך = 'living, conduct'; דרך = 'manner, way'). In fact, in Ecclesiastes *all* of the listed words are usually used figuratively—for example, 'And the dust *returns* [שוב] to the earth' (12.7), or 'Just as [that man] *came from* [out of, יצא] his mother's womb naked he shall *return* [שוב], *going* [הלך] as he *came* [בוא]' (5.15a) and so forth. This raises a theoretical problem for the way in which I am using them to make my argument. It could be said that the figurative uses may somehow nullify the primary meanings suggested.

'The eyes of the wise are in their head, but the fool walks [הלך] in darkness' (2.14a) offers an interesting case in point. Theoretically it could make for a borderline case in that it appeals to the literal sense of walking in order to be understood figuratively. But it is a metaphor.

11. The primary meaning is '(turn to) consider', but see, e.g., Josh. 22.4 and 1 Kgs 10.13, for some physical connotations.

12. See Fox and Porten, 'Unsought Discoveries', p. 37. At this point in their article it is noted that Qoheleth uses verbs of motion and a comparison is made to stories of seeking out physical objects in order to illuminate the question of what Qoheleth sought. The discussion is interesting but has no bearing on the kinds of implications I will draw from the use of motion-words.

Technically, the tenor is the fool to whom is applied the vehicle of walking in darkness (movement). The walking is figurative; we accept that here it means living, conduct and so forth. But is the literal sense lost completely? Can it be separated from the newly created meaning? Indeed, why is 'walking' the chosen vehicle? Metaphors are two things becoming something new. They are the combination of two or more ideas/concepts to create a new idea. Walking and darkness, together with 'the fool', make up the rather negative picture of one who stumbles; who gropes to find something to hold but fails; who is unable to advance in life because of the lack of wit and wisdom to do so. In other words, in the working idea of the impediment of progressive movement the vehicle has retained something of the primary meaning. All of the listed words in one way or another therefore contribute to the overall impression of motion, but some (whether figurative or literal) will be more informative than others. And this is where the real nettle lies: What is their relationship to Qoheleth's quest?

The words of the list that Qoheleth uses to express the quest directly are הלך (2.1), שוב (4.1, 7; 9.11), סבב (2.20; 7.25), תור (1.13; 2.3; 7.25) and פנה (2.11, 12). In all but two of these instances (the infinitive of תור at 1.13 and 7.25), the verbs relate as opening remarks either to other verbs that describe precisely how Qoheleth will search or directly to the content of his discoveries. They set the tone and commence the motion of the quest:

> I said in my heart, 'Come [לכה־נא], I will test you with mirth...' (2.1).

> I set out [תרתי] in my heart to cheer my flesh with wine...(2.3).

> And I considered [turned to consider?, פניתי] all the deeds my hands had done and the toil in which I had toiled to do it...(2.11).

> And I turned [פניתי] to observe wisdom, and madness and folly...(2.12).

> And I turned [סבותי] to despair my heart concerning all the toil at which I toiled under the sun...(2.20).

> And I turned [שבתי] and observed all of the oppressions that are done under the sun. And behold, the tears of the oppressed...(4.1).

> And I turned [שבתי] and observed an absurdity under the sun...(4.7).

> I turned [סבותי], I and my heart, to understand and to search out [לתור] and to seek wisdom and the sum of things...(7.25).

> I turned [שבתי] and observed under the sun:
> The race is not to the swift,
>> nor the battle to the mighty...(9.11).

As if to say, 'I set out, yet I return to where I began and am unable to complete my journey; my heart has come back on itself again and again and again...', Qoheleth is travelling.

Those motion words that are not directly connected to the quest are used in wisdom sayings, vignettes or poems. However, even some of these are indirectly related in that they may be seen to mirror, even extrapolate, the quest's central themes. The best example among these is 5.13-17. I have set out the passage chiastically (and shown Hebrew and italicized theme-words) only in order to show some thematic parallels.

A		There is a grievous *ill* I observed under the sun: riches were *stored up* by their owner to his own *harm*.
	B	But those riches were destroyed in a bad venture. And he had a son, and there was *nothing* for his hand.
	C	Just as [that man] came from [יצא] his mother's womb naked he shall return [שוב], going [הלך] as he came [בא].
	D	And he will not take anything from his toil that he carries [הלך] in his hand.
	CC	This too is a grievous ill: Precisely as he came [בא], so shall he go [הלך];
	BB	and *what profit* has he from toiling for the wind?
AA		Indeed, he *consumes* all his days in darkness, and great *vexation*, and *sickness* and resentment.

This passage is set within a larger investigation into the value of riches (5.10–6.9). However, it is clearly marked apart from what surrounds it[13] in that it has the same subject throughout who is first introduced here ('that man') and who does not appear before or after; in that this section begins with Qoheleth's typical introductory phrase for observations, 'There is a grievous ill...'; and in that the following section begins something new with its הנה (Behold...). After some general remarks (5.10-12), Qoheleth then focuses on a test-case of what happens when someone is controlled by what they search for and desire.

From A to B Qoheleth sets up the problem of the discussion: to him it is grievous and even sickening (חולה) that someone has consumed goods to their own harm (לרעתו; cf. לרע לו at 8.9 and my comments on this in the Postscript, sec. 3). In B he describes how this person then

---

13. I approach this differently from Fredericks who argues that this passage works chiastically in the whole of 5.10–6.9, making, for example, the coming and going here (5.15) parallel to the coming and going of 6.4, both of which fit into the larger elaborate chiasmus (*Coping with Transience*, pp. 71-74).

lost those goods (one would think that, given his attitude to material wealth, this might make Qoheleth happy). There is a resonance between A–B and BB–AA. Key words of harm and illness are mentioned, and the prelude to Qoheleth's question at BB, 'What profit?' (can he have from his pointless toil), is given at B: there was nothing for his hand.

In the centre of this account comes the working image of motion: that man has come and will return, going as he came, and just as he came he will go (C and CC). When he attempts to carry anything away he will fail (D). Like Qoheleth, this man has suffered vexation and illness from experiencing the absurd. Like Qoheleth, this man cannot help but end where he began. Qoheleth is caught in a circular motion in his quest; he can only repeatedly return to it. And what will Qoheleth be able to take with him? (What can this man take from his life?) What profit? Where does this man go? (Do not all go to the same place?—3.20; 6.6—Sheol? [cf. 9.10]) Where will Qoheleth go? The questions raised about this man for the reader can easily be applied to Qoheleth and his quest. So easily, in fact, that it raises the question of whether or not there is a strategy at hand of mirroring Qoheleth's experience in vignettes such as these (cf. 4.7-8, 13-16; 6.1-5; 9.13-16).

Other indirectly related (motion) texts offer mirrors to Qoheleth's own experience. To tease out this element I offer a pastiche, a patch-work of such texts, modified to reflect this aspect of Qoheleth's narrative:

> Much like myself, someone is not satisfied [לא־תשבע] from the good things of their life, and even the stillborn child is better off, 'for in absurdity it came [בא] and in darkness it shall go [ילך], and in darkness its name is covered' (6.3-4). Perhaps I too was better off in darkness, than in the circle of my quest, where I never would have seen (lived in) the light or known (understood) it (6.5); for this is the source of my vexation (1.18).
>
> 'Walk [הלך] in the ways of your heart, and in the sight of your eyes' (11.9b), and enjoy what you can, for you must 'know for certain that concerning all of these things God will bring [בוא] you into judgment' (11.9c). For in the end you will be returned to your beginnings (3.20; 12.7).
>
> 'Better the sight of the eyes [מראה עינים] than the wandering of the soul [מהלך־נפש]. This too is absurdity and a pursuit of wind' (6.9). Better even the vexation that comes from seeing the world as it is than the wandering (quest) of my soul for nourishment and rest. How long will my own soul wander?

There is an interesting canonical twist to Qoheleth's use of הלך: its contrasting use in Proverbs. First it should be noted that at 30 occurrences in Ecclesiastes this word *should* be listed number 8 in Loretz's favourite-word list (רעה, 'evil', also appears 30 times).[14] It is in every sense a 'key' word. Its distribution is spread evenly, occurring in every chapter, and it is often the operative image in texts widely noted to be significant. We have seen the uses Qoheleth has for it: futile wandering, 'inviting' himself (cynically?) to test his own heart, the absurd departure from a world from which you take nothing, and conduct that, to some extent, resembles reckless abandon. Now its primary use in Proverbs, as here, is figurative and not literal. But there is a telling difference. One who walks in Proverbs must walk in integrity (הולך בתם) and securely (ילך בטח, 10.9; cf. 3.23; 19.1). Those who in Proverbs walk in uprightness (הולך ישר) fear the Lord (14.2; cf. 2.20; 15.21). Better is the poor man who walks in integrity (הולך בתם) than the rich whose ways (דרכים) are perverted (28.6; cf. 10.9; 20.7; 28.18). Indeed, wisdom herself sets the wheel in motion by walking in the ways of righteousness and the paths of justice (8.20). And 'Solomon' warns his son not to run with those who entice him to travel in the paths of the unrighteous (1.10-18). For wisdom will call out in the streets to lead him back to the perambulation of the upright (1.20-22). Walking in Proverbs is a moral activity, and when it arrives at Qoheleth's story it takes a deconstructive turn (for the worse?). The only path Qoheleth walks leads to death, Sheol, the unknown or is the path of his own heart.

If one journeys constantly (and repeatedly back to the same place), one needs rest. It comes as no surprise to learn, therefore, that Qoheleth holds rest in the highest esteem. Of course, rest features prominently in narratives that revolve around a quest (for example, one has the impression from reading Bunyan's *Pilgrim's Progress* that when Christian stops for rest in the form of food, wine and comradeship along his long journey, the moment is narratively highlighted and is meant to remain in the memory a long while). Qoheleth makes it abundantly clear that rest is a good thing and that he, along with others under the torment of toil, longs to know it. Note the place of rest in one of the texts discussed above (6.4-5):

> For in absurdity it [the stillborn] came and in darkness it shall go, and in darkness its name is covered. Although it has not seen the sun or understood it, *it finds rest rather than he* [the man of 6.2].

14. As cited in Murphy, *Ecclesiastes*, p. xxix.

And further note these examples:

> What is there for a man in all his toil, and the striving of his heart that
> toils under the sun? For all his days are painful and his work a vexation.
> Even at night his heart does not rest. This too is absurdity (2.22-23).

> Better a handful with rest than two handfuls with toil and a pursuit of
> wind (4.6).

> Sweet is the sleep of the worker whether he eats little or much.
> But the surfeit of the rich man does not allow him to sleep (5.12).

Qoheleth also makes clear that he was himself in dire need of rest due
to the taxing nature of the quest:

> When I set my heart to understand wisdom, and to observe the business
> that is done on the earth—although by day or by night my eyes[15] seeing
> no sleep—I observed all the activity of God…(8.16-17).

That motion and rest feature so prominently suggests that the quest is
to be understood on a physical as well as intellectual level. Such language also offers clues to the narrative aspect of the quest. It enables us
to think about Qoheleth's intellectual motion in very suggestive and
visual terms. Indeed, some readers might find the universal quality of
physical language, even when used figuratively, easier to come to terms
with than abstract intellectual language. The overall impression of
movement should make us stop; that is, give us, Qoheleth's readers,
pause for thought.

3. *Qoheleth's Search and the Actantial Model*

> What I want to discover is the truth of things themselves. What I doubt
> is, in fact, that things are actually as they seem.
>
> Paul Ricoeur[16]

The marriage of wisdom to the notion of searching is not unique to
Qoheleth in the biblical literature (e.g. Job 28; Prov. 8; Sir. 51.13-22
etc.). For example, the author of the Wisdom of Solomon, D. Winston
suggests, displays a 'single-minded…concentrated pursuit after wisdom'.[17] Winston sketches out the way in which that author was set on

---

15. For the emendation to first person see Fox, *Qohelet*, p. 255. Even if this is in
the third person (as NRSV, RSV etc.) the point remains in that Qoheleth includes
himself in his statements about humanity.

16. Paraphrasing Descartes, in *Oneself as Another*, p. 6.

17. 'The Sage as Mystic in the Wisdom of Solomon', in Gammie (ed.), *The*

his own spiritual odyssey. Like the author of Proverbs, the author of
Wisdom sought wisdom herself, and not necessarily things that are
closely related to 'human' knowledge; that is, things deduced from
empirical observation, know-how, book-knowledge and the categories
of knowledge that come from collecting data (as with Solomon in 1
Kgs 4.32-33). In some biblical texts, however, such an implicit criticism of the tireless quest was simply not enough. In what reads like a
corrective intended for Qoheleth, Ben Sira asserts,

> Do not seek for what is too hard for you,
> And do not investigate what is beyond your strength;
> Think of the commandments that have been given you,
> For you have no need of the things that are hidden.
> Do not waste your labor on what is superfluous to your work,
> For things beyond human understanding have been shown you.
> For many have been led astray by their imagination,
> And a wicked fancy has made their minds slip.[18]

But it seems Qoheleth did not heed any such warning (this one came
too late for him in any case!). He conducted his test unashamedly and
with a burning intensity, but what did he look for? Could he say with
the author of the Pseudo-Platonic *Epinomis*, 'For I have sought *this
wisdom* high and low [*anō kai katō*] and so far as it has been revealed
to me I will try to render it plain to you'?[19] What was it that Qoheleth
sought for (far off and deep)? Was it wisdom? Was it 'satisfaction in
life', as Ryken maintains?[20] Or was it the object of his thematic questions; that is, to know what is good for humanity the few days of
their absurd existence?[21] Or did Qoheleth 'exhaust all avenues of

Sage in Israel and the Ancient Near East, pp. 383-97 (383). He comments later that
the author of Wisdom 'appears to be undaunted in his total commitment to the pursuit of the philosophy and science of his age with all its challenges' (p. 389).

18. Sir. 3.21-24; cf. 18.5-8; Wis. 9.13-18; adapted from Goodspeed's translation, *The Apocrypha*, p. 229. I am indebted to Winston's article for drawing attention to the significance of this passage and that of the contrasting references ('The
Sage as Mystic', p. 388).

19. As cited in Winston, 'The Sage as Mystic', p. 385 (italics mine).

20. *Words of Delight*, p. 321.

21. See Fisch, 'Qohelet: A Hebrew Ironist', p. 163, who contrasts this theme to
Mic. 6.8: 'He has showed you O man [אדם] what is good; and what does the Lord
require [דרש] of you but to do justice, and to love kindness, and to walk [הלך]
humbly with your God?' Fisch concludes that Qoheleth finds himself incapable of
sharing in the kind of love and intimacy with his creator that Micah implies, but
settles for a few rainy days instead.

investigation to *understand*..."what God is doing under the sun"'?[22] Or was it some subtle combination of all of these?

In the Introduction I discussed Qoheleth's first announcement of the quest (1.13) but did not investigate what he was searching for. To discover what Qoheleth sought, what he used to find it and what ultimately enabled him to get it or kept him from getting it, I will enlist the help of the actantial model developed by Greimas and Todorov (based largely on the work of Propp), which is meant to account for the basic structure of any narrative. Although the model has been criticized for failing to represent the relationships of complex stories,[23] it is more than adequate for Qoheleth's structurally simple tale.

The actants of the model and what they do are as follows:

Subject the actant that desires/wishes for something
Object the thing that the Subject desires[24]
Power[25] what *enables* the Subject to obtain the Object (and ultimately determines if the Subject is successful)
Receiver the actant (usually the Subject) that ultimately receives the Object
Helper what offers often incidental help in obtaining the Object
Opponent what incidentally opposes the Subject in its search for the Object

A simple example will help to illustrate the model. In the sentence 'Dennis wants to date Rose but she is reluctant to say yes', the Subject is clearly Dennis and the Object is a date with Rose. Since Rose is indecisive she is the Power; that is, she ultimately allows or enables the Subject's success. The Receiver in this case is the Subject (unless there were another competing subject [what Bal calls an anti-Subject] who obtained a date with Rose). The Helper could be many things: Dennis's employment prospects, good looks, charm and so forth. Likewise, the Opponent could consist of the opposites of these things. Helpers and

---

22. A.R. Ceresko, 'The Function of *Antanaclasis* (*ms'* "to Find" //*ms'* "to Reach, Overtake, Grasp") in Hebrew Poetry, Especially in the Book of Qoheleth', *CBQ* 44 (1982), pp. 551-69 (569) (italics Ceresko's).

23. See, for example, Chatman, *Story and Discourse*, pp. 112-13.

24. Objects can be just about anything: a state of existence, a piece of gold and so forth. Bal distinguishes among Objects those of intention, which may include 'wisdom, love, happiness, a place in heaven, a bed to die in...' (*Narratology*, p. 27). Bal's discussion of the model is simply one of the best available, and so it is to her that I will primarily refer.

25. Following Bal (*Narratology*, pp. 28-29) who prefers this to the usual term, 'Sender', since this element can be passive (such as money) *or* active (such as a person's will).

Opponents can be groups of people or things combined into a force, such as society, an army and so forth.

As Bal points out, the model functions on the premise that Subjects of stories undertake 'thinking and action...directed towards an aim' and are intent on either attaining something agreeable or avoiding something disagreeable.[26] And this is what best describes the relationship between the Subject and Object, suggests Bal: the verb 'to wish' (and/or 'to desire'). This is what I will assume of Qoheleth: that his thinking and activities are directed towards an aim.

In Ecclesiastes we have the advantage of the autobiographical form, the predominance of which easily locates the Subject, Qoheleth. The Object, however, is not so easily located.

We may conclude from ch. 2 and elsewhere that Qoheleth at one time *desired* many things and experiences (cf. 5.10; 6.7). But intellectually, Qoheleth applied his mind (sought) in order to understand specifically wisdom and folly (1.17; 7.23,[27] 25; 8.16-17a; 9.1), pleasure (2.1, 3), what has been before him (7.23-24; cf. 1.9; 3.15; 6.10) and all the activity that has been done under the sun (1.13; 8.9, 16-17a; 9.1; cf. 2.11; 3.11b; 10.14b). He also *observed* (ראה) wisdom *in order* to understand it (2.12a; 8.9; 9.1; cf. 7.15-18, 25) and sought to see (ראה) what was good for people to do during their short time under the heavens (2.3; cf. 5.18; 6.12; 8.15). All of these things are to do with the quality of his own understanding (ידע is a favourite word). His express goal was to *better understand*.[28]

Qoheleth himself best sums up the whole Object of his thinking and investigating in an intriguingly simple way when he offers an aside in the midst of a quite specific investigation (7.26-29):

> See, this I have found, said Qoheleth ([*adding*] *one to one to find the sum* [אחת לאחת למצא חשבון], *which my soul has sought continually* [עוד־בקשה], *but which I have not found*): one man among a thousand...(7.27-28).

This is a culminative comment. It is the best image Qoheleth can find to

---

26. *Narratology*, p. 26.

27. Taking the 'all this' of 7.23a to refer to his reflections on wisdom, folly, righteousness and so forth that precede this verse (7.15-22). See my comments above, p. 209 n. 108.

28. It is worth remembering at this point how sorely the frame narrator misunderstood Qoheleth in his summation, 'Qoheleth sought to find words of delight...' (12.10a).

express what his soul has sought continually in its calculating, adding and configuring of wisdom and the world: the sum, a satisfactory and digestible answer. It is significant that Qoheleth uses a simple mathematical problem as the image of his search. He is stating principally that he sought an answer to his calculations and observations that would put things into place and make things understandable and graspable. The answer should be as simple as '2', and such would allow him to understand the world in simple dichotomies: wisdom/folly, long life/death, and so forth.[29] But 2 is, alas, not as simple as it appears. To the Greeks it was a source of mystery.

> The early Greeks were uncertain as to whether 2 was a number at all, observing that it has, as it were, a beginning and an end but no middle. More mathematically, they pointed out that $2 + 2 = 2 \times 2$, or indeed that any number multiplied by 2 is equal to the same number added to itself. Since they expected multiplication to do more than mere addition, they considered two an exceptional case.[30]

As in the speculation of the Greeks, what Qoheleth called the sum was perhaps only a sum in appearance. He could not find it since, despite its simplistic appearance, its quality remained illusive.[31] In fact, Qoheleth uses the same word, חשבון, just a few verses later (v. 29) to refer to the opposite of humanity's simple beginning, which was upright and uncomplicated: the concurrent human search for deception, 'devices' (LXX, λογισμούς; cf. Wis. 1.3; 3.10). Instead of offering closure, the idea of 2 might have opened more possibilities than expected. The Object that his soul had sought continually was an *understanding* that was of an initially naïve quality. This Object was reflexive—to better understand his own experience of the world and hence his own self— but wisdom is tied in with the enterprise, and the nature of wisdom is a problem here.

This leads us to the question of the Helper. Qoheleth used (at least attempted to use) wisdom to his advantage in his search (1.13; 2.3, 9;

---

29. This is the foundation of Qoheleth's realization that true knowledge/perception is in fact neither graspable nor knowable, as I sketched out in Chapter 4.3.

30. D. Wells, *The Penguin Dictionary of Curious and Interesting Numbers* (London: Penguin Books, 1986), p. 41.

31. Ogden concludes similarly, with slightly different emphases: 'That conclusion he sought...was not to be found...for there was sufficient conflicting evidence to establish that *ʾaḥat lᵉʾaḥat*, "one plus one", does not always equal "two"...like wisdom itself, an answer to the riddle was unattainable' (*Qoheleth*, p. 122).

7.23). He consistently held wisdom in high regard (7.11-12, 19; 8.2; 9.13–10.1). The wise profit (2.13) and see the world more clearly than fools (2.14). Qoheleth worked at becoming wise (2.19) and became 'exceedingly wise' in (by?) his test of pleasure (2.15; cf. 7.23). But this is where wisdom the Helper fails him; even with it to guide him while he searches he is not able to find the Object of understanding. Indeed, he is frustrated by the fact that wisdom makes no ultimate difference to one's existence/life, for the wise and the foolish have the same fate regardless. The problem comes into sharp focus at 2.13-14:

> I observed that there is more profit from wisdom than from folly, as [there is] more profit from light than darkness.
> The eyes of the wise are in their head,
>> but the fool walks in darkness.
>> Yet I realized that one fate befalls both of them.

Given the description of material profit in 2.4-10, and the fact that he has just pronounced judgment on the value of toil (2.11), here Qoheleth is likely recognizing the value of wisdom 'generally speaking'. That is, generally speaking, wisdom does help one gain material goods in a much more effective way than folly (1.16; 2.9), just as light generally helps one to see more clearly and to make effective progress in life (see my comments on 2.14a in sec. 2, above). This makes the equivalent fates of the sage and the fool all the more acute and all the more obscure to Qoheleth's understanding. What seems to affect their fate much more than wisdom is what God will choose to do (see below), and such is beyond his understanding as well. Wisdom, in fact, deceives him; wisdom turns from being Helper to becoming Opponent, even to the point of causing him vexation (1.18; cf. 2.15, 19; 7.23). It functions like a false lead in a detective novel. Perhaps because of what it brought him (power, fame, wealth) he initially believed that it implicitly promised him the desire of his heart, understanding.

Besides failed wisdom it may be that there are no other real Opponents. There are factors such as toil, weariness, pain and hate, which frustrate Qoheleth to no end (see esp. 2.17-23), but these are not so much Qoheleth's Opponents as they are built into the structure of the world as Qoheleth sees it. And this brings us to the question of the Power: What ultimately decides whether Qoheleth will obtain the Object, to succeed in understanding all that has happened to him in the realms of wisdom and folly?

As in the above example of Dennis and Rose, we know the Power by knowing the *reasons* for the failure or success of the Subject. Dennis will be successful only if Rose says yes. Qoheleth will be successful if something will allow or disallow him to obtain his goal. While it was wisdom that initially helped him, we must not confuse the Power with the Helper. What ultimately determines Qoheleth's success is the accessibility of understanding itself (that is, of being in a position *clearly* to understand wisdom, conduct, the activity of God etc.).

Qoheleth did succeed in placing himself in a position to test and evaluate the prospects of his becoming wise. He did 'become great', he did amass treasures, he did know folly and madness first hand. And then he considered it all and found that it was הבל. That is, when he pushed farther to understand he came up against an insurmountable barrier. This is especially evident in texts where Qoheleth attempts to obtain the Object but finds himself denied by the *fact* that everything is absurd (1.13-14; 2.11, 15-16, 22-23; cf. 4.4, 8; 6.2; 7.23-24). In each of these instances the Power is the existing structure of deed and consequence; that is, *the way things are*. This insurmountable fact is hinted at from 1.2 and as such suggests again that we are reading tragedy. Things are such that it is not possible to ascertain the how and why of their nature (1.9-10, 15 [cf. 7.13]; 3.11; 9.11-12).[32] So far I have described the passive nature of the Power, but what of the active? Who or what is responsible for this immovable structuration?

There can be no question that God 'is' the Power. Simply put, God is the enabler of human experience; the fate of everyone is somehow under his domain. Now fate is part of the Object in that it is the end/use/purpose of, for example, wisdom and toil (activity) that Qoheleth wants to understand: in the end, where does it take you and leave you? It is in this sense that God is the Power, for Qoheleth cannot

---

32. This has been recognized by others as a key feature of Qoheleth's thought. Stephen Schloesser has put a fine twist on this notion. He argues that Qoheleth turned the traditional notion of wisdom as graspable and of sages themselves as having unsearchable minds (epitomized by Prov. 25.2-3) on its head to mean the opposite. For while it was the glory of kings to search things (words?) out (presumably with the help of God who knew the way), with Qoheleth it was the nature of things (and words?) themselves that was unsearchable, and the minds of kings (i.e. Solomon) themselves subjected to failure ('A King is Held Captive in her Tresses', pp. 205-28, esp. pp. 210-11). He further comments that the Proverbial search for the meaning of words is precisely 'the classical search which third-century philosophy in general [like Qoheleth?] abandoned out of "weariness"' (p. 223 n. 21).

understand just how God influences what happens on the earth. 'Just as you do not understand the way of the life-breath in the formation of bones in the womb, so too you do not understand the activity of God *who does everything'* (11.5), whose influence is everywhere and who determines the end of us all. Qoheleth even goes on to implicate God in his design of the world as by nature inscrutable (3.11; 7.13; 8.17; cf. 9.10). Bewilderingly, God has made the world such *in order that* people will fail to understand it: 'God has set eternity in their hearts *so that* [מבלי אשר; cf. Jer. 2.15] humanity cannot discover the activity that God has done from beginning to end' (3.11b; cf. 6.12; 7.14; 8.17; 9.12; 10.14).[33] God's role in establishing the way things are is essentially negative: 'it is an evil business that God has given to human beings to be busy with' (1.13b; cf. 6.1; 8.6). Yet God has also made it this way so that people will fear his presence (3.14; cf. 8.12-13) and (as we shall later see) he also *empowers* people to enjoy life. This duality reflects further the success of the Power in keeping the Subject from the Object, understanding.

Taken altogether, the actants can be represented as follows:

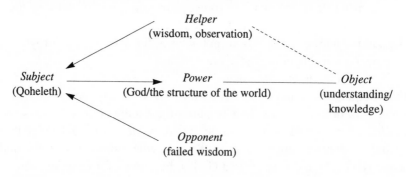

Figure 6

Qoheleth presents actantial analysis with a not uncommon situation in that the Subject and Object are confounded.[34] This confounding,

---

33. Humanity's experience mirrors Qoheleth's quest in that they too are unable to discover what God has done and their own fate. Indeed, humanity in this case may well come close to Bal's notion of a competing anti-Subject. And yet Qoheleth belongs to humanity and therefore the Subject and anti-Subject will both fail in their quest.

34. There also occurs the ironic confounding of Object and Power: the Object of Qoheleth's attempt at understanding is largely (the activity of) the Power itself, God.

however, confirms the relevance of another of Qoheleth's narrative strategies to the quest: autobiography. As we have seen, Qoheleth is introspective. The autobiographical form shows that he is anxious to see his own identity somehow established in a world where everything else is in flux. The discussion of W.K.C. Guthrie about the conclusion of Heraclitus, 'I searched out myself', sheds an interesting light on the matter:

> The verb [to search] has two main meanings: (1) to look for…(2) to question, inquire of somebody, find out… Thus by the two [Greek] words of fr. 101 Heraclitus meant, I suggest… 'I turned my thoughts within and sought to discover my real self…to discover the real meaning of my self-hood; for I knew that if I understood my self I would have understood the *logos* which is the real constitution of everything else as well.'[35]

And by this, continues Olney, Heraclitus 'anticipated the entire history of autobiographical literature'. 'You could not discover the limits of the self', said Heraclitus (frag. 45), 'even by travelling along every path: so deep a *logos* does it have.'[36] Was such the subtext of Qoheleth's search? By travelling (הלך, שוב, יצא, תור etc.) along every path (דרך, סביב etc.) was Qoheleth attempting to know the limits of his own self?[37] Like Heraclitus, Qoheleth was not able to discover those limits since their *logos* (reason/end/use/purpose) was set too deeply. Qoheleth described that realization as הבל and traced its *logos* to the inscrutable Power, God.

4. *Gustave Flaubert's* Bouvard et Pécuchet: *A Comparison*

NATURE: How beautiful Nature is! Say this everytime you are in the country.

Flaubert, 'The Dictionary of Received Ideas'

Qoheleth's tale has been compared to other stories before.[38] One of the

---

35. As cited in Olney, *Metaphors of Self*, p. 7.

36. *Metaphors of Self*, p. 7 (the translation is Olney's own adaptation from standard translations).

37. Fisch agrees that this is the subtext of Qoheleth's search ('Qohelet: A Hebrew Ironist', pp. 158-59).

38. See, for example, L. Kreitzer, who compares particularly the themes of birth/death and life/loss in Ecclesiastes to Hemingway's *A Farewell to Arms*, in Chapter 5, '*A Farewell to Arms*: "A Time to Give Birth and a Time to Die"', in idem, *The Old Testament in Fiction and Film: On Reversing the Hermeneutical*

most intriguing comparisons I have come across is from a Literature PhD thesis by Deborah Pierce, a third of which concerns Gustave Flaubert's *Bouvard et Pécuchet*.[39] Flaubert's novel depicts the experiences of two copyists living in Paris who become inseparable friends, one of whom inherits a substantial fortune. In love with the idea of an idyllic country life, they set out to live 'off the land' on a farm in the town of Chavignolles, Normandy, in 1841. The novel follows their attempts at learning to achieve wealth and success through the aid of knowledge, particularly, if not solely, from books. When they cannot understand the way the world is working, they turn to books of every kind under the sun. Such was the story's encyclopaedic range that Flaubert is said to have consulted over 1500 volumes in its writing, taking 'assiduous' notes on each, even causing his eyesight to go bad.[40] Flaubert spent 16–18 years writing the novel in the late 1860s and '70s up until his death in 1880, but never completed it, leaving us instead with an enticing plan, written in point form, of the final, incomplete tenth chapter.[41] While it is unlikely that Flaubert drew directly from Ecclesiastes for his inspiration, he was aware of the book, stating[42] in the novel that

> our two worthy men, after all their disappointments, felt the need to be simple, to love something, to find peace of mind. They tried Ecclesiastes, Isaiah, Jeremiah. But the Bible frightened them with its prophets roaring like lions, the thunder crashing in the clouds, all the weeping in Gehenna, and its God scattering empires as the wind scatters clouds.[43]

(It is difficult to say whether such a likening of these works was a

Flow (TBS, 24; Sheffield: Sheffield Academic Press, 1994), pp. 170-221. Also, see my remarks in the Introduction, sec. 3.

39. D.L.T. Pierce, Chapter 3, 'Bouvard et Pécuchet: The Gatherers of Wisdom', in *idem*, 'Echoes of the Past in Flaubert's *"L'Education Sentimentale"*, *"Bouvard et Pécuchet"* and *"Salambo"*'' (PhD dissertation; Louisiana State University and Agricultural and Mechanical College, 1992).

40. So Pierce, 'Echoes of the Past', pp. 101, 104. See the 'Introduction' by A.J. Krailsheimer, in *Bouvard et Pécuchet*, p. 9.

41. A second volume, which was to consist of large collections of quotes reflecting concurrent uncritically 'received ideas' (which Flaubert despised), was to follow; there is a translated (at times hilarious) version of this available: 'The Dictionary of Received Ideas', in *Bouvard et Pécuchet*, pp. 291-330.

42. For convenience I will speak of 'Flaubert' and the generally covert narrator of the story interchangeably.

43. *Bouvard et Pécuchet*, p. 223.

satirical remark on Bouvard and Pécuchet's shallow rejection of things they disliked or a reflection of Flaubert's own understanding of them.)

Pierce devotes much of her discussion of the novel to a comparison with Ecclesiastes. She begins the comparison with the following remarks:

> ...upon examining the two works it can be concluded that the import of *Bouvard et Pécuchet* is comprehended in a verse from *Ecclesiastes* which Flaubert might well have used as an epigraph: 'And I applied my mind to seek and to search out by wisdom all that is done under the heavens; it is an unhappy business that God has given to the sons of men to be busy with [1.13].'[44]

One soon discovers that the Object of their quest, of that application of mind that Bouvard and Pécuchet share with Qoheleth, is to better know how to live; to understand how things work; and to know what, exactly, is beautiful. The overall Object, as with Qoheleth, is understanding. As Pierce states, 'Flaubert sets his protagonists...to skim the surface of the world's knowledge...they search for a truth, an unmediated knowledge that will allow them to answer life's questions.'[45] Embedded in that search is a need for security. For example, after learning of some convincing arguments against the faith of his new-found spiritualism, we learn of Pécuchet that 'His need for truth became a raging thirst..."Oh! Doubt! Doubt! I should rather have nothing at all."'[46] Desire often overcomes the pair, leading them to pursue their Object with unbridled fervour and to display ambitions to control their environment and to gain answers (as Qoheleth perhaps naïvely began) that would explain things simply.[47]

Although they do not enlist specifically the help of, for example, wisdom or the powers of observation, Bouvard and Pécuchet rely

44. Pierce, 'Echoes of the Past', p. 77 (italics Pierce's).

45. 'Echoes of the Past', pp. 78, 80. Pierce also terms this aspect in both stories a 'flirtation with the limitless' (p. 85). Compare the narrator's comment at the time when the two of them decide to give up the study of history: 'But they had acquired a taste for history, a need for truth in itself' (*Bouvard et Pécuchet*, p. 121).

46. *Bouvard et Pécuchet*, pp. 210-11.

47. There are many examples of this. In fact, most of the chapters conclude with a failure on one subject and a burning desire to conquer the next. As for their desire for control, take, for example, Flaubert's description of their grandiose thoughts on discovering magic: 'What takes centuries could be developed in a moment, any miracle would be practicable and the universe would be at our disposal' (*Bouvard et Pécuchet*, p. 197).

constantly on their own grasp of the situation, their own grasp of what they have read, their own memory of some principle that they read about—and they are inevitably let down. They cannot grasp the nettle because they fail to understand the significance and true meaning of what they read. Even when they understand one author they are confounded by the fact that another disagrees (such was probably part of Flaubert's stratagem in undermining the value of 'received ideas'). Although they are left in the dark as to the reasons for their failure, readers are left in no doubt. Our two anti-heroes are ignorant, even stupid. Typical is the description of their initial wonder at the possibilities of all that could be learned: 'As they admired some old piece of furniture they felt sorry that they had not lived in the period that it was used, though they knew absolutely nothing about the period in question...Works whose titles they could not understand seemed to contain some mystery.'[48] Even without their knowing it, true knowledge keeps at a distance and keeps things mysterious. There is a sense, therefore, in which their perceived Helper, knowledge, turns into (unperceived?) Opponent.

Underlying their search is the admittance that they cannot understand what they seek. It is an admittance concealed in the guise of questions, such as the following from Pécuchet: 'Where is the rule then, and what hope can we have of success or profit?'[49] Like Qoheleth's, their questions are sadly rhetorical. And here lies the Power: the inaccessibility of understanding. Most importantly, they cannot understand the divorce between deed and consequence, which they experience continually. They follow the rules but they are in turn deceived:

> When they were capable of utterance, they asked themselves the cause
> of so many misfortunes... It was all beyond their comprehension, except
> that they had nearly died [after a fiasco in their chemistry 'lab']...

And, still early on in the story, they misjudge the cause critically:

> ...Pécuchet concluded with these words: 'Perhaps it is because we don't
> know any chemistry!'[50]

But as they continue their search they start to formulate a cause. They

48. *Bouvard et Pécuchet*, pp. 28-29. Compare the following passage: 'If they did not know where they stood with ceramics and Celticism it was because they were ignorant of history, especially the history of France' (p. 118).

49. *Bouvard et Pécuchet*, p. 56.

50. *Bouvard et Pécuchet*, pp. 67-68.

eventually abandon chemistry, linking their failure to the 'crookedness' of the created order: 'Creation is put together in such an elusive and transitory fashion; we should do better to take up something else!'[51] Later on, and more critically, they make a link that I believe constitutes one of the book's key passages. Discussing myths, their conversation runs as follows:

> 'How can you admit', Bouvard objected, 'that fables are truer than the truths of historians?' Pécuchet tried to explain myths, and lost himself in the *Scienza Nuova*. 'Are you trying to deny the plan of Providence?' [asked Pécuchet] 'I don't know it', said Bouvard.[52]

And here lies the source of the Power, which refuses them the attainment of the Object: God has made creation and 'the plan of Providence' inscrutable.

Qoheleth's story shares many qualities with Flaubert's, and some of the suggested reasons behind Flaubert's overall cynical outlook may make us wonder about the impetus behind Qoheleth's outlook. For example, it is commonly held that *Bouvard et Pécuchet* is a stinging satire on the concurrent tendency to take the published word as gospel truth. It is thought that the satire was aimed in particular at the idealistic project of Diderot to create an inexhaustible and authoritative compendium of knowledge, *L'Encyclopédie*.[53] This raises the question of whether Qoheleth's story may have had some social satire in it. Since Qoheleth's character is set in fantastic circumstance, and the things he says are often hyperbolic, this is not too far-stretched an idea. Perhaps Qoheleth is himself a ruse of sorts to make a stinging satire out of those who 'seek for what is too hard' (Sir. 3.21). I am, however, not sure that I believe this (it depends on circumstances that are unknown; with Flaubert we have many advantages in, for example, knowing who the author is). But in that we may account for Bouvard and Pécuchet's folly by such a theory, so we may be open to see an element of satire in Qoheleth's. In fact, the implied circumstance may not even be necessary in that the older Qoheleth provides the necessary sobriety that the image of the cynical Flaubert provides for the satirical theory of his novel's composition. Indeed, as there is sympathy from Flaubert for his fumbling protagonists, there is sympathy from Qoheleth for his misapprehending younger self. It is the balance of sympathy against

51. *Bouvard et Pécuchet*, p. 99.
52. *Bouvard et Pécuchet*, p. 123.
53. Pierce, 'Echoes of the Past', p. 81.

indifference (and mockery), however, that raises another question.

Bouvard and Pécuchet's failures are plainly stated. They attempt to grow orchards and the trees end up dead for being poorly placed. They attempt to make preserves and the fruit rots for improper sealing. Usually their failure is due to a lack of implied common sense,[54] but at all times they are up against insurmountable odds and there is nothing to help them. As a result they become islands to themselves and reject the community around them and attempts at friendship. Failure, for Bouvard and Pécuchet, leads to despair. Flaubert in his depiction of failure offers little sympathy for the two stumbling protagonists. Indeed, they are often regarded as a source of humour at their own expense. Sarcasm abounds. Flaubert describes their blowing up the chemistry lab as 'a noise like a shell bursting' and how afterwards a servant 'found a spatula in the yard'.[55] We learn that during their attempt in their 'lab' to concoct the ultimate cream for baking, 'Pécuchet mumbled calculations, motionless in his long blouse, a sort of child's smock with sleeves; and they considered themselves to be very serious men, doing a useful job.'[56] Also, there is an implied condemnation from Flaubert in that Bouvard and Pécuchet are usually depicted as learning only in a cursory manner, and in a way to suggest that had they restricted their learning to one area and realized their limitations (as opposed to flirting with the limitless) they would have known success. It would be unfair, however, as A.J. Krailsheimer rightly suggests, to think that Flaubert simply used these characters as 'mere butts for [his] sarcasm and satire'.[57] Flaubert often shows sympathy with their plight in striking fashion. He describes their emotions with a seemingly empathetic passion. When the local doctor mocks their attempts at medicine, we read that he 'deeply wounded them'.[58] When Bouvard imagines a loving child, realizing that he will never have one, we read that 'the good fellow wept'.[59] When they are

---

54. Flaubert even depicts them attempting to understand the idea of 'common sense' and then making a mess of it (*Bouvard et Pécuchet*, pp. 208-209).

55. *Bouvard et Pécuchet*, p. 67. Perhaps the most amusing episode is that of Bouvard attempting to manipulate his body heat by wriggling his pelvis about in the bathtub for three hours, on the notion that 'Some scientists maintain that animal heat is developed by muscular contractions...' (pp. 74-76 [75]).

56. *Bouvard et Pécuchet*, p. 66.

57. 'Introduction', p. 15.

58. *Bouvard et Pécuchet*, p. 73.

59. *Bouvard et Pécuchet*, p. 270.

devastated by the destruction of their crops by fire we read that 'Bouvard cried softly as he looked at the fire. His eyes disappeared beneath the swollen lids and his whole face seemed as if it were puffed out with grief.'[60] There is even at times, in the characters' unmasking of the contradictions of books that they read, an implied respect for their however limited critical capacities.

And here lies a curious likeness to Ecclesiastes. The older Qoheleth often implies condemnation of the younger. That is, by instructing the reader to enjoy life and not be vexed by the pain of observation, he castigates his former self. There may even be hints of mockery in the farce-like descriptions of his Solomonic experience ('I got myself male and female singers, and the delights of the sons of humanity: concubines and concubines!', 2.8b). At the same *time* (for he speaks only from one 'later' narrative stance), however, he often identifies positively with the folly of the younger. That is, in lamenting he pities; in describing with poetry the grief that comes from the weight of absurdity he draws us to pity those who experience it with such hardship and endurance, as he once did. There are even hints, in his advice to the young and in his final poem especially, of melancholic longing, as if he somehow missed the vigour and adventure of youth. Such a balance raises questions (with whom do we sympathize? and why?) and our conception of it determines to an extent what we will take the overall meaning of the book to be.

There are other likenesses among the two works that are worth noting.

1. 'Both *Ecclesiastes* and *Bouvard et Pécuchet*', states Pierce, 'return the protagonists, after a series of repetitious searches, to their starting point.'[61] There is a cyclical and perhaps pointless facet to the odyssey of Bouvard and Pécuchet in that there is no real progression in their quest, only 'fixity and death'.[62] Also, they both literally return to their beginning. In the notes for the plan of the projected final chapter they return to Paris and again become copyists. Flaubert's last words in these point-by-point notes are, 'They go to work'.

2. Like Qoheleth, searching led to frustration, even illness. Again and again the protagonists return to start their insatiable quest from nothing, having lost and been (sometimes physically) hurt in the process. 'He

60. *Bouvard et Pécuchet*, p. 51.
61. Pierce, 'Echoes of the Past', p. 81.
62. Pierce, 'Echoes of the Past', p. 83.

was disturbed by doubts', we learn of Pécuchet, '...He wanted to reconcile doctrines with works, critics with poets, grasp the essence of the Beautiful; and these questions exercised him so much that his liver was upset. As a result he got jaundice.'[63]

3. Flaubert's anti-heroes, in the occasional moment of graceful clarity, saw the divorce between deed and consequence clearly and painfully. When they contemplated suicide, they 'tried to imagine [death] in the form of intense darkness...anything was better than this monotonous, absurd, hopeless existence'.[64] After realizing that folly truly disturbed them, they thought about 'the things people said in their village...[and] they felt as if the heaviness of the entire earth were weighing down on them'.[65] The pain of realization imbues Qoheleth's story as well, a feature I will discuss in depth in the Postscript.

Obviously, there are a great number of texts that deal with universal themes such as those I have touched on in this comparison, and the selection of texts for comparison is arguably arbitrary. Comparison, however, like laughter, enables us to hold objects to another light in order to see them in relation to something else, something that may be culturally closer to us. It has offered, in this case, a distinctly modern gauge by which to measure Qoheleth's story against itself (and has also thereby demonstrated the timelessness of Qoheleth's story—not presuming, however, that such a demonstration is necessary). And perhaps it has been beneficial to look at another book whose 'ambiguities can never be resolved because they are part of the irony inseparable from any praise of folly'.[66]

5. Redemption and Remembrance

> [An] attempt at remembering...is at the same time searching for a hidden treasure, for a last delivering word, redeeming in the final appeal a destiny that doubted its own value...[the autobiographer] brings [reconciliation] about in the very act of reassembling the scattered elements of a destiny that seems...to have been worth the trouble of living.
>
> G. Gusdorf[67]

63. *Bouvard et Pécuchet*, p. 145.
64. *Bouvard et Pécuchet*, p. 219.
65. *Bouvard et Pécuchet*, p. 217. Krailsheimer suggests that this text is key to understanding the 'overall plan' of the book ('Introduction', p. 13).
66. Krailsheimer, 'Introduction', p. 16.
67. 'Conditions and Limits of Autobiography', p. 39.

We live in memory and by memory, and our spiritual life is at bottom simply the effort of our memory to persist, to transform itself into hope... into our future.

Miguel de Unamuno[68]

I have already mentioned the fact that Qoheleth gradually moves from quest to expression—from ignorance to search, to knowledge, to the dictum that knowledge is absurd. There is another subtle shift. Most of the texts that directly express the quest occur in the first seven chapters. In the latter part of the book, however, Qoheleth speaks less of the story of his youth and more of his 'present' concern. He addresses the reader with a certainty that betrays the style of questioning that I sketched out above, and that certainty has mostly to do with the fact that he admits his failures and his inability to know—he is certain that he is ignorant. In fact, he is adamant about his ignorance. For he *understood* (ידע) that he failed to understand wisdom and folly (1.17; *passim*). (At least in this regard he is, like a good postmodernist, content without closure.) That hard-won ignorance forms the basis of his strategy in the latter half of the book: the imparting of advice to the addressee.

Qoheleth's advice does not simply arrive out of the blue, however. He explicitly links it to his narrated experience. At 7.13, for example, he asks the reader to 'consider the work of God', and to conclude with him that what God has made crooked cannot be made straight. The sequential reader will remember that in 1.13-15 Qoheleth did precisely the same. He observed and considered what God had given humanity to be busy with as well as all the deeds that are done under the sun, and then concluded that 'What is crooked cannot be made straight, and what is lacking cannot be counted' (1.15). He continues by giving the reader a *reason* to consider his own conclusions: 'I observed everything in the days of my absurdity [in the days of my youth?]' (7.15a). That is, this advice is based on the immoderate circumstance of my youth, when I observed all of the travesties and absurdities of 'justice' (7.15b; cf. 3.16-17).[69] In fact, all of his later words of advice are refined in the fire of his past experience.[70] Overall, the shift is from radical

68. As cited in Kerby, *Narrative and the Self*, p. 21.

69. Even when advice is given on its own it is linked to experience. Passages such as 8.3-5 have Qoheleth's Solomonic experience as their foundation. And 8.16; 9.1; 10.5 are clear examples of Qoheleth establishing an experiential basis for the observations and advice that follow.

70. Longman and I drew similar conclusions independently of one another:

experience to knowledge (although not of a kind that he initially sought).

The importance of advice and Qoheleth's attempt to crystallize it are reflected in the gradual change in narratorial voice—from the density of first-person (ch. 2) to the density of second-person narration (ch. 11). The following graph shows this striking shift in relation to the first-person form.[71]

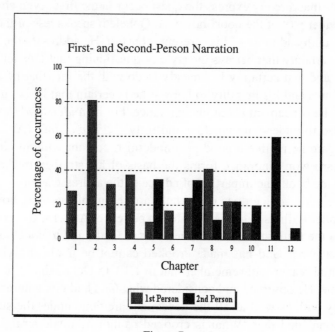

Figure 7

The graph demonstrates well the shift from experience to advice and an overall strategy in which the reader is invited to partake more and more

'[Qoheleth's] experience is the soil out of which his wisdom grows' (*The Book of Ecclesiastes*, p. 19).

71. In various instances the second person is indicated by the pronominal suffix (ךָ), imperative verb forms (e.g. שְׁלַח at 11.1), indirect speech (e.g. אֲשֶׁר תֹּאמַר at 12.1, which governs the remainder of that poem). In the graph I have omitted the second-person verb תַּעֲשֶׂה at 8.4, which is indirect speech at a level removed from Qoheleth's narration ('Who may say to him [the king], "What are you doing [תַּעֲשֶׂה]?"'), and also the two instances of second person as addressed to 'the land' at 10.16-17. For the corresponding first-person graph, see p. 41. For the formula used for calculating the graphs, see pp. 41-42 n. 78.

in the text's story-world, for readers can and do include themselves in the audience that Qoheleth addresses. Allow me to elaborate this point.

The narratee is the character who is addressed in the 'space' of the text itself. At the outer level of the frame this is the frame narrator's son. At the inner level of Qoheleth's narration—in which readers are more involved, since the frame causes amnesia—this is unknown, for Qoheleth never addresses anyone by name or title. However, we can construct from 'hearing one side of the conversation', so to speak, that the person Qoheleth addresses worships at the temple or local 'synagogue' (5.1-5), is a man (11.9), may have a wife (or 'woman') whom he loves (9.9), is young (9.10; 11.9), has servants (7.21), may be a court sage by profession (8.3-5; 10.4, 20) and is probably inquisitive by nature (7.16b; 11.5). This is not so much a narratee as an 'ideal', implied reader. That is, this addressee is able to relate perfectly to all that Qoheleth says on matters with which he too will be familiar. In him Qoheleth would find solace, understanding and a solid drinking partner at the local watering hole. But this person does not exist anymore than Qoheleth does. Any reader can, however, take the place of this implied reader and, as it were, befriend the lonely Qoheleth. And this is made all the easier by the element of second-person narration, which, although the narratee has the above qualities, still does not provide a name. A name would have meant a barrier in this regard and its absence suggests that Qoheleth desired a wide audience to identify as much as possible with this constructed narratee.[72]

There is another element that enables this reading activity. As Brown states, 'underlying Qoheleth's reflections is an explicit awareness that the formation of personal character is a primary goal of wisdom'.[73] This includes the formation not only of his own character (dealt with by the story proper of the quest) but also, and primarily, the character of the

---

72. This readerly transference is also made easier by the act of representation by the frame narrator. Compare Louis Marin's comments in this regard: 'Representative presentation is caught in the dialogic structure of sender and receiver, whoever they may be, for which the frame will furnish one of the privileged spaces of producing "knowing", "believing" and "feeling", of the instructions and injunctions that the power of representation, representing, addresses to the spectator-reader' ('The Frame of Representation', pp. 82-83). Further, see Salyer, 'Vain Rhetoric', p. 190 and p. 443 n. 17 (where he draws on the classic essay of Stephen Crites, 'The Narrative Quality of Experience', *JAAR* 39 [1971], pp. 291-311).

73. 'Character Reconstructed: Ecclesiastes', p. 134.

narratee to whom is addressed his advice. Here is where readers can participate, as it were, in the narrative world, for they are free to suspend disbelief and sense this concern for character formation (which in Qoheleth's case is very appealing since it ultimately concerns, as we shall see, living with/in joy), and in turn test the conditions that Qoheleth lays down for it.

The shift in voice further underscores Qoheleth's 'then' and 'now' narrative stances established by first-person narration. But bringing the relationship between these stances into sharper focus raises questions. Whereas we are able to comprehend much of the 'then' narration of his youth—his circumstance, his desires, his failures and so forth—we know little if anything about the time of his narration, the 'now'. He is, in whatever sense, a king and he is older. But what are the influences on Qoheleth as he speaks in the 'now' dimension? What did he (or 'does he', as a character) *feel* as he narrated? One can speculate that the stance is largely influenced by the act of remembering, for the implied experience involved in retelling his memories is necessarily emotional. Memories (specifically the recollection of events and not merely facts) are by nature emotive and evoke emotions ranging from shame to joy.

Qoheleth's 'now' emotions, however, are not shown to readers. He relates his past, so to speak, expressionlessly. Yet when Qoheleth states that 'I hated life' (2.17-18), is he only referring to his younger disposition? How do we deal with this as a story? Does he still hate life *while* he recounts his tale? When he states that he 'turned to despair' his heart (2.20), is he only referring to his lamentable past? Or does he 'still' despair? I do not think that he does. For, as I stated above, the narrated story redeems Qoheleth's earlier pessimism and despair by virtue of its being set in the past. This is the transforming power of autobiography. And by this we are brought back to the competing themes of success and failure discussed at the beginning of this chapter. Without a doubt Qoheleth has failed in the act of his quest, but his success lies in the telling of his story. Further, by resolving himself to the fact that part of the wisdom of his old age was that he had learned the criteria of the deeper meaning he sought, he redeems the failure of his youth. Since the 'now' can only emerge from the 'brooding consciousness' (Fox) of the 'then', the 'now' is necessarily refined by the fire of the 'then'. If readers lose their grasp of this narrative structure they become in danger of getting lost in the 'then' of Qoheleth's most pessimistic reflection. Indeed, when Qoheleth breaks out with joy it is almost exclusively when he narrates in a 'now' to the 'reader' (see below).

One emphasis of Qoheleth's 'now' advice is on the practical behaviour of the 'reader', and this effects changes in regard to the actors and elements of the actantial model as it applies to his quest. The new Subject is the ideal/implied reader (with which real readers might identify) in that, in Qoheleth's story, it has the role of seeking understanding and respectively failing (humanity *and* Qoheleth fail), but also of seeking God's enablement for a joyful life. The new Object of the new Subject, instead of *understanding*, which brings only grief, is practical living and enjoyment of life. Wisdom can now be a true Helper, without deceit. Whereas wisdom failed Qoheleth in the purpose for which he applied it, it will function adequately for the reader's purpose. This is not in the deeper sense of 'becoming wise', but in the practical sense of effectively 'getting by'. In fact, Qoheleth has nothing bad to say about such wisdom, generally speaking (see above, p. 232). This helps us to make sense of those passages where Qoheleth praises wisdom and its effects, for on the whole they are addressed to the reader, the new Subject. The Opponent will only be its opposite, folly.

As early as 3.22 Qoheleth prepares the way for this shift in the actantial model: 'So I observed that there is nothing better than that humanity should rejoice in their deeds. Indeed, that is their portion; for who will bring them to see what will be after them?' No one can bring them to see or understand the future—their fate—even as it unfolds, but at least they have another, more feasible Object: their portion of joy. Further, they ('humanity', addressee and reader) should not attempt to 'become truly wise' (7.16; cf. 2.15; 7.23-24), for that was Qoheleth's Object and he failed to obtain it. Although they fail in Qoheleth's model (they cannot discover) they may at least rejoice in their deeds and thereby succeed in the new model.

It is important to note (in relation to the 'new' model) that Qoheleth's advice is neither naïve nor uncritical. That is, Qoheleth does not set the reader up for failure in the ways that he failed. The advice that he offers is no more a 'sure thing' than his own enterprise. Indeed, he cites the practical outcome of wisdom for the addressee (11.3) *alongside* the absurd experience of it (11.4-5). He also states that wisdom is generally an advantage (7.11-12, 19; 9.16–10.1), but that fate will not be influenced or changed by it or by anything else under the sun (9.2, 11-12; 10.8-11; *passim*). This is precisely why the wise have no ultimate advantage over fools (6.8). Furthermore, in texts where Qoheleth suggests that God will empower people to enjoy what they have (esp. 2.25-26; 5.18-19; 6.2), joy is not imparted conditionally but is solely a gift of God, the recipient of which is determined by the giver (and there is 'nothing better' than when this gift of God is given; 2.24; 3.12-13; cf. 3.22). It is in these texts that the Power of the new model is established. Whether people can enjoy all of the riches and goods God gives them depends on whether or not he chooses further to empower them to do so. At 2.25 Qoheleth asks, 'Who can eat/enjoy [יאכל] apart from him?'[74] For it is only to those with whom he is pleased that he gives wisdom (but what kind?), knowledge and joy. But to the sinner God gives more toil, and the fruit of that toil to the one who pleases God (2.26). (Note that for Qoheleth, a sinner [part. of חטא] is not necessarily one who offends God, but is one with whom God is displeased for whatever reason[75]—the integrity of God's choice as the Power thereby remains intact.) Qoheleth does not appear to approve of this situation, for he goes on to say in the same verse that this was absurd and a pursuit of wind, but his doctrine (or rather, formulation as the result of empirical observation) is clear. It becomes even more clear in the small but weighty discrepancy observable between 5.19 and 6.2. In both verses there is a common figure: a man to whom God has given riches, wealth and (in 6.2) honour. But in 5.19 God enables that man to enjoy it (והשליטו לאכל ממנו), whereas in 6.2 God does not enable that man to enjoy it (ולא־ישליטנו האלהים לאכל ממנו). Instead, a stranger enjoys it— not a sage or a fool, not a righteous person nor a sinner, but a stranger (נכרי). No reason is given for the difference in God's choice (although note that Qoheleth clearly disapproves of the latter case, which is an evil [6.1], while the former case is good [5.18]). As in Qoheleth's model, the reason for the will of the Power is vexatiously inscrutable.

---

74. That is, God, following the majority of commentaries and LXX in the emen-dation of MT's ממני to ממנו. The previous verse quite blatantly sets the context for such a reading by stating that there is 'nothing better' than to eat, drink and take pleasure in toil, for 'this is from the hand of God' (כי מיד האלהים היא).

75. Qoheleth uses the participle in two senses. The other sense is found at 7.10 where Qoheleth states that there is no one righteous who does good and does not sin (cf. 8.12). With such a moral sense it is not possible to place the sinner and the one who pleases God as opposites since the latter person does not exist. The sense found in 2.26 is also found in 7.26, where the 'sinner' is again contrasted to the one who pleases God. In the end the fate of the moral sinner and the one who 'does good' (albeit imperfectly) are ultimately the same: death (9.1; cf. 2.16).

Other 'joy' texts, however, put the responsibility for joy squarely on
the reader/addressee:

> Go! Eat your bread with joy,
>> and drink your wine with a glad heart;
> For God has already approved your deeds.
> At all times let your garments be white,
>> and let oil not be lacking on your head.
>
> Enjoy life with a woman whom you love, all the days of your absurd life
> that he has given you under the sun—all your absurd days; for this is
> your portion in life, and in the toil at which you toil. All that your hand
> finds to do, do with your strength; for there is no activity, or reasoning,
> or knowledge, or wisdom in Sheol where you are going (9.7-10).

God has ultimately provided the ability to work and to enjoy (he is still
the beginning and end of the individual's self and identity), but he is, as
it were, one step removed. This is a human plane of activity, for *God
has already approved your deeds*—the command is already given. And
in the end God will judge you, as the rabbis I believe rightly understood, not concerning what you have discovered or attained, not concerning what enablement he has bestowed on you to enjoy life, but
concerning the *doing* of these things:

> Rejoice, O young man, in your youth.
>> And let your heart gladden you in the days of your youth.
> And walk in the ways of your heart,
>> and in the sight of your eyes.
> And know for certain that *concerning all of these things*
>> God will bring you into judgment (11.9).

Here the joy is human but the imperative is divine. There is a clear
divide between what the reader/addressee of Qoheleth's advice is *able*
to do and *enabled* to do. It is not that God should be forgotten,[76] nor
that enjoyment means amoral behaviour, but that God has given a heart
that is already capable of rejoicing and that the activities of everyday
life (eating, drinking, dressing, lovemaking) are all able to be infused
with joy.

There are, then, two distinct strains of joy texts. In one God chooses
(as the Power) to enable or not to enable enjoyment. In the other, joy
is accessible through the help of wisdom in daily life, and the

76. Indeed, quite the opposite is the case. Note that fearing God is key to
Qoheleth's advice (3.14; 5.7; 7.18; 8.12-13) and that the most important injunction
of all is to *remember* your creator (see below).

responsibility for that joy is the reader's. Taken altogether the actants of the new model can be represented as follows:

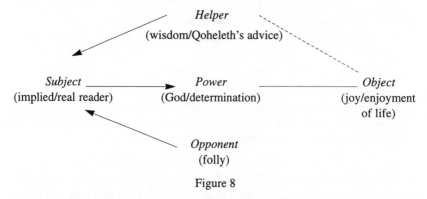

Figure 8

Qoheleth told the story of the failure to obtain his chosen Object, and in this respect the quest was, from the beginning, over. But from that juncture of failure Qoheleth relates what he has learned and points the reader to an obtainable Object. This is great autobiography in that by conveying the wisdom of a deeply lived life the folly of youth is redeemed. Although readers are still caught in his absurd predicament, day-to-day enjoyment and satisfaction is within their own grasp.[77] Qoheleth's quest is therefore by no means the end of the story, for his prevailing concern is to show readers of his story how to live with the absurd.

There is another kind of redemption present in Qoheleth's story, and it applies not only to his earlier narrated experience but also to the absurd condition in which he and the reader find themselves—that redemption is the act of remembering. Qoheleth makes clear that remembering is important (see the Postscript, sec. 4), and in the act of telling his story he has remembered what is presumably important to him. To re-member is to re-construct (Qoheleth has reconstructed a story-world from his experiences), and it is in this sense that Qoheleth redeems his—and the reader's—experience of the absurd; that is, by

77. Fox has recently drawn attention to a similar feature of Qoheleth's advice, namely the reconstruction of meaning: Qoheleth's counsels 'are allowed value for the moment only, but the moment is all we have. These accommodations allow humans to create *little meanings*, local meanings, within the great absurd' ('The Inner Structure of Qohelet's Thought', in A. Schoors [ed.], *Qohelet in the Context of Wisdom* [BETL, 136; Leuven: Leuven University Press, 1998], pp. 225-38 [232]).

simply telling his story. For every story (particularly one which, like Qoheleth's, involves the strategy of recollection) is a making new and a creation of meaning when perhaps there was none to begin with. As Kierkegaard recognized, the whole process of recollecting redeems events that are absurd, cyclical or even meaningless, and creates meaning:

> When the Greeks said that all knowing is recollecting, they said that all existence, which is, has been; when one says that life is a repetition, one says: actuality, which has been, now comes into existence. If one does not have the category of recollection or of repetition, all life dissolves into an empty, meaningless noise.[78]

By recollecting, Qoheleth 'made' his otherwise disjointed experience meaningful as a narrative, thereby transcending the cyclical and the absurd (which constitute the failed outcome of his quest). Note John Sturrock's helpful comments on the autobiographical form:

> A human life can be brought to display meaning only on condition of being turned into a story; once subject to the public order of narrative, it acquires both the gravity of a settled and venerable literary form, and the orientation of hindsight which alone raises the past from an aimless sum of reminiscence into a personal history... A life storied is a life made meaningful...[79]

Making meaning in this way entails making something different from what it once was while maintaining continuity with the past. 'Each time we relate a story', suggests Judith Fishman, 'it is both old and new: there are the events that we draw from our lives that we construct into a text and there is the new—our angle of vision, our selection, our memory...our interpretation, our age, the moment of writing.'[80] This brings us back to the sense of self in Qoheleth's story. The act of memory is intimately connected to self and identity since what we remember is uniquely our own, and through it we relate the way we see the world and interpret those events of our lives that are worthy of remembrance. This contributes to the fictional quality of Qoheleth's story in that his is a reconstruction, for recollection is not the past 'as it actually happened', but *as* we remember it. Narrated recollection

---

78. Written under the pseudonym, Johannes de Silentio, *Fear and Trembling/ Repetition* (ed. and trans. H.V. Hong and E.H. Hong; Princeton, NJ: Princeton University Press, 1983 [1843]), p. 149.

79. *The Language of Autobiography*, p. 20.

80. 'Enclosures', p. 29.

cannot help but imaginatively refigure, interpret and imbue significance to the experience it recollects and to the 'now' experience of the narrator. Indeed, as the philosopher and poet George Santayana notes, more than our empirical faculty, recollection involves the imagination:

> When I remember I do not look at my past experience, any more than when I think of a friend's misfortunes I look at his thoughts. I imagine them: or rather I imagine something of my own manufacture, as if I were writing a novel and I attribute this intuited experience to myself in the past, or to the other person.[81]

Writing fiction and remembering are of the same cloth. Qoheleth's remembering is uniquely his own and as an act of remembrance and imagination, like any good story, easily engages our imaginations.

Of course, Qoheleth's most poignant ode to the act of remembering is his final 'set-piece' (Fisch), the poem of 12.1-7. I will not rehearse the history of its interpretation or discuss what it might refer to (there is plenty of this in the commentaries), for that would detract from the purpose at hand, which is to allow Qoheleth's sense of poetic urgency and the importance of memory here to be felt. I therefore offer my own translation of a passage that, for what it is worth, is among my most treasured anywhere:

> Remember your creator in the days of your youth;
> Before the days of misery come and the years draw nigh,
>   when you will say, 'I have no delight in them';
> Before the darkening of the sun and the light,
>   and the moon and the stars;
> And the clouds return after the rain;
> In the day when the keepers of the house tremble,
>   and the men of strength are bent over;
> And the women at the mill cease since they are few,
>   and the ladies who gaze through the windows are darkened;
> And doors in the street are closed,
>   and the sound of the mill is low;
> And the voice of the bird wanes,
>   and all the daughters of song are brought low;
> When some fear heights,
>   and terrors are in the road;
> And the almond tree blossoms,
>   and the locust is heavy laden,
>   and the caperberry buds;

---

81. Cited in Kerby, *Narrative and the Self*, p. 30.

While humanity goes to their eternal home,
    and the mourners encompass the street;
Before the silver cord is snapped,
    and the golden bowl is crushed;
And a pitcher is broken at the spring,
    and the wheel is crushed in the pit;
And the dust returns to the earth as it was,
    and the spirit returns to God who gave it.

More than anything else this is poetry and demands reading as such. Ellul states the case well when he writes that

> everyone reads this passage like an enigma from which we must find the allegorical meaning of each term...I think the poem is too vast for this, and too 'polysemous' ... It is *first of all* a poem! In other words, it is not at all a problem to solve... First of all we must let the beauty of the text grip us, as we listen to it in silence, like music. We should let the poem strike our emotions first, and allow our sensitivity and imagination to speak before we try to analyze and 'understand' it.[82]

With this in mind I will relate my own reading.

I am reminded of images that grow dim, whether in the memory or before the eyes; of dreams and ideals that were once cherished and strong but have now diminished. I am reminded of the line of a folk song, 'Don't our dreams die hard in the ashes of destiny?'[83] By this I am reminded that everything fades to death. Indeed, as Qoheleth's reader I am reminded that everything eventually darkens, ceases, trembles, fears, closes and wanes in its own time. And yet I am lifted by other images: a bird sings, the seasonal fertility of spring continues (the locust is heavy laden) despite the ceasing of all that is under the sun. The closing images recall the breakdown of an established society: the silver and golden furnishings eventually wear out, the machinery by which we live (the pitcher, the wheel in the pit, all technology for living) becomes broken and will eventually be replaced, along with any meaning that that technology once held for its users. Finally, I am reminded of the end of everyone, and the return to God strikes a note of hope. I am lifted for a moment from all the trappings of the absurd, above what is 'under the sun' in Qoheleth's eyes, and yet I am brought back swiftly to the reality of Qoheleth's experience when I read, '"Absurdity of absurdities", said Qoheleth. "Everything is absurd"'

---

82. *Reason for Being*, p. 285 (italics Ellul's).

83. Mark Heard, 'Another Good Lie', from the album, *Dry Bones Dance* (Ideola Music, 1991).

(12.8). That is my 'felt' reading.

Ellul goes on to convey his own sensitive reading, which is worth citing at least in part:

> As I read this poem...it calls to mind all declines, all breaches, closures, and endings. Not just the decline of an individual nearing death, not just human destiny, but everything: the end of any work which is no longer done, which disappears because no one is present to do it anymore...the end of a village or community...the end of a love replaced by fear; the end of an art, its works shattered, unless they die in our museums... It is the song of the End.[84]

Fisch's reading is also worth citing:

> ...there is something beyond death and vanity [in 12.1-7]. What counts is the life that is given us, the remembering, the testimony. Undercutting and contradicting the grave poetry of dying is the purposeful rhythm of living... Before the days come when the sun, the light, the moon and the stars are darkened, we are to do our remembering, to remember beginnings and endings, to count our days. If we do well...we shall perhaps be remembered in our turn, even after we are returned to dust and the golden bowl is shattered and all its fragile beauty, its fascination, its charm, its near-perfection have been seen as vanity.[85]

Fisch captures well the element of redemption in Qoheleth's closing words. Qoheleth has left behind the intellectual battle, the attempt to address our intellect, and has crafted words of beauty to remind us of the fragility of living and dying. Here is a redemption stunning in its depth and grace, brimming with the wonder of youth (for it places the reader 'in' the opposite of old age and of a world that is only ceasing), yet the sadness of Qoheleth's 'now' is present. The refrain, 'before' the ceasing of everything, is the dominant idea and he cannot reverse the vexation of his own life, but he redeems for himself his experience of the loss of youth and of the futility of his attempts to gain true understanding. Yet the understanding he demonstrates here is, as his final word, incomparably better, for it will not bring the curse of הבל. And here lies his final redemption. By empathetically and elegantly prompting readers to remember (and re-membering itself is a form of redemption) their creator in the face of the end of everything (and this reminder unfolds after the import of living joyfully is related in 11.9), he enables 'those who will hear' to live with the absurdity of dying.

---

84. *Reason for Being*, pp. 285-86.
85. 'Qohelet: A Hebrew Ironist', p. 178.

CONCLUSION

> Better the end of a thing than its beginning.
>
> Qoheleth (Eccl. 7.8)

In my own reading of secondary literature I have been struck by the disparity inherent in the coexistence of a general narrative understanding of Qoheleth's words (as represented in the quotes in sec. 1 of the Introduction, for example) and the aversion to the application of narrative criticism. Although scholars of Ecclesiastes like to imagine that Qoheleth's 'brooding consciousness' is at its centre, clearly it is the emphasis on what Qoheleth said, and not how he said it, or for what reasons he said it in that way, that has been the predominant focus of Qoheleth studies. Why the dysfunctional enterprise?

Perhaps the aversion to narrative approaches lies in the relative mistrust of narratives as a contendable academic form of expression. As Judith Summerfield writes concerning American higher education,

> I suggest...that we loosen what Jimmy Britton calls 'the stranglehold that the expository essay has maintained over writing in American higher education'. He notes, as well, that 'if today's winds of change are any indication at all, narrative will be a candidate for a leading role among those forms of discourse that will replace the expository essay'.[1]

That aversion quite possibly fortifies the reluctance to see in the works we study a narrative form, a reluctance to adopt a way of interpreting. In the case of Ecclesiastes, such a perspective has perhaps also been obscured by the clouds kicked up by those armies of redactors whom we, maybe too easily, imagine to have assaulted and maligned some *Urtext* of Qoheleth's tale.

I have attempted to redress this interpretive imbalance by reading Ecclesiastes using the tools that narrative criticism has to offer. I have not categorically argued that Ecclesiastes can *only* be understood as narrative. Rather, this study has been an experiment in what happens

---

1. 'Framing Narratives', p. 238.

when Ecclesiastes is investigated with confidence in its narrative quality. I have taken an idea and applied it to determine its consequences, and in the process I have necessarily said some things that will appear to be extreme (especially since the narrative approach implies a rejection of other approaches as it involves seeing the text 'one way', as a story). This in turn has left some questions open. While I have showed, for example, that Ecclesiastes can be read as narrative I must admit that the definition of narrative is constantly being expanded and is largely culturally defined.[2] That is, we call Ingmar Bergman's *Through a Glass Darkly* and Samuel Beckett's *Waiting for Godot* stories, even though they do not necessarily operate with functional events in a time sequence of some kind (and if they do it is barely perceptible). But reading something as a narrative, if its discourse so allows, is a readerly decision. Readers can read Ecclesiastes as an unconnected collection of wisdom sayings, or they can just as easily read it with an awareness of its narrative quality and of the features of its story-line.

Such a reading carries the kinds of implications similar to those raised by Solomonic readings. Readers after Martin Luther were 'freed' to discuss critically authorship and the multilayered attributes stemming from textual traditions. This in turn created all kinds of interpretive possibilities, some of which, after the manner of the documentary hypothesis, became virtually doctrinal. As we have seen, the narrative method also creates distinct interpretive possibilities and makes good, as it were, the implied commitment to a narrative approach latent in so much of modern Qoheleth studies. One is a construct of authorship with which readers read (Solomon as author), while the other is a construct of text that asks, How do the events unfurl before the reader as a precipitation of meaning? What are the overall strategies of communication? In what way and on what levels does a story take place?

Another 'open question' is whether this approach has dealt satisfactorily with non-narrative material in Ecclesiastes. I have not considered in depth either the poetry sections or the blocks of wisdom sayings. We have seen, however, how portions of each of these have informed particularly narrative strategies (e.g. 4.1-3; 7.23-29; 12.1-7). But there are other considerations in my favour. The first is that the poems can be

---

2. For a recent discussion of the problem of defining narrative, see Chatman, *Coming to Terms*, pp. 6-21.

seen as mirror-texts for the whole of Qoheleth's experience. The time poem (3.1-8), for example, has been seen by Zimmermann to reflect Qoheleth's life experience—as a microcosm of the larger story.[3] Also, all of the 'non-narrative' material is in a narrative setting (see Figs. 1 and 3) and there are no 'markers' to suggest that they should be considered to be outside of the story proper. The narrative integrity (of voice, person, stance and so forth) throughout the whole is firmly intact; indeed, it evidences stylistic strategies. Finally, Qoheleth's advice (much of which appears in the blocks of wisdom-sayings in chs. 7 and 10), refined in the fire of his earlier experience, is spoken in the second person and functions largely to redeem the story/life of the protagonist, Qoheleth.

A word is in order about the Postscript that follows. The Postscript explores themes that are made possible by Qoheleth's narrative form; that is, the expression of an individual's experience of the absurd. In a sense it has arisen from what precedes it in that this book is precisely about Qoheleth's way of knowing, his interaction with the world and the inherent redemptive potential of his story (it also complements many of the particular issues raised in the Excursus and Chapters 6 to 8). Indeed, that Qoheleth's words are in any way comparable to the personal reflections of others is suggestive of their power as autobiography.

In closing I would like to explain how I came to apply the narrative approach to Ecclesiastes. After one of my readings I was struck by the vitality of character that held the strings of observation together, the elements of time played on my mind and a good story emerged clearly from what was sometimes a murky reading experience. Therefore, this whole study arises from and pays homage to a reading experience. This brings me to the role of the imagination in reading that I discussed in Chapter 8.5 and that I would like to describe briefly here.

In my reading experience I can easily imagine Qoheleth telling his story, and can visualize a setting: a one-man play. For this is one context in which we may be told a story and allow the teller of the story to detract into maxims that convey the story's essence or aims. Such a setting also aids in the important realization that Qoheleth's story emanates from a person: that is, the narrative character that is more

3. See *Inner World*, pp. 44-49. Zimmermann argues that the narrativity of the poem reflects Qoheleth's 'life-script'. Compare my comments concerning texts that might mirror Qoheleth's quest (pp. 182, 184).

cohesive than what we have usually allowed for. When we read Proverbs we imagine the voice of Solomon, of wisdom, or perhaps for the more 'educated', the voice of many redactors is heard (for some it may be the voice of God), but when we read Qoheleth we hear the uni-voice of the cynic. Or is it the joyful optimist? Or is it the unique Hebrew intellectual? Whoever it is, it is Qoheleth the individual and it is his story that we hear. Of course, the frame narrator is the stage itself, and Qoheleth sits in a chair in a drafty room with a fireplace and *many* books on his shelves. Behind him flash the scenes of his youth while he tells his story: vineyards, kingdoms, oppressions of peoples, images of toiling, searching and of intermittent rest. Sometimes he gets up from his chair to speak directly to the audience, relating soberly what is most important to store away, to remember, to know and to rejoice in. And this is where the real contribution of a narrative approach lies: the elucidation of that central figure who searches for relief from his absurd condition.

Postscript

QOHELETH AND THE EXISTENTIAL LEGACY OF THE HOLOCAUST*

> He who has a 'why' to live for can bear almost any 'how'.
>
> Victor Frankl, Holocaust survivor

> There is no why.
>
> Simeon Levi, Holocaust survivor[1]

This is a comparative reflection, and I feel the need to make two things clear about it from the start. First, Qoheleth's subject matter is, in one sense, in no way comparable to the Holocaust.[2] The Holocaust is a unique event in human history, and I do not presume to belittle the uncommon suffering of its victims by presuming an *experiential* likeness between their observations and those of Qoheleth (either diachronically or by regarding Qoheleth strictly as a narrative character). My interest lies in the themes that have emerged from reflections on the Holocaust—from its survivors and its commentators—and that bear likeness to some of Qoheleth's themes.[3] Second, I do not regard the Holocaust as merely 'an example' of the existential themes under review (whereas Qoheleth's thought *is* merely 'an example'). Again, its uniqueness must be remembered. Why, then, am I making the thematic comparison at all? My reasons are twofold.

First, comparisons at any level have the potential to shed interpretive light. Because of my lack of expertise in Holocaust studies and philosophy, I intend to

---

* This Postscript appears in a slightly shorter from as 'Qoheleth and the Existential Legacy of the Holocaust', *HeyJ* 38.1 (1997), pp. 35-50.

1. Both quotes cited by Leon Stein, 'The Holocaust and the Legacy of Existentialism', in Y. Bauer *et al.* (eds.), *Remembering for the Future* (3 vols.; Oxford: Pergamon Press, 1989), II, pp. 1943-55 (pp. 1951, 1945, respectively). Frankl's quote is directly from Nietzsche and it, along with another Nietzschean quote ('What does not kill me makes me stronger'), formed the starting point of Frankl's controversial psychological theories.

2. Or 'Shoah', as it is often called. Shoah (שׁוֹאָה) is the modern Hebrew word for the Nazi Holocaust, meaning 'catastrophe' or 'devastation'.

3. The distinction between focus on reflections as against historical analyses is, as S.M. Bokolsky has shown, an important one. In his essay, 'The Problem of Survivor Discourse: Toward a Poetics of Survivor Testimonies' (in Bauer *et al.* [eds.], *Remembering for the Future*, I, pp. 1082-1092), Bokolsky discusses cases where the testimony of Holocaust survivors differs from academic historical accounts and the problems such confliction raises. '[Students] of the Holocaust', says Bokolsky, 'do not listen to survivors to learn about historical facts' (p. 1087). The same point can be emphasized concerning my approach. The truth I am after is that of the memory of experience, or even the experience of memory.

shed light only on the themes of Qoheleth—any illumination beyond this is hoped for, but incidental. The second and more important reason is my own interest, which was initially sparked by a visit to the Yad-va-Shem[4] Holocaust museum in Jerusalem. From my own subsequent reading and viewing of films on the subject (such as Claude Lanzmann's *Shoah* [1985],[5] and Agnieszka Holland's *Europa, Europa* [1991]), I have been struck by the recurrent themes of absurdity, fate and death, and the thematic resemblance of them to Qoheleth's narrative. The step towards this study was, therefore, a natural one.[6] While some have drawn significant parallels between, for example, the Holocaust and Job,[7] Ecclesiastes and existentialism (see below, n. 32), and existentialism and the Holocaust,[8] I have not come across any study that links the three I am attempting to link.[9] I will turn to what precisely forms the links below.

1. *Existentialist Themes: Material for a Response*

Existentialism for a long while dominated arenas of continental philosophical thought and has had a far-reaching influence on humanities areas such as philosophy, theology and drama. Defining existentialism is made a complex task by the fact that so many diverse thinkers have claimed the nomen as their own. While

4. יד ושם, lit. 'hand and name'—symbols of the importance of remembering. The phrase originates from Isa. 56.5: 'I will give in my house and within my walls a monument and a name [יד ושם] better than sons and daughters; I will give them an everlasting name [שם עולם] which shall not be cut off' (RSV).

5. Stein said of *Shoah* in 1989 that it was arguably 'the greatest film of the Holocaust yet made' ('Legacy of Existentialism', p. 1953).

6. It would be unfair of me not to admit, I think, another reason for my interest. With many others, at the time of writing, my attention turned to the 50-year commemorations of VE day, and of the liberation of Belsen and other camps. A revival of general public interest seems to have accompanied these as well. I refer to a host of television specials and Steven Spielberg's film, *Schindler's List* (1994).

7. See Stein, 'Legacy of Existentialism', p. 1949. Holocaust survivor Elie Wiesel, in his semi-autobiographical novel *Night*, describes the talk that surrounded him at night in the barracks of Auschwitz: 'Some talked of God, of his mysterious ways, of the sins of the Jewish people, and of their future deliverance. But I had ceased to pray. How I sympathised with Job! I did not deny God's existence, but I doubted his absolute justice' (trans. S. Rodway; London: Robson Books, 1987 [1960], p. 53). It is worth noting here that I am in agreement with the sympathy underlying Frank Crüsemann's comment, 'Koheleth brings Job to its logical conclusion' ('The Unchangeable World', p. 61).

8. I will be drawing heavily (as I already have for the title of this Postscript) from Leon Stein's engaging and perceptive essay entitled, 'The Holocaust and the Legacy of Existentialism'. There he details the host of existential reactions that the Holocaust engendered—from its survivors (Victor Frankl, Filip Müller and others) to its reactionaries (Richard Rubenstein, Reinhold Niebuhr, Claude Lanzmann and others).

9. It is worth noting, however, that in his photo-essay depicting each verse of Ecclesiastes, R. Short offers a photo of an Auschwitz survivor displaying the tattooed numbers on his forearm in order (I presume) to depict an irony in the meaning of 3.18, 'I said in my heart concerning human beings, "God is purging them to show them that they themselves are animals"' (*A Time to Be Born—A Time to Die*, ad loc.).

Søren Kierkegaard is widely regarded as the 'founder' of modern existentialism, others point to Augustine, even Socrates. Even the mainly post-World War II writers who are regarded as clearly existential (e.g. Sartre, Camus, Heidegger) differ among themselves on such central notions as the existence of God and the nature of human responsibility. Perhaps the best approach is to discuss existentialism in terms of its defining themes. Key themes I will focus on are the role of extreme circumstances, (confrontation with) absurdity and (particularly in relation to the existential legacy of the Holocaust) the individual struggle with or against death and fate.

As A. MacIntyre suggests, 'stress on the extreme and the exceptional experience is common to all existentialism'.[10] One prime example of this comes from the Preface (*Exordium*) of Kierkegaard's *Fear and Trembling*, in which four versions of Abraham's sacrifice of Isaac (the Akedah) are imaginatively devised and contemplated. In each one the emphasis is laid on a different aspect of that most extreme of experiences. In version III Abraham is racked with guilt by the notion that his willingness to sacrifice the best that God had given him was the most terrible sin he could imagine. In version IV it is Isaac who returns having 'lost the faith', and who refuses to speak of the event for the remainder of his life.[11] In each it is the ramifications of the extremity of the ordeal that is drawn out and reflected upon.[12] In the absurdist dramas of the 1950s and '60s (of Beckett and Camus in particular), the heroes find themselves in drastic and at times unrealistic situations, and it is the flair and drama employed that has brought criticism on existentialism for being too out of touch and not concerned with the 'ordinary'.[13] As we shall see, however, its obsession with the extreme has made existentialism amenable to reflection on the Holocaust.

For the existentialist, extreme circumstances breed the realization of the absurd. The extremity itself is defined by that frustration of hope or desire in a circumstance that suggests its opposite. In other words, it is the divorce between deed and consequence (see the Excursus) that defines the extreme. When one experiences the

---

10. 'Existentialism', in P. Edwards (ed.), *The Encyclopedia of Philosophy*, III (New York: Macmillan, 1967), pp. 147-59 (149).

11. *Fear and Trembling/Repetition*, pp. 13-14.

12. Isabel Wollaston has recently argued that the Akedah has functioned historically as an archetype for the traditional Jewish response to catastrophe. Simply put, in her essay, '"Traditions of Remembrance": Post-Holocaust Interpretations of Genesis 22' (in J. Davies, G. Harvey and W.G.E. Watson [eds.], *Words Remembered, Texts Renewed* [JSOTSup, 195; Sheffield: Sheffield Academic Press, 1995], pp. 41-51), Wollaston draws some significant parallels between Holocaust reflections and the Akedah, showing how modern Jewish appropriations of the biblical story operate with two basic strategies: (1) the Holocaust is a 'sacred parody' of the Akedah, and (2) the Holocaust is a 'literal recall' of the story, a tale of 'monumental faithfulness'. It is interesting to note the idea of 'holocaust' present in the Akedah. Isaac is offered as a sacrifice wholly consumed by fire (עֹלָה).

13. MacIntyre makes the following helpful statement in this regard: 'It would be...illuminating to see existentialism as the fusion of a certain kind of dramatization of social experience with the desire to resolve certain unsolved philosophical problems' ('Existentialism', p. 153).

failure of, for example, a set of rules in a supposedly closed and secure social system, that circumstance is extreme by virtue of one's consciousness of the illogical relationships within it. Hence the absurd drama does not consist merely of the world and its systems, which are absurd in themselves, but also of humanity's participation, made up of the confrontation between the 'wild longing for clarity whose call echoes in the human heart'[14] and the illogicity of the world; these together *create* the absurd. The absurd itself is consciousness of that confrontation and defines, to a large degree, modern existentialism.

The struggle with or against death and fate is the broadest of the existentialist themes I will touch on. These two certainties loom above the horizon of the absurdist drama and must either be rallied against or bravely accepted. Although it is a theme that pulsates through literature—from Hamlet's soliloquy to Hemingway's Frederic and Catherine in *A Farewell to Arms*—for the existentialist it is an all-encompassing issue. For example, in Samuel Beckett's most celebrated play, *Waiting for Godot*, the whole process of waiting takes on a quality of Sheol-like proportions. Two 'bums' named Estragon and Vladimir, the 'protagonists' around whom the play revolves, partake in idle but clever banter throughout the first act (being occasionally interrupted by a curious wanderer named 'Pozzo'), and return to do the same in the second. The dialogue is infused with nebulous references to death and fate. Principally, neither of our heroes can leave as they are waiting for Godot, and although they are unsure why they continue, they do so, in circular frustration. In the second act Vladimir commences, in the same place as the first act concluded, with a song:

> A dog came in the kitchen
> And stole a crust of bread
> Then cook up with a ladle
> And beat him till he was dead.
>
> Then all the dogs came running
> And dug the dog a tomb—
> And wrote upon the tombstone
> For the eyes of dogs to come:
>
> A dog came in the kitchen...[15]

Of course, the resolution to the dilemma of Vladimir's song differs depending on whom one reads, but the dilemma itself remains essentially the same: life in its futility is circular, and attempting to escape it, and death within it, is futile.

2. The Existential Drama Made Real

The Holocaust brought each of these themes into sharp and painful relief. As Stein states the case, 'Existentialism in all its forms—from Friedrich Nietzsche to Jean

---

14. A. Camus, *The Myth of Sisyphus* (trans. J. O'Brien; New York: Vintage Books, 1991 [1942]), p. 21.
15. New York: Grove Press, 1954, pp. 37-38.

Amery—became a pervasive, unifying theme in the reaction of Western culture to the Holocaust. Existential thinkers and writers struggled to create meaningful responses to an overwhelming event that had shattered traditional frameworks of meaning.'[16] This is because the Holocaust *embodied* existential themes in such a frighteningly real way that the critique of the 'out of touch' drama of the existentialist could not be levied. Nietzschean myth had become flesh. Sartre's dictum, 'existence precedes essence', became a response to the inhuman notion that (as in the manner that Nazis regarded Jews, Slavs and Gypsies) people were abstract objects whose essence was tragically pre-judged.[17] Challenges to the way in which Western culture was able to divorce itself from the responsibility of its view of the human subject, particularly early on in the War, had to be made.

The theme of extreme situations is perhaps the most obvious that emerges from the Holocaust ordeal. The very idea of Holocaust, the extermination of a people based on who they are and not what they had done (that is, not fitting the classical notion of 'criminal') can only be couched in extremist terms. It required the employment of literally thought-less categories of the person, and made, for the Jewish people, existence itself a crime. And then there are the inconceivable facts. For example, of the 400,000 victims of the Polish concentration camp, Chelmo (German = Kulnhof), 2 survived.[18] Among the remains of the camp at Belsen today stand memorials which mark the deaths on those sites of, for example, 800, 1000 and even 5000 people. It is not possible to reflect upon the Holocaust without thinking in the most extreme of terms.

Of course, such facts do not really need rehearsing, but in the circumstances they reflect, the existential dilemma was made real for every Jew. There is the story, for example, of Solomon Perel, who at the age of 13 changed his identity to escape from the camps. He 'served' in the Hitler Youth and daily faced his crisis of identity alone, until he no longer knew who he was.[19] Even those who accepted their identity had to face the fact that their oppressors did not regard them as human. In the camps, those who used the word 'body' or 'victim' to describe the Jewish dead were beaten. Instead, they were forced to use the Nazi word of choice, *Figuren*.[20] The incomparable suffering led many to feel as though their very selves had been hollowed out. In his novel, *Night*, Elie Wiesel describes such an experience. He reflects poignantly on his feelings after witnessing the burning of children not much younger than himself:

> It was no longer possible to grasp anything. The instincts of self-preservation, of self-defense, of pride, had all deserted us...the child I was had been consumed in the flames. There remained only a shape that looked like me.[21]

16. 'Legacy of Existentialism', p. 1943.
17. Stein, 'Legacy of Existentialism', p. 1943.
18. Their names are Mikhaël Podchlebnik and Simon Srebnik and they are featured in Claude Lanzmann's film, *Shoah*.
19. As told in the film, *Europa, Europa*, based on Perel's autobiography.
20. As described by R. Glazar in Lanzmann's *Shoah*.
21. *Night*, p. 46. He later reflects that he detested the feeling of disjunction between body and self which the intense physical suffering caused (pp. 91-92).

The extremities of the experience of the Holocaust were a theft of hope, and in existential terms, a theft of the freedom to determine and preserve the self.

In the concentration camps, those who were intellectually sensitive found themselves tortured by the extremity of their experience and the unanswerable questions that it raised.[22] A recurrent theme of Holocaust literature and film is the inability to comprehend the inhumanity, and the pain involved in trying. Sensitive victims could say with Qoheleth, 'With much wisdom (perception, awareness) comes much vexation, and those who increase knowledge increase pain' (1.18). The most tortuous of those unanswerable questions was surely 'Why?', and attempting to answer it amounted to the fullest confrontation with the absurd.

First, there are the bitter ironies, which, especially in retrospect, reflect the absurd. Before the war, 80% of the Polish town of Oświęcim (which 'became' Auschwitz) were Jewish. As is well known, Jews were often among the social élite of Germany—doctors, lawyers, scientists—and had won a high percentage of Germany's pre-war Nobel prizes. At the conclusion of part 1 of *Shoah*, Claude Lanzmann illustrates the absurdity of the mechanical and dehumanizing policies of the Nazis by reading a letter issued from the headquarters of the Reich at the height of the War. The letter specifies, in the most calculating terms and without a hint of irony, the changes needed for 'gas vans' used to kill Jews. For example, since a lightbulb inside the vans was noted usually to have a calming effect, the letter recommended its use only at the beginning and end of journeys, so as to make loading and unloading easier. Images of an industrial city flash on the screen, highlighting the victory of technology over the human. The absurd thus becomes frighteningly clear.

And there are ironies of experience. Polish citizens of Treblinka witnessed some of the wealthier Jews from France and Holland arriving by train to the concentration camp in first-class compartments, under the impression that they were arriving to work in new jobs. Women on such trains were often seen applying cosmetics in anticipation of impressing their new 'employers'.[23] A deadlier and truly absurd irony was observed by Elie Wiesel. His first confrontation with real suffering at Auschwitz led him to question his existence. When he realized that the world had remained silent while he witnessed appalling sights, he asked himself if it were really possible, and had to pinch himself to prove he was alive.[24] The silence of the world was not what he had expected. His basic trust in God (he was a devout student of the Talmud) and humanity had led him to expect an outcry. Its absence was absurd.

The examples are, of course, endless. But what was the intellectual response? Leon Stein masterfully shows how Camus and others responded to the Holocaust through writing novels such as *The Painted Bird* (Kosinski, 1965) and treatises

22. See Stein, 'Legacy of Existentialism', p. 1953.

23. From Lanzmann's *Shoah*. Also in *Shoah*, and in a similar vein, historian Raul Hilberg relates stories of how the Nazis often stole the property of Jews in order to pay the travel costs they incurred for sending the same Jews to the death camps. Many of the Jews in effect paid, as Lanzmann puts it, for 'the privilege of being gassed'.

24. *Night*, p. 41.

such as *The Myth of Sisyphus* (Camus, 1942).[25] For Camus, the myth captured well the essence of the absurd. Sisyphus's apparent resignation to futile labour was a model for bravery in the face of the absurd. 'Yet the Holocaust showed', says Stein, 'that Camus's "myth of Sisyphus" was real and deadly: "In Auschwitz men and women carried gigantic rocks back and forth to no purpose."'[26]

It was inevitable that the Holocaust experience caused many to reflect on their own fate, particularly the prospect of death. Because of the essential sameness of everyone's prospects, the question of fate transcended the individual and was made communal. Distinctions among people became blurred. As deportation began in his ghetto, Elie Wiesel recognized such an awareness within the community: 'There were no longer any questions of wealth, of social distinction, and importance, only people all condemned to the same fate—still unknown.'[27] Facing the unknown meant a denial of choice, and the denial of choice, both the individual's and the community's, heightened the struggle with fate. This was something which, as Thomas Keneally contends, Oskar Schindler came to realize. Keneally relates how Schindler purchased a burial place in a local churchyard for some Jews who were found dead in an abandoned rail car. When the parish priest told him that he could only offer plots reserved for suicides, Schindler reportedly answered that 'these weren't suicides. These were the victims of a great murder.'[28] For the Jews there was little liberty of choice.[29]

The awareness of fate laid so heavy on some that often guilt was experienced by those who managed to escape. Inge Deutschkron, a Jew who lived in hiding in Berlin all through the War, felt that by surviving she had wrongly escaped fate itself.[30] Richard Glazar, a Treblinka survivor, recalls the feelings of foreboding he

25.   Although likely not a direct response to the Holocaust, this work is proffered by Stein as an implied critique.

26.   'Legacy of Existentialism', p. 1948. Stein is citing T. Des Pres, from his *The Survivor*.

27.   *Night*, p. 30.

28.   *Schindler's List* (London: Hodder & Stoughton, 1994 [orig. *Schindler's Ark*, 1982]), p. 387. Keneally relates elsewhere how witnessing the execution of the ghetto police ('the most faithful...as well as the most grudging') had convinced Schindler that the ability to 'win over' life even through scheming or 'obedience' had been completely obliterated (pp. 275-76).

29.   Of course, one must be wary of simplifying the notion of choice, of ascribing to Jews what Simone de Beauvoir has called an 'atavism of resignation' or the nonsense that is 'the mystery of the Jewish soul'. Indeed, her comments are well worth noting here: Jews who were capable of an uprising at the Treblinka camp showed that 'their helplessness in the face of their executioners was not the expression of some secret blemish...[but] was due to the circumstances' (in the Preface to Jean-François Steiner's *Treblinka* [London: Weidenfeld and Nicolson, 1967 (1966)], pp. x, xiii). Further, Victor Frankl once wrote that there remained to the prisoner a 'freedom to bear oneself "This way, or that way", and there *was* a "this or that"' (as cited in J. Hassan, 'The Survivor as Living Witness', in Bauer *et al.* [eds.], *Remembering for the Future*, I, pp. 1093-1104 [1095], from Frankl's *Group Therapeutic Experiences in Concentration Camps*). My point here, then, is not unlike that of de Beauvoir's: stolen (Jewish) choice was the fallen victim of absurd circumstance.

30.   As related in *Shoah*. J. Hassan comments that feelings of guilt were due partly to the sense of a loss of shared experience with other survivors, which in turn brought on feelings of isolation from the wider community of Jewish Holocaust survivors ('The Survivor as Living Witness', p. 1101).

related to a friend while in the camp:

> We're shipwrecked, but still alive,
> and we can do so little
> but watch out for every wave, ride it,
> and brace ourselves for the next wave.
> Ride the waves at all costs, nothing more (from *Shoah*).

The metaphor seems sadly appropriate. Waves are predictable and continuous, each one feeding the other in a relentless circle. There is a reminiscence of Qoheleth here: 'All streams flow to the sea, but the sea is not full; to the place where the streams flow, there they flow again' (1.7). Stein describes an instance of poetic consent to fate from Lanzmann's *Shoah*. It is the final scene in which

> a resistance fighter returns to the Warsaw ghetto and finds himself utterly alone: 'I said to myself, "I'm the last Jew. I'll wait for morning and for the Germans"'... Here was pure *amor fati*, a love of fate, overwhelming in its serenity. Nietzsche would have envied him.[31]

While not all may agree with Stein's reference to Nietzsche, the bold acceptance of fate is lucidly present and shows again existentialism's amenability to reflection on the Holocaust.

3. *The Disillusioned Rationalist and the Holocaust*

Not a little attention has been given to the idea that Qoheleth is a precursor of sorts to existentialism.[32] This is mainly because Qoheleth shares some distinctive qualities with the existentialists. Indeed, it seems it would not be untrue to fix on Qoheleth A. MacIntyre's designation of the existentialist, 'disappointed rationalist'.[33] Besides what I have already touched on above,[34] allow me to outline further some of those qualities.

In terms of the above themes, Qoheleth is indeed an extremist. Like the dramatists, he has a flair for expressing the absurd in dramatically extreme terms. For

---

31. 'Legacy of Existentialism', p. 1953.
32. So Kenneth W. James, 'Ecclesiastes: Precursor of Existentialists', *TBT* 22 (1984), pp. 85-90; Peter, 'In Defence of Existence'; Fox, *Qohelet*, esp. sec. 0.2. Other writers have picked up on significant existential themes. The core thesis of Frank Crüsemann's article, 'The Unchangeable World', is the breakdown in Qoheleth's thought of the relationship between deed and consequence (further on which, see below). Gordis explores Qoheleth's world-view in terms akin to existentialism, emphasizing especially Qoheleth's sensitivity to the contradictory nature of events he has observed (in Chapter 14 of *Koheleth*, 'The World-View of Koheleth', pp. 112-22). Brown, following Fox's lead, compares at length Qoheleth's thinking to existential themes, including Camus's *Myth of Sisyphus* ('Character Reconstructed: Ecclesiastes', esp. pp. 129-48). F.W. Nichols compares Ecclesiastes to Beckett's *Waiting for Godot* ('Samuel Beckett and Ecclesiastes: On the Borders of Belief', *Enc* 45 [1984], pp. 11-22). Nichols also mentions Vladimir's 'A dog came in the kitchen' song (see above, p. 263) in relation to Qoheleth.
33. 'Existentialism', p. 147.
34. That is, that הבל is best translated 'absurd'; see the above examples and discussion in the Excursus.

example, nothing could be more absurd for a Hebrew sage than to play, as Qoheleth did, with the persona of Solomon. Under Qoheleth's auspices, Solomon's guise took on mythic proportions and his failure to succeed in Solomon's world (that is, the reliable world of retribution, wisdom and folly—for who is a fool and who is a sage in Qoheleth's eyes?) is a sublime piece of absurdist drama. The Solomonic scenario is Qoheleth's most potent rejection of the easy notion of retribution. The rejection was ultimately rooted, as Kenneth James states, in Qoheleth's realist principles: 'Qoheleth...recognizes the vanity of accepting the Hebrew theory of retribution, if by so doing the person becomes blind to the realities of pain and pointlessness which often form a part of a good person's life.'[35] Qoheleth's world is polarized in two extremes: that of the King of wisdom, and that of the embittered sage who no longer knows even what wisdom or existence is.

Furthermore, Qoheleth presents himself to us as an observer of extreme situations. A good example of this is 4.1-3:

> Again I saw all the oppressions that are done under the sun.
> And behold, the tears of the oppressed;
>> and there was no comforter for them.
> Yet from the hand of their oppressors was power—
>> and there was no comforter for them.
> And I considered the dead who had already died
>> [better off] than the living who still live.
> But better than both of them
>> is the one who has not yet been—
>> who has not seen the evil activity that has been done under the sun.

Qoheleth here reflects the experience of the sensitive sufferer in the camps. Although his later narrative stance will override his pessimism, his sensitivity brings him to the hopeless conclusion that non-existence is to be preferred to this kind of existence (cf. 6.3). For the oppressed whom he observes, oppression is the theft of hope, of a reason to live, even exist—a conclusion that echoes much of Holocaust reflection.

As a result of his seemingly painful experience, Qoheleth advocated an avoidance of the extreme:

> I observed everything in the days of my absurdity. There is a righteous man perishing in his righteousness and there is a wicked man whose life is prolonged by his wickedness. Do not be greatly righteous, nor become exceedingly wise. Why be dumbfounded? Do not be greatly wicked and do not be a fool. Why should you die in a time not your own? Better that you take hold of the one and from the other not withdraw your hand—yet the one who fears God escapes both of them (7.15-18; cf. 1.8).

Qoheleth speaks as a weary observer, worn down by the days of his absurdity. He offers the examples of the ends of both the righteous and the wicked as a generalization, a metaphor for 'everything' he has observed during his absurd existence, and he refuses to be dumbfounded by them. One does not, after all, know what will happen. Excess in the realms of righteousness and wisdom can result in

---

35. 'Ecclesiastes: Precursor of Existentialists', p. 86.

stupefication (שׁמם, to be shocked, appalled; cf. Job 21.5). Excess in the realms of wickedness and folly may end in an unexpected death. Yet Qoheleth has witnessed those who escape the rules: the righteous who die by their righteousness (אבד בצדקו) and the wicked who live long by their corruption (מאריך ברעתו). In his honest appraisal he can only hope to avoid the pain of perception. The thematic parallels to approaches to thinking about the Holocaust are doubtless striking.

The absurd is an organizing principle of Qoheleth's thought, a standard of observation and thinking about the world, and his honest confrontations with it are easily recognizable as thematic links to themes of the absurd in Holocaust reflection. Qoheleth observed the world and yet he did not attempt to reconcile its phenomena within a cohesive system of thought.[36] He is here racked with despair from his observations (2.17-18; 4.1-2; *passim*), there generous in his joy from the same (5.18; 8.15; *passim*); here bleak (1.2, 13; *passim*), there sanguine (7.19; 9.7-8; *passim*). Elsewhere the reader catches a glimpse of a more balanced vision of life (3.1-8; 8.6; 9.1-3a). There is a host of plain contradictions in the book's internal logic as well.[37] Indeed, Qoheleth was, as Fox has outlined,[38] much like Camus's hero of the absurd who refuses to surrender to the explanations of institutions (divine or otherwise), or of the everyday, and chooses to observe the contradictory phenomena of life without reserve.[39] Hence the root of his contradiction. Qoheleth's insistence on honest confrontation lies behind his blunt and often contradictory observations on everyday existence and, like an ancient Elie Wiesel, he recognized that such unfettered observations could prove a vexation in themselves (7.16-17). Qoheleth experienced life as Camus's hero—without screens.[40]

One of Qoheleth's prominent themes relates directly to the content of Holocaust

36. It is worth noting that Qoheleth was not a lone voice in the Hebrew Bible in his observation of the absurd. In Lamentations, for example, is the continual recognition that there appears to be little reason for the suffering of Israel. The theme culminates in the final prayer that finishes boldly in an insecure tone, with the questions, 'Why have you forgotten us completely? Why have you forsaken us these many days? Restore us to yourself, O Lord...renew our days of old—unless you have utterly rejected us, and are angry with us beyond measure' (Lam. 5.20-22, NRSV; cf. 1.11–2.1; esp. 1.17, 21).

37. For example, Qoheleth asserts both that all toil is הבל and yields nothing (2.11, 18; 6.7), but also that enjoyment of one's toil is the greatest possible occupation—a gift from God (2.24; 4.9; 5.19-20; 8.15).

38. In the Introduction of *Qohelet*, esp. pp. 13-16.

39. Compare Camus's comments: 'The leap in all its forms, rushing into the divine or eternal, surrendering to the illusions of the everyday or of the idea—all these screens hide the absurd. But there are civil servants without screens, and they are the ones of whom I mean to speak' (*Myth of Sisyphus*, p. 91).

40. Cf. esp. 2.15. Also, see 1.18; 7.3; 11.10. So Fox on 7.16-17: 'Qohelet is teaching the avoidance of an extreme of wisdom (such as he himself acquired) because (we may deduce from the context) it makes one aware of inequities such as those described in 7:15, and this awareness will leave one shocked' (*Qohelet*, p. 234). In a more lyrical vein, Gordis described the sensitive aspect of Qoheleth's observations thus: 'This cry of a sensitive spirit wounded by man's cruelty and ignorance, this distilled essence of an honest and courageous mind, striving to penetrate the secret of the universe, yet unwilling to soar on the wings of faith beyond the limits of the knowable, remains one of man's noblest offerings on the altar of truth' (*Koheleth*, p. 122).

reflection: the failure of words to express the absurd. Note the following comments compiled from interviews with Holocaust survivors by S.M. Bokolsky:

> If the oceans were ink and the sky was paper, there would not be enough ink or paper to tell of one hour in Auschwitz.

> You cannot say in an hour, or a day or a week what it was like in those years. It is not possible to tell you.

> There is not enough tape, not enough paper, not enough time and not enough words to make you understand what we went through.

> I cannot tell you—I cannot. There are no words to tell you.[41]

Language fails to express the enormity and inherent absurdity of the event, of each experience of it. For Qoheleth as well, the failure of language is another contribution to the absurdity of his own experience:

> All words are wearisome—
>> One cannot express [it].
> An eye is not satisfied with seeing,
>> and an ear is not filled from hearing (1.8).

> For with many dreams and absurdities [there are] many words—
> But fear God (5.7).

> Since there are many words that increase absurdity, what profit is there for humanity? (6.11).

> Who is like the sage? And who knows the interpretation of a thing? (8.1).

Actually, not even the sage knows (8.17). Since the word for 'thing' (דבר) at 8.1 can also mean 'word' or 'act' (as in 'The *acts* of King X'), the judgment is wide-sweeping. The failure comes in attempting to make sense of what one observes: the *object* of one's perception and understanding. It is a general failure that Qoheleth links to God's concealment of the comprehension of his works (3.11-14; 11.5 and elsewhere). It is a refrain found in Holocaust reflection: there is no why, there is no expression and there is no understanding.

Qoheleth's fixation with death has long been recognized as an important theme of the book,[42] one linked intrinsically to the fate of humanity. Qoheleth's attitude to death in itself was, however, not despairing. Qoheleth rejects death (not to be confused with Ecclesiastesan non-existence) as an alternative even to the vexation of existence (as in, for example, 6.7-9). Indeed, not 'death in itself', says Frank Crüsemann, 'but only an early and untimely death was regarded as reason for despair; in itself death made life shine more brightly'.[43] This is spelled out clearly and poetically in 9.11-12 (cf. 9.1-3; 10.8-11):

---

41. 'The Problem of Survivor Discourse', p. 1083.

42. See Murphy, *Ecclesiastes*, p. lviii; *idem*, 'Recent Research on Proverbs and Qoheleth', *CRBS* 1 (1993), pp. 119-40 (133-34).

43. 'The Unchangeable World', p. 67.

> And again I observed under the sun:
> The race is not to the swift,
>   nor the battle to the mighty.
> Neither yet is there bread to the wise,
>   nor yet riches to those who understand,
>   nor yet favour to the knowledgable.
> For a time of calamity will befall all of them.
> Indeed, humanity does not know their time.
> Like fish that are caught in an evil net
>   and birds caught in the snare,
> So will human beings be snared by an evil time,
>   when it falls upon them suddenly.

Like the operative principle of the absurd (the race is not necessarily to the swift), the time and quality of death remains obscured to human understanding. There is no fear, only the acknowledgment that knowledge is thwarted (cf. 3.2, 19; 8.8). As Elie Wiesel recognized by more painful means, the future is frightfully unknown and the evil net may lie in wait, and choice is, as in Qoheleth's analogy of the hapless hunted animal, another victim of thievery.

Consciousness of human finitude and death is a theme that courses throughout Qoheleth's narrative. The following passage (8.6-9) can be taken as representative:

> Indeed, for every matter there is a time and a procedure,
>   yet the misery of humanity prevails upon them.
> For they do not know what will be;
>   for who will tell them how it will be?
> No one has authority over the wind to retain the wind
>   and no one has authority over the day of death.
> And no one has discharge from war,
>   nor will evil deliver those who practice it.
> All this I observed while giving my heart to all the activity that has been done under the
> sun, at a time when one person has authority over another to the other's harm.

The prospect of the unknown ('humanity', Qoheleth included, 'does not know what will be') is precisely what makes Qoheleth so aware of the fate that befalls everyone. Since he has realized that he is powerless in the face of death (that he has no authority over it, ואין שלטון ביום המות, 8.8; cf. 9.5) he gives himself no choice but to be painfully cognizant. Yet what really enlarges the passage is its final phrase (8.9b). Qoheleth alludes to a reason for his awareness: his implied social situation. This has all happened 'at a time when one person has authority over another to the other's harm' (עת אשר שלט האדם באדם לרע לו). Even as a fictive situation, the implication of the context is important. The *reason* for the infliction of harm is concealed and, if we give Qoheleth the benefit of the doubt, he is powerless to stop it. Here is a consciousness of human impotence in the face of the unknown on a sociopolitical scale.

There are likely other qualities that Qoheleth shares with the existentialists,[44]

---

44. For example, James contends that Qoheleth shares with the existentialists 'the commitment to existence as the primary condition for finding the meaning of life' ('Ecclesiastes: Precursor of Existentialists', p. 86).

and there certainly remain more links to Holocaust reflection to explore. Here are a few examples.

1. Both strains of reflection are set in contrast to an ideology of reduction and unthinking retribution (for Holocaust victims a frightfully real one, for Qoheleth a likely fictive one),[45] each 'at a time' when the overturning (or virtual shattering) of traditional frameworks of meaning is occurring.

2. The *subject* (the experiencing self who makes decisions) is brought into sharp relief. In the case of Qoheleth it is always the formation of his own self that is in question—what will become of the sage who opts to search out everything under the sun?[46] In the case of the Holocaust, the theft of choice established the subject's centrality.

3. Qoheleth apparently rejected the nationalism of the Yahwists, and his observations reflect a community in exile. While there is no notion of nationalism, there is one of community. In his 'two are better than one' sayings (4.9-12), for example, he endorses companionship in difficult circumstance. As Judith Hassan remarks of the way in which Holocaust survivors coped, 'In the concentration camp, individuals stood a far better chance of surviving if they were part of a pair or group.'[47]

4. One may note a possible derivation of the word שׁוֹאָה from biblical Hebrew. The noun shares the same root as שָׁא, a word that, like הבל, is used to qualify the futility of idols and of false or deceitful words. It is one of the few words that comes closest to the meaning of הבל.[48] The noun itself is found in the prophets and wisdom literature to mean a tempest or ruin, which in a bitter twist of irony for its modern use, constitutes divine wrath (e.g. Isa. 10.3; Ps. 35.8).

5. Important questions remain to be explored in terms of the place of God in the whole comparison. If for some Holocaust victims God was to be implicated, while for others God was to be trusted in the face of human evil (in an act of 'monumental faithfulness'), how is Qoheleth's apparent resignation to the absurd, in a world for which God is seen to be responsible, to be reconciled? Indeed,

45. Of course, there has been no shortage of proposals for the historical milieu of Ecclesiastes, but we need not 'know' it to discern the clashing of ideology implied in Qoheleth's notion of הבל (the expected cosmology, which Qoheleth's experience opposes, can only exist as ideology, a presumably inherited one). It is also well demonstrated by his conflicting relationship with the frame narrator who seeks to restrict meaning while Qoheleth cannot contain it (God's works are unknowable, wisdom is a pursuit of wind). Furthermore, Qoheleth has 'seen' a paradigm shift in power (5.7-9; 10.5-7) and inexplicable evils under the sun (4.1-3; 8.11-13), and such contributes to the sense of ideological unease in his narrative world.

46. Beyond what I have already suggested above about Qoheleth's notion of the *subject* (Chapter 7), if G. Whitlock is correct, there may be some existential significance in the biblical meaning of רוח. Extrapolating from the Joshua texts, and in reference to existentialist theologian Paul Tillich, Whitlock suggests that people need רוח from God in order to muster the 'courage to be', to exist—that is, to be human and not 'merely a clod of earth' ('The Structure of Personality in Hebrew Psychology', p. 6).

47. 'The Survivor as Living Witness', p. 1093. Hassan goes on to discuss the specific activities such as sharing food and the importance of 'organizing' (pp. 1100-1101).

48. Cf. Exod. 23.1; Ps. 24.4; Isa. 1.13; Jer. 2.30; 18.15. It is used *with* הבל at Ps. 31.7, where the psalmist describes those whom the Lord hates and who pay regard to vain idols (הבלי-שׁוא).

Qoheleth's virtual celebration of 'the everyday', coupled with his bold joy in a deceitful world devoid of rationale, stands either as an insult or a resonating intertext to the memory of the Holocaust victim.

4. *Survival and Memory*

In a world once familiar, Holocaust victims were made to feel alienated. Camus offered a thoughtful rendering of the problem:

> A world that can be explained even with bad reasons is a familiar world. But, on the other hand, in a universe suddenly divested of illusions and lights, man feels an alien, a stranger. His exile is without remedy since he is deprived of the memory of a lost home or the hope of a promised land...[and] there is a direct connection between this feeling and the longing for death.[49]

For many that longing proved too strong, but the same longing drove some victims to grasp for reasons for living that understandably suggest desperation. For example, Keneally tells of a woman at her wits' end in Auschwitz who makes motions to throw herself against an electric fence. The reason her friend offers to stop her seems to us, as Keneally comments, 'perversely sane': 'If you do that, you'll never know what happened to you.' Yet in this case it sufficed.[50] How can human value be affirmed in such a situation? Maybe this particular woman sought, for a change, to conquer the unknown. She would have bitter-sweet victory over at least one absurd fate. She would *choose* to escape the hunter's trap.

Qoheleth's reason for living seems an odd twist to that woman's story. One must push ahead with life and live fully, in spite of the fact (if not for the very reason) that you do not know what lies ahead:

> In the morning sow your seed
> and in the evening do not let your hands be idle.
> For you do not know whether this or that will be advantageous
> or if both alike will be good.
> Sweet is the light
> and it is good for the eyes to see the sun.
> Indeed, if one should live many years
> let that person rejoice in all of them.
> But let that person also remember the days of darkness,
> for they will be many.
> All that comes is absurd (11.6-8).

Here is reason to live life as fully as possible. In a manner quite different from that in Keneally's example,[51] ignorance of the future is a motivation to continue living

---

49. *Myth of Sisyphus*, p. 6.

50. *Schindler's List*, pp. 348-49.

51. Perhaps more akin to her story is Qoheleth's seemingly desperate sentiment, 'Better a name than good oil [טוב שֵׁם מִשֶּׁמֶן טוֹב] and the day of death than the day of one's birth' (7.1; cf. 9.4). Death offered escape from the absurd world (a return to the eternal home, 12.5; cf. 12.7) and the establishment of remembrance through a name. Both were better than the day of birth since, as Whybray points out, at birth the future is still 'entirely unknown' (*Ecclesiastes*, p. 113).

with all one's capabilities, although many ominous days may lie in wait.

One way survival was managed in the camps was through the determination to remember and be remembered, so that the world would not forget the atrocity of the whole event. The determination was widespread, and one does not have to listen long to, for example, a Holocaust documentary to hear a reference to it. As Stein comments, 'Along with many victims, Alexander Donat said that the drive to bear witness was a "sacred mission that would give me the strength to endure everything".'[52]

The importance of memory to Qoheleth can hardly be overstated. He frequently recognized the danger of losing the memory of past generations (and presumably the lessons thereby learned):

> There is no remembrance of the sage or the fool forever; in the coming days everything will have already been forgotten. How the sage dies just like the fool! (2.16b).

> This too I observed—[an example of] wisdom under the sun—and it seemed great to me: [There was] a small city with a few men in it, and a great king came to it and surrounded it, and built great siegeworks against it. And a poor wise man was found there who delivered the city by his wisdom. Yet no one remembered that poor man (9.13-15).

Sometimes the recognition echoes the form of a lament:

> There is no remembrance of the people of old;
>   nor yet of the people to come—[those] who will be.
> [There] will be no remembrance of [either of] them,
>   [along] with those who will be after (1.11).

By implication Qoheleth recognized the importance of the act of remembrance. The very idea that no one is, in the end, remembered, forms a lamentable part of the inscrutable condition of the world. Indeed, he fits well a description of Camus's 'true rebel': 'the artist who fights for decency and memory in an absurd world'.[53]

5. *Conclusion*

> I believe in the sun
> though it is late
> in rising
> I believe in love
> though it is absent
>
> I believe in God
> though he is
> silent...
>
>   Anonymous[54]

---

52. 'Legacy of Existentialism', p. 1952.

53. Cited in Stein, 'Legacy of Existentialism', p. 1949.

54. Translated from the French by H. Schiff, in *idem* (ed.), *Holocaust Poetry* (London: HarperCollins, 1995), p. 184. A note in this edition states, 'Text from an unsigned inscription found on the wall of a cave in Cologne where Jews had been hiding.'

Holocaust survivor Filip Müller said of his experiences in Auschwitz, 'We felt abandoned by the world...we came to know what life was. *Where there is life there is hope*...we hoped against hope...and survived.'[55] With Qoheleth he could perhaps say,

> Yet for one who is joined to all the living there is hope, for [even] a living dog is better off than a dead lion. For the living know that they will die, but the dead do not know anything. And there is no longer a recompense for them since the memory of them has been forgotten. Also, their love, their hate and their envy have already perished, and there is no portion for them ever again in all that has been done under the sun (9.4-6).

Qoheleth identifies perhaps the most culturally despised of animals in the ancient Near East and asserts, contrary to expectation, that even such a creature has hope. But as Qoheleth develops the comparison (essentially between the dead and the living) it becomes clear that there are reasons for this hope. The knowledge that they will die may seem a strange reason for hope, but not when we consider that the dead cannot know *anything*. In this respect hope is, as the commentaries suggest, simply being certain of what will happen. But the most important part of the comparison is not that the dog is alive, but that it is joined to the realm of *all* the living. Filip Müller's comment is, significantly, in the first-person plural. Even for those who know the absurdity of judgment based on essence, there is hope in companionship. And the idea that there is no longer a recompense for the dead, a reward (שכר), because their memory is forgotten, imbues the hope of the living with real worth. The fact that the dead will never know what it is to live (to *experience* love, hate and even envy), and that their portion on this earth is gone forever, makes the seemingly meagre hope of the living shine brightly.

As Qoheleth set up the bleak picture of the absurd divorce he left himself no option but despair (because he *observed* the divorce). Yet Qoheleth did, for some reason, have hope. Francis Nichols compares Qoheleth's obstinate hope to the soothing words of parents to their children in the night: 'Everything will be alright.' But how do they know?[56] Qoheleth has confidence in the answer that God will give to the human heart in the midst of grief. The joy expressed in 5.19-20 will help victims of the absurd to 'rarely remember the (painful) days of their lives'—to find healing not in the absence of recollection, but in the absence of the misery it has long engendered—'for God will answer them in the joy of their heart'.[57] But perhaps even more vitally, like many Holocaust survivors, Qoheleth found hope in the simple act of narrative, of re-membering, re-constructing all the days of 'my absurdity' (הבלי, 7.15).

55. From Lanzmann's *Shoah* (italics mine).
56. 'Samuel Beckett and Ecclesiastes', p. 20.
57. On this translation, see p. 198 n. 84.

BIBLIOGRAPHY

1. *On Ecclesiastes*

Barton, G.A., *The Book of Ecclesiastes* (ICC; Edinburgh: T. & T. Clark, 1959 [1908]).

Barton, J., 'Ecclesiastes: An Example', in *idem*, *Reading the Old Testament* (London: SCM Press, 1984), pp. 61-76.

Bickerman, E., 'Koheleth (Ecclesiastes) *or* The Philosophy of an Acquisitive Society', in *idem*, *Four Strange Books of the Bible* (New York: Schocken Books, 1967), pp. 139-67.

Blumenthal, J. (designer), *Ecclesiastes, or The Preacher* (series of wood engravings) (New York: Spiral Press, 1965).

Breton, S., 'Qoheleth Studies', *BTB* 3 (1973), pp. 22-50.

Brown, W.P., 'Character Reconstructed: Ecclesiastes', in *idem*, *Character in Crisis* (Grand Rapids: Eerdmans, 1996), pp. 120-50.

Burkitt, F.C., *Ecclesiastes: Rendered into English Verse by F. Crawford Burkitt* (London: Macmillan, 1936).

Burns, G., 'The Hermeneutics of Midrash', in R. Schwartz (ed.), *The Book and the Text* (Oxford: Basil Blackwell, 1990), pp. 189-213.

Castellino, G., 'Qoheleth and his Wisdom', *CBQ* 30 (1968), pp. 15-28.

Ceresko, A.R., 'The Function of *Antanaclasis* (*mṣ'* "to Find" //*mṣ'* "to Reach, Overtake, Grasp") in Hebrew Poetry, Especially in the Book of Qoheleth', *CBQ* 44 (1982), pp. 551-69.

Christianson, E.S., review of *The Book of Ecclesiastes (NICOT)*, by Tremper Longman III, *HS* 40 (1999), forthcoming.

—'Qoheleth the "Old Boy" and Qoheleth the "New Man": Misogynism, the Womb and a Paradox in Ecclesiastes', in A. Brenner and C. Fontaine (eds.), *Wisdom and Psalms: A Feminist Companion to the Bible (Second Series)* (FCB [Second Series], 2; Sheffield: Sheffield Academic Press, 1998), pp. 109-36.

—'Qoheleth and the/his Self among the Deconstructed', in A. Schoors (ed.), *Qohelet in the Context of Wisdom* (BETL, 136; Leuven: Leuven University Press, 1998), pp. 425-33.

—'Qoheleth and the Existential Legacy of the Holocaust', *HeyJ* 38.1 (1997), pp. 35-50.

Crenshaw, J., 'Qoheleth's Understanding of Intellectual Enquiry', in A. Schoors (ed.), *Qohelet in the Context of Wisdom* (BETL, 136; Leuven: Leuven University Press, 1998), pp. 205-24.

—Review of *Qohelet and his Contradictions*, by M.V. Fox, *JBL* 109 (1990), pp. 712-15.

—*Ecclesiastes* (OTL; London: SCM Press, 1988).

—'Youth and Old Age in Qoheleth', *HAR* 10 (1986), pp. 1-13.

—'Qoheleth in Current Research', *HAR* 7 (1983), pp. 41-56.

Crüsemann, F., 'The Unchangeable World: The "Crisis of Wisdom" in Koheleth', in W. Schottroff and W. Stegemann (eds.), *God of the Lowly: Socio-Historical Interpretations of the Bible* (Maryknoll, NY: Orbis Books, 1979), pp. 57-77.

De Boer, P.A.H., 'A Note on Ecclesiastes 12.12a', in R. Fischer (ed.), *A Tribute to Arthur Vööbus* (Chicago: Lutheran School of Theology, 1977), pp. 85-88.

Delitzsch, F., 'Ecclesiastes', in *idem, Commentary on the Old Testament*, VI (Grand Rapids: Eerdmans, 1980 [1875]).

Dell, K.J., 'Ecclesiastes as Wisdom: Consulting Early Interpreters', *VT* 44 (1994), pp. 301-29.

Dornseiff, F., 'Das Buch Prediger', *ZDMG* 89 (1935), pp. 243-49.

Eaton, M., *Ecclesiastes* (TOTC; Downer's Grove, IL: InterVarsity Press, 1983).

Ellul, J., *Reason for Being: A Meditation on Ecclesiastes* (trans. J.M. Hanks; Grand Rapids: Eerdmans, 1990).

Etting, E. (illustrator), *Koheleth: The Book of Ecclesiastes* (New York: New Directions, 1940).

Eybers, I.H., 'The "Canonization" of Song of Solomon, Ecclesiastes and Esther', in W.C. van Wyk (ed.), *Aspects of the Exegetical Process* (OTWSA, 20; Pretoria West: NHW Press, 1977), pp. 33-52.

Farmer, K., *Who Knows What Is Good?: A Commentary on the Books of Proverbs and Ecclesiastes* (ITC; Grand Rapids: Eerdmans, 1991).

Fisch, H., 'Qohelet: A Hebrew Ironist', in *idem, Poetry with a Purpose: Biblical Poetics and Interpretation* (ISBL; Indianapolis: Indiana University Press, 1988), pp. 158-78.

Fox, M.V., 'The Inner Structure of Qohelet's Thought', in A. Schoors (ed.), *Qohelet in the Context of Wisdom* (BETL, 136; Leuven: Leuven University Press, 1998), pp. 225-38.

—'Wisdom in Qoheleth', in L.G. Perdue *et al.* (eds.), *In Search of Wisdom* (Louisville, KY: Westminster/John Knox Press, 1993), pp. 115-31.

—*Qohelet and his Contradictions* (JSOTSup, 71; Sheffield: Almond Press, 1989).

—'Frame-narrative and Composition in the Book of Qohelet', *HUCA* 48 (1977), pp. 83-106.

Fox, M.V., and B. Porten, 'Unsought Discoveries: Qohelet 7.23–8.1a', *HS* 19 (1978), pp. 26-38.

Fredericks, D.C., *Coping with Transcience: Ecclesiastes on Brevity in Life* (TBS, 18; Sheffield: JSOT Press, 1993).

Galling, K., 'Kohelet-Studien', *ZAW* 50 (1932), pp. 276-99.

Garrett, D., 'Ecclesiastes 7.25-29 and the Feminist Hermeneutic', *CTR* 2.2 (1988), pp. 309-21.

—'Qoheleth on the Use and Abuse of Political Power', *TrinJ* 8 (1987), pp. 159-77.

Ginsberg, H.L., *Studies in Koheleth* (New York: Jewish Theological Seminary of America, 1950).

Ginsburg, C.D., *Coheleth (Commonly Called the Book of Ecclesiastes)* (London: Longman, 1861).

Goldin, J., 'The End of Ecclesiastes: Literal Exegesis and its Transformation', in A. Altmann (ed.), *Biblical Motifs: Origins and Transformations* (Cambridge, MA: Harvard University Press, 1966), pp. 135-58.

Good, E., 'The Unfilled Sea: Style and Meaning in Ecclesiastes 1.2-11', in J. Gammie *et al.* (eds.), *Israelite Wisdom: Theological and Literary Essays in Honor of Samuel Terrien* (Missoula, MT: Scholars Press, 1978), pp. 59-73.

—'Qoheleth: The Limits of Wisdom', in *idem, Irony in the Old Testament* (Sheffield: Almond Press, 1981 [1965]), pp. 168-95.

Gordis, R., *Koheleth—The Man and his World* (New York: Bloch Publishing, 1962).

Harrison, C.R., 'Qoheleth among the Sociologists', *BibInt* 5.2 (1997), pp. 160-80.

—'Qoheleth in Social-Historical Perspective' (PhD dissertation; Duke University, 1991).

Hendry, G.S., 'Ecclesiastes', in D. Guthrie and J.A. Motyer (eds.), *The Eerdmans Bible Commentary* (Grand Rapids: Eerdmans, 1970), pp. 570-78.

Hengel, M., 'Koheleth and the Beginning of the Crisis in Jewish Religion', in *idem, Judaism and Hellenism* (trans. J. Bowden; 2 vols.; London: SCM Press, rev. edn, 1974 [1973]), I, pp. 115-30.

Hirshman, M., 'The Greek Fathers and the Aggada on Ecclesiastes: Formats of Exegesis in Late Antiquity', *HUCA* 59 (1958), pp. 137-65.

Holm-Nielsen, S., 'The Book of Ecclesiastes and the Interpretation of It in Jewish and Christian Theology', *ASTI* 10 (1976), pp. 38-96.

—'On the Interpretation of Qoheleth in Early Christianity', *VT* 24 (1974), pp. 168-77.

Isaksson, B., *Studies in the Language of Qoheleth* (AUUSSU, 10; Uppsala: Almqvist & Wiksell, 1987).

James, K.W., 'Ecclesiastes: Precursor of Existentialists', *TBT* 22 (1984), pp. 85-90.

Jarick, J., *Gregory Thaumaturgos' Paraphrase of Ecclesiastes* (SBLSCS, 29; Atlanta: Scholars Press, 1990).

Johnston, D., *A Treatise on the Authorship of Ecclesiastes* (London: MacMillan and Co., anonymous edn, 1880).

Kaiser, O., 'Qoheleth', in J. Day, R.P. Gordon and H.G.M. Williamson (eds.), *Wisdom in Ancient Israel: Essays in Honour of J.A. Emerton* (Cambridge: Cambridge University Press, 1995), pp. 83-93.

Kamano, N., 'Character and Cosmology: Rhetoric of Ecclesiastes 1,3–3,9', in A. Schoors (ed.), *Qohelet in the Context of Wisdom* (BETL, 136; Leuven: Leuven University Press, 1998), pp. 419-24.

Knobel, P.S. (trans.), *The Targum of Qohelet* (The Aramaic Bible, 15; Edinburgh: T. & T. Clark, 1991).

Kreitzer, L., '*A Farewell to Arms*: "A Time to Give Birth and a Time to Die" ', in *idem, The Old Testamnent in Fiction and Film* (TBS, 24; Sheffield: Sheffield Academic Press, 1994), pp. 170-221.

Kushner, H.S., *When All You've Ever Wanted Isn't Enough* (Sydney: Pan Books, 1987).

Lauha, A., *Kohelet* (BKAT, 19; Neukirchen–Vluyn: Neukirchener Verlag, 1978).

Loader, J.A., *Polar Structures in the Book of Qohelet* (BZAW, 152; Berlin: W. de Gruyter, 1979).

Lohfink, N., 'Qoheleth 5.17-19—Revelation by Joy', *CBQ* 52 (1990), pp. 625-35.

Longman III, Tremper, *The Book of Ecclesiastes* (NICOT; Grand Rapids: Eerdmans, 1998).

Loretz, O., 'Zur Darbietungsform der "Ich-Erzählung" im Buche Qohelet', *CBQ* 25 (1963), pp. 46-59.

Luther, M., 'Notes on Ecclesiastes', in J. Pelikan (gen. ed.), *Luther's Works*. XV. *Notes on Ecclesiastes, Lectures on the Song of Solomon, Treatise...* (St Louis: Concordia Publishing, 1972), pp. 1-187.

Lux, R., ' "Ich, Kohelet, bin König..." Die Fiktion als Schlüssel zur Wirklichkeit in Kohelet 1:12–2:26', *EvT* 50 (1990), pp. 331-42.

Margoliouth, D.S., 'The Prologue of Ecclesiastes', *Exp* 8.2 (1911), pp. 463-70.

McKenna, John E., 'The Concept of *hebel* in the Book of Ecclesiastes', *SJT* 45 (1992), pp. 19-28.

McNeile, A.H., *An Introduction to Ecclesiastes* (Cambridge: Cambridge University Press, 1904).

Miller, D.B., 'Qohelet's Symbolic Use of הבל', *JBL* 117.3 (1998), pp. 437-54.

Murphy, R.E., 'Recent Research on Proverbs and Qoheleth', *CRBS* 1 (1993), pp. 119-40.

—*Ecclesiastes* (WBC, 23a; Dallas: Word Books, 1992).

—'The Sage in Ecclesiastes and Qoheleth the Sage', in J.G. Gammie (ed.), *The Sage in Israel and the Ancient Near East* (Winona Lake, IN: Eisenbrauns, 1990), pp. 263-71.

—'Qohelet Interpreted: The Bearing of the Past on the Present', *VT* 32 (1982), pp. 331-37.

Nichols, F.W., 'Samuel Beckett and Ecclesiastes: On the Borders of Belief', *Enc* 45 (1984), pp. 11-22.

Ogden, G., *Qoheleth* (Readings; Sheffield: JSOT Press, 1987).

—' "Vanity" It Certainly Is Not', *BT* 38.3 (1987), pp. 301-307.

—'Historical Allusion in Qoheleth iv 13-16?', *VT* 30 (1980), pp. 309-15.

Paterson, J., 'The Intimate Journal of an Old-Time Humanist', *RL* 19.2 (1950), pp. 245-54.

Pawley, D., 'Ecclesiastes: Reaching Out to the Twentieth Century', *BR* 6 (1990), pp. 34-36.

Payne, M., 'The Voices of Ecclesiastes', *CL* 15 (1988), pp. 262-68.

Perry, T.A., *Dialogues with Kohelet: The Book of Ecclesiastes* (University Park, PA: Pennsylvania State University Press, 1993).

Peter, C.B., 'In Defence of Existence: A Comparison between Ecclesiastes and Albert Camus', *BTF* 12 (1980), pp. 26-43.

Plumptre, E.H., 'The Author of Ecclesiastes', *Exp* 2 (1880), pp. 401-30.

Polk, T., 'The Wisdom of Irony: A Study of *Hebel* and its Relation to Joy and Fear of God in Ecclesiastes', *SBTh* 6.1 (1976), pp. 3-17.

Ryken, L., 'Ecclesiastes', in L. Ryken and T. Longman III (eds.), *A Complete Literary Guide to the Bible* (Grand Rapids: Zondervan, 1993), pp. 268-80.

—'Ecclesiastes', in *idem*, *Words of Delight: A Literary Introduction to the Bible* (Grand Rapids: Baker Book House, 1987), pp. 319-28.

Salters, R.B., 'Qoheleth and the Canon', *ExpTim* 86 (1974-5), pp. 339-42.

Salyer, G.D., 'Vain Rhetoric: Implied Author/Narrator/Narratee/Implied Reader Relationships in Ecclesiastes' Use of First-Person Discourse' (PhD dissertation; University of California at Berkeley, 1997).

Schloesser, S., ' "A King is Held Captive in her Tresses": The Liberating Deconstruction of the Search for Wisdom from Proverbs through Ecclesiastes', in J. Morgan (ed.), *Church Divinity* (Bristol: Cloverdale Corporation, 1989–90), pp. 205-28.

Schoors, A., *The Preacher Sought to Find Pleasing Words: A Study of the Language of Qoheleth* (OLA, 41; Leuven: Peeters, 1992).

Seow, C.-L., *Ecclesiastes: A New Translation with Introduction and Commentary* (AB, 18C; New York: Doubleday, 1997).

—'Qohelet's Autobiography', in A.B. Beck *et al.* (eds.), *Fortunate the Eyes that See: Essays in Honor of David Noel Freedman in Celebration of his Seventieth Birthday* (Grand Rapids: Eerdmans, 1995), pp. 275-87.

Sheppard, G., 'The Epilogue to Qoheleth as Theological Commentary', *CBQ* 39 (1977), pp. 182-89.

Sheridan, S., 'The Five Megilloth', in S. Bigger (ed.), *Creating the Old Testament* (Oxford: Basil Blackwell, 1989), pp. 293-317.

Short, R., *A Time to Be Born—A Time to Die* (New York: Harper & Row, 1973).

Spina, F.A., 'Qoheleth and the Reformation of Wisdom', in H.B. Huffmon *et al.* (eds.), *The Quest for the Kingdom of God: Studies in Honor of George E. Mendenhall* (Winona Lake, IN: Eisenbrauns, 1983), pp. 267-79.

Stone, E., 'Old Man Koheleth', *JBR* 10 (1942), pp. 98-102.

Viviano, P., 'The Book of Ecclesiastes: A Literary Approach', *TBT* 22 (1984), pp. 79-84.

Whitley, C.F., *Koheleth: His Language and Thought* (BZAW, 148; Berlin: W. de Gruyter, 1979).

Whybray, R.N., *Ecclesiastes* (NCB; Grand Rapids: Eerdmans, 1989).

—'Ecclesiastes 1.5-7 and the Wonders of Nature', *JSOT* 41 (1988), pp. 105-12.

—'Prophecy and Wisdom', in R. Coggins *et al.* (eds.), *Israel's Prophetic Tradition* (Cambridge: Cambridge University Press, 1982), pp. 181-99.

—'Qoheleth, Preacher of Joy', *JSOT* 23 (1982), pp. 87-98.

Williams, J.G., 'Proverbs and Ecclesiastes', in R. Alter and F. Kermode (eds.), *The Literary Guide to the Bible* (London: Collins, 1987), pp. 263-82.

Wilson, G.H., '"The Words of the Wise": The Intent and Significance of Qohelet 12.9-14', *JBL* 103.2 (1984), pp. 175-92.

Wright, A.G., 'Additional Numerical Patterns in Qohelet', *CBQ* 45 (1983), pp. 32-43.

—'The Riddle of the Sphynx Revisited: Numerical Patterns in the Book of Qoheleth', *CBQ* 42 (1980), pp. 38-51.

—'The Riddle of the Sphinx: The Structure of the Book of Qoheleth', *CBQ* 30 (1968), pp. 313-34.

Wright, J.S., 'The Book of Ecclesiastes', in J.D. Douglas *et al.* (eds.), *New Bible Dictionary* (Leicester: Inter-Varsity Press, 2nd edn, 1982), pp. 295-96.

—'The Interpretation of Ecclesiastes', *EvQ* 18 (1946), pp. 18-34.

Zimmermann, F., *The Inner World of Qohelet* (New York: Ktav, 1973).

2. On Narrative

Alter, R., *The Art of Biblical Narrative* (London: George Allen & Unwin, 1981).

Auerbach, E., *Mimesis* (Princeton, NJ: Princeton University Press, 1968).

Bakhtin, M., *The Dialogic Imagination: Four Essays* (ed. M. Holquist; trans. E. Holquist and M. Holquist; Austin: University of Texas Press, 1981 [1975]).

Bal, M., *Narratology: Introduction to the Theory of Narrative* (trans. C. von Boheemen; Toronto: University of Toronto Press, 1985).

Bar-Efrat, S., *Narrative Art in the Bible* (JSOTSup, 70; Sheffield: Almond Press, 1989).

Barthes, R., *Criticism and Truth* (ed. and trans. K. Pilcher; London: Athlone, 1987).

—'Introduction to the Structural Analysis of Narratives', in *idem, Image, Music, Text* (ed. and trans. S. Heath; London: Fontana Press, 1977), pp. 79-124.

—'The Death of the Author', in *idem, Image, Music, Text* (ed. and trans. S. Heath; London: Fontana Press, 1977), pp. 142-48.

—'Myth Today', in *A Barthes Reader* (ed. with an introduction by S. Sontag; London: Cape, 1982 [1956]), pp. 93-149.

Barthes, R. *et al.*, *Structural Analysis and Biblical Exegesis* (trans. A.M. Johnson, Jr; PTMS, 3; Pittsburgh: Pickwick Press, 1974 [1971]).

Berlin, A., *Poetics and Interpretation of Biblical Narrative* (BLS, 9; Sheffield: Almond Press, 1983).

Booth, W., *The Rhetoric of Fiction* (Harmondsworth: Penguin Books, 2nd edn, 1983).

Brooks, P., *Reading for the Plot: Design and Intention in Narrative* (Oxford: Clarendon Press, 1984).

Buth, R., 'Word Order Differences between Narrative and Non-Narrative Material in Biblical Hebrew', in *10th World Congress of Jewish Studies: Procedures* (Jerusalem: World Union of Jewsish Studies, 1990), pp. 9-16.

Caws, M.A., *Reading Frames in Modern Fiction* (Princeton, NJ: Princeton University Press, 1985).

Chatman, S., *Coming to Terms: The Rhetoric of Narrative in Fiction and Film* (Ithaca, NY: Cornell University Press, 1990).

—*Story and Discourse: Narrative Structure in Fiction and Film* (London: Cornell University Press, 1978).

Coward, R., and J. Ellis, *Language and Materialism: Developments in Semiology and the Theory of the Subject* (London: Routledge & Kegan Paul, 1977).

Crites, S. 'The Narrative Quality of Experience', *JAAR* 39 (1971), pp. 291-311.

Cruttwell, P., 'Makers and Persons', *HudR* 12 (1959–60), pp. 487-507.

Culler, J., *On Deconstruction: Theory and Criticism after Structuralism* (repr., London: Routledge, 1989 [1983]).

Dittmar, L., 'Fashioning and Re-fashioning: Framing Narratives in the Novel and Film', *Mosaic* 16.1-2 (1983), pp. 189-203.

Eagleton, T., *Literary Theory: An Introduction* (Oxford: Basil Blackwell, 1983).

Elliott, R.C., *The Literary Persona* (Chicago: University of Chicago Press, 1982).

Eslinger, L., 'Narratorial Situations in the Bible', in V.L. Tollers and J. Maier (eds.), *Mappings of the Biblical Terrain: The Bible as Text* (London: Bucknell University Press, 1990), pp. 72-91.

Fishman, J., 'Enclosures: The Narrative within Autobiography', *JAdC* 2 (1981), pp. 23-30.

Forster, E.M., *Aspects of the Novel* (Harmondsworth: Penguin Books, 1962 [1927]).

Foucault, M., 'What Is an Author?', *PrtRev* 42 (1975), pp. 603-14.

Frey, J., 'Author-Intrusion in the Narrative: German Theory and Some Modern Examples', *GR* (1948), pp. 274-89.

Frye, N., *The Great Code: The Bible and Literature* (Toronto: Academic Press Canada, 1982).

Genette, G., *Narrative Discourse* (trans. J. Lewin; Oxford: Basil Blackwell, 1980 [1972]).

Gittes, K.S., 'The Frame Narrative: History and Theory' (PhD dissertation; University of California, 1983).

Greimas, A.J., 'Narrative Grammar: Units and Levels', *MLN* 86 (1971), pp. 793-806.

Gusdorf, G., 'Conditions and Limits of Autobiography', in J. Olney (ed.), *Autobiography: Essays Theoretical and Critical* (Princeton, NJ: Princeton University Press, 1980), pp. 28-48.

Hardy, B., 'Towards a Poetics of Fiction: An Approach through Narrative', in M. Meek *et al.* (eds.), *The Cool Web: The Pattern of Children's Reading* (London: The Bodley Head, 1977), pp. 12-23.

Iser, W., 'Narrative Strategies as a Means of Communication', in M.J. Valdés and O.J. Miller (eds.), *Interpretation of Narrative* (Toronto: University of Toronto Press, 1978), pp. 100-17.

Kerby, A.P., *Narrative and the Self* (SCT; Bloomington: Indiana University Press, 1991).

Olney, J., *Metaphors of Self: The Meaning of Autobiography* (Princeton, NJ: Princeton University Press, 1972).

Olney, J. (ed.), *Autobiography: Essays Theoretical and Critical* (Princeton, NJ: Princeton University Press, 1980).

Pelc, J., 'On the Concept of Narration', *Semiotica* 2–3 (1971), pp. 1-19.

Polzin, R., *Biblical Structuralism* (Philadelphia: Fortress Press, 1977).

Prince, G., *Narratology: The Form and Functioning of Narrative* (Berlin: Mouton, 1982).

Rimmon-Kenan, S., *Narrative Fiction: Contemporary Poetics* (London: Methuen, 1983).

Romberg, B., *Studies in the Narrative Technique of the First-Person Novel* (Stockholm: Almqvist & Wiksell, 1962).

Spence, D., 'Narrative Recursion', in S. Rimmon-Kenan (ed.), *Discourse in Psychoanalysis and Literature* (London: Methuen, 1987), pp. 188-210.

Sprinker, M., 'Fictions of the Self: The End of Autobiography', in J. Olney (ed.), *Autobiography: Essays Theoretical and Critical* (Princeton, NJ: Princeton University Press, 1980), pp. 321-42.

Sturrock, J., *The Language of Autobiography: Studies in the First Person Singular* (Cambridge: Cambridge University Press, 1993).

Summerfield, J.F., 'Framing Narratives', in T. Newkirk (ed.), *Only Connect: Uniting Reading and Writing* (Upper Montclair: Boynton/Cook, 1986), pp. 227-40.

White, H., 'The Value of Narrativity in the Representation of Reality', *CritInq* 7 (Autumn 1980), pp. 5-27.

3. *Other Works*

Allen, L.C., *Psalms 101–150* (WBC, 21; Waco, TX: Word Books, 1983).

Alter, J., 'Television's False Intimacy', *Newsweek International* (27 June 1994), p. 25.

Alter, R., *The Art of Biblical Poetry* (New York: Basic Books, 1985).

Aurelius, M., *The Meditations of Marcus Aurelius* (trans. J. Collier; rev. A. Zimmern; London: Walter Scott, 1887).

Baldick, C., *The Concise Oxford Dictionary of Literary Terms* (Oxford: Oxford University Press, 1990).

Barr, J., *The Garden of Eden and the Hope of Immortality* (Minneapolis: Fortress Press, 1992).

—*Holy Scripture: Canon, Authority, Criticism* (Philadelphia: Westminster Press, 1983).

Barton, J., *Oracles of God: Perceptions of Ancient Prophecy in Israel after the Exile* (London: Darton, Longman & Todd, 1986).

Bauer, Y. *et al.* (eds.), *Remembering for the Future* (3 vols.; Oxford: Pergamon Press, 1989).

Beauvoir, S. de, 'Preface', in J.-F. Steiner, *Treblinka* (London: Weidenfeld and Nicolson, 1967 [1966]), pp. vii-xiii.

Beckett, S., *Waiting for Godot* (New York: Grove Press, 1954).

Beckwith, R., *The Old Testament Canon of the New Testament Church* (Grand Rapids: Eerdmans, 1985).

Boivin, M.J., 'The Hebraic Model of the Person', *JPsT* 19.2 (1991), pp. 157-65.

Bokolsky, S., 'The Problem of Survivor Discourse: Toward a Poetics of Survivor Testimonies', in Y. Bauer *et al.* (eds.), *Remembering for the Future* (3 vols.; Oxford: Pergamon Press, 1989), I, pp. 1082-92.

Brenner, A., 'Job the Pious? The Characterization of Job in the Narrative Framework of the Book', *JSOT* 43 (1989), pp. 37-52.

Brockington, L.H., 'The Problem of Pseudonymity', *JTS* 4 (1953), pp. 15-22.

Broyde, M.J., 'Defilement of the Hands, Canonization of the Bible, and the Special Status of Esther, Ecclesiastes, and the Song of Songs', *Judaism* 44.1 (Winter 1995), pp. 65-79.

Brueggemann, W., 'The Social Significance of Solomon as a Patron of Wisdom', in J.G. Gammie (ed.), *The Sage in Israel and the Ancient Near East* (Winona Lake, IN: Eisenbrauns, 1990), pp. 117-32.

Cady Stanton, E., *The Woman's Bible* (2 vols.; Edinburgh: Polygon Books, 1985 [1898]).

Camus, A., *The Myth of Sisyphus* (trans. J. O'Brien; New York: Vintage Books, 1991 [1942]).

Childs, B.S., *Introduction to the Old Testament as Literature* (Philadelphia: Fortress Press, 1989 [1979]).

Clements, R.E., 'Solomon and the Origins of Wisdom in Israel', *PRS* 15 (1988), pp. 23-35.

Clines, D.J.A., 'Deconstructing the Book of Job', in *idem, What Does Eve Do to Help? and Other Readerly Questions to the Old Testament* (JSOTSup, 94; JSOT Press, 1990), pp. 106-23.

—*Job 1–20* (WBC, 17; Dallas: Word Books, 1989).

Clines, D.J.A. (ed.), *The Dictionary of Classical Hebrew* (4 vols.; Sheffield: Sheffield Academic Press, 1993–98).

Cohen, I., 'The Heart in Biblical Psychology', in H.J. Zimmels, J. Rabbinowitz and I. Finestein (eds.), *Essays Presented to Chief Rabbi Israel Brodie* (2 vols.; London: Soncino Press, 1967), I, pp. 41-57.

Craigie, P., 'Psalms and the Problem of Authorship', in *idem, Psalms 1–50* (WBC, 19; Waco, TX: Word Books, 1983), pp. 33-35.

Crenshaw, J., *Old Testament Wisdom: An Introduction* (London: SCM Press, 1982).

Davidson, A.B., *An Introductory Hebrew Grammar* (New York: Charles Scribner's Sons, 24th edn, 1932).

Dimant, D., 'Pseudonymity in the Wisdom of Solomon', in N.F. Marcos (ed.), *La Septuaginta (V Congreso de la IOSCS)* (Madrid: CSIC, 1985), pp. 243-55.

Duro, P., 'Introduction', in *idem* (ed.), *The Rhetoric of the Frame: Essays on the Boundary of the Artwork* (Cambridge: Cambridge University Press, 1996), pp. 1-10.

Duro, P. (ed.), *The Rhetoric of the Frame: Essays on the Boundary of the Artwork* (Cambridge: Cambridge University Press, 1996).

Eissfeldt, O., *The Old Testament: An Introduction* (trans. P.R. Ackroyd; Oxford: Basil Blackwell, 1974).

Eybers, I.H., 'Some Light on the Canon of the Qumran Sect', in S.Z. Leiman (ed.), *The Canon and Masorah of the Hebrew Bible: An Introductory Reader* (New York: Ktav, 1974), pp. 23-36.

Fabry, H.-J., '*lēḇ; lēḇāḇ*', *TDOT*, VII, pp. 399-437.

Fishbane, M., *Biblical Interpretation in Ancient Israel* (Oxford: Clarendon Press, 1985).

Flaubert, G., *Bouvard et Pécuchet* (trans. A.J. Krailsheimer; London: Penguin Books, 1976 [1881]).

Gammie, J.G. (ed.), *The Sage in Israel and the Ancient Near East* (Winona Lake, IN: Eisenbrauns, 1990).

Geyer, J., *The Wisdom of Solomon* (London: SCM Press, 1963).

Ginzberg, L., *The Legends of the Jews* (7 vols.; Philadelphia: The Jewish Publication Society of America, 1968).

Gruchy, J. de (ed.), *Dietrich Bonhoeffer: Witness to Jesus Christ* (The Making of Modern Theology; London: Collins, 1988).

Halperin, D., 'The Book of Remedies, the Canonization of the Solomonic Writings, and the Riddle of Pseudo-Eusebius', *JQR* 72 (1982), pp. 269-92.

Hartley, L.P., *The Go-Between* (Harmondsworth: Penguin Books, 1958).

Hassan, J., 'The Survivor as Living Witness', in Y. Bauer *et al.* (eds.), *Remembering for the Future* (3 vols.; Oxford: Pergamon Press, 1989), I, pp. 1093-1104.

Höffken, P., 'Das EGO des Weisen', *TZ* 41 (1985), pp. 121-34.

Hoffman, Y., *A Blemished Perfection: The Book of Job in Context* (JSOTSup, 213; Sheffield: Sheffield Academic Press, 1996).

Humphreys, W.L., 'The Motif of the Wise Courier in the Book of Proverbs', in J. Gammie *et al.* (eds.), *Israelite Wisdom: Theological and Literary Essays in Honor of Samuel Terrien* (Missoula, MT: Scholars Press, 1978), pp. 177-90.

Kanaris, J., 'Calculating Subjects: Lonergan, Derrida, and Foucault', *Method: Journal of Lonergan Studies* 15 (1997), pp. 135-50.

Kemp, W., 'A Shelter for Paintings: Forms and Functions of Nineteenth-Century Frames', in Eva Mendgen *et al.*, *In Perfect Harmony: Picture and Frame, 1850–1920* (Amsterdam: Van Gogh Museum, 1995), pp. 14-25.

Keneally, T., *Schindler's List* (London: Hodder & Stoughton, 1994 [orig. *Schindler's Ark*, 1982]).

Kierkegaard, S., *Fear and Trembling/Repetition* (ed. and trans. H.V. Hong and E.H. Hong; Princeton, NJ: Princeton University Press, 1983 [1843]).

Kraemer, D., 'The Formation of Rabbinic Canon: Authority and Boundaries', *JBL* 110.4 (1991), pp. 613-30.

Krailsheimer, A.J., 'Introduction', in *Bouvard et Pécuchet* (trans. A.J. Krailsheimer; London: Penguin Books, 1976 [1881]), pp. 7-16.

Kreitzer, L., *The Old Testament in Fiction and Film: On Reversing the Hermeneutical Flow* (TBS, 24; Sheffield: Sheffield Academic Press, 1994).

Laurin, R., 'The Concept of Man as a Soul', *ExpTim* 72 (1961), pp. 131-34.

Lee, H., *To Kill a Mockingbird* (Harmondsworth: Penguin Books, 1964 [1960]).

Leiman, S.Z., *The Canonization of Hebrew Scripture: The Talmudic and Midrashic Evidence* (Hamden, CT: Archon Books, 1976).

Lichtheim, M., *Ancient Egyptian Literature* (3 vols.; Berkeley: University of California Press, 1973).

Longman III, Tremper, *Fictional Akkadian Autobiography* (Winona Lake, IN: Eisenbrauns, 1991).

MacIntyre, A., 'Existentialism', in P. Edwards (ed.), *The Encyclopedia of Philosophy*, III (New York: Macmillan, 1967), pp. 147-59.

Marin, L., 'The Frame of Representation and Some of its Figures', in P. Duro (ed.), *The Rhetoric of the Frame: Essays on the Boundary of the Artwork* (Cambridge: Cambridge University Press, 1996), pp. 79-95.

Marrou, H.I., *A History of Education in Antiquity* (trans. G. Lamb.; London: Sheed and Ward, 1956).

Marter, E.W., 'The Hebrew Concept of "Soul" in Pre-Exilic Writings', *AUSS* 2 (1964), pp. 97-108.

Meade, D., *Pseudonymity and Canon* (WUNT, 39; Tübingen: J.C.B. Mohr, 1986).

Mendgen, E. *et al.*, *In Perfect Harmony: Picture and Frame, 1850–1920* (Amsterdam: Van Gogh Museum, 1995).

Middleton, J.R., and B.J. Walsh, *Truth Is Stranger Than It Used to Be* (Gospel and Culture; London: SPCK, 1995).

Monaco, J., *How to Read a Film* (Oxford: Oxford University Press, 1981).

Nowell, I., 'The Narrator in the Book of Tobit', in D.J. Lull (ed.), *SBL 1988 Seminar Papers* (Atlanta: Scholars Press, 1988), pp. 27-38.

Penny, N., 'Back to the Wall', *London Review of Books* 17.18 (21 September 1995), pp. 12-13.

Pierce, D.L.T., 'Echoes of the Past in Flaubert's *"L'Education Sentimentale"*, *"Bouvard et Pécuchet"* and *"Salambo"*' (PhD dissertation; Louisiana State University and Agricultural and Mechanical College, 1992).

Polanyi, M., *The Study of Man* (Chicago: University of Chicago Press, 1959).

Polka, B., 'Freud, Science, and the Psychoanalytic Critique of Religion: The Paradox of Self-Referentiality', *JAAR* 62.1 (1994), pp. 59-81.

Polzin, R., *Moses and the Deuteronomist: A Literary Study of the Deuteronomistic History*. I. *Deuteronomy, Joshua, Judges* (Bloomington, IN: Indiana University Press, 1980).

Porten, B., 'The Structure and Theme of the Solomon Narrative', *HUCA* 38 (1967), pp. 93-128.

Porter, S., 'Two Myths: Corporate Personality and Language/Mentality Determinism', *SJT* 43 (1990), pp. 289-307.

Rad, G. von, *Wisdom in Israel* (trans. J.D. Martin; London: SCM Press, 1972 [1970]).

Ricoeur, P., *Oneself as Another* (trans. K. Blamey; Chicago: University of Chicago Press, 1994).

Robinson, S., 'Lying for God: The Uses of Apocrypha', in G. Gillum and C. Criggs (eds.), *Apocryphal Writings and the Latter-Day Saints* (Religious Studies Monograph Series, 13; Provo, UT: Religious Studies Center, Brigham Young University, 1986), pp. 133-54.

Rowland, C., *The Open Heaven* (London: SPCK, 1982).

Rutherford, B., *The Meditations of Marcus Aurelius: A Study* (Oxford: Clarendon Press, 1989).

Schiff, H. (ed.), *Holocaust Poetry* (London: HarperCollins, 1995).

Scott, R.B.Y., 'Solomon and the Beginnings of Wisdom', in M. Noth and D.W. Thomas (eds.), *Wisdom in Israel and in the Ancient Near East* (VTSup, 3; Leiden: E.J. Brill, 1955), pp. 262-79.

Seybold, D., *'hebhel; hābhal'*, *TDOT*, III, pp. 313-20.

Sheppard, G., 'Canonization: Hearing the Voice of the Same God through Historically Dissimilar Traditions', *Int* 36 (1982), pp. 21-33.

Sherwood, Y., *The Prostitute and the Prophet: Hosea's Marriage in Literary-Theoretical Perspective* (JSOTSup, 212; GCT, 2; Sheffield: Sheffield Academic Press, 1996).

Simon, J., *The Art of the Picture Frame: Artists, Patrons and the Framing of Portraits in Britain* (London: National Portrait Gallery, 1996).

Simpson, W.K. (ed.), *The Literature of Ancient Egypt* (London: Yale University Press, 1973).

Smith, M.S., 'The Heart and Innards in Israelite Emotional Expressions: Notes from Anthropology and Psychobiology', *JBL* 117.3 (1998), pp. 427-36.

Stein, L., 'The Holocaust and the Legacy of Existentialism', in Y. Bauer *et al.* (eds.), *Remembering for the Future* (3 vols.; Oxford: Pergamon Press, 1989), II, pp. 1943-55.

Steinbeck, J., *Of Mice and Men* (London: Heinemann, 1966 [1937]).

Traber, C., 'In Perfect Harmony? Escaping the Frame in the Early Twentieth Century', in Eva Mendgen *et al.*, *In Perfect Harmony: Picture and Frame, 1850–1920*

(Amsterdam: Van Gogh Museum, 1995), pp. 221-47.

Waltke, B., 'Superscriptions, Postscripts, or Both', *JBL* 110.4 (1991), pp. 583-96.

Waltke, B., and M. O'Connor, *An Introduction to Biblical Hebrew Syntax* (Winona Lake, IN: Eisenbrauns, 1990).

Wells, D., *The Penguin Dictionary of Curious and Interesting Numbers* (London: Penguin Books, 1986).

Whitlock, G., 'The Structure of Personality in Hebrew Psychology', *Int* 14 (1960), pp. 3-13.

Whybray, R.N., 'Prophecy and Wisdom', in R. Coggins *et al.* (eds.), *Israel's Prophetic Tradition* (Cambridge: Cambridge University Press, 1982), pp. 181-99.

Wiebe, M., 'The Wisdom in Proverbs: An Integrated Reading of the Book' (PhD dissertation; University of Sheffield, 1982).

Wiesel, E., *Night* (trans. S. Rodway; London: Robson Books, 1987 [1960]).

Wilson, R.R., 'The Hardening of Pharoah's Heart', *CBQ* 41 (1979), pp. 18-36.

Winston, D., 'The Sage as Mystic in the Wisdom of Solomon', in J.G. Gammie (ed.), *The Sage in Israel and the Ancient Near East* (Winona Lake, IN: Eisenbrauns, 1990), pp. 383-97.

Wolff, H.W., *Anthropology of the Old Testament* (trans. M. Kohl; London: SCM Press, 1974 [1973]).

Wollaston, I., ' "Traditions of Remembrance": Post-Holocaust Interpretations of Genesis 22', in J. Davies, G. Harvey and W.G.E. Watson (eds.), *Words Remembered, Texts Renewed* (JSOTSup, 195; Sheffield: Sheffield Academic Press, 1995), pp. 41-51.

INDEXES

INDEX OF REFERENCES

BIBLICAL REFERENCES

Old Testament		7.3	183	1.13	100
Genesis		7.13	184	1.15	100
1.2	188	7.14	183	4.2	109
1.30	204	8.15	183	4.10	102
2.7	186, 204	8.32	183	4.14	102
3	203	9.7	183	4.41-43	61
4.2	85, 113	9.34	183	6.1	102
4.4	113	10.20	183	6.5-6	185
4.9	113	10.27	183	6.5	187
6.5	196	14.4-5	184	11.19	102
6.17	187	18.20	106	12.8	61
7.15	187	23.1	271	12.32	109
7.22	187	26.33	92	27.1	61
9.4-6	187	32.4	190	27.9	61
9.21	185	36.1-2	100	27.11	61
12.11	85	36.4	100	29.1	61
14.18	131	36.8	100	29.4	163
18.5	184			32.21	79, 80
24.45	197	*Leviticus*		32.22-25	61
27.4	186	17.10-11	187	32.44-45	61
37.2	85			32.48	61
37.19	105	*Numbers*		33.1	61
41.2	85	13.32	27	34.10	61
45.3	26	14.34	27		
49.6	186	15.39	116, 152,	*Joshua*	
49.24	106		199	2.11	184
		21.4	202	5.1	184
Exodus		31.19	186	7.5	184
1.20	102	31.28	186	10	131
3.12	102			11.11	187
4–14	183	*Deuteronomy*		14.8	184
4.16	102	1.1	61	22.4	222
4.21	183	1.2	61		
6.9	202	1.5	61		

Judges
18.2 103
19.5 184
19.6 184
19.8 184
19.9 184

1 Samuel
12.24 116
24.16 129
25.7 146
25.25 80
30.19 88

2 Samuel
13.33 196
14.1-21 132
16.7 80
16.20–17.23 132
17.10 184
19.19 196
19.22 130
19.23 26
24.10 184

1 Kings
1–11 143, 163
3.5-9 167
3.8-9 102
3.9 163, 164
3.12-13 131
3.12 163
3.14 31
4.1 130
4.11 133
4.20-28 104
4.29-30 131
4.29 164
4.30-31 164
4.31-34 146
4.31 164
4.32-33 228
4.33-34 102
5.7-12 133
5.12 152
7.15 190
8.1-2 129
8.14 129

8.22 129
8.55 129
8.65 129
9.1-11 133
10.13 222
10.23 131
10.24 163
11 130
11.1-8 144
11.3 144, 145
11.4 31
11.9-40 165
11.13 166
11.14 166
11.23-25 166
11.41 77
14.19 77
14.29 77
15.7 77
15.23 77
15.31 77
16.5 77
16.13 79
16.14 77
16.20 77
16.26 79
16.27 77
21.13 80
22.39 77

2 Kings
9.24 191
17.15 80, 81
21.1-17 144
21.10-15 144
21.16 144
21.17 144

1 Chronicles
13.4 102
22.19 184, 187
25.8 103
29.25 131

2 Chronicles
1.15 132
9.23 163
10 130

11.18 129
13.8 129
23.3 129
30.12 163
32.33 129
33.1-20 144
33.10-17 144
33.18-19 144
35.3 103

Ezra
2.55 129
2.57 129
3.1 102
7.27 163
8.2 129

Nehemiah
2.12 163
7.5 163
13.25-26 144

Esther
6.6 108

Job
1.1–2.13 62
1.1 62
1.2-3 62
1.2 62
1.6–2.13 62
1.8 114
1.22 62
2.3 62
2.10 101
3.16 29, 201
5.6 100
5.27 103
7.6 82
7.7 101
7.11 188, 206
7.16 80
9.29 80
10.8-11 183, 189
10.18-22 183, 189, 190
11.7-8 94
14.9 63

14.22	187	58.4-5	105	8	208, 227
15.2-6	100	61.10	79	8.4-36	35
15.3	100	62.10	80	8.15	136
15.4	100	63.6	114	8.20	226
20.3	189	64.6	185	9.8	101
21.4	202	71.21	136	9.17-18	64
21.5	268	72	134	10	104
21.34	80	72.4-14	134	10.1-2	64
23.16	184	77.6	185, 188	10.1	64, 147
24.2	85	78.33	80	10.9	226
25.1	62	80.1	106	10.21	196
26.1	62	86.11	163	12.15	99
27.1	62	86.17	136	13.2	101
27.11	102	94.11	79, 80,	13.4	101
27.12	80		82	13.11	80
28	208, 227	103.1	188	13.12	200
28.12-14	216	103.2	188	13.21	101
28.21-22	216	104.15	184	13.22	133
28.27	103	104.29	188	14.2	226
29.1	62	106.48	102	14.30	82
30.9	188	110.1	138	14.31	135
30.26	101	119	102	15.21	226
31.35	80	119.91	89	15.33	100
32.1-5	188	119.99	102	16–22	158
32.8	189	131.2	188	16.14	140
32.18-19	188	139.13	191	16.15	139, 140
34.4	101	144.4	79	18.2	185
34.14-15	187	144.15	102	18.15	99
37.7-8	116	146.7	135	19.1	226
42.10-17	63			19.8	185
42.10	63	*Proverbs*		19.10	140
		1–9	11, 97	19.14	133
Psalms		1.1-8	64	19.20	64
1.2	114	1.1-7	97	19.27	64
4.1	188	1.1	64, 75	20.7	226
4.2	188	1.3	97	21.1-2	184
23.1	106	1.5-6	99, 100	21.6	79, 80
23.4	136	1.5	100	22.11	140
24.4	271	1.6	100	22.16	135
25.4-5	102	1.7	100, 116	22.17	64, 185
31.7	271	1.10-18	226	22.20-21	100
31.8	79	1.20-22	226	23.12	185
32.2	188	1.22-33	35	23.15	64
35.8	271	2.20	226	24.21	140
39.6	79, 82	3.7-8	116	24.30-34	35
39.7	79	3.23	226	25.1	104
39.12	79	4.1-3	35	25.2	103
51.6	185	7	104	25.2	146

Reference	Pages
25.2-3	233
25.6	140
28.6	226
28.10	101
28.16	135
28.18	226
29	64, 134
29.2	102
29.13	135
30	64
30.1-9	35
30.1	77
30.3-4	64
30.6	152
31	64
31.1	77
31.2-5	64
31.9	136, 141
31.30	80, 81

Ecclesiastes

Reference	Pages
1–6	45, 220
1–2	40, 147, 206
1.1-11	47
1.1-3	28
1.1-2	11, 31, 45, 57, 69, 74, 76, 93, 141, 167, 217
1.1	46, 65, 74, 77, 128, 129, 147, 167
1.2-11	23, 77, 78
1.2	29, 32, 45-47, 73, 74, 77-79, 88, 89, 92, 93, 96, 115, 129, 147, 167, 233, 268
1.3–12.7	162
1.3-11	46, 47, 68, 78; 141
1.3	27, 45, 101, 219, 220
1.4–12.7	44
1.4-11	68
1.4-7	89, 220
1.4	167
1.6	85
1.7	29, 266
1.8	29, 77, 101, 109, 190, 201, 214, 267, 269
1.9-10	168, 233
1.9	43, 45, 209, 230
1.10	77
1.11	102, 141, 273
1.12–12.7	47
1.12–6.9	220
1.12–2.26	128, 147, 205
1.12–2.17	129, 143, 167
1.12–2.11	22, 35
1.12-26	22, 129
1.12-13	26-28, 69, 206
1.12	31, 39, 42, 46, 47, 65, 74, 93, 130, 132
1.13–6.9	47
1.13-15	243
1.13-14	85, 233
1.13	28, 29, 32, 45, 84, 101, 147, 163, 164, 167, 185, 194, 195, 198, 206, 223, 229-31, 234, 237, 268
1.14-15	206
1.14	27, 45, 84, 87-89, 92, 93, 147, 206
1.15	83, 103, 138, 147, 164, 220, 233, 243
1.16-17	164, 195, 206
1.16	31, 39, 40, 74, 131, 132, 141, 147, 194, 195, 207, 232
1.17	45, 84, 94, 101, 113, 147, 163, 194, 230, 243
1.18	49, 109, 202, 206, 225, 232, 264, 268
2–11	44
2	31, 44, 45, 128, 132-34, 137, 143, 147, 197, 207, 230, 244
2.1-11	132, 162, 164
2.1-3	207
2.1-2	163
2.1	29, 39, 45, 74, 84, 87, 147, 194,

Ecclesiastes (cont.)
197, 206,
209, 223,
230
2.2-3 206
2.2 74, 147,
209, 219
2.3 27, 45,
101, 137,
184, 194,
223, 230,
231
2.4-10 206, 232
2.4-8 132, 163
2.4 40
2.7 74, 205
2.8 132, 133,
145, 241
2.9 31, 40,
74, 101,
132, 164,
231, 232
2.10 133, 194,
201
2.11 27, 39,
40, 45,
84, 87-
89, 92,
93, 132,
133, 147,
163, 220,
223, 230,
232, 233,
268
2.12 39, 94,
101, 132,
147, 223,
230
2.13-23 133
2.13-14 232
2.13 39, 101,
132, 137,
232
2.14-15 87
2.14 39, 49,
203, 222,
232

2.15-16 233
2.15 39, 45,
49, 74,
82, 147,
194, 208,
209, 232,
247, 268
2.16 49, 82,
89, 90,
101, 203,
248, 273
2.17-23 202, 232
2.17-20 207
2.17-18 246, 268
2.17 45, 84,
87-89,
92, 93,
117, 132,
147, 203
2.18-26 132
2.18-19 88, 168
2.18 39, 45,
132, 268
2.19 45, 82,
147, 208,
221, 232
2.20 39, 45,
132, 177,
194, 198,
223, 246
2.21 45, 82,
84, 88,
133, 147
2.22-23 227, 233
2.22 45, 194,
198
2.23 45, 82,
85, 147,
194, 198
2.24-25 101
2.24 39, 132,
133, 137,
147, 200,
248, 268
2.25-26 248
2.25 194, 248
2.26 45, 82,
84, 88,

101, 143,
147, 194,
248
3 204
3.1-8 257, 268
3.1 27, 45,
105
3.2 137, 270
3.8 132
3.9 101
3.10-11 37, 163,
164
3.10 28, 198,
205
3.11-14 269
3.11 38, 44,
89, 90,
117, 158,
163, 164,
194, 197,
213, 230,
233, 234
3.12-13 248
3.13 133
3.14-15 38, 198
3.14 234, 249
3.15 43, 209,
230
3.16-22 28
3.16-17 111, 134,
137, 138,
243
3.16 29, 32,
45, 137,
147, 209
3.17 39, 74,
97, 105,
117, 147,
194, 209
3.18-21 88, 203,
205
3.18 39, 74,
147, 194,
204, 205,
209, 260
3.19 45, 82,
88, 92,
93, 147,

Ecclesiastes (cont.)
    202, 203, 270
3.20   88, 89, 205, 225
3.21-22   221
3.21   202, 204
3.22   137, 147, 247, 248
4.1-3   110, 134, 213, 256, 267, 271
4.1-2   29, 32, 268
4.1   28, 39, 45, 135-37, 142, 147, 164, 223
4.2-3   135
4.2   39
4.3-4   84
4.3   45, 117, 190
4.4   28, 39, 45, 82, 84, 137, 147, 213, 233
4.6   45, 84, 85, 227
4.7-8   82, 88, 225
4.7   28, 39, 45, 137, 147, 223
4.8   39, 45, 49, 82, 84, 200, 214, 219, 233
4.9-12   101, 138, 271
4.9   268
4.10   203
4.12   138
4.13-16   29, 140, 225

4.13   106, 136, 139-41
4.14-16   141
4.14   141
4.15   45, 137, 158
4.16   45, 82, 84, 102, 141
5.1-7   116, 137, 139
5.1-5   245
5.1   29, 74, 194
5.2-7   105
5.2-4   139
5.2-3   77
5.2   27, 137, 204
5.3   104, 109
5.4-7   116
5.5   139
5.6   195, 198
5.7-9   271
5.7   77, 82, 89, 109, 249, 269
5.8-9   136
5.8   74, 105, 134, 135, 137, 142
5.9   74, 139
5.10–6.9   224
5.10-12   224
5.10   45, 82, 230
5.11   109, 220
5.12   227
5.13-17   224
5.13   45, 84, 105
5.15   84, 222, 224
5.16   220
5.17-19   198
5.18-19   198, 248
5.18   39, 45, 90, 133,

    205, 230, 248, 268
5.19-20   268, 274
5.19   248
6   213
6.1-5   200, 201, 225
6.1-2   84
6.1   45, 234, 248
6.2   45, 82, 84, 226, 233, 248
6.3-6   29
6.3-5   190
6.3-4   225
6.3   29, 30, 74, 109, 209, 214, 267
6.4-5   226
6.4   29, 30, 224
6.5   29, 30, 225
6.6   89, 225
6.7-9   201, 202, 269
6.7   201, 214, 230, 268
6.8   49, 101, 220. 247
6.9   45, 82, 84, 201, 225
6.10–12.7   47
6.10–11.6   220
6.10   209, 230
6.11   82, 89, 109, 203, 220, 269
6.12   45, 82, 89, 220, 230, 234
7   47, 103, 257
7.1-14   29
7.1   213, 272

Ecclesiastes (cont.)

7.2	163, 194, 196
7.3	194, 199, 268
7.4	194
7.6-27	35
7.6-7	85
7.6	45, 82
7.7	101, 194
7.8	202, 255
7.9	202
7.10	248
7.11-12	101, 232, 247
7.11	201
7.12	220
7.13-14	29, 30
7.13	83, 103, 117, 138, 147, 164, 220, 233, 234, 243
7.14	44, 205, 234
7.15-22	230
7.15-19	209
7.15-18	230, 267
7.15-16	82
7.15	31, 82, 88, 89, 243, 268, 274
7.16-17	137, 268
7.16	245, 247
7.18	198, 249
7.19-22	29, 94
7.19	134, 232, 247, 268
7.21-22	196
7.21	163, 194, 196, 245
7.22	194
7.23-29	105, 256
7.23-24	90, 93, 208, 209, 230, 233, 247

7.23	74, 94, 101, 147, 208, 230, 232
7.24	94, 220
7.25-29	143, 144, 209
7.25-26	94
7.25	39, 101, 194, 223, 230
7.26-29	124, 145, 230
7.26	39, 95, 145, 194, 248
7.27-29	95
7.27-28	230
7.27	11, 46, 47, 71, 74, 95
7.28	200
7.29	94, 101, 145, 231
8	103
8.1-2	101
8.1	77, 139, 220, 269
8.2-9	134, 142
8.2-5	138
8.2	39, 41, 134, 138, 232
8.3-5	243, 245
8.3	104
8.4	138, 244
8.5-6	97
8.5	194
8.6-9	270
8.6-8	139
8.6	105, 234, 268
8.7	209
8.8	205, 270
8.9	45, 163, 194, 230
8.10	45, 74, 137

8.11-13	271
8.11	82, 194, 196, 198
8.12-13	38, 198, 234, 249
8.12	39, 82, 248
8.14	45, 74, 82, 85, 147
8.15-17	195
8.15	39, 45, 133, 205, 230, 268
8.16-17	94, 101, 227, 230
8.16	30, 31, 137, 147, 163, 194, 243
8.17	44, 45, 90, 101, 105, 117, 137, 147, 164, 234, 269
9.1-3	82, 137, 268, 269
9.1	45, 88, 92, 163, 194, 196, 205, 230, 243, 248
9.2	88, 247
9.3	45, 84, 194, 196, 197
9.4-6	274
9.4	272
9.5	203, 270
9.6	45
9.7-10	31, 249
9.7-8	199, 268
9.7	158, 184, 194
9.9	45, 82, 89, 245

Ecclesiastes (cont.)

9.10	187, 225, 234, 245
9.11-12	233, 247, 269
9.11	45, 101, 137, 147, 223
9.12	145, 234
9.13–10.1	232
9.13-18	101
9.13-16	140, 141, 225
9.13-15	29, 30, 273
9.13	45
9.16–10.1	247
9.16-17	141
9.16	39, 74
9.17	77
10	47, 257
10.1-4	29
10.2	194
10.3	194
10.4	140, 202, 245
10.5-7	30, 32, 134, 139, 140, 271
10.5	45, 84, 243
10.7	158
10.8-20	29
10.8-11	247, 269
10.11	105
10.12	77
10.14	209, 220, 230, 234
10.16-17	74, 134, 139, 140, 244
10.16	134
10.19	89, 184
10.20	105, 140, 245
11	44, 203, 244
11.1	244

11.3	247
11.4-5	247
11.5	89, 90, 202, 205, 234, 245, 269
11.6-8	272
11.6	117
11.7	201
11.8	45, 88
11.9-10	31, 199
11.9	29, 30, 116, 117, 151-53, 194, 225, 245, 249, 254
11.10	82, 89, 194, 203, 268
12.1-7	105, 252, 254, 256
12.1	31, 104, 244
12.2	201
12.3	203
12.5	272
12.6-7	114
12.7	187, 188, 202, 204, 205, 222, 225, 272
12.8-14	11, 46, 47, 97
12.8	30, 32, 42, 45-47, 74, 88, 92, 93, 96, 99, 115, 254
12.9-14	97
12.9-10	46, 67, 75, 96, 99, 114
12.9	29, 96, 99, 102, 103, 106,

	108, 129, 146
12.10-11	96, 158
12.10	74, 75, 77, 96, 104, 176, 230
12.11-14	97
12.11-12	67, 108, 110
12.11	106, 107, 146
12.12-14	114
12.12	46, 99, 106, 108, 109, 112
12.13-14	96, 99, 115, 117
12.13	89, 96, 115, 150, 198

Song of Songs

1.1	92
3.11	198
4.12–5.1	133
5.5	40
5.6	40
6.2	133
6.11	133
8.11-12	133

Isaiah

1.13	271
5.17	85
10.3	271
30.7	80, 82
30.29	198
32.1	136
39.9-10	158
40.11	106
41.7	105
42.5	102
49.1-3	191
49.4	80
51.19	136
56.5	260
57.13	79

Jeremiah			*Ezekiel*			*Malachi*	
1	191		11.19-20	184		3.5	135
1.1	73		21.26	137			
1.4-10	183		33.4-6	106		Apocrypha	
1.4-9	190		34.12	106		*Tobit*	
2.5	80, 81		36.26	184		1.1	65
2.15	234		44.5	185		1.2-11	65
2.30	271					1.3-4	65
4.23-26	136		*Daniel*			1.3	65
8.17	105		1.4	102		14.11-15	65
8.19	79		4.13	185			
9.14	102		4.36	103		*Wisdom of Solomon*	
9.20	102		10.12	163		1.3	231
10.1-15	81					3.10	231
10.3	80		*Hosea*			9.13-18	228
10.4	105		7.11	185			
10.8	79		12.1	113		*Ecclesiasticus*	
10.15	80					2.1	66
14.22	79		*Amos*			3.21-24	228
15.5	136		1.1	73		3.21	239
15.16	199		4	135		7.16	102
16.19	80					12.13	105
18.15	271		*Jonah*			18.5-8	228
23.16	80		2.9	79		38.24	100
24.7	163					42.15–43.26	117
31.10	106		*Micah*			43.27	117
31.33	163		2.7	202		47.9	103
32.33	102		6.8	228		51.13-22	66, 227
39.8	102					51.23-30	66
			Habakkuk			51.23	66
Lamentations			2.18	102		51.26-27	66
1.11–2.1	268						
1.17	268		*Zephaniah*			New Testament	
1.21	268		1.1	73		*John*	
4.17	80					1.49	169
5.20-22	268		*Zechariah*				
			10.2	80			

OTHER ANCIENT REFERENCES

Qumran			*Šab.*			Talmuds	
1QS			3	152		*b. Meg.*	
6.7	151					7a	150-52
			Yad.				
Mishnah			3.5	151		*b. Šab.*	
Ed.						30b	150
5.3	150, 151						

Tosefta
Yad.
2.14   149, 150, 152
3.5   149, 151

Midrashim
Lev. R.
28.1   150

Qoh. R.
1.1-2   158
1.3   150

3.11   159
10.4   143
11.9   152

Targums
Targ. Qoh.
1.1-2   133
3.12   167
4.1-3   142
4.15   167
7.27   167
9.7   167
12.8-10   146

Christian Authors
Augustine
City of God
20.3   168
20.13   168

Origen
de Princ.
5.3   168

Classical
Heraclitus
frag.
45   174, 235

INDEX OF AUTHORS

Alter, J. 175
Amery, J. 263
Ananth, D. 122

Bal, M. 19, 25, 34, 71, 74, 91, 162, 229, 230, 234
Baldick, C. 42
Bar-Efrat, S. 185, 197
Barr, J. 149, 186, 187, 192
Barthes, R. 19, 76, 179, 210
Barton, G.A. 84, 150, 208
Barton, J. 22, 153, 154, 158, 166, 170, 217
Barucq, A. 128
Beardsley, M. 161
Beauvoir, S. de 265
Beckett, S. 256, 261, 262, 266
Beckwith, R. 109, 150, 151
Best, S. 179
Bickerman, E. 155, 159, 170
Blumenthal, J. 25, 75
Boer, P.A.H. de 106
Boivin, M.J. 191, 192
Bokolsky, S.M. 259, 269
Bonhoeffer, D. 214
Booth, W. 24, 29, 73, 77, 87, 128, 160-62, 169
Brenner, A. 62, 63
Breton, S. 20
Brooks, P. 32, 33, 120
Brown, W.P. 36, 37, 207, 208, 210
Broyde, M.J. 145, 149, 150, 152
Brueggemann, W. 112, 143
Bruss, E. 178
Burkitt, F.C. 24, 87
Burns, G.L. 108

Camus, A. 83, 86, 261, 262, 265, 266, 268
Castellino, G. 22
Caws, M.A. 45, 53, 56, 57, 119, 120
Ceresko, A.R. 229
Chatman, S. 24-28, 30, 55, 57, 160, 161, 229, 256
Childs, B.S. 62, 63, 97, 124, 128, 156
Christianson, E.S. 94
Clines, D.J.A. 62, 63
Cohen, I. 183, 185, 191
Conrad, J. 120, 161
Coward, R. 182
Craigie, P. 158
Crenshaw, J. 20, 22, 38, 103, 111, 113, 124, 128, 129, 133, 134, 145-47, 156, 185
Crites, S. 245
Crüsemann, F. 87, 260, 266, 269
Culler, J. 165

Davidson, A.B. 99
Delitzsch, F. 171
Dell, K.J. 153
Derrida, J. 179
Dimant, D. 147, 157
Dittmar, L. 57, 59, 60, 119, 121
Donat, A. 273

Eaton, M. 99, 124, 146, 156, 177
Edel, L. 177
Eissfeldt, O. 130, 157
Ellermeier, F. 128, 141
Elliott, R. 37, 176, 179
Ellis, J. 182
Ellul, J. 110, 130, 145, 253, 254
Eslinger, L. 59, 71

Etting, E. 25
Eybers, I.H. 148, 151, 153

Fabry, H.-J. 183, 184, 186, 191, 196, 197
Fisch, H. 23, 34, 142, 177, 210, 217, 218, 228, 235, 252, 254
Fishbane, M. 103
Fishman, J. 178, 251
Flaubert, G. 217, 235-37, 239, 240, 242
Forster, E.M. 43, 78
Foucault, M. 155, 156, 179, 181

Fox, M.V. 9, 13, 19-21, 23, 26, 37, 46, 49, 58-61, 65, 74, 81, 83, 86, 89, 90, 94, 99, 103, 104, 106, 107, 110, 111, 115, 122, 124, 146, 148, 162, 177, 196, 208, 222, 227, 246, 266
Frankl, V. 259, 260, 265
Fredericks, D. 86, 124, 224
Frye, N. 21

Galling, K. 128, 177
Garrett, D. 136, 138
Genette, G. 21, 30, 34, 42, 70, 71, 72
Geyer, J. 155
Gillum, G. 156
Ginsberg, H.L. 106, 128, 130, 137
Ginsburg, C.D. 107, 132, 152, 171
Ginzberg, L. 151, 166
Gittes, K. 68, 69, 121
Glazar, R. 263
Goldin, J. 97, 106, 109
Good, E. 23, 77, 78, 86
Gordis, R. 49, 106, 114, 117, 128, 135, 138, 150, 153, 205, 208, 266, 268
Greimas, A.J. 229
Grotius, H. 170
Gruchy, J. de 214
Gundry, R. 192
Gusdorf, G. 36
Guthrie, W.K.C. 235

Halperin, D. 151
Harrison, C.R. 157
Hassan, J. 265, 271
Haupt, P. 170
Heidegger, M. 261

Hengel, M. 34, 154, 157
Hirshman, M. 169
Höffken, P. 22, 162
Hoffman, Y. 62, 63
Holm-Nielsen, S. 148, 165, 167, 168
Hopkins, G.M. 212
Humphreys, W.L. 158

Isaksson, B. 22, 39, 40
Iser, W. 20

Jacob, E. 192
James, K.W. 266, 267, 270
Jarick, J. 88, 153, 167, 168
Johnston, D. 171

Kaiser, O. 134
Kamano, N. 10, 31, 134
Kanaris, J. 178, 179
Kellner, D. 179
Kemp, W. 54
Keneally, T. 265, 272
Kerby, A.P. 180-82, 243, 252
Knobel, P.S. 146, 165
Kraemer, D. 149
Krailsheimer, A.J. 236, 240, 242
Kreitzer, L. 235
Kushner, H. 218, 219

Lacan, J. 181, 210
Lanzmann, C. 260, 263, 264, 266, 274
Lauha, A. 177
Laurin, R. 187, 191
Lazarus, M. 186
Lee, H. 30
Leiman, S.Z. 149, 150
Levi, S. 259
Lohfink, N. 95, 198
Longman, T. III 9, 23, 35, 37, 47, 85, 115, 123, 124, 128, 135, 140, 148, 152, 155, 243
Loretz, O. 22, 44, 65, 142, 205, 226
Lundin, R. 214
Luther, M. 156, 170, 256
Lux, R. 162

MacIntyre, A. 261, 266
Marin, L. 52, 53, 245

Marrou, I.H. 154
Marter, E.W. 191
Martin, S. 25, 76
McEvenue, S. 191
McKenna, J.E. 85
Meade, D. 155, 156
Michael, I. 175, 176
Middleton, J.R. 179, 214
Miller, D.B. 90
Monaco, J. 55
Müller, F. 260, 274
Murphy, R.E. 44, 82, 96, 100, 101, 103,
    114, 117, 124, 139, 167, 192, 208,
    220, 226, 269

Nichols, F.W. 266
Niebuhr, R. 260
Nowell, I. 60

O'Connor, M. 40
Ocean, H. 54
Ogden, G. 82, 124, 141, 231
Olney, J. 210, 212, 235

Paterson, J. 21, 33, 34
Payne, M. 23
Penny, N. 53, 54
Perry, T.A. 130, 131, 154, 197
Peter, C.B. 83, 86
Pierce, D.L.T. 236, 237, 239, 241
Plumptre, E.H. 33, 34
Polanyi, M. 110, 111
Polk, T. 81, 86
Polka, B. 181
Polzin, R. 19, 61, 62, 90
Porten, B. 94, 143, 222
Prince, G. 21, 22, 49
Proust, M. 43, 72

Rad, G. von 111
Ricoeur, P. 180
Rimmon-Kenan, S. 24, 25, 160
Robinson, S. 156
Romberg, B. 57, 58, 124
Rose, M. 54
Rousseau, J.-J. 57, 124
Rowland, C. 157
Rubenstein, R. 260

Rudolph, W. 142
Russell, B. 175
Rutherford, B. 142
Ryken, L. 22, 23, 35, 115, 216, 218, 228

Salters, R.B. 128, 134, 139, 148, 150
Salyer, G. 10, 23, 29, 34, 37, 38, 130,
    132, 154, 245
Santayana, G. 252
Sartre, J.P. 261
Schiff, H. 273
Schloesser, S. 153, 215, 233
Schoors, A. 40
Schrag, C. 210
Schwarz, H. 54
Scott, R.B.Y. 106, 146
Seow, C.-L. 10, 22, 27, 35, 36, 128, 130,
    133, 134, 138, 197
Seybold, D. 79, 80, 84, 93
Sheppard, G. 97, 104, 106, 109, 117,
    128
Sherwood, Y. 63
Short, R. 25, 260
Showalter, E. 165
Silentio, J. de 251
Simon, J. 52-54, 122, 123
Smith, M.S. 192
Spence, D. 44
Spina, F. 131
Sprinker, M. 174, 179
Stanton, E.C. 145
Stein, L. 13, 259, 260, 262-66, 273
Steinbeck, J. 55
Steiner, J.-F. 265
Stevens, W. 118
Stone, E. 34, 175, 176
Sturrock, J. 33, 37, 176, 251
Summerfield, J. 70
Swinburne, A.C. 221

Tennyson, A. 173
Thaumaturgos, G. 171
Tillich, P. 271
Traber, C. 52, 121-23

Vaughan, H. 216
Viviano, P. 23, 98

Walsh, B.J. 179, 214
Waltke, B. 40, 158
Wells, D. 231
Whitlock, G. 191, 271
Whybray, R.N. 13, 21, 49, 68, 95, 96,
    100, 105, 136, 137, 140, 147, 148,
    198, 201, 220
Wiebe, M. 60, 64, 67, 118, 120
Wiesel, E. 260, 263-65, 270
Williams, J.G. 22
Wilson, G. 96, 97, 109, 124
Winston, D. 228
Wolff, H.W. 183, 184, 186, 187, 195

Wollaston, I. 261
Woolf, V. 45, 70
Wright, A.G. 19, 45, 98, 220
Wright, C.H.H. 155
Wright, J.S. 115
Wright, R. 70

Yates, W.B. 79

Zimmerli, W. 37, 128
Zimmermann, F. 21, 23, 34, 116, 121,
    143, 145, 177, 257

JOURNAL FOR THE STUDY OF THE OLD TESTAMENT
SUPPLEMENT SERIES

149   Eugene Ulrich, John W. Wright, Robert P. Carroll & Philip R. Davies (eds.), *Priests, Prophets and Scribes: Essays on the Formation and Heritage of Second Temple Judaism in Honour of Joseph Blenkinsopp*

150   Janet E. Tollington, *Tradition and Innovation in Haggai and Zechariah 1–8*

151   Joel Weinberg, *The Citizen–Temple Community* (trans. Daniel L. Smith Christopher)

152   A. Graeme Auld (ed.), *Understanding Poets and Prophets: Essays in Honour of George Wishart Anderson*

153   Donald K. Berry, *The Psalms and their Readers: Interpretive Strategies for Psalm 18*

154   Marc Brettler and Michael Fishbane (eds.), *Min'ah le-Na'um: Biblical and Other Studies Presented to Nahum M. Sarna in Honour of his 70th Birthday*

155   Jeffrey A. Fager, *Land Tenure and the Biblical Jubilee: Uncovering Hebrew Ethics through the Sociology of Knowledge*

156   John W. Kleinig, *The Lord's Song: The Basis, Function and Significance of Choral Music in Chronicles*

157   Gordon R. Clark, *The Word Ḥesed in the Hebrew Bible*

158   Mary Douglas, *In the Wilderness: The Doctrine of Defilement in the Book of Numbers*

159   J. Clinton McCann (ed.), *The Shape and Shaping of the Psalter*

160   William Riley, *King and Cultus in Chronicles: Worship and the Reinterpretation of History*

161   George W. Coats, *The Moses Tradition*

162   Heather A. McKay and David J.A. Clines (eds.), *Of Prophets' Visions and the Wisdom of Sages: Essays in Honour of R. Norman Whybray on his Seventieth Birthday*

163   J. Cheryl Exum, *Fragmented Women: Feminist (Sub)versions of Biblical Narratives*

164   Lyle Eslinger, *House of God or House of David: The Rhetoric of 2 Samuel 7*

166   D.R.G. Beattie and M.J. McNamara (eds.), *The Aramaic Bible: Targums in their Historical Context*

167   Raymond F. Person, *Second Zechariah and the Deuteronomic School*

168   R.N. Whybray, *The Composition of the Book of Proverbs*

169   Bert Dicou, *Edom, Israel's Brother and Antagonist: The Role of Edom in Biblical Prophecy and Story*

170   Wilfred G.E. Watson, *Traditional Techniques in Classical Hebrew Verse*

171   Henning Graf Reventlow, Yair Hoffman and Benjamin Uffenheimer (eds.), *Politics and Theopolitics in the Bible and Postbiblical Literature*

172   Volkmar Fritz, *An Introduction to Biblical Archaeology*

173   M. Patrick Graham, William P. Brown and Jeffrey K. Kuan (eds.), *History and Interpretation: Essays in Honour of John H. Hayes*

174   Joe M. Sprinkle, *'The Book of the Covenant': A Literary Approach*

175   Tamara C. Eskenazi and Kent H. Richards (eds.), *Second Temple Studies. II. Temple and Community in the Persian Period*

176   Gershon Brin, *Studies in Biblical Law: From the Hebrew Bible to the Dead Sea Scrolls*

177   David Allan Dawson, *Text-Linguistics and Biblical Hebrew*

178   Martin Ravndal Hauge, *Between Sheol and Temple: Motif Structure and Function in the I-Psalms*

179   J.G. McConville and J.G. Millar, *Time and Place in Deuteronomy*

180   Richard L. Schultz, *The Search for Quotation: Verbal Parallels in the Prophets*

181   Bernard M. Levinson (ed.), *Theory and Method in Biblical and Cuneiform Law: Revision, Interpolation and Development*

182   Steven L. McKenzie and M. Patrick Graham (eds.), *The History of Israel's Traditions: The Heritage of Martin Noth*

183   John Day (ed.), *Lectures on the Religion of the Semites (Second and Third Series) by William Robertson Smith*

184   John C. Reeves and John Kampen (eds.), *Pursuing the Text: Studies in Honor of Ben Zion Wacholder on the Occasion of his Seventieth Birthday*

185   Seth Daniel Kunin, *The Logic of Incest: A Structuralist Analysis of Hebrew Mythology*

186   Linda Day, *Three Faces of a Queen: Characterization in the Books of Esther*

187   Charles V. Dorothy, *The Books of Esther: Structure, Genre and Textual Integrity*

188   Robert H. O'Connell, *Concentricity and Continuity: The Literary Structure of Isaiah*

189   William Johnstone (ed.), *William Robertson Smith: Essays in Reassessment*

190   Steven W. Holloway and Lowell K. Handy (eds.), *The Pitcher is Broken: Memorial Essays for Gösta W. Ahlström*

191   Magne Sæbø, *On the Way to Canon: Creative Tradition History in the Old Testament*

192   Henning Graf Reventlow and William Farmer (eds.), *Biblical Studies and the Shifting of Paradigms, 1850–1914*

193   Brooks Schramm, *The Opponents of Third Isaiah: Reconstructing the Cultic History of the Restoration*

194   Else Kragelund Holt, *Prophesying the Past: The Use of Israel's History in the Book of Hosea*

195   Jon Davies, Graham Harvey and Wilfred G.E. Watson (eds.), *Words Remembered, Texts Renewed: Essays in Honour of John F.A. Sawyer*

196   Joel S. Kaminsky, *Corporate Responsibility in the Hebrew Bible*

197   William M. Schniedewind, *The Word of God in Transition: From Prophet to Exegete in the Second Temple Period*

198   T.J. Meadowcroft, *Aramaic Daniel and Greek Daniel: A Literary Comparison*

199   J.H. Eaton, *Psalms of the Way and the Kingdom: A Conference with the Commentators*

200 Mark Daniel Carroll R., David J.A. Clines and Philip R. Davies (eds.), *The Bible in Human Society: Essays in Honour of John Rogerson*

201 John W. Rogerson, *The Bible and Criticism in Victorian Britain: Profiles of F.D. Maurice and William Robertson Smith*

202 Nanette Stahl, *Law and Liminality in the Bible*

203 Jill M. Munro, *Spikenard and Saffron: The Imagery of the Song of Songs*

204 Philip R. Davies, *Whose Bible Is It Anyway?*

205 David J.A. Clines, *Interested Parties: The Ideology of Writers and Readers of the Hebrew Bible*

206 Møgens Müller, *The First Bible of the Church: A Plea for the Septuagint*

207 John W. Rogerson, Margaret Davies and Mark Daniel Carroll R. (eds.), *The Bible in Ethics: The Second Sheffield Colloquium*

208 Beverly J. Stratton, *Out of Eden: Reading, Rhetoric, and Ideology in Genesis 2–3*

209 Patricia Dutcher-Walls, *Narrative Art, Political Rhetoric: The Case of Athaliah and Joash*

210 Jacques Berlinerblau, *The Vow and the 'Popular Religious Groups' of Ancient Israel: A Philological and Sociological Inquiry*

211 Brian E. Kelly, *Retribution and Eschatology in Chronicles*

212 Yvonne Sherwood, *The Prostitute and the Prophet: Hosea's Marriage in Literary-Theoretical Perspective*

213 Yair Hoffman, *A Blemished Perfection: The Book of Job in Context*

214 Roy F. Melugin and Marvin A. Sweeney (eds.), *New Visions of Isaiah*

215 J. Cheryl Exum, *Plotted, Shot and Painted: Cultural Representations of Biblical Women*

216 Judith E. McKinlay, *Gendering Wisdom the Host: Biblical Invitations to Eat and Drink*

217 Jerome F.D. Creach, *Yahweh as Refuge and the Editing of the Hebrew Psalter*

218 Gregory Glazov, *The Bridling of the Tongue and the Opening of the Mouth in Biblical Prophecy*

219 Gerald Morris, *Prophecy, Poetry and Hosea*

220 Raymond F. Person, Jr, *In Conversation with Jonah: Conversation Analysis, Literary Criticism, and the Book of Jonah*

221 Gillian Keys, *The Wages of Sin: A Reappraisal of the 'Succession Narrative'*

222 R.N. Whybray, *Reading the Psalms as a Book*

223 Scott B. Noegel, *Janus Parallelism in the Book of Job*

224 Paul J. Kissling, *Reliable Characters in the Primary History: Profiles of Moses, Joshua, Elijah and Elisha*

225 Richard D. Weis and David M. Carr (eds.), *A Gift of God in Due Season: Essays on Scripture and Community in Honor of James A. Sanders*

226 Lori L. Rowlett, *Joshua and the Rhetoric of Violence: A New Historicist Analysis*

227 John F.A. Sawyer (ed.), *Reading Leviticus: Responses to Mary Douglas*

228 Volkmar Fritz and Philip R. Davies (eds.), *The Origins of the Ancient Israelite States*

229 Stephen Breck Reid (ed.), *Prophets and Paradigms: Essays in Honor of Gene M. Tucker*

230 Kevin J. Cathcart and Michael Maher (eds.), *Targumic and Cognate Studies: Essays in Honour of Martin McNamara*

231 Weston W. Fields, *Sodom and Gomorrah: History and Motif in Biblical Narrative*

232 Tilde Binger, *Asherah: Goddesses in Ugarit, Israel and the Old Testament*

233 Michael D. Goulder, *The Psalms of Asaph and the Pentateuch: Studies in the Psalter, III*

234 Ken Stone, *Sex, Honor, and Power in the Deuteronomistic History*

235 James W. Watts and Paul House (eds.), *Forming Prophetic Literature: Essays on Isaiah and the Twelve in Honor of John D.W. Watts*

236 Thomas M. Bolin, *Freedom beyond Forgiveness: The Book of Jonah Re-Examined*

237 Neil Asher Silberman and David B. Small (eds.), *The Archaeology of Israel: Constructing the Past, Interpreting the Present*

238 M. Patrick Graham, Kenneth G. Hoglund and Steven L. McKenzie (eds.), *The Chronicler as Historian*

239 Mark S. Smith, *The Pilgrimage Pattern in Exodus* (with contributions by Elizabeth M. Bloch-Smith)

240 Eugene E. Carpenter (ed.), *A Biblical Itinerary: In Search of Method, Form and Content. Essays in Honor of George W. Coats*

241 Robert Karl Gnuse, *No Other Gods: Emergent Monotheism in Israel*

242 K.L. Noll, *The Faces of David*

243 Henning Graf Reventlow, *Eschatology in the Bible and in Jewish and Christian Tradition*

244 Walter E. Aufrecht, Neil A. Mirau and Steven W. Gauley (eds.), *Aspects of Urbanism in Antiquity: From Mesopotamia to Crete*

245 Lester L. Grabbe, *Can a 'History of Israel' Be Written?*

246 Gillian M. Bediako, *Primal Religion and the Bible: William Robertson Smith and his Heritage*

248 Etienne Nodet, *A Search for the Origins of Judaism: From Joshua to the Mishnah*

249 William Paul Griffin, *The God of the Prophets: An Analysis of Divine Action*

250 Josette Elayi and Jean Sapin (eds.), *Beyond the River: New Perspectives on Transeuphratene*

251 Flemming A.J. Nielsen, *The Tragedy in History: Herodotus and the Deuteronomistic History*

252 David C. Mitchell, *The Message of the Psalter: An Eschatological Programme in the Book of Psalms*

253 William Johnstone, *1 and 2 Chronicles, Vol. 1: 1 Chronicles 1–2 Chronicles 9: Israel's Place among the Nations*

254   William Johnstone, *1 and 2 Chronicles, Vol. 2: 2 Chronicles 10–36: Guilt and Atonement*

255   Larry L. Lyke, *King David with the Wise Woman of Tekoa: The Resonance of Tradition in Parabolic Narrative*

256   Roland Meynet, *Rhetorical Analysis: An Introduction to Biblical Rhetoric* translated by Luc Racaut

257   Philip R. Davies and David J.A. Clines (eds.), *The World of Genesis: Persons, Places, Perspectives*

258   Michael D. Goulder, *The Psalms of the Return (Book V, Psalms 107–150): Studies in the Psalter, IV*

259   Allen Rosengren Petersen, *The Royal God: Enthronement Festivals in Ancient Israel and Ugarit?*

260   A.R. Pete Diamond, Kathleen M. O'Connor and Louis Stulman (eds.), *Trouble with Jeremiah: Prophecy in Conflict*

261   Othmar Keel, *Goddesses and Trees, New Moon and Yahweh*

262   Victor H. Matthews, Bernard M. Levinson and Tikva Frymer-Kensky (eds.), *Gender and Law in the Hebrew Bible and the Ancient Near East*

264   Donald F. Murray, *Divine Prerogative and Royal Pretension: Pragmatics, Poetics and Polemics in a Narrative Sequence about David (2 Samuel 5.17–7.29)*

266   J. Cheryl Exum and Stephen D. Moore (eds.), *Biblical Studies/Cultural Studies: The Third Sheffield Colloquium*

269   David J.A. Clines and Stephen D. Moore (eds.), *Auguries: The Jubilee Volume of the Sheffield Department of Biblical Studies*

270   John Day (ed.), *King and Messiah in Israel and the Ancient Near East: Proceedings of the Oxford Old Testament Seminar*

272   James Richard Linville, *Israel in the Book of Kings: The Past as a Project of Social Identity*

273   Meir Lubetski, Claire Gottlieb and Sharon Keller (eds.), *Boundaries of the Ancient Near Eastern World: A Tribute to Cyrus H. Gordon*

275   William Johnstone, *Chronicles and Exodus: An Analogy and its Application*

276   Raz Kletter, *Economic Keystones: The Weight System of the Kingdom of Judah*

277   Augustine Pagolu, *The Religion of the Patriarchs*

278   Lester L. Grabbe (ed), *Leading Captivity Captive: 'The Exile' as History and Ideology*

279   Kari Latvus, *God, Anger and Ideology: The Anger of God in Joshua and Judges in Relation to Deuteronomy and the Priestly Writings*

291   Christine Schams, *Jewish Scribes in the Second-Temple Period*

292   David J.A. Clines, *On the Way to the Postmodern: Old Testament Essays, 1967–1998 Volume 1*

293   David J.A. Clines, *On the Way to the Postmodern: Old Testament Essays, 1967–1998 Volume 2*